Amelia R. Brown is Senior Lecturer at the University of Queensland in Brisbane, Australia. She has published widely on ancient Greece in the late antique and early Byzantine periods.

"Amelia R. Brown's study of the transformation of Corinth from a late Roman to an early Byzantine city between the third and the sixth century CE is a singular achievement. Using all available evidence – written sources, inscriptions, archaeological materials – with enormous expertise, Brown presents a detailed analysis of the entire city, its public places, religious sites, commercial and domestic spaces, waterways and other infrastructure, to demonstrate how, where and when exactly the Greek-Roman city became a Greek, Roman and Christian one. This book will become a model for all interested in the late Roman world and its aftermath. Through her detailed focus on Corinth, one of the most connected cities in the Mediterranean, Brown has offered a signal contribution to the age-old question of the fate of cities at the end of the Roman Empire: yes, there was decline and fall, but also practical continuity and, in the end, a transformed yet still recognizable Corinth."

– Susanna K. Elm, Sidney H. Ehrman
Professor of European History,
University of California, Berkeley

CORINTH IN LATE ANTIQUITY

A Greek, Roman and Christian City

AMELIA R. BROWN

BLOOMSBURY ACADEMIC
LONDON • NEW YORK • OXFORD • NEW DELHI • SYDNEY

BLOOMSBURY ACADEMIC
Bloomsbury Publishing Plc
50 Bedford Square, London, WC1B 3DP, UK
1385 Broadway, New York, NY 10018, USA

BLOOMSBURY, BLOOMSBURY ACADEMIC and the Diana logo
are trademarks of Bloomsbury Publishing Plc

First published 2018 by I.B. Tauris & Co. Ltd.
Paperback edition first published 2019 by Bloomsbury Academic

A catalogue record for this book is available from the British Library.

A catalog record for this book is available from the Library of Congress.

ISBN: HB: 978-1-7845-3823-1
PB: 978-1-3501-2498-1
ePDF: 978-1-7867-3358-0
ePub: 978-1-7867-2358-1

Series: Library of Classical Studies 17

Typeset by OKS Prepress Services, Chennai, India

To find out more about our authors and books visit
www.bloomsbury.com and sign up for our newsletters.

For Amy Summer and Mark Erasmus

CONTENTS

LIST OF FIGURES

Unless otherwise stated, all figures are reproduced courtesy of the American School of Classical Studies at Athens, Corinth Excavations, with thanks to James Herbst for the Corinth plans and credit to Ino Ioannidou and Lenio Bartzioti for the Corinth photographs.

ACKNOWLEDGEMENTS

I owe thanks first of all to my advisors from the University of California at Berkeley, where the Ph.D. dissertation which led to this book was completed in the Graduate Group in Ancient History and Mediterranean Archaeology in 2008. Susanna Elm nurtured my interest in Late Antiquity, and Ronald S. Stroud introduced me to epigraphy, Demeter, the American School of Classical Studies at Athens (ASCSA) and, most importantly, the ASCSA Corinth Excavations. Maria Mavroudi and Chris Hallett provided important guidance on the use of manuscripts and the study of Roman sculpture, respectively, and I also benefitted from courses taught by Andrew Stewart, Emily Mackil, Erich Gruen and the late Crawford Greenewalt.

I am grateful to the American School of Classical Studies at Athens for awarding me the John Williams White and Edward Capps Fellowships, during which I began research on my dissertation, and for ASCSA seminars taught by Carolyn Snively and John Pollini. I am grateful for guidance and academic support to the staff of the ASCSA Corinth Excavations, especially Director Guy D.R. Sanders, as well as Assistant Director Ioulia Tzonou-Herbst, Architect James Herbst, photographer Petros Dellatolas, Katherine Petrole and incoming Director Christopher Pfaff. I must single out for special thanks Assistant Director Emerita Nancy Bookidis, who gave me detailed feedback which I appreciate and have tried to follow. I appreciate conversations with Director Emeritus Charles K. Williams II and Numismatist Emeritus Orestes Zervos, and the remarkable photographs of Corinthian finds by the late Ino Ioannidou and Lenio Bartzioti. Thanks also to the three anonymous reviewers for I.B.Tauris and the editors; any errors that remain are mine.

I am deeply grateful to the Princeton University Center for Hellenic Studies for granting me the Hannah Seeger Davis Post-Doctoral Research Fellowship in 2009 to begin preparation of this book and to all my Princeton mentors in Late Antiquity, especially Dimitri Gondicas, Peter Brown, Tia Kolbaba, Slobodan Curcic, Brent Shaw and the Bakirtzis family. Thanks also to the University of Queensland for a New Staff Research Start Up grant to continue with my Corinthian research in Australia.

In the years since I first came to Corinth in the summer of 2001, I have benefitted from too many academic discussions, treks, conversations and friendships to list and properly appreciate. So, thanks first to my Berkeley colleagues, especially Jon Frey, Isabelle Pafford, Jorge Bravo, Michele Ciaccio and Kurt Lampe. Thanks to my ASCSA Regular Member colleagues, especially Jamie Donati, Amalia Avramidou, Eph Lytle, Sarah James and Dimitri Nakassis. Thanks to my ASCSA Associate Member colleagues, especially David Pettegrew (organizer of the walk to Kenchreai), Bill Caraher, Theo Kopestonky, Jeremy Ott and Angela Ziskowski (organizer of the walk to Perachora). Thanks to Margaret Mullett for hosting me at Dumbarton Oaks; R.R.R. Smith and Bryan Ward-Perkins for welcoming me to Aphrodisias and including me in the Last Statues of Antiquity research project, website and book (Brown 2016a; Smith and Ward-Perkins 2016); and Troels Myrup Kristensen and Lea Stirling for including me in research projects and books on pilgrimage and sculpture in Late Antiquity based at Aarhus University (Brown 2012b, 2016b; Kristensen and Stirling 2016).

Down Under, I appreciate my colleagues and students at the University of Queensland and the Australian Archaeological Institute at Athens, and especially insights from Caillan Davenport and Estelle Strazdins. Thanks to past and present Corinth Excavations staff members Takis Notis, Thanassis Notis, Panos Kakouros, Tasos Kakouros and Jennifer Palinkas for help in the field, as well as Evangelia Kondyli-Kakkava, Tasia Stamati and Anna Kouvaleska at Hill House. I deeply appreciate conversations and collegiality over the years with so many learned Corinthian scholars, notably Betsey Robinson, Paul Scotton, David Scahill, Michael Ierardi, Rebecca Sweetman, Mary Sturgeon, Mary E. Hoskins Walbank, Kathleen Slane, Sarah Lepinski, Katerina Ragkou, Cathy de Grazia Vanderpool, Eric Poehler, Steven Ellis, Allison Emmerson, Eleni Hasaki, Elli Tzavella, James

Wiseman, David Romano, Irene Romano, Connie Stroud, Joseph L. Rife, Elizabeth Gebhard, Tim Gregory and Lita Tzortzopoulou-Gregory. Finally, thanks to my parents, my sister Lisa Brown, my husband Graham Elliott and my children, who have each helped my research on Corinth in their own way. *Sine qua non*.

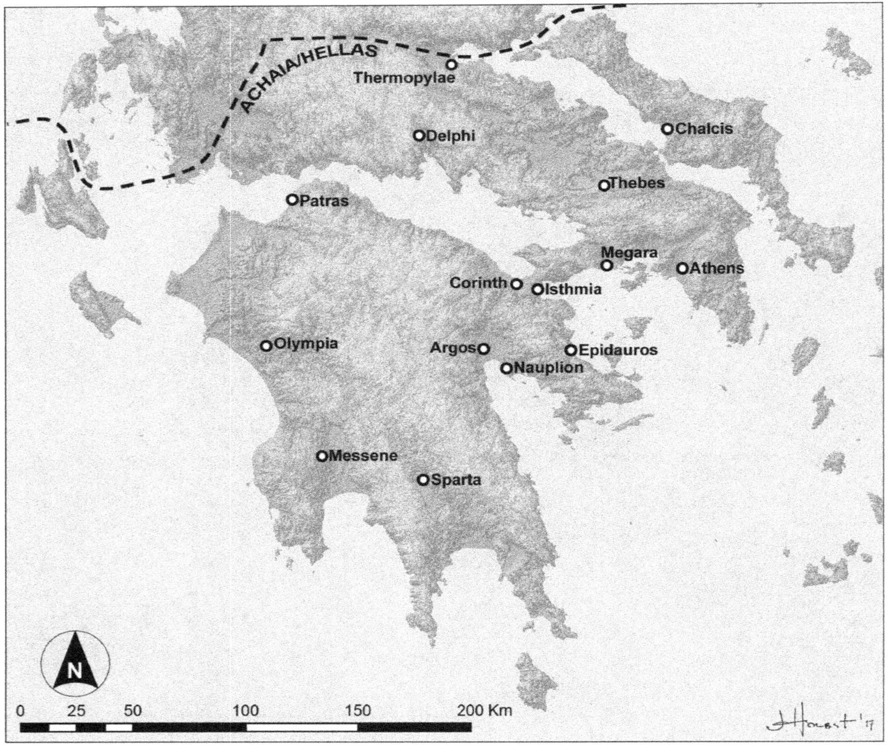

Figure 1 The Roman province of Achaia (Byzantine Hellas).

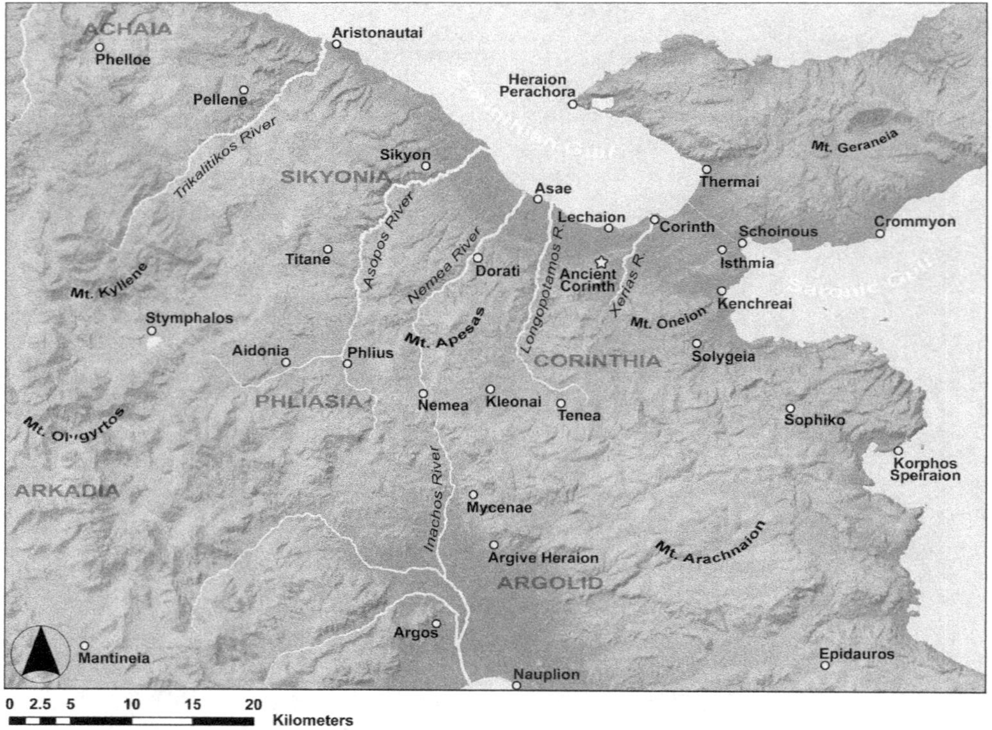

Figure 2 The Corinthia and Northeastern Peloponnese.

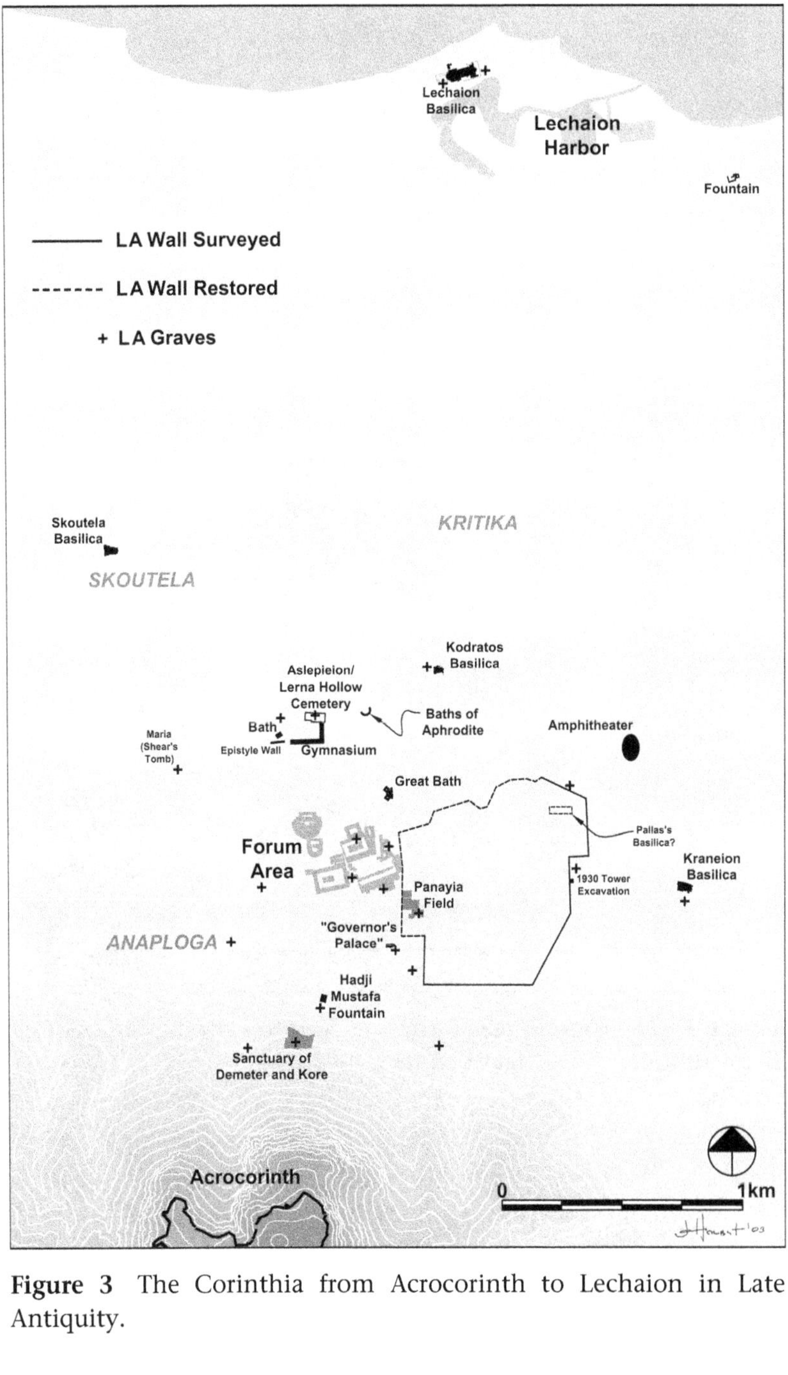

Figure 3 The Corinthia from Acrocorinth to Lechaion in Late Antiquity.

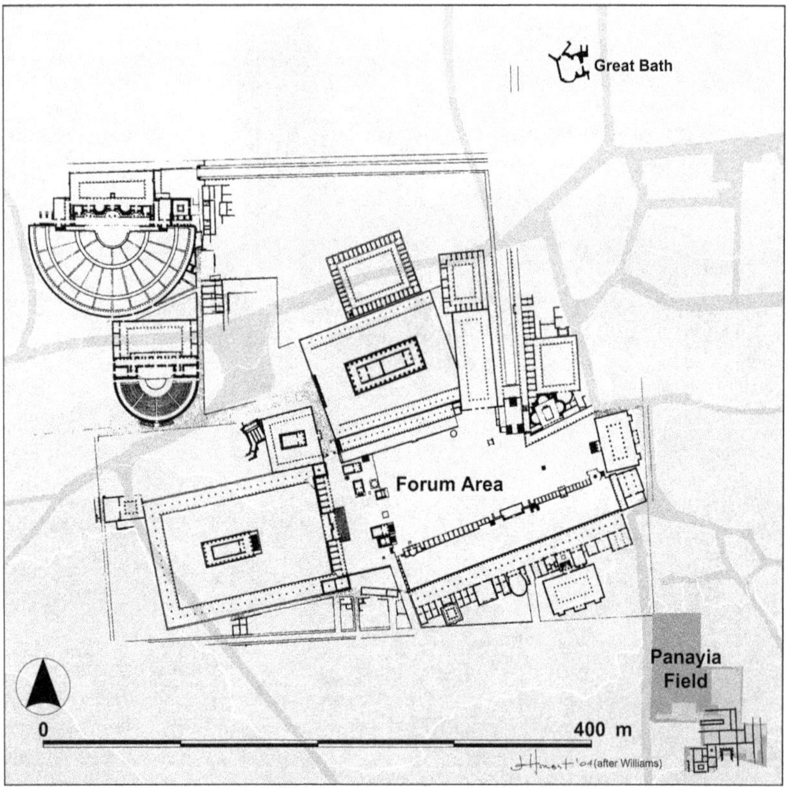

Figure 4 The Forum Area of Ancient Corinth with the Panayia Field Excavations and the Great Bath.

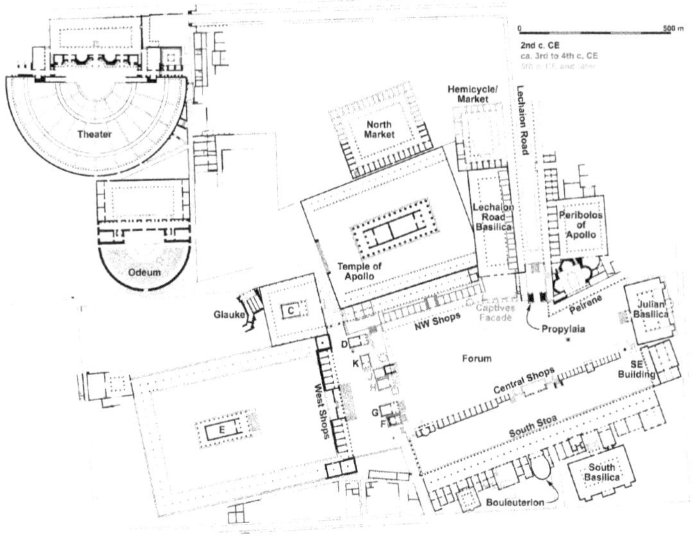

Figure 5 Public buildings in the Forum Area of Ancient Corinth in Late Antiquity.

Figure 6 The Forum Area in Byzantine and Frankish Corinth.

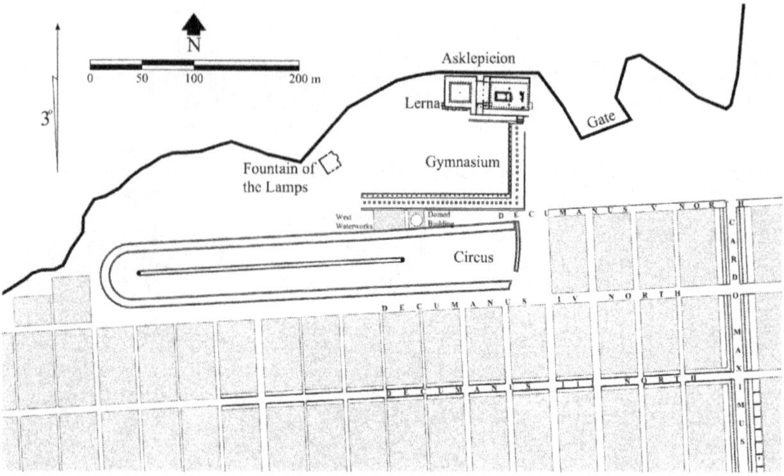

Figure 7 The northern area of Ancient Corinth with the Circus and the Old Gymnasium. (Courtesy of Corinth Computer Project.)

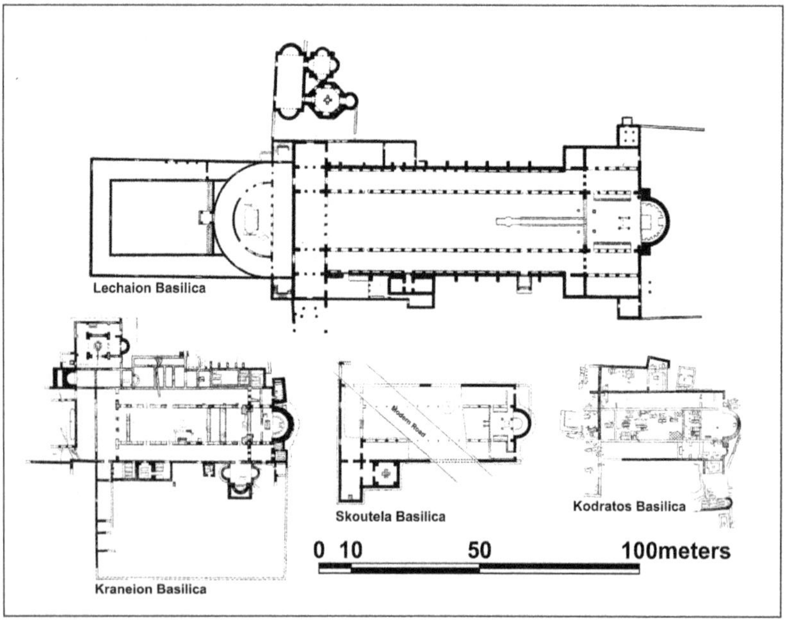

Figure 8 Plans of four Christian basilica churches excavated at Corinth.

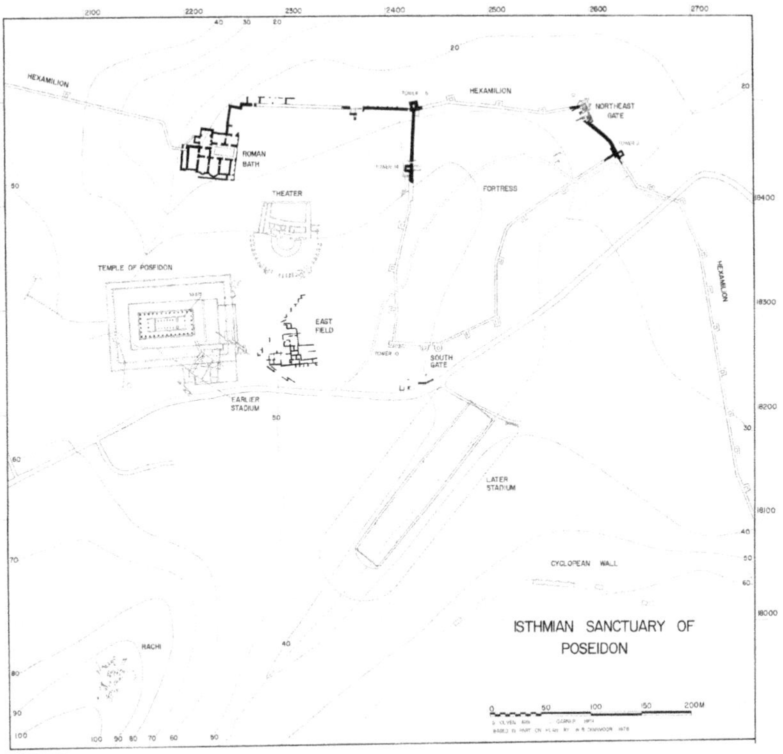

Figure 9 Plan of Isthmia. (Courtesy of The Ohio State University Excavations at Isthmia.)

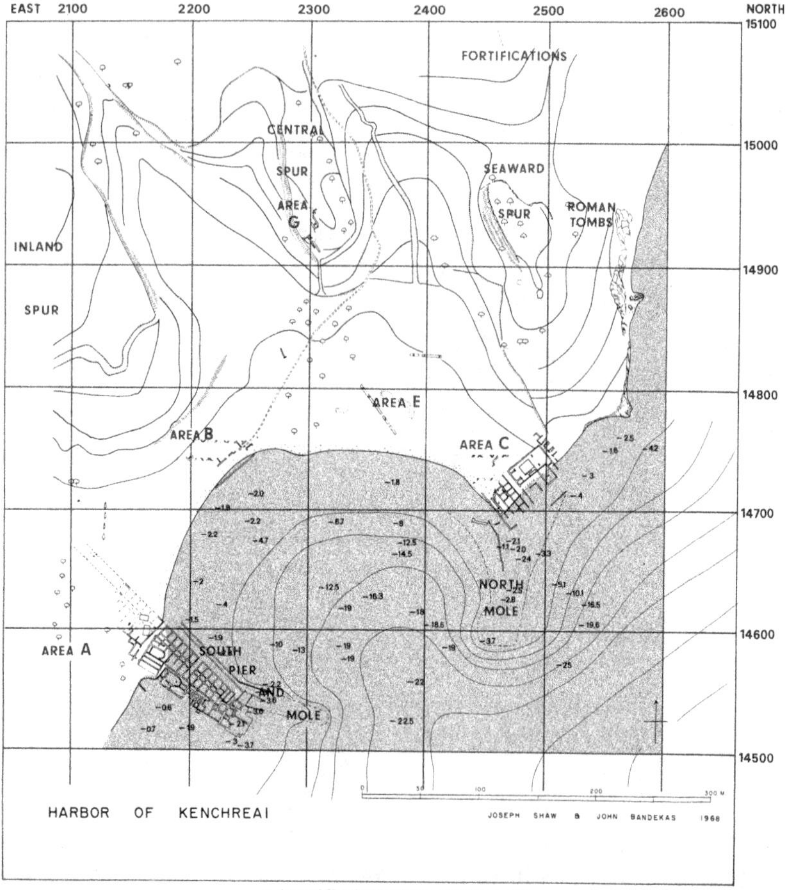

4. Area of Kenchreai Explored by Excavation.

Figure 10 Plan of Kenchreai. (From Scranton et al. 1978 (*Kenchreai* 1), Figure 4, Courtesy of The American Excavations at Kenchreai.)

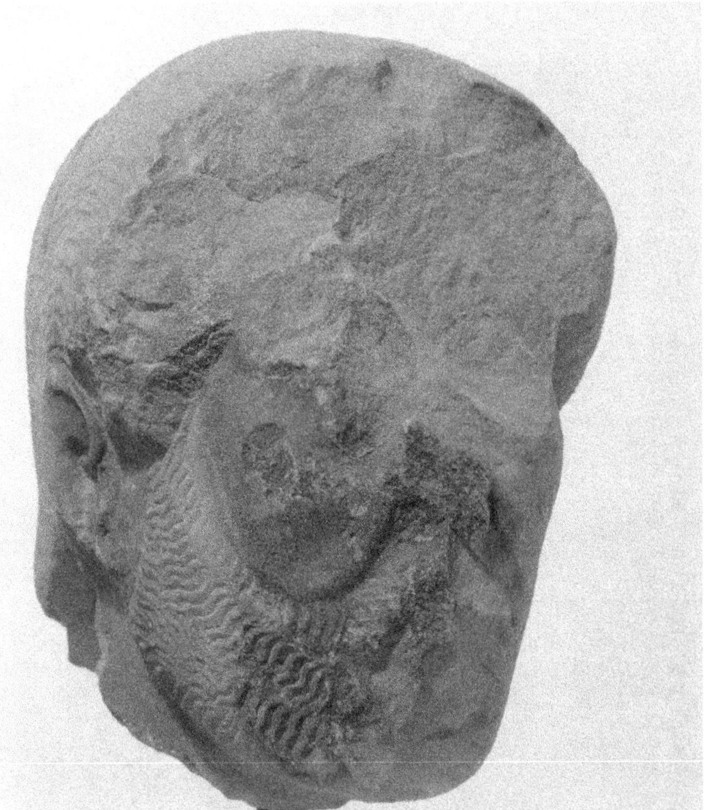

Figure 11 Marble male head, probably of the fifth century, Corinth Museum inv. no. S-909.

Figure 12 Marble male head marked with a cross, probably of the fifth century, Corinth Museum inv. no. S-919. (Photo by Petros Dellatolas. Reproduced Courtesy of American School of Classical Studies at Athens, Corinth Excavations.)

INTRODUCTION

SIGNIFICANCE, SCHOLARSHIP AND STRUCTURE

The Significance of Late Antique Corinth

In 1908, three marble portrait heads were found by the Fountain of Peirene near the Forum of Ancient Corinth: the bearded pagan priest on this book's cover, a second bearded man whose face was smashed, and a stubbly-faced man with a small cross carved into his forehead (see cover image, Figures 11–12 for the heads, and Figures 3–6 for the Forum).[1] Who were they? When they were alive, probably in the fourth or fifth century to judge by their hairstyles, they represented the traditional authorities and institutions of Roman and late antique Corinth: the colonial City Council, the imperial Governor of Achaia, and the officials of Greco-Roman polytheistic religion. Their portraits also embodied tradition in their material and original display context, carved from marble at the command of these authorities, and doubtless set up for public view on or near the Forum, atop busts or bodies on inscribed bases, in thanks for their service to the city of Corinth and its people. A century or so later, however, these heads were violently broken from their bodies, one was marked with a Christian cross, and they were all discarded down the drain. The Early Christian authorities of Byzantine Corinth tore down portraits like these, along with theaters and temples, and melted most of their marble into lime mortar, yet they also still administered a city called Corinth on the Isthmus of central Greece, maintaining civic infrastructure like stoas, shops, streets, fountains and baths, and building new Christian churches and fortification walls.

These three heads, and their findspot by the Peirene Fountain and the Roman Forum in sixth-century fill, bear witness to the Corinthian chapter of the dramatic transformation of cities around the Mediterranean Sea in Late Antiquity.[2] The purposeful disposal of these heads, and the rest of Corinth's public sculpture, speaks to the wider paradox which bedevils our understanding of Late Antiquity. How could cities supposedly suffering from centuries of decline put up so many colonnades, churches and fortification walls in the fifth and sixth centuries? Why were age-old urban traditions like public honorific portraiture, and the portraits themselves, discarded like so much rubbish at the same time? The conversion of people and then civic space to Christianity provides a partial answer, but it does not entirely explain the changes and continuities in civic authorities, urban institutions and public buildings which transformed Corinth, and other Greco-Roman cities, in Late Antiquity. The paradox, in fact, is that in order to maintain civic infrastructure, to build monumental new churches and city walls, and even to purposefully dispose of, or reuse, so much ancient sculpture and architecture, there had to be a functioning city with civic authorities and an urban population at Corinth, as elsewhere in Late Antiquity. Corinth's shifting urban topography, and the people responsible for it, reveals what declined and disappeared, but also what emerged transformed, and what was newly built, in order to support public urban life on the Isthmus from the third to the sixth century.

Corinth is well suited to a study of this paradox of Late Antiquity, because of its ancient significance, defined borders and extensive excavation over more than a century. Corinthians established urban institutions and authorities some three millennia ago near the flowing waters of the Peirene Spring, below Acrocorinth and above the narrow Isthmus and its two seas (see Figures 1–6). The area of Ancient Corinth (*Archaia Korinthos*) was a civic center for administrative, commercial, sacred and defensive purposes, between protective heights and agricultural plains, overlooking harbors and highways, for centuries before Pausanias in the middle of the second century described his Κόρινθος δὲ καὶ ἡ ἐπὶ τῷ ἰσθμῷ χώρα, "Corinth and the land around the Isthmus."[3] Pre-Roman Greek Corinth flourished as a major *polis* of Archaic, Classical and Hellenistic *Hellas* (Greece). Greek Corinthians were notorious tyrants, merchants, potters, bronze-smiths and courtesans. They fought against the Persians, their fellow Greeks, and then the Romans, who sacked Corinth in 146 BCE. Corinth was refounded on the orders of Julius Caesar himself, who sent colonists in 44 BCE to renovate, supplement and romanize the old Corinthian civic center and institutions into a Roman colony, *colonia Laus Julia Corinthiensis*. In Late Antiquity, Corinth was the seat of the proconsul of Achaia, the governor of the imperial Roman province of Achaia (all Greece south of Thermopylae), and also St John Chrysostom's "first city of *Hellas*," since Corinth's Christian archbishop oversaw about 46 bishops in the province.[4]

Corinth's central political, economic and religious role in southern Greece in Late Antiquity is attested by a wealth of literary, epigraphic and archaeological evidence. This combination of ancient significance and surviving evidence provides an opportunity to closely investigate the transformation of urban life in a provincial capital city from the high Roman Empire to the Early Byzantine era. The evidence from Corinth reveals how authorities and residents of one significant city responded concretely, at the social and spatial levels, to large-scale changes in civic administration, commerce and culture sweeping across the Mediterranean. Roman Imperial urban life was transformed utterly at Corinth, as elsewhere around the Mediterranean, yet in the same landscape and with important continuities of civic identity and infrastructure. Throughout Late Antiquity, between the third and sixth centuries, the Corinthian authorities and people maintained, renovated, abandoned, demolished or built anew almost all their ancient civic institutions and amenities. By the late sixth century, Corinthian political, economic and religious offices and public spaces were all still in existence, but fundamentally changed. What can Corinth tell us today about the realities of urban change in Late Antiquity, the people who directed them and their underlying causes?

Urban change in Late Antiquity was shaped by both natural and human agents. Through the examination of continuity and change at Corinth, I link historical events, individuals and groups in the city with their specific role in transforming civic spaces. The Corinthian authorities passed from a City Council, and an imperial governor sent from Rome, to a Christian archbishop administering Corinth together with local *archontes* (leaders) and imperial officials sent from Constantinople. The Corinthian civic center changed from a colonial Roman Forum with a *Bouleuterion* (*Curia*, Council House), *Bema* (Rostra), civic basilicas and temples to a meandering *Plateia* (public square) with Christian churches, an episcopal palace and intramural burials. The waters of the Peirene Spring still flowed from public fountains and (smaller) baths in Byzantine Corinth, among paved streets, shops and colonnades of stoas. However, these civic amenities were repaired, and new churches and fortification walls constructed, out of torn-down statues, pagan sanctuaries and public entertainment venues. Byzantine Corinth survived as a new kind of city: seat of an archbishop and his flock, sometime-stronghold of an imperial general, and home to Corinthians still pursuing a *politikê zoê*, an urban life, transformed yet still in a city perched between Acrocorinth and the plains, harbors and highways of the Isthmus.[5]

Late Antiquity was a significant time for the Corinthians. After the foundation of Constantinople, in particular, Corinth was again on the front line of political, economic and religious change in the Roman Empire, subject to forces both natural and human, from earthquakes and so-called barbarian invasions to polytheist, Jewish and Christian religious controversies. Between Rome and Constantinople, Thessalonike and Alexandria, Corinth was always potentially one of the most connected cities in the ancient Mediterranean. Real connections, formed between actual people through letters, shipments and physical travel, tied the raw potential of Corinth's geographic location on the Isthmus into the political, economic and religious networks of the Later Roman Empire. These human networks left their mark in literary and epigraphic texts, and in the material goods excavated at Corinth or exported abroad. Every pot was once made, transported and used by someone. Human networks conveying letters and material goods also carried immaterial ideas about authority, culture (*paideia*) and spirituality too, shaping urban life and then its physical environment.[6] For, to paraphrase Bob Dylan, "the times were a changin'," and Rome really did fall (several times) in Late Antiquity. Why? Some changes to urban life were remarked on at the time, as apocalyptic or miraculous, while others went without contemporary notice. The Fall of Rome as the end of an empire as well as an urban way of life has been studied for centuries as *a* (and often *the*) central question in Western Civilization, from Gibbon onwards.[7] The challenge is to understand what Corinthian civic authorities and institutions can tell us about the specific causes of, and responses to, urban continuity and change in Late Antiquity. How did Corinth pass into the Middle Ages with its name and position astride the Isthmus unchanged, but so utterly reshaped? Other cities changed too, of course, but few are as significant as Corinth for the combination of ancient importance and currently available evidence.

The Scholarship of Late Antique Corinth: Texts, Archaeology and History

Scholars have access to, and continue to unearth, a notable wealth of ancient epigraphic, literary and archaeological evidence for late antique Corinth. There are hundreds of inscriptions carved by and for the Corinthians themselves from the third to sixth centuries (though today most are fragmentary, and the corpus is weighted heavily towards Christian epitaphs). Pausanias wrote an extended description of the historical and mythological landscape of later second-century Corinth, and historians from Dexippus to Procopius commented on contemporary events in southern Greece. Some valuable historical data survives in Byzantine and early modern sources too. More detail on the relevant epigraphic and literary texts, and comments on their authorship, genre and chronology may be found in Appendix I.

Yet it is the archaeological excavations which really distinguish Corinth as a special place to study: the Corinth Excavations of the American School of Classical Studies at Athens have continued almost annually since 1896, and the Greek government, the Archaeological Society of Athens, and other institutions have extended archaeological research even further. Extensive parts of Ancient Corinth from all eras have been uncovered and studied, especially around the Roman Forum, the civic center of late antique Corinth. The areas excavated, methods used, publications produced, and preservation of the finds have been to the benefit of the study of all eras of ancient and medieval history, including Late Antiquity. However, chronology at Corinth rests, as elsewhere, on arguments based on literary sources, inscriptions, coins, stratigraphy and stylistic analysis, especially of pottery. Very few buildings at Corinth bear closely dated inscriptions, and most are dated by coins, pottery, stratigraphy and construction style. While coins rarely change in date, multiple but (almost) always forward-moving interpretations may be given to single coins and even entire hoards.[8] Late antique pottery is the subject of energetic study at Corinth, but can provide close dating for buildings only if recently excavated or kept in the past.[9] A detailed history of the Corinth

Excavations of the American School of Classical Studies at Athens in relation to the study of Late Antiquity may be found in Appendix II.

Scholarship on Roman and late antique Corinth, and Greeks under the Roman Empire, still suffers from old prejudices about the superiority of ancient Greek over Roman, free over subordinate, and innovative over derivative ancient political systems, art and literature.[10] Historical research on Corinth began with early modern scholars drawing on ancient literary sources, especially Pausanias, to study the history of pre-Roman Corinth, and gradually drawing on the material evidence of the Corinthian landscape, visible inscriptions or collections of Archaic pottery. After archaeological excavations started at Corinth in the late nineteenth century, historians gradually began to write about the Greek and then the Roman and late antique history of Corinth with reference to archaeological discoveries. However, the archaeologists on site were reading Pausanias too, and so historians drew not on separate strands of evidence but on ancient texts and material culture already intertwined.

Robert Scranton's 1957 Corinth Excavations volume on Medieval Corinth (*Corinth* XVI) is still fundamental, though outdated, with alternating chapters summarizing the literary and archaeological evidence from Late Antiquity and the Middle Ages as understood in the mid-twentieth century.[11] Scranton published descriptions and plans of all the archaeological evidence which he thought to be post-Roman and pre-Modern, including many buildings and walls removed by the early excavators (see Figure 6). Other scholars from the early Corinth Excavations linked their finds with the history of Roman, Late Roman (late antique) or Byzantine (medieval) Corinth, especially Gladys Davidson Weinberg.[12]

However, the history of Corinth in Late Antiquity has been enriched fundamentally in recent years by the pottery research of Kathleen Slane and the excavations directed by Demetrios Pallas, Guy D.R. Sanders and Timothy E. Gregory. Slane has published extensively on Roman and late antique pottery at Corinth, and her work underpins much of the historical research conducted at the site in recent years.[13] From the 1950s to 1980s, Pallas used his excavation of two Early Christian churches, the Kraneion and Lechaion basilicas, as the basis for numerous articles on the archaeology of late antique (Early Byzantine) Corinth.[14] Anna Avraméa, Demetrios Athanasoulis and other scholars have continued the work of Pallas, exploring the history and archaeology of late antique and Byzantine Corinth.[15]

As Director of the ASCSA Corinth Excavations from 1997 to 2017, Sanders published articles on late antique Corinth questioning the traditional coin and text-based historical interpretations, worked in tandem with Kathleen Slane on revised pottery chronologies, and directed excavations southeast (1997–2007) and south (2007–17) of the Forum.[16] He has mentored students and scholars at the ASCSA Corinth Excavations with interests in all eras, including my own interest in Late Antiquity. Finally, as Director of The Ohio State University Excavations at Isthmia, the Eastern Korinthia Archaeological Survey (EKAS), and other projects in and outside the Corinthia, Gregory has tackled numerous historical and archaeological questions of late antique and Byzantine Corinth, especially the Slavic invasions and Christianization.[17] He has also mentored generations of students to research the late antique Corinthia, especially the area of Isthmia, including Richard Rothaus, P. Nick Kardulias, R. Scott Moore, William Caraher, Jon Frey and David Pettegrew.[18]

Most modern histories of Greek or Roman Imperial Corinth also contain important research relevant to the landscape and monuments of Late Antiquity.[19] Since the late 1970s, interest in late antique Corinth has grown steadily: James Wiseman's historical narrative of Roman Corinth up to 267 remains relevant, as does work on Roman civic administration, topography and Pausanias' itinerary by Mary E. Hoskins Walbank, Corinth Excavations Director Emeritus Charles K. Williams, II, David Romano and Athanasios Rizakis.[20] Wider excavations in the Corinthia under the auspices of the ASCSA directed by Elizabeth Gebhard and Paul Clement at Isthmia, Robert L. Scranton and then Joseph L. Rife at Kenchreai, and now Paul Scotton at Lechaion, have uncovered and published extensive remains from Late Antiquity, as has work by Greek and other European scholars.[21] Late antique epigraphy at Corinth has benefitted recently from research by Pallas, Denis Feissel, Michael B. Walbank and especially Erkki Sironen, editor of the new *IG* IV^2 3 on Corinthian inscriptions of the fourth to sixth centuries.[22] Important articles are in the Corinth Excavations centenary volume;[23] the triad of conference volumes on pagan and Early Christian religion and society at Roman Corinth;[24] the recent conference volume on Isthmia;[25] and the publication of the 2009 conference at Loutraki organized by the Greek Archaeological Service and German Archaeological Institute.[26]

However, the only monograph to date to focus solely on Late Antiquity at Corinth was published by Rothaus in 2000, though it is an almost unedited version of his 1993 Ph.D. dissertation from OSU. He studied the Christianization of the Corinthia in Late Antiquity closely in his work, and assembled much of the evidence for shifts in cult practices and sacred space at Corinth which I draw on in Chapters 6 and 7. However, the force of his arguments was blunted by uncritical use of archaeological evidence and poor copy-editing.[27] A monograph on the history of Roman Corinth with relevance for Late Antiquity was also published by Donald W. Engels. His economic treatise on Roman Corinth is organized thematically, focusing mainly on first- to second-century evidence, with occasional use of later material.[28] His work is hampered by uncritical use of economic theories, bias against Late Antiquity, and misconceptions about Corinthian agriculture, but remains widely cited, and did signal an important shift in emphasizing provision of urban services rather than consumption as the key quality of Corinth and other ancient cities. Finally, David Pettegrew's recent monograph examines the Isthmus of Corinth and the eastern Corinthia throughout Antiquity, and into Late Antiquity, outlining how the same basic landscape of the Isthmus was considered sacred, commercial and/or strategic in different eras for different reasons, and how historical sources relate to the ceramic finds of EKAS.[29]

Here, however, the aim is to draw on all the available sources for the Corinthian city center and urban public life to document the history of shifting urban institutions and authorities in Late Antiquity. I cover not only religious continuity and change in Chapters 6 and 7, but also the transformation of administration, urban infrastructure and traditional aspects of urban public life in Chapters 1 to 5, with the key role played by construction of fortification walls discussed in Chapter 8. In each chapter, I also explore Corinth's broader significance in understanding how these people, their authorities and their urban history at this physical crossroads might contribute to interpreting urban change in other cities across the Mediterranean in Late Antiquity.

When we look beyond Corinth at scholarship of cities and urbanism in Greece and around the Mediterranean in Late Antiquity, there are many archaeological reports and conference papers, but few synthetic works.[30] Archaeological reports cover whole buildings or parts of city-sites, and new evidence appears constantly, but this scholarship is often fragmented, informed by specialist skills and the tendency to link material culture to documented historical events (sometimes in circular fashion).[31] Late antique conference volumes with a civic theme are steadily rising in numbers, combining bibliographic essays, archaeological reports on parts of cities, and analyses of specific urban phenomena.[32] Some works, as here, chart the course of one city in Late Antiquity, while a few survey all urban life in that era. Among the former are recent histories of Athens, Thessalonike, Rome, Antioch and Alexandria, all integrating archaeology and texts to construct an urban narrative.[33]

General surveys of ancient cities and urban life, especially in Greece, tend to start early in Antiquity, and so devote less space to later periods, while authors who do include Late Antiquity emphasize decline and decay.[34] Recently, however, several works have focused on cities and urban life in Late Antiquity, including both textual and archaeological sources, and have made explicit arguments as to how and why the city as an institution supposedly declined at the end of Antiquity in specific regions, whether Greece, Asia Minor or North Africa.[35] The role of a coastal location on the Mediterranean Sea is contested, as are the necessary features of a city, and the relative importance of politics, economics or religion in urban change. Many institutions and structures of the ancient urban way of life were abolished or abandoned in Late Antiquity, most notably what Cyril Mango has dubbed monumentality.[36] Helen Saradi contrasts the literary sources on continuity with the archaeological evidence for change in the sixth-century city; Hendrik Dey emphasizes how economic activity and monumental topography (especially colonnaded streets) were maintained into the Middle Ages "to frame the exercise of spiritual authority."[37] Caraher outlines how the trope of abandonment of urban public buildings (especially temples) and the countryside alike shape ancient and modern characterizations of Late Antiquity.[38] Sharp differences of opinion and argument remain, however, while conference volumes often emphasize regional variation rather than draw general conclusions.

There is a clear need for new historical narratives of the human agents of continuity and change in late antique cities, especially in Greece. The majority of archaeologists in Greece now excavate small areas of monumental, pre-Roman cities or sanctuaries, do salvage excavation of small separate plots of land or conduct intensive surveys. The rise of survey archaeology, social science theories and questioning of old pottery chronologies has yielded masses of new data and new interpretations, unevenly published, but often sharply at odds with older evidence and assumptions.[39] Among historians, on the other hand, there is similarly an interest in social and cultural history, the history of individuals, the female, poor and rural folk passed over in ancient texts or early modern scholarship.[40] From this perspective, I have a very traditional focus on authorities in power, rather than the poor, and their texts, statues and monumental public buildings. These are the materials, along with pottery, coins and graves, which archaeology in Greece has mainly uncovered, and they have shaped the history written about ancient Greece and urban life there. However, the main thrust of historical writing on ancient Greek cities, like the *Polis* project, continues to focus on the cities and monuments of the Classical era.[41] Moreover, only one of the conference volumes cited above on cities in Late Antiquity, for example, included any case studies from Greece.[42] Another long-standing problem in scholarship on ancient cities is the tendency to stay within modern socio-political boundaries, especially among Greece, Turkey, Italy and the Balkan countries (I am not immune to this either). There is thus a pressing need to study cities in Greece, and elsewhere, against the backdrop of vigorous research on the causes of urban change all around the Mediterranean Sea in Late Antiquity.

Comparison of late antique cities at opposite ends of the Mediterranean by Jorge López Quiroga, along with research by Daniel Osland at Emerita Augusta in Spain and Christopher Lightfoot at Amorium in Turkey, leads to conclusions which my work at Corinth supports: urban public infrastructure and related economic activity was directly maintained by newly Christian civic elites and the Christian clergy on the basis of their own interests.[43] They supported the continuation of only certain limited aspects of ancient urban life in their new political, economic and especially religious circumstances, notably urban needs related to water supply, commerce, communications, defense and the practices of Christianity. In the chapters which follow, I outline the details of this process at Corinth and the evidence for the people involved from the third to sixth centuries, revealing not only how these changing civic elites reshaped their city by their choices, but also how the activities of the rest of the urban population were shaped in turn to suit the interests of the elites. I will show how the Corinthians as a whole, but especially the elites who had the money and will to do so, responded concretely to external shifts in politics, economics, religion and culture to transform but still preserve their city into the late sixth century.

Structure

Chapters are organized thematically around traditional ancient Greco-Roman civic authorities and institutions to reveal what persisted, disappeared, and was transformed by the response of Corinthian officials, and the broader populace, to the political, economic and religious pressures of Late Antiquity. The ideal civic institutions of an ancient Greek city under the Roman Empire were defined famously by Pausanias' *Guide to Greece*, in relation to their absence from little Panopeus in Boeotia, just north of Corinth.[44] In the middle of the second century, the starting point of my research, Pausanias pointed out the notable civic institutions which Panopeus lacked: *archeia* (official buildings), public buildings designated for administration and government by *archontes* (leaders or officials), and an *agora* (latin *forum*), an open marketplace where the *archeia* would stand alongside stoas, shops and workshops as the commercial center of the city. Panopeus even had no "water led to a fountain," no *gymnasion* (gymnasium) or *theatron* (theater). What it did have were a landscape linked to mythology, cult spaces for the practice of traditional Greek polytheistic religion, and strong fortification walls. I have used Pausanias' definitions to guide my chapters on continuity and change in the urban institutions of late antique Corinth.

Chapter 1 starts with the natural landscape of the Corinthia, and the literary evidence for the changing civic authorities (*archontes*) who administered Corinth in Late Antiquity, from the colonial City Councillors, Greco-Roman priests, and imperial Governors of Achaia to the Christian archbishop and his clergy. Chapter 2 then surveys the continuities and changes in the Corinthian authorities' central public spaces of civic administration and government, their *archeia* (official buildings): the Forum, the *Bouleuterion* (*Curia*, or Council House), civic basilicas, a *Praetorium* (Governor's Palace) and an episcopal palace. These last two buildings have not been located for certain, but would have resembled the excavated Corinthian urban and rural villas.

Chapter 3 emphasizes the continuities in civic amenities of commerce, water supply and communications which the Corinthian authorities maintained, such as stoas, shops, fountains, baths, streets and harbors. The Forum continued throughout Late Antiquity as a civic center and a Greek *agora* (market) maintained by the authorities and used by all levels of people, with surrounding stoas and shops, and paved roads running to the harbors, Acrocorinth and neighboring cities. The central amenity of urban life at well-watered Corinth, however, unlike Panopeus, was always management of the natural springs, and although small-scale fountains and baths gradually replaced the monumental Roman imperial structures, and many drains were blocked or replaced, public control of a continuous supply of clean fresh water for drinking and washing remained central to urban living and bathing at Corinth throughout Late Antiquity.

Chapter 4 offers a stark contrast to the continuities of Chapters 1, 2 and 3, as it shows how the traditional public spaces of assembly and entertainment, chiefly the Isthmian festival site, but also the *gymnasia* (gymnasiums), circus, stadium, odeum and *theatron* (theater) of Corinth were adorned and frequented in the third and fourth century, but then gradually demolished for building material and lost to public use in the fifth and sixth centuries. A similar rupture with long-standing urban traditions, and with a similar chronology of dramatic change in public attitudes, can be observed in the creation and destruction of public sculpture, the focus of Chapter 5.

Chapters 6 and 7 cover what was lost, and what gained, in the profound fifth- and sixth-century Christianization of the Corinthian sacred landscape, both built and experienced. The slow loss of traditional Greco-Roman temples, cults, rituals, festivals and inter-linked mythology around the Forum Area in the fifth and sixth century is the focus of Chapter 6, and their replacement with Christian (and Jewish) sacred spaces and practices. The faster, earlier-to-change rupture in the sacred landscape of the civic periphery, harbors and fortresses in the later fourth and fifth centuries forms Chapter 7, climaxing with many monumental Christian churches built in these areas in the sixth century. In the second century, Panopeus and Corinth alike shared a Greco-Roman polytheistic religion connected with cult buildings old and new, which were destroyed, abandoned or replaced unevenly by churches and Christian practices in Late Antiquity, creating a revised sacred topography and a new set of stories for the city.

Finally, Chapter 8 looks at the most monumental and expensive structures besides churches built in Late Antiquity at Corinth: the massive fortification walls for protection in times of trouble which were put up across the Isthmus, around the city center and on Acrocorinth. These fortification walls were created anew (or in the case of Acrocorinth rebuilt) largely using building material from the old venues of public assembly, entertainment, culture and religion. They were built to supplement the natural defenses of the narrow Isthmus and high Acrocorinth, and to protect the populace and the public buildings of the city center, in response to decisions and spending by imperial authorities, but probably by employing local Corinthians to actually conduct the work. The populace of late antique Corinth, and the civic authorities, whether colonial, imperial or ecclesiastical, all had human needs to fulfill, but they also made practical and ideological decisions to intervene in their natural and built environment for public as well as private benefit. The fifth- and sixth-century authorities not only renovated old structures for administration and commerce, transport and food-supply, water and hygiene, but they also built monumental new structures for Christian collective worship, and monumental, but often in the future largely symbolic, high fortification walls for protection.

A city is made up of people, both the authorities and the population at large, not just buildings in a landscape. There are real challenges in recovering the actions and intentions of individuals in the past, and the specific uses and forces shaping urban spaces, especially over decades and centuries. So besides Pausanias' civic ideals, I also try to recover some of Luke Lavan's "activity areas" of overlapping civic, commercial and cultural space in Late Antiquity.[45] Ideally, the study of such activity areas stays connected to evidence both textual and archaeological, and restores change over time to the study of ruined buildings, placing them back into landscapes filled with people to occupy and use them, and deposit artifacts.[46] Civic space in Chapter 2 thus spans local, imperial and ecclesiastical politics and construction, whether of public buildings or fine houses.[47] Commercial space in Chapter 3 encompasses the economy of Corinth, its professions, shops, workshops, industries and commerce, and the response of the individual Corinthians and the authorities to economic uncertainty and pressure.[48] Cultural space in Chapters 4–7 then covers the intertwined religious and (for lack of a better term) secular cultural spaces where this authority played out alongside and intertwined with dramatic religious change: so-called pagan temples and their cults were all replaced by churches (though the Jewish synagogue survived); artistic and athletic spectacles ceased to happen almost entirely, as their traditional venues of public entertainment were destroyed to make way for fortifications, or abandoned; public sculpture was melted down or dumped in drains.[49] My subtitle "Greek, Roman and Christian" alludes to the threefold civic culture at Corinth in Late Antiquity, which was shared more broadly across the Eastern Roman Empire, but especially prominent in a Greek city, refounded by the Romans, which traced its Church to the Apostle Paul. Within each chapter, I also try to revive multiple and overlapping uses which were likely present in each ancient space, based on building type, location, artifacts and chronology.

The urban transformations of Corinth in Late Antiquity fall into two sharply different eras. In the third and fourth century, the pace of adding new statues, inscriptions and public buildings slowed down, but these continued to be created, and generally in traditional styles. Inner-city venues for public entertainment were renovated into arenas, while remodeling of stoas, shops and roads took place around the Forum, and at rich villas in and outside the city. The later fourth century was an especially tumultuous time for local elites, the Governor of Achaia, the Church and the entire cityscape of Corinth. Earthquakes and so-called barbarian invasions spurred change alongside Christian conversion and upheaval in imperial administration.

The fifth and sixth centuries saw a very different sort of city gradually develop: Corinthians stopped erecting or maintaining statues, temples, sites for public entertainment and most old monumental public buildings. They melted down, demolished or cut up most of what they had, in order to build monumental churches and fortification walls, as well as more modest versions of traditional public buildings such as stoas, shops, fountains and baths. The communal Christian festivals, and the churches, became central to civic life, and the traditional public gathering places, along with the artistic, athletic and spectacular events once held there, were abandoned or actively demolished. Corinthians did continue to patronize and renovate some old public spaces around the Forum in the later sixth century, but they also built their new stoas, shops, fountains and baths on a much smaller scale, and with much reused rather than new material. Byzantine Corinth, however, is a subject for another book.

In what follows, I offer an organized account of the major changes to urban life in late antique Corinth, from both the historical and archaeological evidence, and ask why urban life was changing so dramatically in Late Antiquity, and who (or less often what) was responsible. I explore some of the major areas of these changes – in civic spaces of administration, commerce, entertainment, religion and defence – and identify ways in which the Corinthians responded by adapting their own urban environment to external and internal pressures. In Late Antiquity, Corinth was always considered a city, by its own inhabitants, its leaders and outsiders. Corinth was a community of people living in close proximity, and maintaining both common urban institutions and public buildings. The Corinthians first transferred their allegiance and office-holding from a local City Council under an imperial governor to a more amorphous group of local Christian *archontes* (leaders) under the archbishop, his clergy and an imperial military general. They gradually changed how they celebrated their leaders and decorated their city (without statues), what they bought and where it came from (cheaper quality, more local production), and how they marked births, deaths and festivals (at the Christian church, or Jewish synagogue). By the end of the sixth century, the Corinthians had changed the way they did almost everything, but they did not in the process abandon their city, their urban way of life, or their identity as Corinthians.

CHAPTER 1

LANDSCAPE AND CIVIC AUTHORITIES IN LATE ANTIQUE CORINTH

The history of the city of Corinth in all eras unfolded in the activities of people enhancing and exploiting the resources of the natural landscape of the Corinthia, shaping it through construction and cultivation, receiving ships or travelers at the Isthmus, rebuilding after earthquakes, and withdrawing to Acrocorinth in times of trouble. Corinthians, visitors and immigrants all contributed to this process, and so to history, but civic authorities in control of resources shaped the city in the most monumental way, and appear most prominently in the historical record. These included (mostly male and wealthy) local *archontes* (leaders), landowners, councillors of the colonial City Council, priests of the traditional Greco-Roman (or Imperial) cults, the Governor of Achaia, his staff and many other imperial officials. From the fourth century, the newly legal and increasingly powerful Christian archbishop of Corinth and his clergy increasingly overlapped with the local *archontes*, and took up some of their responsibilites around the city, while also overturning many traditional areas of civic patronage.

The Landscape of Late Antique Corinth

Corinthian history is intertwined with the natural topography, geology, climate, resources, opportunities and limitations of the landscape of the Corinthia, the territory of the city of Corinth.

Geographers, generals and poets alike have long admired the Corinthian landscape, with the city center commanding two seas, the narrow Isthmus of land in between, and a fertile coastal plain below the natural crag of Acrocorinth (see Figures 1–10, 1.1–1.5).[1] Natural springs, stones, earthquakes, rainfall, flora and fauna all still shape the possibilities and limitations of urban life today, as in millennia past, in the Corinthia, the territory of the city of Corinth, at the northeastern corner of the Peloponnesian peninsula.[2] Here, the Isthmus forms a natural landbridge between the Peloponnese and central Greece, dividing the Corinthian Gulf on the west from the Saronic Gulf to the east.[3] North of the Isthmus, the Geraneia mountains and Perachora (or Peraea) peninsula stab westwards into the Corinthian Gulf, forming the border with Megara, today part of Attica.[4] To the south, Mt. Kyllene's foothills step down from the west at Mt Apesas (Phokas) and then curl around to the east to cradle the Corinthian plain, reaching the Saronic Gulf at Mt Oneion and its eastern hill Stanotopi, with steeper peaks and mountain valleys just to its south, including Solygeia (modern Galataki), Sophiko and coastal Korphos (probably the ancient Speiraion cape and harbor).[5] This mountain range divides Corinthia from Arcadia, Argolis and then Epidauria to the south, with their upland valleys and the ancient cities of Phlius (Agios Georgios, Modern Nemea), Kleonai (Agios Nikolaos, near the Nemean festival site at Ancient Nemea) and coastal Epidauros (the city was on the north coast below Epidauros' more famous Sanctuary of Asklepios).

To the west, the deep gorges of the seasonal torrents of the Longopotamos (Rachiani) and then Nemea (Koutsomadiou or Zapantis) Rivers separate Corinthia from ancient Sikyonia (ancient Sikyon is modern Vasiliko, with its harbor Kiato), the Asopos (modern Agiorgitikos) River valley, and then the narrow coastal plain of Achaia, with its "ever changing mixture of bold promontory, gentle slope, and cultivated level … crowned on every side by lofty mountains," which Colonel Leake once praised.[6] At the heart of the Corinthia, the natural bastion of Acrocorinth rises up above a skirt of rocky terraces descending unevenly to the coastal plains below, cut off from Mt Oneion by the Leukon (Xerias River) valley to the east.[7] The Corinthia thus has two seashores as natural boundaries, permeable sites for sailing in or out, to west or east, but also more solid southern and northern mountain boundaries, where civic,

Figure 1.1 Ancient Corinth and Acrocorinth, looking south from Lechaion in 1810, with columns of Temple of Apollo at center, panorama by Von Stackelberg (Published in Williams 1829, vol. 1, pl. 9.)

Figure 1.2 Ancient Corinth and Acrocorinth, looking south from Lechaion in 2017. (Photo by author.)

military and later ecclesiastical circles of authority radiating out from the *Bouleuterion* (Council House), fortress or cathedral extended along narrow roads to neighboring cities.

Today, the village of Ancient Corinth occupies the city center of ancient Corinth, sitting on raised terraces north of Acrocorinth with a panoramic view of the Gulf of Corinth, the Isthmus, and the proverbially fertile coastal plain, the Vocha, which extends west towards ancient Sikyonia, and northeast as far as modern Corinth on the coast of the Isthmus (Figures 2–3, 1.2–1.3).[8] Modern Corinth, *Korinthos,* is now the political, economic and ecclesiastical city center of the Corinthia, but it was founded only after an 1858 earthquake, and sited on the west side of the Isthmus between two ancient ports, Poseidonia and Lechaion. Lechaion has been identified by visible ruins, mounds of dredged sand, and a shallow artificial lagoon marking the man-made harbor which once served the Corinthian Gulf, the Ionian and Adriatic Seas, and the Western Mediterranean.[9] On the eastern side of the Isthmus, Kenchreai (modern *Kenchries*), south of Poseidon's Sanctuary at Isthmia, was the main port in Late Antiquity for accessing the Saronic Gulf, the Aegean Sea and the eastern Mediterranean (Figure 10).[10] The modern Corinth Canal was cut across the narrowest point of the Isthmus, alongside the ancient roadways and fortification walls which once ran from the western harbor of Poseidonia (modern Corinth) to Schoinous (modern Kalamaki), the ancient port of Isthmia, on the east side of the Isthmus.

Geologically, the Corinthia, like most of Greece, is a skeleton of hard limestone mountains under a body of former seabeds, with a skin of recently deposited coastal sediments. Acrocorinth is ringed with layers of uplifted and tilted former seabeds: soft limestones, conglomerates and corals overlying even softer marls, resources extracted since Antiquity (but not including any marble).[11] Corinthian limestone was quarried directly from the surface, notably from the fossilized sand dunes of oolithic limestone which run through the ancient city center and to the east.[12] At the edges of these limestone and conglomerate terraces, the underlying marl layers yield clays for the famous Corinthian ceramics.[13] These layers are also relatively impervious to water, and thus channel groundwater out along the northern edges of the terraces to form east-west bands of natural springs. The use of these natural springs by the ancient Corinthians has been well studied: atop Acrocorinth, along its northern base, and along the northern edges of the upper and lower terraces of the ancient city, some 24 springs emit cool, fresh water year-round.[14]

Medium-sized earthquakes (4 to 5) are very common in Poseidon's Corinthia, but only rarely do earthquakes do extensive damage, or generate tsunamis, uplift or subsidence. A series of segmented faults form the southern side of the Corinthian and Saronic Gulfs, part of the larger African-European plate boundary.[15] Ambraseys claims no earthquake of the past 300 years in Central Greece has exceeded 7.5, and the 15–20 km. length of the faults probably makes this an upper limit for this region.[16] Specific pre-modern earthquakes mentioned in texts or visible in the landscape are rarely precisely datable, and the types of tectonic activity common in the Corinthia must be carefully combined with any ancient account, or archaeology.[17] Stephen Miller has pointed out that although the strong earthquakes of 1858 (7.0) and 1861 (7.3) caused extensive damage to houses in both Ancient Corinth and Ancient Nemea, the ancient columns still standing at both sites were unharmed. The Nemean temple's fallen columns, neatly splayed outwards, along with the flexibility of multi-drum columns, mean that the ancient destruction of the Temple of Zeus at Nemea was largely done by human hands, with implications for other colonnades throughout the Corinthia.[18]

No written account of a fourth-century earthquake specifically names Corinth. Libanius refers to earthquakes in 363 in Greece and Palestine in his *Funeral Oration* for the emperor Julian; his phrasing is echoed by the historian Zosimus, who describes an earthquake in Greece after the death of Valentinian on 17 November 375.[19] In both cases, the *topos* is used of "every city in Greece but one was destroyed" after the death of an emperor. Rothaus thus suggests the second earthquake of 375/6 is a literary fabrication, though he does not cite the epigraphic evidence outlined below.[20] Jerome, in a commentary on Isaiah, also recorded the 363 quake in Palestine, then made fuller reference to another quake of 21 July 365, affecting Sicily, many islands and the coast of Epirus.[21] This is almost certainly the quake and tsunami which Ammianus dates in the second year of the joint reign of Valens and Valentinian (365/6), and which he says affected Alexandria, Sicily, Crete and the southwestern coasts of the Peloponnese and Epirus.[22]

Corroborating evidence for a late fourth-century earthquake affecting Corinth, and the interest of local officials in making repairs to public buildings afterwards, comes from an inscription built into a gate at Nauplion (the port of Argos), origin unknown, which honors a *scholastikos* (rhetorician, or advocate) for repairing "a basilica" under the emperor Valens (and Gratian?, 375–8?) damaged "by earthquakes and movement of the seas (tsunamis)," κατὰ σισμοὺς καὶ τοὺς θαλαττὶο[υς \ κατακλυσμοὺς?].[23] The clearest archaeological evidence for late fourth-century earthquake damage at Corinth comes from the Great Bath on the Lechaion Road, repaired *c.*400, and the Governor of Achaia's restoration of colonnades in front of the West Shops and South Stoa under Valens and Valentinian (see Chapter 3). The southern harbor mole at Kenchreai was also probably shaken and sunk by seismic activity *c.*400 (see Chapter 7, and Figure 10). Thus, although Corinth is not explicitly mentioned in any literary source for a fourth-century earthquake, there is damage to public buildings at Corinth and repairs in the late fourth century which could be seismically motivated.

In the sixth century, Malalas explicitly records that Corinth suffered an earthquake in 520/1, the third year of Justin's reign, when that emperor sent aid to the city, perhaps even making repairs to the Forum, where he was honored in an inscription.[24] Procopius invokes earthquakes at Corinth twice for rhetorical value discussing the reign of Justin's nephew and successor Justinian. He uses them to give the negative side of Justinian's era of authority in the *Secret History*, enumerating the natural disasters which either Justinian caused as a demon incarnate, or which God caused as punishment for the Roman Empire from 518 to about 558/9.[25] He emphasizes in particular the loss of life in Corinth and eight other cities, first victims of earthquake, and then the plague from 541/2 on. Corinth is significant enough to be listed last, a pendant to Antioch listed first. Procopius emphasizes the scale and range of diasters and "destruction of humanity," not recovery, for a very long list of places. However, he also refers to earthquakes at Corinth while praising Justinian for

Figure 1.3 Ancient Corinth, the Corinthian Gulf and Perachora, looking north from the slopes of Acrocorinth in 2017. (Photo by author.)

Figure 1.4 Ancient Corinth Forum Area, looking north from the South Stoa across the Forum at the Temple of Apollo, Northwest Shops and modern village church on the right (east). (Photo by author.)

building the Hexamilion Wall across the Isthmus in his *Buildings*.[26] It is likely that he is referring first of all in the *Secret History* and the *Buildings* to the quake of 520/1, for which Malalas says the emperor Justin sent relief (see above). Procopius may also, when he speaks of

Figure 1.5 Lechaion Road, looking north from the Propylaia, with Peirene Fountain, the Peribolos of Apollo and the modern village *Plateia* and church of Ancient Corinth on the right (east). (Photo by author.)

plural earthquakes in the *Buildings*, be including lesser damage caused by a quake in 551/2. He mentioned this earthquake in the last book of his *Wars* as damaging Boeotia, Achaia and the Crisaean (Corinthian) Gulf, Chaeronea, Coronea, Patras, Naupactus and Delphi, and causing a tsunami in the Malean Gulf between Boeotia and Thessaly near Thermopylae.[27] This sounds like a quake or series of quakes along the faults west of Corinth in 551/2, but not one strong enough at Corinth to warrant imperial aid.

The Corinthian climate is Mediterranean, with hot dry summers and cool wet winters.[28] On the mountains, terraces, and coastal plains, natural vegetation and agriculture coexist, watered by the natural springs, seasonal torrents and a low level of annual rainfall, which tends to fall in short, intense cloudbursts. The natural vegetation is similar to Antiquity in type and elevation, with pine, fir and oak forests on the mountain slopes changing to shrubby maquis or low lying phrygana lower down.[29] The large trees necessary for ancient ship-building and architecture were once common on slopes, particularly on the north side of Mt Geraneia.[30] The Hellenistic fortified refuge of Oenoe in these northern mountains of the Perachora peninsula, and adjacent modern logging, probably indicate the presence of forestry there in Antiquity.[31] Uncultivated areas of the Corinthia provided firewood in all eras, as did trimming of vines and olive groves. Wild herbs, nuts and berries were gathered for consumption and medicine, along with the Kermes oak insect (*pinokokki* on *quercus coccifera*) for red cocchineal dye, for example, or acorns for tanning hides.[32]

Alongside this native vegetation, a mixed agriculture of fields, flocks and groves was certainly practiced by Corinthians long before, and long after, Late Antiquity, shaped by altitude, available water and soil quality, as well as population, urban demands and larger-scale market forces.[33] The major division in planting was between the drier, poorer soils of the lower mountain slopes and terraces, and the thicker, better soils of the more well-watered coastal plain. Today, the Mediterranean triad of grains, olives and vines coexists with the cultivation of legumes, vegetables and new fruits in the Corinthia, despite suburban housing and industry. In the seventeenth century, the gardens of Ancient Corinth were famous for citrus trees introduced in the Middle Ages, while the plain was divided into large estates where tenant farmers cultivated grains, lentils and vegetables.[34] These large estates were broken up after Greek independence, and since then the plain has grown cash crops, shifting from currants to tobacco and then, since EU accession, currants, tomatoes, flowers and vegetables.[35] Since the 1970s, bulldozers have been used to create new agricultural terraces and reorient communication routes.[36] Flocks of sheep mixed with goats still graze alongside Corinthian fields and groves, but tractors replaced the bovines and equines once kept for traction in the twentieth century.[37]

The intensity of agriculture and the relative proportions (and types) of crops and domestic animals have certainly changed frequently in the Corinthia since Late Antiquity, but farming methods and technologies advanced little before the middle of the twentieth century.[38] Sanders argues convincingly that historians like Salmon and Engels underestimate the fertility of the ancient Corinthia by offering estimates for average cereal-yields well below early modern, or even ancient, data from the Corinthia, as well as from better-documented neighboring Argolis and Attica. He also demonstrates from a range of early modern sources how yields vary from year to year, and how much was required to support subsistence, on the same sorts of fields as farmed in Antiquity around the Corinthia.[39] Ancient authors praised Corinthia's abundant vineyards, but disapproved of the harsh wine produced by them, which was largely for local consumption.[40] Comparisons between the Corinthia, Argolis and Attica, as well as between Corinth and other Roman colonies, show that the Corinthia probably supported a population of about 30,000 in the second century, and into Late Antiquity.[41]

Local and Imperial Authorities in Late Antique Corinth

Corinthians inhabiting this landscape in Late Antiquity were governed at first by a colonial City Council (*Curia*, or *Boule*) composed of eligible landowners, the decurions, who chose magistrates, or civic officials (*archontes*), from among themselves to supervise civic services, collect taxes, and administer local cults. At the imperial level of administration, Corinth was the capital city of the province of Achaia, the official seat of the Governor of Achaia and his staff.[42] In the third and fourth centuries, the City Council, local elites and the Governor of Achaia appear frequently in inscriptions, and sometimes in literary sources, as patrons of public building and administration in Corinth. However, both the City Council and the Governor of Achaia largely drop out of the written record in the early fifth century, with the decurions apparently disappearing into imperial service abroad, retiring to their villas in the countryside, or joining the Christian hierarchy, which exercised growing power over local civic as well as ecclesiastical affairs. From the sixth century, though, the local landowners (and former decurions) were officially joined by imperial law with the Metropolitan archbishop of Corinth and his clergy into a new council of *archontes*, who are attested elsewhere as appointing civic officials like a *defensor* (*ekdikos*), *pater* and/or *curator* (*logistes* or *ephoros*) of the city.[43] Into the Byzantine era, then, there were still *archontes* of Corinth officially responsible for civic services in close alliance with the archbishop and clergy of the Church, and still under the auspices of imperial authorities like a *Strategos* (General) of Hellas (the *theme* name which replaced the province of Achaia), and the Praetorian Prefect of Illyricum or Eparch at Thessalonike.

As the official representative of Roman imperial authority, the Governor of Achaia and his staff were responsible for collecting imperial taxes, judging legal cases, hearing petitions, and handling a steadily growing number of local issues.[44] Literary and epigraphic sources help to establish the role of the governor at Corinth, and in Achaia, before and after the tetrarchic reforms of Diocletian, after the rise of Constantine, and then into the sixth century.[45] The Governor of Achaia in the second and third centuries was a senatorial proconsul of praetorian rank, a *vir clarissimus proconsul* (Greek ὁ λαμπρότατος ἀνθύπατος). Diocletian, however, reorganized the provinces after his accession in 284, and demoted the post of Governor of Achaia (along with other imperial posts) to the equestrian rank of a *vir perfectissimus praeses* (Greek ὁ διασημότατος ἡγεμών). Constantine, however, extended his imperial rule over Greece in 317, again reorganizing the provinces and restoring the governorship of Achaia to a senatorial province for a *vir clarissimus* of consular rank. Thus, to serve as Governor of Achaia in Corinth remained one of the plum posts of the Later Roman Empire throughout the third and fourth centuries, and even into the fifth century.[46]

After Diocletian's reforms and the creation of the Tetrarchy, Corinth also became part of a new three-tiered system of political and military imperial administration in the Balkans, under the Emperor of the East. The grand Prefecture of Illyricum encompassed the southern

Balkans, and had its capital and Praetorian Prefect at first at Sirmium (and later Thessalonike), with below that a diocese and Vicar of Moesia (later Macedonia, also at Thessalonike), and below that the old Roman province of Achaia, still with Corinth as its capital city for the Governor of Achaia. The province of Achaia extended, as before, from the Peloponnesus north through Attica, Boeotia, Locris and Phocis to a frontier on the northwest with Epirus and on the northeast with Thessaly (along the strategic pass of Thermopylae) (Figure 1).

Other than the restoration of the rank of the Governor of Achaia, Constantine made no other known benefaction at Corinth, although he did make benefactions to other cities in Greece, especially Athens, according to his successor Julian.[47] Inscriptions erected in honor of Constantine, or his sons, often along with fellow tetrarchs, are found throughout Greece.[48] However, at Corinth there is nothing for him or his family found to date but one single statue base, a reused garland altar turned upside down and inscribed by "the city of the Corinthians" in honor of "the victorious Augustus / Flavius Constans," probably the son of Constantine rather than the seventh-century imperial visitor Constans II.[49] Inscribed plaques honor a few emperors of the fourth to sixth centuries, and perhaps record local benefactions directed by them to Corinth via their officials (see below, Chapter 5). Justinian's official Victorinus in the sixth century was clearly responsible in some way for financing and building fortification walls throughout Illyricum, and also for Corinth and Greece, according to the Hexamilion inscriptions (see below, Chapter 8). Imperial authority and patronage at Corinth apparently passed in the middle of the fifth century from the Governor of Achaia to other imperial officials responsible for military and sometimes other sorts of public infrastructure.

Both Wiseman, and more recently Haensch, have questioned whether Corinth was in fact the official seat of the Governor of Achaia, and hence the capital city of that province.[50] However, Corinth's status as the provincial capital of Achaia seems clear from both the literary and epigraphic record, particularly from the first century onwards, and in context with other cities in Achaia like Athens, Messene and Patras.[51] Corinth is "the head of the whole province of Achaia" in Apuleius' *Metamorphoses*, where the story is partly set in the second-century city.[52] Aelius Aristides praised second-century Corinth as "even the common city of the Greeks, a sort of metropolis and mother for them."[53] This second-sophistic rhetorical elision, from Archaic Corinth as notable colonizer and metropolis, to contemporary Roman Corinth as provincial capital, and thus metropolis of Hellas, finds epigraphic expression on a statue base of third-century lettering from the Corinthian Forum. Here an otherwise unknown orator, Peducaeus Cestianus of Apollonia (a Corinthian colony), was honored in Greek with permission of the *Boule* (City Council) by Κόρινθος / ἡ μητρόπολις, "Corinth / the Metropolis."[54] The sixth-century chronicler Malalas also calls Vespasianic Corinth the *metropolis* of *Hellas*, while his contemporary Hierocles displayed his erudition by listing the city in his geographic work as "once Ephyra, metropolis of all Hellas."[55] These and other Early Byzantine authors were influenced, no doubt, by the Church hierarchy, since Corinth was the seat of the Metropolitan archbishop, but also by the shift in nomenclature from the province of Achaia to the *theme* of Hellas, which kept Corinth as the seat of the *Strategos* (General).

The governor appears frequently in Corinthian inscriptions of the third to fourth century as a benefactor of the city, and especially its public buildings, in the name of the ruling emperor(s), as the conferor of honors to local benefactors, or as the recipient of honors from the city. Only one inscribed edict of a Governor of Achaia is well-preserved: a fourth- or fifth-century declaration on correct procedure in the law courts from a certain Fl. Ulpius Macarius. The Governor of Achaia most famous outside of Greece was undoubtedly Aur. Valerius Tullianus Symmachus, who received two constitutions preserved in the Theodosian Code while in office at Corinth in 319 (*CTh* 2.4.1, 2.15.1).[56] No other city in Achaia has so many gubernatorial honors, attestations of his presence, or civic functionaries mentioned in inscriptions from the first century into Late Antiquity (see Chapter 5 for further on statues and statue bases). Inscriptions and *testimonia* of the fourth through early fifth century continue to reveal the Governor of Achaia, his staff and other imperial officials active in Corinth, while epitaphs show civic administration still carried out into the sixth or seventh century (dating on *formulae* and letter forms).[57] Public officials, members of the governor's staff or the staff of the City continue to appear in late antique inscriptions even when these become mainly Christian epitaphs.[58] Public honorific inscriptions as a whole decrease sharply from the third to fifth century, while epitaphs, mostly for Christians, rise steadily from the later fourth century to a peak in the sixth century, and continue into the seventh century. Among the public officials, both local and imperial, catalogued by Michael B. Walbank in his study of the inscriptions of the Christian community of Corinth he finds an assessor (*protos*), *lictors* (*rhabdouchoi*), clerks (*orthographos, taxeotes*), a councillor (*bouleutes*), an ex-prefect (*apo eparchon*), financial officials (*singoularioi*), guards (*exkoubitores, boukellarioi*) and stewards (*domestikoi, oikonomos*).[59] Especially noteworthy for serving the civic administration of sixth-century Corinth are Julian the bathhouse keeper (*balnikarios*), an unnamed inspector of weights for the city (ζυγοστάτης τῆς πόλεως), and Theodore the muleteer of the bishop (taking over from the *cursus publicus*, the public postal service).[60] Achaia is listed in the *Notitia Dignitatum* of *c.*395 as one of two provinces in the East with a proconsular Governor (the other was Asia), who was served by an extensive staff of assistants and secretaries, and entitled to four uses of the *cursus publicus* (public postal service).[61]

In 395, the emperor Theodosius died, and the Governor of Achaia is attested as present at Corinth when the Gothic general Alaric invaded the Peloponnesus and occupied Greece with his so-called barbarian Gothic army. Alaric's forces were apparently in and around Corinth for over a year, until they were supposedly defeated in battle by a similarly disruptive army under the half-Vandal general Stilicho in the western Peloponnesus, and retreated northwards into Epirus (and eventually to sack Rome in 410).

Inscriptions place the Governor of Achaia and his staff at Corinth at the turn of the fourth to fifth century, after Alaric's invasion, occupation and retreat of 395–7. To judge from some very small epigraphic fragments, the western side of the Forum (maybe even the Northwest Shops) was an area where public documents were posted in Late Antiquity. Five fragments of a list of names with the abbreviation of omicron over tau may represent a third-century cadaster.[62] Sironen disassociates a fragment with the name of the emperor Honorius from this cadaster, identifying the fragment instead as the heading for a lost edict posted between 393–408.[63] Another fragment of a public document found near the Amphitheater records a *diatyposis* (decree passed by a provincial council), which was passed and posted at Corinth under the emperors Arcadius, Honorius and Theodosius, probably in 401/2.[64] Sironen argued that this is the Corinthian copy of a better-preserved inscription of this *diatyposis* found in Megara (but now at the Aegina Museum).[65] The Megara inscription records a meeting of representatives of all the Hellenic cities of the province of Achaia which was held by the Governor of Achaia Claudius Varius at Corinth in the year 401/2, to discuss grain levies to be deposited at Corinth's *horrea* (warehouses) by the cities of the Peloponnesus, and administered there by a *praepositus horreorum* (an administrator of warehouses). This means in the early fifth century the Governor of Achaia still had a place to receive guests and issue regulations, and Corinth still had facilities to entertain official visitors and store large quantities of grain. See Chapter 3 for the harbors where these *horrea* would have been located.

The evidence for the Governor of Achaia at Corinth fades after these early fifth-century documents, and he seems only to be attested once more epigraphically, as the recipient of a fragmentary edict on fortification wall construction sent down by the Praetorian Prefect of Illyricum to the ἀ]νθύπατε τῆς Ἑλ[λάδος (proconsul of *Hellas*, Governor of Greece).[66] Only the central portion of the end of the edict survives, inscribed on an Ionic epistyle block which was apparently reused as a stele for posting the edict publicly, and then later reused again as building material in the South Stoa. The fortification wall construction (τειχοποιΐα) could relate to the city walls of Corinth or the Hexamilion Wall across the Isthmus, and the text has been dated by letter forms to the sixth century. An imperial official, *Comes* Diogenes, is attested in the late fifth century, under the emperor Leo or Zeno, by a statue base which honors him for restoring towers and baths in Megara, and in other Hellenic cities, perhaps including Corinth (he is perhaps the recipient of one of the two *chlamydatus* official portrait statues from Megara).[67]

Under Theodosius II, however, the focus of imperial patronage in southern Greece seems to have shifted to Athens. A large public building south of the Little Metropolis in Athens, possibly once the *Diogenion* or Gymnasium of the Ephebes, is known from an inscribed epistyle block to have been "built up from the foundations by the Proconsul of Hellas, Severus Aëtius," between 396–401; the formula honoring the emperors is the same as that on the rebuilt West Shops and South Stoa colonnades in Corinth (see below in Chapter 2).[68] Next at Athens came the construction of a monumental palace in the

Athenian Classical Agora *c*.410–25, the so-called Gymnasium of the Giants, and contemporary benefactions by the Praetorian Prefect of Illyricum Herculius, the emperor Theodosius II and the native Athenian empress Eudocia.[69]

Imperial officials like the Praetorian Prefect of Illyricum, the Governor of Hellas mentioned above, or Justinian's wall building official Victorinus were surely still present at Corinth from time to time in the fifth and sixth century, and the work of administering the city, collecting taxes, building fortification walls and maintaining some public civic services continued. From the early fifth century, it is Corinth's Christian authorities who appear increasingly in the historical and epigraphic record, and who seem to have taken up many of the old responsibilities of the City Council, the Governor of Achaia, and the old public officials, eventually under the nominal authority of the *Strategos* (General) of the new *theme* of Hellas (the old province of Achaia).

Early Christian Authorities at Corinth

In Late Antiquity, Corinthians traced the origins of their Christian community and its authorities back to the apostle St Paul in the middle of the first century, on the basis of his letters to Corinth, and the later account of his visit to Corinth and trial in *Acts*, both of which were included in their bibles.[70] By the second century, the bishop of Corinth had asserted a position of authority over Christians in southern Greece beyond Corinth too, by virtue of Corinth's status as provincial capital of Achaia, and as the receipient of St Paul's letters and apostolic ministry. St Paul, and his editor-biographers, were well aware of the importance of focusing their efforts on provincial capitals and prominent cities with Jewish populations like Corinth. As a church hierarchy solidified in the later second and third centuries, the archbishop of Corinth maintained his primacy over bishops throughout Achaia, and, as in the secular world, exercised his authority under the auspices of an official in Thessalonike, an archbishop who was subject to the Western Church under the Archbishop of Rome (the Pope).[71] Our surviving texts on the Early Church at Corinth largely emerge out of episodes of conflict: between Christians and Jews in the second and early third century, between Christians and Roman imperial authorities in the mid-third to early fourth centuries, and among self-identifying Christians throughout.[72] In the later fourth century and fifth there is even some textual evidence for conflict between Christians and Hellenes (polytheists or pagans).

Evidence for the conflict between Christians and the Roman imperial authorities at Corinth survives, as at other cities, mainly in much later lists of names of Christian martyrs, with their date of execution (and later commemoration), and the names of the officials who ordered it. Vassiliki Limberis points out how late in date and problemmatic as historical sources are these lists of names and dates for Corinthian martyrs, and how subject to confusion with other martyrs.[73] Only two Corinthian martyrs achieved fame in the wider church, St Quadratus and St Leonidas, whose cults will be discussed in Chapter 7 in relation to the churches likely built in their honor in the north cemetery of Corinth and at the harbor of Lechaion respectively. Otherwise, we read that in the era of Gordian III and Philip the Arab (238–49), Helikonis of Thessalonike was tortured and martyred at Corinth, on 10 March, under the procurator Justin, then Victorinus and six others were tortured and martyred on 31 January under the procurator Tertius, probably during the Decian persecution.[74] The undated martyr Deacon Tymonis was remembered on 19 April, as were Crispus and Gaius on 4 October.[75] Corinth's last martyr, apparently under Diocletian, was supposedly a young official who freed a virgin desired by the proconsul from a brothel, and was hence thrown to the beasts.[76]

Thus among Greek cities with contemporary martyrdom stories, Corinth is notable for the fact that most concern large groups of martyrs executed in March/April; there is a possible connection here with the celebration of Easter and Passover provoking negative attention from the Jewish community and Roman authorities, the biennial Isthmian games in the spring, or the usual time for the governor to hold court at Corinth when he arrived at the beginning of the sailing season. We also see a combination of Latin and Greek names, and a number of Christians from outside the city, mostly from Achaia or southern Illyricum. In the third and early fourth centuries, then, the tribunal of the Julian Basilica and the other civic basilicas of Corinth were likely the scene for the trials of these or other Christians at Corinth, required to offer incense to the genius of the reigning emperor present in portrait-form (see Chapter 2).[77]

In the fourth century, the Corinthian archbishops Hesiodos, Epictetus, Dionysius II, Dorotheos and then finally Alexander oversaw the activities of about 46 suffragan Christian bishops at the head of now legal churches throughout Achaia.[78] With Archbishop Alexander, the clergy of Corinth re-emerge into the wider discourse of Christianity outside Achaia.[79] John Chrysostom corresponded with Alexander, and then *c.*400 called Corinth 'the first city of Greece' in his homily on St Paul's *Letter to the Corinthians*.[80] Later in this same homily he also judged St Paul similar yet superior to Diogenes the Cynic, who spent much of his life at Corinth, in the area of the Kraneion, as Chrysostom would have known.[81]

Just a few years later, a scandal arose at Corinth regarding Perigenes, a Corinthian clergyman first appointed bishop of Patras, refused by his new flock there, and then accepted as Archbishop of Corinth by his legitimate higher authority Pope Boniface (but not by his fellow bishops).[82] In 419, all the bishops of Achaia, Thessaly and Epirus subject to the Vicar of Thessalonike held a synod at Corinth to resolve what they called an illegal double bishopric. Over 100 men would have gathered at Corinth, but where would they have met: in an undiscovered church, some subsidiary part of a church complex, or in the episcopal palace? The *Bouleuterion* in the South Stoa could even have been used for this early fifth-century synod.[83] The Thessalian bishops called on Perigenes to resign from Corinth, while those of Achaia appealed to Pope Boniface, who confirmed Perigenes as long as Rufus, his Vicar in Thessalonike, approved.[84] He seems to have done so, and Perigenes remained in office.

Two years later, the Thessalian bishops apparently saw an opening to appeal to Archbishop Atticus of Constantinople, and Arcadius' son Theodosius II, over the head of the Pope in Rome. While Pope Boniface and Patriarch Atticus exchanged accusatory letters, the emperor Theodosius II sent a decree in his and his uncle Honorius' name to the Praetorian Prefect of Illyricum, Philip, on 14 July 421.[85] This law includes the customary fervent endorsements of the old and traditional, but also a very new and unusual defense of the authority of the Archbishop of Constantinople in Illyricum, just as if he were Archbishop of Rome:

> The same Augusti (Honorius and Theodosius) to Philippus, Praetorian Prefect of Illyricum. We command that the ancient

> practice and the pristine ecclesiastical canons which have been in force up to the present shall be observed throughout all the provinces of Illyricum and that all innovations shall cease. Then, if any doubt should arise, such cases must be reserved for the synod of priests and their holy court, not without the knowledge of the most revered man of the sacrosanct law, the Bishop of the City of Constantinople, which enjoys the prerogative of ancient Rome. Given on the day before the ides of July in the year of the consulship of Eustathius and Agricola (14 July 421).[86]

Meanwhile back in Italy Pope Boniface and the emperor Honorius were exchanging letters as well, and at last Honorius persuaded Theodosius II and Patriarch Atticus in Constantinople to defer to Rome's ecclesiastical authority in Illyricum, and let Perigenes stay on as bishop of Corinth.[87] Perigenes then represented Corinth at the Third Ecumenical Council at Ephesus in 431, and died in office in 435.[88] This law, however, remained on the books, and the letters of Popes to bishops in Greece and the Balkans, and to the Emperors in Constantinople in the fifth and sixth century, are full of more and more angry expressions of authority over Illyricum, authority which was slowly waning as the bishops of its provinces turned to Constantinople whenever they objected to something handed down from Rome.

In the first half of the fifth century Corinth still had the resources as a city to host a synod of bishops from Achaia and other provinces of Illyricum too. Her archbishops were conscious of a special status in the emerging political and ecclesiastical struggle between West and East, but did not consistently pick sides. Archbishop Peter of Corinth called another synod of Achaian bishops to his city in 446, this time for the Emperor Leo, and he was chided by the Pope for it; this same Peter was also at Chalcedon in 451, and again favored the Emperor over the Pope.[89] His nephew Kyriakos the Anchorite, whose father was also a priest, became a monk in Palestine.[90] Archbishop of Corinth Eustathius is known only from his epitaph, as he was interred (or re-interred) *c.*500 in the St Quadratus Basilica, which he may have had a role in building (Chapter 7).[91] The clergy of Corinth thus received visitors in the city, traveled abroad, and engaged in correspondence with colleagues around the eastern Mediterranean and as far west as Rome throughout Late Antiquity.

It was apparently in the fifth century that Corinth's Metropolitan Archbishop, his clergy and Christian *archontes* (leaders) gradually supplanted the old City Council and the Governor of Achaia as the responsible local civic authorities. Yet the *Bouleuterion* (Council House) was still usable, and some sort of local authority must have maintained and rebuilt the public infrastructure of stoas, shops, streets, fountains and baths, probably the landowners and former councillors in cooperation with the Christian clergy, as legislation prescribed. But were the Christian officials of these centuries drawn from the same families as the City Councillors had been? How did the imperial officials like the Praetorian Prefect of Illyricum, Philip, handle this shift? The archbishops were seemingly locals, not outsiders, and it was a gradual shift most likely.[92] The old aristocracy only slowly gave up on honoring one another with statues and inscribed poems (see Chapter 5). But they were becoming Christian by the later fourth century, then becoming bishops and building basilica churches by the sixth century, all while maintaining the Fountain of Peirene and fortifying Corinth.

The Corinthian Archbishop Photius sent the deacons Dionysius and Callinicus to the 5th Church Council in Constantinople in 553, and is probably to be identified with the Φώτιος . . . ἐπίσκοπος (Photius . . . bishop) in a prayer inscribed on a column found on Acrocorinth.[93] He had a long term of office under the emperor Justinian as a patron and leader of the city of Corinth, and may even have built a church on Acrocorinth where the prayer was once inscribed as his epitaph (see below, Chapter 7). The Epiphanius in a sixth-century inscription, an invocation of the Holy Trinity found at the west end of the South Stoa, may also have been a sixth-century archbishop.[94]

Christian epitaphs of fifth- to seventh-century script add a range of ecclesiastical offices and clergy below the archbishop to our picture of Corinthian church (and increasingly civic) administration in Late Antiquity. These include, in decreasing order of rank below the archbishop, presbyters, deacons and a deaconess, a sub-deacon (*hyperetes*), a male and a female intendant (*mizoteros/a*), the sextons (*dekanoi*) Andreas and George, and a reader (*anagnostes*).[95] The presence of women as well as men is thus attested in positions of authority in the Church at Corinth, as elsewhere (and as in earlier times). These officials are involved in the selling as well as the buying of graveplots, and, in the case of the sextons, in digging them. Yet they would also have had income from the Church, and official responsibilities outside of services and festivals, giving them authority in the city. There are no monks or holy men in the epitaphs, though men and women besides Victorinus call themselves a slave (*doulos/e*), perhaps piously or perhaps showing real service, and a certain Ioannes is remembered as an ascetic vegetarian (or more likely market gardener).[96]

In 591, Archbishop Anastasius of Corinth was named in letters of introduction from Pope Gregory the Great as his emissary to the Patriarch in Constantinople, and later removed from his seat after a dispute with his superior Hadrian, the Archbishop of Thessalonike.[97] Another correspondent of Pope Gregory, on the topic of clerics avoiding military service, was the Archbishop John of Corinth.[98] An odd group of late antique inscriptions, and notably Christian invocations, came from the western area of the Forum, many written on paving slabs; Scranton suggested that rooms in the Northwest Shops may have served as a prison in the sixth to seventh century, and Michael B. Walbank suggests that the *boukellarioi* (guards) mentioned in two texts were probably in the service of the Church as well as the city, and "cursed by their victims."[99] Even in the 680s, Corinthian bishops are still recorded as acting as emissaries between the Pope in Rome and the Patriarch in Constantinople, so the clergy of Corinth were certainly extant in the seventh century, in the city or traveling between Rome and Constantinople, even after Slavic settlement and then Arab raiding of the Peloponnesus.[100]

CHAPTER 2

THE FORUM AND SPACES OF CIVIC ADMINISTRATION

Corinthian civic and imperial authorities took the lead in construction, renovation or demolition of public buildings in the course of administering the city of Corinth, as well as in the course of many other commercial, sacred or cultural activities. In the name of the Corinthians, these authorities also honored one another for their generosity and benefaction, first with texts and statues, then later just with texts. In Late Antiquity, they also shifted from governing Corinth from the traditional spaces of civic administration around the Forum to the newly built churches and their own palatial homes, whether *villae urbanae* or *rusticae* (urban or rural villas), a *praetorium* (Governor's Palace) or an episcopal residence. The political infrastructure of *archeia* (government buildings) which partly characterized Corinth as a city required both money and initiative to maintain. This political infrastructure included administrative buildings around the Forum like civic basilicas, and construction at the broader interface between public and private spaces in the civic center of Corinth and beyond: the stoas, shops, streets, fountains, baths and harbors which are discussed in Chapter 3. The maintenance of buildings for civic administration, justice and deliberation around the Forum showed the people of Corinth in Late Antiquity the interests and agendas of the authorities, whether these were municipal, imperial or Christian. The construction or enhancement of houses and churches, meanwhile, communicated a different message. Roman houses were always used to some extent for public business, but rarely paid for by the public purse if their occupant was neither the emperor nor his representative. However, I have included them in this chapter as spaces of administration in Late Antiquity. Christian churches, on the other hand, began as houses and then gradually in the fifth century became separate new public assembly buildings (*ekklesiai*) under both local and imperial patronage. It is unlikely, however, that civic funds were devoted to church building at Corinth before such funds became entirely the responsibility of the Church, and so I will consider churches as public religious buildings in Chapters 6 and 7. From the third to sixth century, however, the Forum was always a central urban space to display the exercise of government over the city of Corinth, and its public buildings were modified many times over to suit shifting administrative bodies and models of urban public patronage.

The Forum of Corinth in the Early Third Century

By the early third century, the Corinthian Forum was an architectural palimpsest: monumental pre-Roman Greek public buildings and architecturally enhanced natural springs embedded in a Roman colonial Forum laid out in the early Augustan age, which had itself been transformed by some 250 years of renovations and additions by the City Council, the Governor of Achaia, Roman emperors, and other local and imperial benefactors (Figures 4–5, 1.3–1.5). The result served Corinthians and visitors alike as the civic, commercial and cultural center of the city, the architectural framework for a wide range of ordinary and extraordinary public activities, just like other ancient forums and *agorai* (markets) around the Roman Empire. The Forum was a particular focus of the early excavations at Corinth, and digging has also continued sporadically there down to the present day, along with scholarship, particularly on individual buildings.[1] I combine this ongoing research with the testimony of ancient authors, notably Pausanias, to discuss the Forum's overall appearance and uses throughout Late Antiquity in this and the following chapters. Pausanias was mainly interested in Greek religion and antiquities, however, so it is often hard to restore what Pausanias noted, as well as what he passed over, in his description of his Corinthian Agora (the Roman Forum), and combine it with the evidence of the Corinth excavations (especially since so many late antique, medieval and early modern layers have been removed).

After the early third century, only a few completely new buildings were added to the Forum, but its pavements, stoas, shops, fountains and baths were constantly redecorated, and new public portrait statues were erected into the fifth century. Fragments of public documents, imported and unfinished goods, and thousands of coins testify to the operation of civic government and commerce side by side around the Forum: cases judged, deals made, crowds of people coming and going. Some buildings were ruined, notably the Julian Basilica and Central Shops in the later fourth century, and the Theater, Odeum and probably some temples in the fifth century, but the majority of imperial Roman non-religious structures on the Forum were continuously repaired into the sixth century, as far as can be determined today. In the later fifth and sixth century, a real sea change happened with the destruction or reuse of most public sculpture and inscriptions, the construction of fortification walls, the appearance of burials, and the construction of churches. Through the end of Antiquity, however, the Forum was ringed mainly with public buildings, and pavements, stoas, shops, roads, fountains and baths were maintained at public expense, as befitting a city center.

Caesar made the decision to refound Corinth in 44 BCE (before the Ides of March), but most of the actual settlement and re-establishment of the city sacked a century before was left to his heir Octavian (later Augustus), with some initial involvement from Marc Antony.[2] The Forum of the refounded *Colonia Laus Julia Corinthiensis* was laid out soon after 44 BCE as a rectangular open space just north of the intersection of the new colony's main north-south *Cardo Maximus* (the Lechaion Road) and the east-west *Decumanus Maximus*.[3] This plan intentionally accommodated significant pre-existing natural and built elements and communication routes of the Corinthian landscape.[4] The Forum occupied a low natural east-west valley, formerly the site of Classical and Hellenistic racecourses.[5] The Archaic Temple of Apollo already filled most of the hill to the north of this valley, while a monumental Hellenistic stoa on its south side atop a low ridge, the South Stoa, was also renovated, probably to serve as offices and shops. Other pre-Roman buildings were restored on the sloping ground near the short sides of the new Forum: the Glauce

Fountain above the Theater on the northwest, and the Peirene Fountain on the Lechaion Road to the northeast.[6]

The reuse of all these Greek buildings in a new colonial Forum, and its placement on open space in between them, evokes the question of whether this area previously held the Agora of the Greek city of Corinth. The identity of the Greek Agora with the Roman Forum was accepted without question by most early excavators, particularly after the discovery of Peirene, the Theater and the South Stoa.[7] Scranton, however, theorized that it was only the *Hellenistic* Agora of pre-Roman Corinth, and Mr Williams challenged this entire identification on the basis of a lack of water, flat space and any other civic buildings, preferring the unexcavated ground north of Temple Hill and downhill from Peirene as the location of the Greek Agora.[8] Jamieson C. Donati now argues that the concentration of the Archaic Temple of Apollo, racecourses, adjacent fountains, Theater and monumental South Stoa, along with literary testimonia, epigraphic finds and pre-Roman buildings excavated by Mr Williams, do indeed favor locating the Greek Agora beneath the Roman Forum.[9] But while the pre-Roman terrain of the Forum is now better defined, and seems favorable for an Agora, the position of Peirene and absence of excavation under the modern village, its *Plateia* and the excavation dump to the north and east still pose an important challenge in reconstructing the pre-Roman Greek city center.[10]

In any case, each side of the new colony's Forum was soon further elaborated architecturally with newly built structures common to contemporary Roman colonies. A long, narrow stoa divided the north side of the Forum from Temple Hill (Northwest Stoa); on the south a line of small chambers, the Central Shops, framed benches and a speaker's platform, the Bema, in front of the refurbished South Stoa.[11] The first civic basilica was placed laterally along the east side of the Forum, the Julian Basilica, with a smaller public building to its south, the Southeast Building; a civic basilica was also built to the south of the South Stoa, the South Basilica, and a third along the east side of Temple Hill, with an entry from the north side of the Forum, the Lechaion Road Basilica.

Roman-style podium temples were built on two levels at the west end of the Forum; three small temples (Temples F, G, K), the Fountain of Neptune/Poseidon and the Babbius Monument were on the west flank of the Forum itself. Two larger temples (Temple E, Temple C) behind them were set within peribolos walls, with another row of small chambers in front of these on the Forum side, the West Shops. Finally, Roman arches covered roads exiting from the northeast (Pausanias' Propylaia), the northwest, and the southwest corners of the Forum; these are likely the roads identified by Pausanias as leading northeast to Lechaion, northwest to Sikyon and southwest to Acrocorinth, respectively.[12] The Lechaion Road, just below the Propylaia, was wide enough to form a sort of lower Forum, with stoas fronting shops on both sides (the Lechaion Road Shops), and behind them on the east a meatmarket (the Macellum), bronze foundry, latrine and baths, along with the venerable Fountain of Peirene.[13]

Throughout the first two centuries after the founding of the colony of Corinth, local and occasionally imperial donors added extensively to this mix of old Greek and new Roman buildings in the city center, particularly after a severe earthquake in 77/8.[14] The Peribolos of Apollo replaced the Macellum on the Lechaion Road.[15] On the west of the Forum, by the small podium temples, the Neptune/Poseidon Fountain with dolphins given by Babbius, and his monument, were replaced by two more small podium temples built in honor of the emperor Commodus (Temples H, J). Ben Millis argues that the small south-facing Temple K was replaced by the east-facing Temple D, slightly to its north, in the early third century.[16] The Lechaion Road Basilica gained the massive new sculpted façade of Persian captive caryatids; the adjacent North Stoa was supplemented by the heavy vaulted row of Northwest Shops along the same line.[17] The Theater gained a new stage building faced with relief sculpture under Hadrian, and Herodes Atticus refurbished the Odeum just to its south. Massive public baths were built at Corinth around the year 200 to the north of the Forum: the Great Bath on the Lechaion Road (unexcavated brickwork standing north of the Theater may also represent a second large bath of similar date). The Forum and Lechaion Road were lined with marble bases holding statues of civic honorands, and divine statue groups were placed in the temples and other buildings. Many buildings were faced both inside and out with marble revetment, and further adorned with inscribed dedications, reliefs and sculpture. The Greek language, long spoken in Roman Corinth, and probably by the majority, joined the Latin language under Hadrian for public and private inscribed texts, and then largely replaced Latin later in the second century.[18]

The Forum and Civic Administration in Late Antiquity

Therefore, the person who entered the Forum at Corinth in the third century through the monumental Roman triumphal arch (Greek Propylaia) in its northeastern corner encountered a grand paved rectangular space, a monumental civic center ringed with old and new Greek and Roman buildings with varied (and often overlapping) political, commercial and cultural functions. Although this open space is today the dusty ground with traces of pavement revealed by the Corinth excavations, literary sources, epigraphy and archaeology allow the restoration of a forest of statues in front of stoas, arches and columns in Late Antiquity, and crowds of real living people too. The Propylaia remained the monumental entryway for an open Forum throughout Late Antiquity, and indeed into at least the tenth century, first with steps and then, by the Middle Byzantine era, a monumental ramp leading up to the Forum from the Lechaion Road.

The authority of the City Council, the Governor of Achaia, the Greco-Roman gods, and emperors past and present was expressed through architecture, sculpture and activities around the Forum. The Propylaia itself bore relief sculptures of weaponry, imperial sacrifice and barbarian submission, perhaps celebrating Trajan's Parthian campaign.[19] Pausanias says it was crowned by statues of Corinth's patron god Helios with his son Phaethon in their chariots.[20] The themes of victory over eastern barbarians were echoed in the adjacent Captives Façade, concealing the Lechaion Road Basilica just west of the Propylaia, and facing onto the Forum: a row of monumental Parthian captives stood on bases depicting *Nikai* (Victories), captives and trophies, celebrating the victorious eastern campaign of a still-mysterious emperor (Lucius Verus or Alexander Severus?).[21] On the Lechaion Road nearby was a post-Hadrianic monument to Roma, with a female personification of the city seated on a marble throne formed from the seven hills of Rome carved in relief, and the pediment of Temple E also featured Roma (see Chapter 5).[22]

Opposite the Propylaia, the Bema in the middle of the Central Shops could be used by the Governor of Achaia or other leaders to address crowds gathered in the Forum.[23] Behind the line of the Bema and Central Shops, the south side of the Forum was formed by the massive Hellenistic South Stoa.[24] Broneer suggested that several rooms in the refurbished South Stoa were imperial offices, and this upper southern Forum as a whole was specifically dedicated to civic administration, which seems likely.[25] One former shop of the South Stoa was heavily renovated into a horseshoe-shaped chamber with a bench all along the back wall and a door facing north, fitting perfectly the outline of a Roman colonial *Bouleuterion* (Council House)(Figure 5).[26] Here the decurions (councillors), annually elected duovirs (two leading men) and many lesser magistrates of the city might have met and worked into the fifth century.[27]

Paul Scotton places the Governor's main tribunal in the southern apse of the Julian Basilica, the monumental civic basilica which formed the east side of the Forum, and which possibly held an *aerarium* (treasury) in its basement cryptoporticus.[28] Governor Gallio famously rejected the Jews' bid to bring St Paul to trial when he was sitting in judgment at Corinth, on the Bema in Broneer's reconstruction, or in the Julian Basilica.[29] The Governor also had the choice of the Lechaion Road Basilica behind the Captives' Façade, or the South Basilica behind the Bema and South Stoa for his public business, legal judgments and hearing petitions.[30] The greatest concentration of recognizable imperial portraits and early Roman dedications at Corinth comes from the Julian Basilica, showing it served as a locus for imperial cult, with statues, altars and dedications to imperial family members, the Augustan *Nemesis* and the *Genius* of the Colony.[31] A statue of Augustus was displayed, and the divine Julius Caesar by the tribunal, while Augustus' grandsons Gaius and Lucius, and a head possibly of Nero, were probably put out of sight in the cryptoporticus already in the second century; Pausanias may have seen the head of the reigning emperor Marcus Aurelius atop a cuirassed marble body cut around his neck socket which was found nearby.[32]

In the third to early fourth century, the Governor sitting in judgment was thus flanked by statues of the founders of the Empire, the renovators of the Julian Basilica, and probably the current Emperor as well, with new heads on the old bodies. A bust found in this area, which could be wearing the chlamys of late antique imperial office, was also carved for the insertion of multiple portrait heads, like the cuirassed statue from the Julian Basilica. This could be a mount for even later imperial portrait heads for the use of the Governor when holding court, though only one very battered head was found nearby (for more on sculpture, see Chapter 5).[33] Late fourth-century coins found among these statues in the rubble of the Julian Basilica indicate that the building did not survive long into the fifth century, and most marble revetment, statuary or inscriptions largely went into the lime kilns in the fifth or sixth century, especially when the Southeast Building was rebuilt over the Julian Basilica's south aisle and tribunal.[34] However, that very rebuilding does attest to continued public building, and perhaps even civic administration, on this eastern side of the Forum in Late Antiquity.

The Southeast Building, just south of the Julian Basilica, may have once been the *Tabularium*, the library or archives building of the colony.[35] This may be the place mentioned in an oration published among those of Dio, but attributed to Favorinus, a Hadrianic sophist, and supposedly delivered by him at Corinth, in which he complains of the removal of a statue of himself from the Library (8. *ta biblia*) of the Corinthian Agora (Forum), where it had been erected at public expense, just because he was out of favor with Hadrian. Whether this is an imaginary address, or was actually given by Favorinus, it testifies to a library or archives on the Corinthian Forum.[36] This oration also forms an important piece of evidence for Hellenic education and sophistic display in Roman Corinth, activities depicted when Philostratus placed a Cynic philosopher and his students there in the mid-first century.[37] The famous doctor Galen is said to have studied at Corinth in the late second to early third century; Athenaeus then featured both him and an otherwise unknown colleague from Corinth named Myrtilus in his literary symposium of the *Learned Banqueters*.[38] Pausanias (2.1.6) described frescoes of the contest between Poseidon and Helios for control of Corinth in the Southeast Building, which have actually been excavated.[39]

Scranton once suggested that the Julian Basilica was modified in the fifth century to serve as a church, with the episcopal palace in the Southeast Building. However, Scotton now judges that the so-called apse of the Julian Basilica is of indeterminate date and purpose (without further excavation), and that the medieval tombs in the Julian Basilica were placed in proximity to the Southeast Building. It was the Southeast Building, renovated in the sixth century with an extension at its northern end over the old tribunal, three aisles, and a new entry from the south, which Scotton suggests could even have been a church of St Paul.[40] This tempting suggestion would keep the center of administration of Corinth located on the Forum, commemorate the trial of St Paul, and help explain the Byzantine burials in the ruins of the Julian Basilica. For more on Christian use of the Forum Area in Late Antiquity, see Chapter 6.

Domestic Spaces of Authority, Production and Consumption: *Villae Urbanae* and *Rusticae*

Traditional civic administration lost the buildings in the area of the Forum around the fifth century, but it then moved into the houses of the *archontes*, where production and consumption was already based: the *praetorium* (palace) of the Governor of Achaia, or other imperial officials, the episcopal residence of the Archbishop of Corinth, the house churches, and the dwellings of rich to middling to poor. Though no house at Corinth can be certainly linked with any specific individual, archaeology does show the resources employed in elaboration of domestic space, displaying the interests and status of civic authorities and driving commerce in the *agora* (the Forum, or market).

Just above the Forum to the southeast, the inner-city neighborhood of Panayia Field is named from the late medieval Panayia Church which once stood in this area, and which was replaced by the modern Panayia Church just to the north (Figures 4, 1.3–1.5, 2.1–2.3). Small-scale discoveries by the ASCSA Corinth Excavations and the Greek Archaeological Service in this elevated area east and southeast of the Forum have been significantly enriched by over a decade of recent ASCSA Corinth Excavations digging in the Panayia Field (1995–2007), yielding buildings from every era of Late Antiquity.[41] A major north-south road along the east side of the neighborhood was used into the sixth century, with the drain kept open beneath.[42] In the third century, a wealthy domus or urban villa can be reconstructed from a small garden pool, wells and a few walls which remain from that era. This third-century domus may have been decorated with sculptural finds from north of this area, like a lost Dionysos with a Nymph and Pan, or the small marble statuette of Armed Aphrodite, patron goddess of Corinth (Figure 2.1).[43]

This domus was replaced by an even larger townhouse or urban villa under the Tetrarchy, and occupied by an elite Corinthian family throughout the fourth century. Most likely occupying an entire city block, this fourth-century domus, the Panayia Villa, had at least two

Figure 2.1 Marble statuette of Armed Aphrodite, Corinth Museum inv. no. S-2548.

peristyle courtyards, two small fountains, a courtyard with a *euripus* basin, marble and mosaic floors, and frescoed walls (Figure 2.2).[44] A collection of nine marble statuettes of gods and goddesses from one small room likely represent the remnants of a household shrine of the fourth century, including Artemis, Asklepios, Roma, Dionysos, Herakles, Pan and a figure conventionally called Europa. Though a few were fragmentary, most were in good condition, with paint and gilding. These pieces are important evidence not only for sculptural taste and polytheistic domestic religious practice in fourth-century

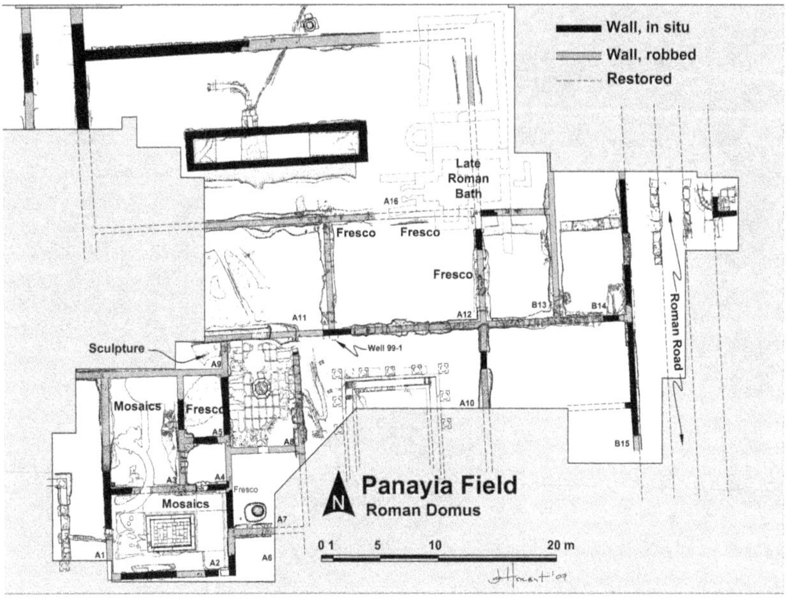

Figure 2.2 Panayia Field Excavations, fourth century.

Corinth, but also demonstrate the continued production of small-scale sculpture in Greece long after the so-called Herulian invasion.[45] The Mosaic House just south of the Forum and west of Panayia Field also contained mosaic floors and a collection of small-scale sculpture, including some of the same figures as in the Panayia Villa.[46] The fine arts in fourth-century Corinth certainly found patrons in private homes as well as public buildings, to judge by the mosaics, frescoes and sculpture collection of these and other urban and rural villas.[47] The Panayia Villa was destroyed by fire sometime after 360, perhaps caused by an earthquake.[48] However, in the fifth century another grand domus extending out of the excavation area was built, with an apsidal dining room (Figure 2.3).[49] It is tempting to link this fifth-century domus with ecclesiastical use, or at least Christian inhabitants, whose descendants would build and patronize the adjacent Panayia Bath and the so-called Long Building in the next century (see Chapter 6).

Farther south and just uphill from the Panayia Villa, a small section of the grandest urban domus so far discovered in Corinth was exposed by the Greek Archaeological Service, the so-called

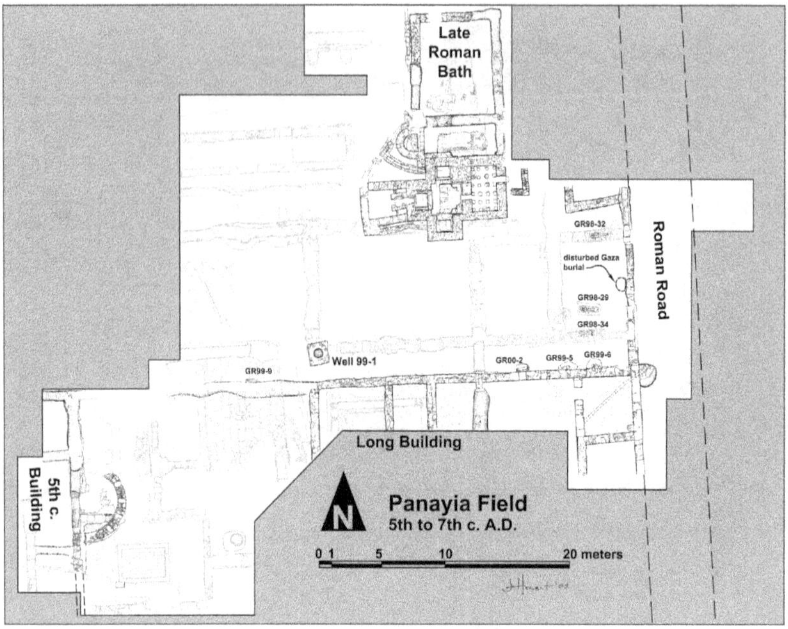

Figure 2.3 Panayia Field Excavations, sixth century.

Governor's Palace, containing a monumental brick-built nymphaeum with central pool and flanking apsidal dining rooms (Figure 3).[50] Though this building does not compare with the Palace of Galerius in Thessalonike, this may have been the *praetorium* (official palace) for the use of the Governor of Achaia in Corinth.[51] To the north of the Forum, both behind the shops on the East of Theater north-south road, and opening off from the east-west Theater-Bath road, the House of the Opus Sectile Panel was a domus decorated with frescoes, a glass opus-sectile panel with fish and eels, and a reused Classical pebble-mosaic floor where a small excavated storeroom held amphoras, cooking and serving vessels and well-used lamps.[52] This was probably the first of several grand houses along the east-west Theater-Bath Road, now buried beneath the excavation dump.[53] There were other finely appointed and maintained *villae urbanae* in Corinth into the sixth century too, to judge from the opus sectile floors, brick walls and other salvage operations of the Greek Archaeological Service. Some of this material is still visible in open trenches in Ancient Corinth, and published in newspapers, the *Deltion* or surveys of Corinthian archaeology as a whole.[54]

Above and south of the road to Sikyon, west of the Forum, is the Corinthian neighborhood of Anaploga, around the modern church of Agioi Anargyroi.[55] A striking monumental marble head of a divinity was brought in from this area, and stray architectural members also led to the excavation of buildings, water systems and a cemetery along the road leading up from the Forum Area to Anaploga in the early 1960s.[56] An elaborate mosaic floor of the later second or third century with panels of peacocks and roosters was excavated from one room of a building with frescoed walls located near a natural spring, possibly a sanctuary or an urban villa, high up away from farmland and the Forum to take advantage of the fine view.[57] This Anaploga Sanctuary or Villa was renovated in the fourth century, after which a very fine and expensive glass cage-cup found in the area was probably displayed there.[58] The Anaploga Sanctuary or Villa was then destroyed in the early fifth century, to judge from coins over the floor; unlike in Panayia Field, no later rebuilding of rich houses or religious structures has been discovered in this area.[59] However, a very large structure from Late Antiquity with mosaics, an opus-sectile floor, and a bath was excavated by the Greek Archaeological Service in 1985, just at the edge of the upper city terrace at the northeast of Corinth by the Kraneion Basilica, probably another urban villa (or even a palace) positioned to enjoy the view of the Gulf of Corinth below.

At the northwest corner of Corinth was another natural spring, Kokkinovrysi, just south of the road to Sikyon as it descended to the plain from the lower city terrace.[60] This well-watered spot shaded by the edge of the terrace was the site for a sanctuary of the Nymphs and another suburban Roman villa still occupied in Late Antiquity. Shear's Roman Villa, excavated by T. Leslie Shear in 1925, was richly decorated with frescoes and mosaics of Europa, Dionysos and bucolic scenes, just like an urban domus, but it was also sited at the edge of the best agricultural land in the Corinthia, equipped with olive and wine presses and other industrial installations.[61] Gladys Davidson Weinberg discovered a fifth-century pottery kiln by the Tile Works near Shear's Roman Villa, which was certainly occupied in the fourth century, and perhaps in the fifth century too.[62] If this industrial area was used at the same time as Shear's Roman Villa, it illustrates well the ideas of Corinthian landowners, ideas about the mixture of craft, farming and leisure appropriate to a villa on the edge of the city. In Epirus, William Bowden concluded that urban decline was linked with the retreat of the aristocracy to the countryside in Late Antiquity.[63] However, Corinthian landowners built and elaborated grand urban and rural houses throughout Late Antiquity, with as many urban villas excavated to date as rural ones.

Several *villae rusticae* have been excavated in the Corinthia, rural houses which were centers of agricultural production like the villas on the edge of Corinth, and also locations of display of luxury to honored guests, and retreats for their owners from the bustle of the city. Demetrios Pallas dated one excavated rural villa to the third century in the eastern Corinthia at Pano Magoula.[64] Other luxurious villas used into Late Antiquity lay on eastern headlands of the Corinthian coast, and on islands in the Saronic Gulf.[65] Material culture of Late Antiquity from Almyri and Korphos, mosaics from near Sophiko, and a villa excavated at Akra Sophia all probably derive from *villae rusticae* on the Saronic Gulf side of the Isthmus. Roman ruins near Assos (modern Agios Charalambos, near Zevgolatio) on the coast to the west of Lechaion, beyond the Longopotamos river gorge, probably represent ancient Asae, the village of the northwestern Corinthia (Figure 2).[66] This is where the Road to Sikyon that ran beside the Skoutela Basilica reached the coast and turned west, and before it crossed the western border of the Corinthia at the Nemea river. By the church of Agios Charalambos, a fine small bath complex was built in Late Antiquity, and renovated as late as the sixth century; perhaps it belonged to a rural villa, or even the ancient village.[67] There were also Roman sherds, and thus Corinthians visiting or living on the Halcyonides Islands, the modern Kala Nesia in the Corinthian Gulf, and in villages on the peninsula of Perachora.[68]

The most recently published *villa rustica* of the late antique Corinthia is the Katounistra Villa, which stood on the hillside just east of Loutraki (ancient Thermai), overlooking the Isthmus, the Corinthian Gulf and Ancient Corinth on the opposite shore.[69] Alongside an ancient route over Mt Geraneia, where there was a Han in the early modern era, this villa was also built beside a natural spring. The excavated corner of this monumental villa was first consructed in the second century with a large apsidal hall and numerous rooms, while fourth-century mosaic floors, marble decoration (including a fountainhead of Eros (or Palaemon) on a dolphin) and a bath complex were also found. Some of the lamps date from the sixth century, and were marked with crosses. The excavator concluded that this was a luxurious and productive residence for a Corinthian family over centuries, even after their conversion to Christianity.

All evidence points toward the Corinthia being a "busy countryside" in Late Antiquity, as David Pettegrew has argued using the survey data from the Eastern Korinthia Archaeological Survey (EKAS).[70] Cynthia Kosso suggests deliberate imperial involvement in encouraging intensive agriculture, and Corinthian landowners were certainly active in the countryside in Late Antiquity, both in villa construction and in agricultural production, apparently largely for local consumption.[71] Between Corinth and the harbor at Lechaion was the richest cultivated countryside, the Vocha plain, interlaced with roads, and with a band of cemeteries dividing it from the northern edge of the city of Corinth.[72] The ridges of the Eastern Corinthia, west and south of Isthmia and Kenchreai, have recently been surveyed by EKAS, with the recovery of much late antique pottery from the fields and villas of this less desirable but still fertile farmland among the cemeteries, quarries and roads east of the Kraneion neighborhood.[73]

The issue of long-lasting land division, or centuriation, of the Corinthia in Late Antiquity is controversial, but a network of property divisions based on colonial and also probably Flavian planning was certainly maintained in Late Antiquity.[74] David Romano and his Corinth Computer Project team have argued for pre-colonial, colonial and Flavian centuriations extending all across the Corinthia on the basis of roads, modern fields and certain ancient monuments. One issue is actual boundaries to land parcels, while another is the actual owners of the parcels. Whatever division of land was made in the first century BCE among the colonists, however, or remade in the Flavian era, parallels with other Roman colonies suggest that the general trend was for land to be held by gradually smaller numbers of wealthy families in the second and third centuries.[75] There are references in third- and fourth-century inscriptions to families owning land in both Patras and Corinth.[76] These families invested in rural as well as urban villas in Late Antiquity, and doubtless used their homes alongside the episcopal residence (and later the churches) as centers for administration, agricultural production, conspicuous consuption, leisure and religious practices.

CHAPTER 3

COMMERCE, WATER SUPPLY AND COMMUNICATIONS

The excavated areas of Ancient Corinth display deep continuities in the repair of civic infrastructure throughout Late Antiquity despite the ruin of three civic basilicas and numerous temples. Civic patrons still maintained and even enhanced their Forum's ancient infrastructure of civic amenities related to commerce, water supply and communications in the third to sixth centuries, especially investing in stoas, shops, streets, fountains and baths. Beyond the Forum, a network of roads remained open in all directions to neighboring regions, and especially to the harbors of Lechaion and Kenchreai, where moles, piers and other harbor facilities were regularly maintained into the sixth century. There is a visible decline in the monumentality of civic infrastructure throughout Late Antiquity, for example, the ruin of the Hadrianic aqueduct, but there is also a notable emphasis by recorded patrons, especially the Governor of Achaia, on restoration of colonnaded stoas, fountains and harbors. López Quiroga argues that parallels in surviving cities of the far western and eastern Mediterranean in Late Antiquity result from urban elites still pursuing their economic interests and survival in an urban context.[1] This model of maintaining services for the city, such as streets, shops and water supply, out of economic self-interest fits the activities of the Corinthian authorities. However, they still had some interest in civic monumentality, too, in the colonnades, inscriptions and statues financed as part of renovations around the Forum, along the Lechaion Road and at the harbors, especially in the fourth century.

Around the Forum, the marble colonnades with porticoes (Greek stoas) in front of the West Shops and the South Stoa were both restored in the later fourth century in the name of the reigning emperors. The Central Shops of the Forum were then replaced by a set of broad paved stairs and small fountains, probably in the early fifth century (Figure 5).[2] These initiatives represent a desire to retain monumentality and commercial as well as administrative functionality around the Forum, replacing ruined civic basilicas with maintenance of the rows of small shops behind shady stoas on the northwestern, western and southern sides of the Forum. Though linked in terminology, the inscribed dedications on the epistyles of the renovated West Shops and South Stoa colonnades are in very different lettering, and may not even belong to the same campaign of renovation. The West Shops' inscription is carefully engraved in neat lettering in one line running atop two fasciae of the original epistyle blocks of this building. The reconstruction is credited on the inscribed epistyle blocks in Greek to the Governor of Achaia, whose name Sironen restores as Flavius Varronianus, in the name of a reigning emperor Vallentinian (*sic*) and his co-emperor(s). If Valens was his co-emperor, as restored by Sironen most recently, it would fall in the years 364–75.[3]

The South Stoa's inscription, however, lacks any name of a governor, and is carved in two lines of sloppy lettering across both the epistyle and frieze sections of two reused blocks (perhaps originally three), which were newly erected to span the southwards continuation of the Lechaion Road running through the center of the South Stoa to the South Basilica and beyond. The restoration was again done under a reigning emperor Vallentinian (*sic*) and his co-emperor(s). John H. Kent, Feissel, Rizakis and now Sironen have restored the South Stoa's epistyle inscription by comparison with the West Shops' epistyle inscription, though Sironen freely admits that it is unclear if the governor was also responsible.[4] Given the close proximity of the South Stoa epistyle repair to the *Bouleuterion* (Council House), it is tempting to suggest that the *Boule* (Council) might have even undertaken this repair as a more slipshod counterpart to the finer efforts of Governor Varronianus on the West Shops. Kent argued that both epistyles represented repair work of 366/7 after the earthquake of 365, though there is no explicit evidence that earthquakes damaged either building, and certainly the rebuilding might also be linked to the age of both buildings and the interests of the governor.

Both repairs certainly took place under the reign of at least two emperors in the later fourth century, and on both epistyles the first emperor honored was Vallentinian (*sic*). Thus there is a certain date range for rebuilding of 364–75 (Valentinian and Valens, with Gratian after 367) and possibly 383–92 (Valentinian II and Theodosius, with Arcadius after 383).

These repairs to the colonnades and porticoes in front of the West Shops and South Stoa, and then the new fountains and paving over of the Central Shops, form part of widespread evidence for significant architectural reconstruction, provision of civic amenities like shady stoas and fountains, and continued monumental character in the Forum in the later fourth and early fifth centuries. Even after the Julian and Lechaion Road Basilicas were ruined, the West Shops and South Stoa were enhanced, and the new Hemicycle Market was built on the Lechaion Road's west side opposite the renovated Peribolos of Apollo.[5] This era *c*.400 was long-connected with the so-called end of ancient Corinth, beginning with the earthquakes of 365 and/or 375, and culminating in the invasion and occupation of Alaric's Gothic army between 395 and 397 (see Chapter 1). Broneer's fire in the South Stoa was even redated by Slane from the later third to the later fourth century, on the basis of pottery in the destruction layer.[6] Scranton blamed earthquakes and Alaric for later fourth-century damage, but concluded that fifth-century renovations would have been made to the Forum in any case.[7] The condition of the standing masonry of the Northwest Shops, West Shops and South Stoa today signal that in the fifth and sixth centuries, and long afterwards, they continued to form core infrastructure for the western end of the Forum, even if only for reuse as housing (Figure 6). Earthquakes may have shaken Corinth in the later fourth century, and Alaric's army certainly came (and went) with the assistance of the governor, but in the fifth century the Forum was still the center of Corinthian public life, commerce and communications.

Broad sidewalks, colonnades, shady stoas and shops lined both sides of the paved Lechaion Road from where it left the Forum at the Propylaia throughout Late Antiquity, running straight northwards towards the harbor of Lechaion (Figures 3–5, 1.1–1.5).[8] The Lechaion Road Basilica on the west side seems to have been ruined *c*.400, perhaps by an earthquake, but the roadside shops below it, and on the east side of the Lechaion Road, were thoroughly renovated about then, and finds of coins inside them date through the reign of Justin II (565–78), while the shops themselves were in use into at least the ninth century.[9] In Late Antiquity, the colonnaded road or *embolos* was a basic feature of cities throughout Greece, Italy and Asia Minor.[10] The best-preserved and published example is the street of Byzantine shops at Sardis, while the Arcadian Way at Ephesus between the Theater and the Harbor is also comparable to Corinth's Lechaion Road.[11]

A monumental ramp leading down out of the Forum was constructed over the Lechaion Road's Roman stairs and pavement using marble *spolia* (including elements of the Propylaia), statue bases and even statue bodies after Late Antiquity. Dismantled in the early years of the ASCSA Corinth Excavations, Scranton argued that this ramp was built as late as the tenth century based on coins found underneath it, and that the Lechaion Road and shops along it were in active use up through the eleventh century.[12] Hendrik Dey has recently put the late antique preservation of the monumentality of Corinth's Lechaion Road in context, arguing that its wide paved roadway, sidewalks, colonnades and shops were maintained by the Christian or imperial authorities into the tenth century as a space for commerce and for civic and religious processions.[13] However, a shift in street use and market habits does seems to have taken place gradually after the sixth century in Middle Byzantine Corinth. The Forum proper eventually became narrower (though with an extension still to the west up in front of the West Shops), the repaved and raised Lechaion Road with its monumental ramp led down from the Forum's northeast end, and then the modern village *Plateia* was formed as a widening of the east-west road running east from just north of the end of the ramp. The end result, by about the eleventh century, was something like an extended S-shaped bazaar, or shopping district, rather than a Roman Forum (Figure 6).

Behind the stoas and rows of small shops along the Lechaion Road in Late Antiquity were further commercial spaces, the *periboloi* or colonnaded shops encircling courtyards (Figure 5). A relief of a ship on the first-century entablature of the Peribolos of Apollo, built atop the *Macellum* (Roman market) just off the east side of the Lechaion Road and north of Peirene Fountain, suggests the original benefactor was a merchant, and this space had a primarily commercial function. The Peribolos of Apollo was repaved with mosaic floors in the third century by a member of the tribe *Aemilia*, a citizen, and perhaps a merchant too, and used throughout Late Antiquity with many further renovations.[14] To the northeast and north of Temple Hill were two more commercial *periboloi*: the Hemicycle and the North Market.[15] The Hemicycle *peribolos* was built in the fourth century, opposite the Peribolos of Apollo and facing the Lechaion Road, and probably had a commercial function. Both the Hemicycle and the Peribolos of Apollo were then subdivided in the fifth or sixth centuries, for workshops and possibly domestic use, while the frontage on the Lechaion Road remained as shops. Broneer argued that two denizens of the rooms behind the Hemicycle were engaged in commerce but crushed when it collapsed in the later sixth century, to judge by their position buried in rubble with bags of coins still at their waists.[16]

The neighborhood called East of Theater by excavators nestled between the Theater, Temple Hill and the excavation dump, in the angle of two well-excavated roads, the perimeter road along the Theater's eastern cavea wall (East Theater Road) and the colonnaded road which once ran east from a gate in the northeast Theater courtyard to the Great Baths on the Lechaion Road, and beyond (Theater-Bath Road) (Figures 4–5, 7).[17] In contrast to the monumental public buildings around the Forum, or along the Lechaion Road, there were small separately built shops, workshops and shrines along East Theater Road and around the northeast Theater courtyard, while the grander sidewalks and colonnades of Theater-Bath Road concealed large houses to its south.[18] East Theater Road had commercial spaces devoted to fulling, blacksmithing and glass-production in the second to third centuries.[19]

The original purpose for any forum (or Greek *agora*) was commercial, and the emphasis above on maintaining colonnades or stoas around paved squares and along roads should not distract attention from the use of the small rows of shady chambers behind them, the shops and workshops of Corinth in Late Antiquity. In the open rectangular Forum itself, in the many small chambers built along its north, west and south sides, along the upper Lechaion Road, and in the *periboloi*, Corinthians would surely have found urban services and products for sale (food, drinks, gambling, sex, wholesale goods, repairs), workshops for production, and then houses.[20] Weinberg emphasized the commercial functions of the Julian, Lechaion Road and South Basilicas, placed as they were just at the east, north and south entrances of the Forum.[21] Though stoas with colonnades in front and small rooms behind are conventionally termed *shops* by archaeologists, their actual use as such is rarely explored. Some were indeed used for offices, shrines or houses, yet not only the architecture but also the comparative evidence confirms that most were in fact used for selling goods and services, as well as for associated functions like storage and manufacturing, and housing for the shopkeepers and craftspeople.[22] Diocletian's Price Edict was set up at Corinth, as at many other cities in the Peloponnesus (though only one small fragment of the Latin preface to the edict was found in the Gymnasium Excavations), but we do not know how many of its commodities or services were available at the Corinthian markets.[23]

Epitaphs from Corinth also give us some idea of the occupations of Christian Corinthians outside of public officials and the clergy in the later fourth to seventh century, the era when inscribed tombstones became popular for those who could afford them. These occupations, from doctors, poets and teachers, to barbers, millers, and goatherds (or dealers in goatskins), span a very wide and mainly urban range, comparable to the ancient cities of better-documented Egypt.[24] Erkki Sironen has edited the Greek texts of these tombstones most recently in *IG* IV^2 3, while Michael B. Walbank has followed Nikos A. Bees, Denis Feissel and Anna Avraméa in compiling and commenting on an illuminating list of professions broken down by type.[25] Besides the jobs already mentioned, he lists workers in metal, marble and stucco; food suppliers like butchers, poultry-raisers, pheasant-breeders, fishermen and pickle-sellers; makers and sellers of candles, cloaks, tunics, shoes and furs; and a fireman (πυροξαλλ[ος?]), an innkeeper (or tavernkeeper, κάπηλος) and a banker (τραπεζίτης).[26] These people were all engaged in their trades in and around the Forum at Corinth in Late Antiquity, and especially along the Lechaion Road.

Though Corinth ceased to mint her own coinage under the Severans, *c.*209,[27] literally thousands of fourth-century coins have been found in the Forum excavations, more than from any other century but the twelfth, with lesser quantities of fifth- and sixth-century coins excavated too.[28] Sanders argues that pottery and stratigraphy from the Panayia Field Excavations reveal that the fourth-century coins found in large numbers at Corinth provide only a *terminus post quem* for associated structures, and do not necessarily date the last use or destruction of those structures in the fourth century.[29] His discovery of fifth-century *minimi*, especially of Anastasius, through sieving has helped to clarify the difference between fourth- and fifth-century contexts, but it seems clear that fourth-century coins stayed in circulation long into the fifth century at Corinth. What does this say about the Corinthian economy in Late Antiquity? Some sort of commerce continued into the sixth century in and around the Forum, and much of it was still monetized. The large numbers of discarded fourth-century coins may also speak to monetary reforms which drove them out of use. An official steelyard weight in the form of an imperial bust was found by the West Shops, probably Constantine or one of his sons, showing the official monitoring of weights and measures continued under imperial authority.[30]

Archaeological evidence also supplements epigraphy for what was made and sold in these shops in and around the Forum: glass made locally, or imported from Egypt,[31] metal,[32] marble sculpture,[33] lamps, ceramics and many sorts of perishable goods transported and stored in amphoras.[34] Lamps were both local and Attic, while ceramics used for cooking, storing and eating were mainly local, Attic or from the Aegean, with only a few expensive fine African wares imported from further afield, in contrast to previous and subsequent eras.[35]

The South Stoa, West Shops and Northwest Shops around the Forum were the heart of Corinth's commercial district throughout Late Antiquity, but also extended down the Lechaion Road and north of Temple Hill. In the Forum, as noted above, both the West Shops and South Stoa colonnades were rebuilt at least in the case of the West Shops by the Governor of Achaia in the late fourth century. The Peribolos of Apollo and the North Market also underwent repairs in Late Antiquity, but no benefactor is known.[36] However, permanent shops built and maintained at public expense were only one part of commerce around the Forum, where temporary booths and seasonal markets may also have occurred.[37] Together, all these different sorts of commercial activities certainly testify to a commitment on the part of the City Council, imperial officials and Christian clergy to provide and maintain areas, opportunities and routes for commerce in the traditional heart of the city. This was also the case with ensuring a steady supply of fresh water in Late Antiquity.

Fresh Water Supply: Springs, Fountains and Baths

The fresh water springs of the Corinthian landscape flow naturally all year round, and are especially abundant in the urban area of

Ancient Corinth. These springs were by necessity still maintained to some extent by Corinthian authorities throughout Late Antiquity, and channeled into pipes, conduits, drains, fountains and pools. However, the natural springs were monumentalized and adorned beyond the urban necessity of supplying water to the public for drinking or washing (and beyond the more basic need of preventing flowing water from natural springs from rushing down the streets). Some fountains and baths were even maintained or constructed at some distance from the natural springheads. Much of the imperial Roman system of fresh water supply to public fountains and baths was elaborated with marble in the third to sixth centuries, often with the civic benfactor still lauded in inscriptions. Several late antique donor inscriptions survive from the Fountain of Peirene (see below), and one fragmentary poetic text of unclear origin appears to laud an official for care of a "spring" (πηγὴ[ν]) and "waters" (ὑ]δάτων) with reference to "Paphia" (Aphrodite) in the fifth century.[38]

Betsey Ann Robinson's extensive work on the fountains of the Forum, especially the venerable Fountain of Peirene, complements that of Mark Landon and Yannis Lolos on the other natural springs and water systems of the Corinthia.[39] Some of the Roman imperial water systems did go out of use at defined moments in Late Antiquity, particularly the Hadrianic aqueduct from Stymphalos, and many of the massive drains under and north of the Forum were blocked in the later fifth and especially sixth centuries. However, Peirene Fountain remained the central, monumental and public source of fresh water at the Forum into the sixth century, while the Lerna Fountain at the Asklepieion and the Fountain of the Lamps to its west were converted to Christian use in the fifth century (Figures 5, 7).[40] A culture of water remained central to Corinthian public life and the priorities of civic authorities throughout Late Antiquity. For reasons of both necessity and ideology, some fresh water systems from springs and drains to fountains and baths were maintained from the city center out to the neighborhoods, suburbs, harbors, Isthmia and even atop Acrocorinth.

The Fountain of Peirene is fed by a natural spring which emerges from the northern edge of the terrace just below the Forum; its water formed the valley of the upper Lechaion Road, and probably even dictated the emergence of the Corinthian urban center around it. Elaborated architecturally since the Archaic era, Peirene was renovated anew just after the foundation of Roman Corinth.[41] In the third century, according to B.A. Robinson, we should imagine a rectangular court faced in colorful marble extending north from the natural rock face with its row of drawbasins behind a two-storey columned façade, frescoes of fish depicted as swimming below the waterline in the drawbasins, and sculpture adorning both a basin at the south side of the court (perhaps Scylla), and a single apse at the north side (for further on the sculpture of Peirene, see Chapter 5). In the center of the court, steps led down to the rectangular lower level visible today, where water poured out into channels along the long sides.[42] Peirene remained a favored location for Corinthians to demonstrate their civic euergetism throughout Late Antiquity, as it was central, venerable and supplied copious fresh drinking water (as well as fed baths and fountains below it to the north, like the Roman Baths and Great Bath on the Lechaion Road). An unknown late third-century donor put up a balustrade with a pierced marble latticework screen, inscribed in part, "and near the waters of Peirene," καὶ ἐφ' ὑδά[των — — —] Πιρήν[ην.[43] At the same time, or a bit later, small stone water stairs were installed below some of the spouts on the lower level of the court, and then lateral basins were built in front of the side arches of the spring façade too.

Even more elaborate than the rebuilding of the colonnades of the West Shops and South Stoa was the construction of a new monumental triconch court at Peirene, probably in the fourth century. B.A. Robinson argues persuasively that the three monumental apses still prominent today on the north side of the spring façade, and long attributed to Herodes Atticus, were built at the earliest after the middle of the third century, and most likely in the second half of the fourth century, and thus clearly not by him.[44] She offers compelling stratigraphic and especially architectural comparative evidence from across the Roman empire in the fourth century of similar triconch structures. A statue of Herodes' wife Regilla was thus most likely erected (or re-erected) in one apse, perhaps on the model of her great Nymphaeum at Olympia, but her base in Peirene, like her base as Tyche from the Western Forum, bears a verse text in late antique lettering, and is reused (see Chapter 5, Figure 5.4).[45] The new monumental Fountain of Peirene triconch at the center of Corinth partly used *spolia* from the previous fountain court, and other buildings, but the interiors of the three apses were lined in marble, and decorated with honorific portraits and female divinities, some also repaired, and probably reused like Regilla's base.[46] This close attention to civic water sources in Late Antiquity, and their elaboration with sculpture, even pagan statues, is typical of the development of cities all over Greece, Asia Minor and the Early Byzantine Empire.[47]

It is difficult to date several further additions to Peirene more closely than to the fifth or sixth century, but this public fountain certainly benefitted from generous benefactions and monumental adornment into the middle of the sixth century. Peirene's interior space was first enhanced with a central circular basin over the old rectangular court, complementing the half-circles of the three apses, and the arches along the spring façade, keeping the water accessible to large groups of people.[48] Next, the spring façade itself was decorated, and perhaps shaded, by a parallel colonnade supporting a curious entablature composed of projecting marble beams carved with acanthus on their ends, and a reused series of epistyle blocks bearing a red-painted dedication by a donor.[49] This entire so-called outlooker screen and colonnade was composed of reused architectural members, with columns cut down to size, beam-ends carved to match, and the second-century epistyle's Latin inscription chiseled off so that the new, Greek inscription could be painted directly onto the epistyle blocks, thanking someone for paying for "all the visible decoration in Peirene" in the second half of the fifth or early sixth century.[50] It is tempting to associate this latter benefaction with the emperor Justin's aid to Corinth after the earthquake of 520/1, but it could as easily be the work of a local, perhaps even a clergyman. Peirene certainly continued to be maintained as a practical source of water and decorated as a civic building throughout Late Antiquity at the junction of the Forum and Lechaion Road, the civic center of Corinth. It was probably only in the seventh or eighth century that Peirene's water was directed into new channels built of *spolia* rather than its ancient drains, and diverted to new public fountains to the north somewhere under the modern village of Ancient Corinth, in the area just west and north of the modern village *Plateia* (near the Great Bath on the Lechaion Road). The ancient Fountain of Peirene itself was then converted into a chapel.[51]

North of the Peirene Fountain, opposite the Hemicycle and just north of the Peribolos of Apollo, Roman Baths were excavated on the

Lechaion Road, which are sometimes called the Baths of Eurykles. Just like the Great Bath on the Lechaion Road farther north, they were supplied with water from Peirene. Pausanias (2.3.5) mentions baths built at Corinth by Roman Spartan aristocrat Eurykles just after he describes the Peribolos of Apollo, and then he also mentions baths built by Hadrian elsewhere. Pausanias' Eurykles might be the early colonial or early Hadrianic Spartan benefactor of that name, and donor of a phase of these Roman Baths in either case.[52] The Roman Baths lay just behind the eastern shops lining the Lechaion Road, and included a public latrine, and cold, warm and hot rooms built in rubble and mortar.[53] They were probably in use through *c.*400, when they were replaced with structures interpreted as a private house and a glass-maker's quarters, occupied through the rest of Late Antiquity.[54]

The Great Bath on the Lechaion Road lies to the north of the ASCSA Corinth Excavations area (Figure 4). Its brick ruins have always been partially visible, standing just north of the modern village *Plateia* of Ancient Corinth. From its scale alone, the Great Bath is certainly the major bathing complex of third-century Corinth, then certainly used and repaired throughout Late Antiquity.[55] Damage in the late fourth century attributed to an earthquake was swiftly repaired, and the Great Bath was restored again in the early sixth century for public use.[56] One of the sixth- or seventh-century conduits for Peirene's water probably led to a public fountain in the area too. Hadrian's baths mentioned by Pausanias might then be the unexcavated brick ruins north of the Theater by the Old Gymnasium mentioned before, though this brickwork is said to be later, or even the famous baths at Lechaion described below.

Three smaller baths east, west and south of the Forum were built and used in the fifth and sixth centuries, and may represent constructions for either public or private bathing.[57] Southeast of the Forum, the Panayia Bath was small but lavish in décor, constructed over part of the ruined fourth-century domus, perhaps for the public use of the neighborhood, the occupants of the fifth-century house to the southwest, or the enigmatic Long Building to the south (Figure 2.3).[58] The Hill House Bath to the west of the ASCSA Corinth Excavations' Hill House and the Odeum is similar in scale, and likely contemporary to the Panayia Bath, and perhaps also designed for neighborhood use.[59]

A bath revetted in marble was constructed in the west section of the South Stoa in the fifth century, between a Roman latrine and the lavish Marble Room. These South Stoa Baths may have been for the use of the City Council, clergy or administrators working in the offices of the South Stoa, or for the public.[60] Near the Forum, on the line of the ancient Sikyon Road to the west, was a second Roman-era fountain beyond the Fountain of Glauce, with a mosaic floor.[61] Repairs were made to the important Peirene drain leading north under the Peribolos of Apollo *c.*300, and a third public latrine was also built on the west of the Forum by the Fountain of Glauce in the middle of the fourth century (the other two latrines were in the Roman Baths on the Lechaion Road and in the South Stoa).[62]

In the center of the South Stoa, on the south side of the Forum, a marble-encrusted fountain by the *Bouleuterion* (Council House) supplied fresh water to the public, and may have held statues on either side of the deep basin; in the Central Shops, cool *exedrae* (benches in niches) stood on either side of the Bema, and later fountains were installed in that area too.[63] The Great East-West Drain under the South Stoa contained coins through the reign of emperor Leo I (457–74), remaining in use until that time.[64] These Forum Area fountains and new smaller bath buildings, along with the Great Bath on the Lechaion Road, demonstrate the continued provision of public baths in Corinth despite the shift to many small baths and only one large one, perhaps after the destruction of Corinth's aqueduct, and in line with a shift happening in other Greek cities from large to small baths.[65]

To the south of the Forum, the upper city terrace slopes gently upwards, then it turns into the steeper, rockier incline of Acrocorinth itself. This geological transition is marked today, as at the other terrace-breaks, by an east-west line of natural springs tapped in the Roman era: the early modern Hadji Mustafa Fountain spring on the road up Acrocorinth (currently the source of Ancient Corinth's most potable water), and Kakavi spring to the east.[66] Somewhere above these natural springs, perhaps just adjacent to Hadji Mustafa Fountain, or farther east, the Hadrianic aqueduct from Stymphalos would have ended in a castellum or reservoir, like the *dexamene* (cistern) on Lycabettus in Athens, with pressure lines distributing the water down from there throughout the city, particularly to its public baths.[67]

On Acrocorinth, Upper Peirene Fountain was used as a source of clean, fresh drinking water into the nineteenth century, and pottery, coins and lamps show that the natural spring-fed pool was continuously maintained as a source of fresh water throughout Late Antiquity and beyond.[68] Formulaic inscriptions on the walls of the Fountain request that a number of different people, some of whom are *marmarioi* (marble workers), be remembered by an unnamed deity at the spring, perhaps as Broneer suggested, Bellerophon, or Aphrodite herself; the Roman terms and letter-style of the Greek texts date most of these graffiti to the second or third century.[69]

This interest in continued fresh water supply and bathing in Late Antiquity extended to the harbors, Isthmian Sanctuary of Poseidon and villas of the Corinthia too. The only building at the Isthmian Sanctuary of Poseidon known to have remained in use after the construction of the Hexamilion Wall and Fortress was Isthmia's large brick Roman bath complex, just inside the new Hexamilion Wall, to the west of the Fortress, and possibly still public.[70] At Lechaion, a Nymphaeum constructed southeast of the harbor in the third century may have been a public structure, or part of a large contemporary villa; both buildings were renovated in the sixth century.[71] Ampelius may have been referring to third-century Lechaion, or less likely Kenchreai, when he included in his wonders of the world: "at Corinth along the sea is the great flank of a bath, which one person cannot comprehend."[72] A second large bath building on the north side of the harbor where the Lechaion Basilica would be built was constructed already in the fifth century, perhaps along with adjacent houses. A marble *trapezophoros* (table support) in the form of a nymph or Aphrodite probably formed part of the decoration, continuing Lechaion's bath culture into the sixth century.[73]

Christian clerical and lay statements of approval for public baths and bathing in Late Antiquity far outnumber those of censure.[74] Regular use of public baths by all levels of society remained usual at Corinth as well as other cities around the Mediterranean into the sixth century and beyond. At Thessalonike, Philippi and Stobi, for example, baths were immediately adjacent to inner-city churches built in the early sixth century.[75] The bath complexes at Corinth all would have once been adorned with sculpture and marble, and formed part of the essential public buildings of Corinth's city center and harbors, as well as a necessary component of most rural villas.[76]

Communication Routes: Corinthian Roads, Harbors and the Isthmus

Beyond the open rectangular Forum with stoas around it, on all sides the Roman colonial city plan of straight streets intersecting at right angles stretched out, and butted up against extant traces of Corinth's Greek city plan and natural features like Temple Hill and Peirene Valley (Figures 3, 7). Corinth was rebuilt on a regular grid of streets with the Forum at its center shortly after the Roman colony was established, and many streets were paved and maintained with sidewalks and even colonnades with stoas throughout Late Antiquity. The precise details of the placement and extent of the grid, however, beyond the excavated sections mentioned above, have attracted much debate, linked to the research on broader centuriation of the landscape referred to in Chapter 2.[77] Most excavated roadways, like the Lechaion Road (the north-south *Cardo Maximus*), the east-west Theater-Bath Road, the north-south road on the east side of the Panayia Field, and the east-west road south of Temple E (probably the *Decumanus Maximus*), were continuously serviced and resurfaced into the sixth century, and the drains underneath or alongside them kept clear.

Corinth was the communications center for the Corinthia, the Peloponnesus to the south, and central Greece to the north throughout Late Antiquity, whether one came (or left) by land or by sea (see Figures 1–2).[78] Ancient land routes from the north passed through the Isthmus, and then, overseen from Acrocorinth, led west, south and southeast to the coasts or interior of the Peloponnese peninsula.[79] Besides Corinth and its harbors, other subsidiary centers of population (villages) and villas once dotted the coasts and slopes of the Corinthia. Some villages persisted from Antiquity through Late Antiquity and up to the present day in roughly the same location, while others were abandoned (or newly founded in modern times), mainly at springs, crossroads or passes.[80] The route Pausanias took, climbing upwards and south past the Egyptian shrines out of the Corinthian Forum, was probably the road leading to Corinth's main southern or Phliatic Gate, the beginning of the major road from Corinth south through Kleonai (with a branch there for Phlius, hence the name of the gate), and on through the Dervenakia Pass into Argolis and the deeper Peloponnesus.[81] Pausanias also notes a second southern road from Acrocorinth, which ran to Tenea and then up to the Agionorion or Kleisoura pass, through the southern mountains to Berbati and then Argolis as well. In the southern Corinthia, ancient Tenea is probably modern Chiliomodion, where ruins of fortification walls, a theater and a third-century portrait head mark the only Corinthian village mentioned by Pausanias on the route south from Acrocorinth.[82] South of ancient Tenea, another smaller Roman village was located at Klenia, at the entrance to the pass.[83] The fourteenth-century castle of Agionoros today guards the very top of the pass, and architectural *spolia* in and around the village reveal that it also goes back to Roman times, with churches built in the Byzantine era.[84] The Nyphitsa Cave at Kalyvaki just south of Ano Klenia yielded Roman-era dedications, and represents the small-scale personal cults once practiced all over the Corinthia, but not closely studied here.[85]

North of the Isthmus from Corinth there were at first two coastal roads, one on each shore of the Isthmus. On the west side of the Isthmus, the road ran from Lechaion and Poseidonia to ancient Thermai (modern Loutraki), with branches from there west to the Heraion at the tip of Perachora peninsula, north over the pass on Perachora to come out at Oenoe along the Halcyon Gulf, or eastwards into the Geraneia mountains towards Megara.[86] The road along the Halcyon Gulf also split, going either north into Boeotia (where shepherds once exchanged Oedipus), or east into Megara via coastal Aegosthena (modern Porto Germeno). The Scironian cliffs at the farthest northeast border of the Corinthia were proverbially dangerous in Antiquity, but there were at least two Roman villages and a road on the Saronic Gulf coast before these cliffs, first Sidous (modern Sousaki) and then Crommyon (modern Agioi Theodoroi).[87] Late Roman walls just north of the Corinth canal's eastern mouth at modern Kalamaki, and then a chapel with sherds around it about a mile farther north at Agios Charalambos, may belong to the ancient settlement of Schoinous, the harbor for Isthmia at the eastern side of the narrowest point of the Isthmus.[88]

Corinth's ancient northern harbor of Lechaion was located at a natural marsh and lagoon which once flowed into the sea of the Corinthian Gulf on the coast directly north of Ancient Corinth (Figure 3). Two outer harbors were along the sandy shoreline, and an inner harbor was formalized by dredging the lagoon in Antiquity. Today the lagoon is a seasonal, shallow pool cut off from the sea.

The entrance channel, although filled in modern times at its former mouth, is a shallow, narrow basin flanked by high sand dunes, probably from the accumulations of successive past dredgings, but never dated.[89] Ancient texts record that Lechaion was once an active port with warehouses, baths, sanctuaries and fine coastal houses ringing the inner harbor.[90] Pallas excavated the Lechaion Basilica on its northern side, and recent ongoing archaeological exploration by the Lechaion Harbor and Settlement Land Project directed by Paul Scotton has so far confirmed extensive remains to the east and south of the inner harbor. Epigraphic evidence shows Aphrodite *Epilimenia* (Harborside) and Poseidon were both worshipped at Roman Lechaion; Pausanias noted a *hieron* (sanctuary) of Poseidon and a bronze statue.[91] There is a small island in the center of the artificial inner harbor basin, where Shaw suggested Pausanias' bronze statue of Poseidon might have stood, on a now-fallen Carystian marble column (if not inside the Sanctuary of Poseidon) (Figure 1.2).[92] Possibly also once standing on this island, or closer to the shore, was the statue of Flavius Hermogenes on the large triangular base found at Lechaion, and today in the Corinth Museum courtyard, which bears an inscription honoring him while Governor of Achaia (*c*.340–60) from both the *Boule* (City Council) and *Demos* (Assembly) of Corinth as "patron and founder of the harbor," εὐεργέτην καὶ κτίστην τοῦ λιμένος.[93] To earn these titles, Governor Hermogenes likely dredged, or otherwise rebuilt and enhanced, Lechaion Harbor in the middle of the fourth century. Such efforts indicate that the imperial government and the Governor still valued Lechaion then as a port for travel and trade with the West. Recent underwater work by the Lechaion Harbour Project directed by Bjørn Lovén and Dimitris Kourkoumelis has revealed that the moles at the entry to the harbor were built from wooden caissons filled with rubble and floated into place around the fifth century.[94]

Lechaion, the western and more sheltered Corinthian harbor, may have been the site of *horrea* or grain warehouses, like those referred to in the Corinthian copy of the Megarian inscription of 401/2 mentioned above.[95] A massive Classical foundation with later Roman buttressing excavated by the Service in 2003 near the south end of the western Long Wall on the plain was identified as a warehouse.[96] Large quantities of grain arranged by the Governor of Achaia in such a regulation to be shipped to Corinth were likely to support an imperial garrison. Grain was collected near Thermopylae from the Aetolian, Boeotian and Euboean cities, and was brought by sea, almost certainly to a harbor-side granary. Granaries have been excavated at Patara, Andriace (port of Myra, southern Lycia), Barbegal (France) or Caesarea Maritima.[97] Grain brought by sea from Thermopylae was probably unloaded at Kenchreai, then brought by cart to Lechaion or stored in warehouses at Kenchreai.

Corinth's ancient eastern harbor town, Kenchreai, certainly also once had large-scale harbor facilities.[98] In contrast to Lechaion, here the coastline formed a natural cove, which was further enhanced by the construction of two long moles or breakwaters, with a pier atop the southern one (Figure 10). In parallel with Lechaion, the shore seems to have been filled still in Late Antiquity with fine houses, sanctuaries and warehouses.[99] A large double-sheaved pulley block from the Kenchreai dockside in particular testifies to the significant scale of the harbor cranes which must once have existed there.[100] The most important finds for Late Antiquity were the unique glass panels from the southern pier, dated to the late fourth century, and the ruins of the Early Christian basilica church at the base of the southern mole.[101] Late Roman sherds and perhaps walls from the Saronic Gulf harbor at ancient Cape Speiraion (modern Korphos), near the Corinthia's southeastern border with the Epidauria, also testify to its use in Late Antiquity as a subsidiary harbor southeast of Kenchreai.[102]

In the third century, efforts to cut a canal through the Isthmus were considered a folly of the past, though traces of first- to second-century digging were still visible at the west side of the Isthmus, and a relief of Herakles adorned one old scarp.[103] A paved road probably remained usable for transporting people and cargo in wheeled vehicles from coast to coast across the Isthmus.[104] Parts of a stone-paved road excavated at the western side of the Isthmus could be interpreted as the *diolkos* (dragway) mentioned by Strabo as the route for trans-Isthmian transport of people, goods and (very rarely) warships.[105] David Pettegrew and other scholars have sharply questioned the use of the *diolkos* as a route for dragging ships across the Isthmus, as well as the frequency and volume of trans-Isthmian trade, yet the excavated roadway is paved and deeply rutted, revealing its use to transport heavy carts most likely filled with goods from coast to coast, and perhaps on occasion from ship to ship.[106]

There was a decline in communication between the governments of West and East, first during Alaric and Stilicho's conflict in the Peloponnesus of 395–7, then especially after the sack of Rome by Alaric's forces in 410, as milestones were no longer updated after that era by emperors along the Via Egnatia.[107] This may mean that less-trafficked roads, like those in the Corinthia, or southern Greece, received fewer repairs from the imperial government. Yet Corinthian and Greek bishops continued to go to Church councils and neighboring sees; landowners traveled between far-flung properties; and imperial armies (along with more northern barbarians) were on the march. New imported luxury goods and fine pottery in small quantities continued to appear in the fifth and sixth century, not only in Corinth, but in relatively remote inland areas to the south of the Corinthia, like the Berbati Valley farmhouse near Mycenae.[108]

In the middle of the sixth century, the historian Procopius gives an extended description of the Justinianic plague's emergence in Egypt, and its spread from there to Constantinople and every other land, "killing many," in and after the year 541.[109] Primary textual evidence for this plague is also seemingly contained in a number of novels of Justinian, certainly one of 542 in support of bankers, because all know there is currently "a danger of death spreading in every place," and probably also in others issued soon after legislating on those who died without heirs and combatting increases in both prices and wages.[110] This Justinianic plague of 541/2 continues to attract attention throughout the Mediterranean, as archaeologists search for solid evidence of its impact, and historians use comparative approaches to expand our understanding of it beyond these texts.[111] Most agree that it was bubonic plague, the killer of as much as a third of the population in some cities, and a serious factor in the decline of the entire Eastern Empire's economic complexity and military potential in the later sixth century.[112]

Corinth is one of the few cities to be explicitly linked with severe effects from the plague, which at least indicates that despite the earthquakes mentioned above, in 541/2 the city was still the sort of densely populated and maritime city most affected by the plague. Moreover, it is likely that, as in Constantinople, the plague would have recurred throughout the rest of the sixth century in Corinth too, further reducing the population.[113] Yet in Gaza the venerable monk Barsanouphius wrote a letter expressing hope for the future in the piety of "John at Rome, Elias at Corinth, and another in Jerusalem."[114] Papyrus business documents in Egypt, the source of the plague, scarcely show any change at all in the 540s, and some of the comparative studies undertaken recently suggest that a loss of manpower can actually have a stimulating effect on the economy of a city.[115] Corinth, however, almost certainly suffered from the reduction of able-bodied population which the plague caused in the middle of the sixth century. It was at just that time, however, that the Hexamilion Wall and fortresses were marked by Victorinus as completed in the name of Justinian, after the organized demolition of Corinth's spaces of civic assembly, entertainment and Greco-Roman religion.

CHAPTER 4

SPACES OF CIVIC ASSEMBLY AND ENTERTAINMENT

Corinth had at least five spaces of civic assembly and entertainment in Late Antiquity, monumental public buildings where the populace could assemble to watch performances of music, dance, drama, oratory, gladiators, beast hunts, athletics or chariot racing. Attendance at these spectacles, and their provision by the civic authorities in the context of public festivals, was a celebrated aspect of Greco-Roman urban life. They come back to life in the cycle of vivid paintings uncovered in 1926 on the arena wall of the Corinthian Theater, which showed life-sized *venatores* (professional beast hunters) fighting lions, a bull and a leopard, and with some third- or fourth-century graffiti commenting on the scenes.[1] In the city center of Corinth, the nearly continuous renovation of the pre-Roman Theater space after the foundation of the colony was accompanied by the construction of an adjacent Odeum, and a Roman Amphitheater, a Circus (Hippodrome), a running track and probably an updated gymnasium and stadium on the northern edge of the city (Figures 3–7). Farther afield, a Corinthian *agonothetes* (games-giver) continued to host a biennial festival at the Sanctuary of Poseidon at the Isthmus into the fourth century, with music and athletics at its Theater and Stadium. However, the fifth and sixth centuries witnessed a dramatic decline in training, performing and public assembly for entertainment outside the market or the church, as well as the pillaging of these Corinthian public buildings for their stone (mainly for fortification walls). Thus audiences at Corinth, as at other cities, enjoyed some two centuries of dynamic renovation, investment and entertainment in their public assembly spaces into the late fourth century, and then lost those spaces, and probably the opportunity to perform or observe most forms of entertainment, to their despoilment for construction of fortification walls in the fifth and sixth centuries.[2] This was a profound change in the civic landscape of Corinth, as well as in the public culture of urban life, and was likely driven by the decisions of imperial officials first to divert civic funds to construction of fortification walls, and then to reduce the cost of the latter by building with material taken directly from spaces of civic assembly and entertainment. These decisions certainly accorded with the disapproval of spectacles of all kinds voiced by Christian clergy, and probably aligned with the Christian faith of the majority of imperial officials from the fifth century onwards.

Theater, Odeum and Amphitheater

The Corinthian Theater and adjacent Odeum just up the hill could be reached easily from the northwest gate of the Forum on the paved East of Theater Road, as well as from the major roads coming into Corinth from the west, north or east (Figures 3–5).[3] Together, these two central public performance spaces took advantage of the natural slope between upper and lower city terraces, and formed an impressive complex for public assembly and entertainment in the third to fourth centuries, with paved ramps, courtyards and stoas in adjacent public spaces. Their extensive and expensive renovation to present various spectacles of public entertainment to gathered crowds throughout the third and fourth centuries contrasts with their robbing out for building fortification walls in the fifth century, forming one of the most distinctive ruptures in the provision of public spaces in late antique Corinth.

The Theater was one of Corinth's most venerable and also most newly renovated public monuments in the third and fourth centuries.[4] Corinthian civic authorities rebuilt the Greek Classical Theater on Roman lines with surrounding public spaces in the first and second centuries, then made extensive modifications to the orchestra to fit it out as an arena for the spectacles of gladiators and beast-hunts depicted in paintings on the areana wall in the early third century.[5] The Theater was full of honorific statuary, and boasted a monumental marble *scaenae frons* covered in reliefs of the Labors of Hercules and the Amazonomachy.[6] Further free-standing statuary was added in the third century: Robinson identified the hind-quarters of a horse found in the Theater as the seated centaur Chiron, from a statue group of Chiron teaching Achilles how to box, poorly finished but perhaps put up rapidly for the expected visit of Caracalla, the New Achilles, just before 217 (which may be associated with the arena renovation).[7] Portraits were put up in the third and fourth century as well, probably by the stage or at the edge of the cavea: two portrait heads, a *chlamydatus*-wearing official and the hand of a second were found, and the base of a "boy comedian" (παῖδα κωμωδόν), honored with a statue and list of his victories by his father, with the permission of the *Boule* (City Council).[8]

In the fourth century, the arena was further renovated to serve for water spectacles as well, with a reservoir in the old East Hall, and then in its last phase of use, seating was extended once more in the cavea down to the floor of the orchestra "for civic events and public entertainment."[9] A drain from the Theater arena contained coins of Constantius II to Theodosius, testament to use of the Theater for public assembly throughout the fourth century and into the early fifth, yet the Theater's stone stage and seats were then apparently robbed out for use as *spolia* in fortification wall building *c*.425–50.[10] However, excavations in 2011 at the northwest corner of the Theater revealed commercial and communal activities throughout the fifth century in the area: a fountain replaced by a public well in the Lesser Plaza west of the North Peristyle of the Theater, and the use of the Theater's West Hall as a dump for tons of bones of recently-slaughtered cattle and sheep, whose meat apparently fed great numbers of banqueting Corinthians at public events held to the north or west of the old Theater, in the area of the Old Gymnasium.[11] The North Peristyle's outer walls and *spolia* from the Theater may have also contributed to construction of the late antique fortification wall around the city of Corinth (see below Chapter 8).

Just uphill from the Theater was a second public performance space, the covered theater or Odeum, whose renovation was attributed to Herodes Atticus. This is one of the very few public buildings at Corinth which we can put a name to, since besides Pausanias' bare notice of its existence, Herodes' biographer Philostratus, writing *c*.200, mentions "a roofed theater built by him for the Corinthians, not as great as that at Athens, but without many famous things elsewhere to equal it."[12] It remained as financed by Herodes, and probably used for lectures and drama until the middle of the third century when, after a fire, it was renovated, like the Theater, to serve as a small arena through the fourth century.[13] Williams suggests that the Odeum arena was a gladiatorial practice ground for the Theater, and the Amphitheater to the northeast of the city was therefore no longer in use from the middle of the third century.[14]

The Corinthian Amphitheater was carved into the soft limestone bedrock at the very northeast edge of the upper city terrace, in the Kraneion neighborhood (Figure 3). Dio Chrysostom mocked the location as, "outside the city in a glen, a place that is able to hold a crowd but otherwise is dirty and is such that no one would even bury a free-born citizen there."[15] Still clearly visible today in the landscape, the structure of the Amphitheater has never been excavated archaeologically. Welch makes comparative arguments for its construction in the early days of the colony, since it is relatively small; Williams argues that the conversion of the Theater and Odeum to arenas in the middle of the third century signaled the end of its use.[16] However, many spectacles would have been staged by local benefactors as part of imperial cult celebrations, and multiple performance venues were used simultaneously in other cities in Late Antiquity.[17] In texts through the early third century, gladiatorial and beast-hunt spectacles held in the Amphitheater at Corinth attracted negative attention, as a foil for Athens, and as symbolic of Corinthian *romanitas* due to its resettlement by veterans (Plutarch *Caes.* 57, Augustus *Res Gestae* 28) and freedmen (Strabo 8.6.23, Crinagoras of Mytilene *AnthPal* 9.284).[18] However, the civic officials of Athens as well as other uncolonized cities of Greece began to hold such games too under the Empire, and then to modify their theaters and stadiums to better accomodate them.[19]

In Apuleius' satyrical *Metamorphoses*, the narrator encounters a newly appointed Corinthian official hiring gladiators and collecting animals in Thessaly for a three-day *munera* (festival) to be held in Corinth's Amphitheater; after being ridden to Corinth, the narrator (who has been turned into an ass) describes part of the mythological dramas, Pyrrhic dances and mimes of the event itself.[20] Beast hunts are further attested at the Amphitheater by a Greek inscription copied by Cyriac of Ancona from a base with figures of *venatores*, once the support for a bronze statue erected by the beast hunters (θηραίτορες ἄνδρες) of Corinth for their doctor Trophimos "near the entrances for the beasts."[21] A third-century epitaph of a gladiator from this area displays an image of him in his professional gear with the palm of Victory, and indicates there was indeed a cemetery by the Amphitheater, perhaps even one reserved for those who competed there (Figure 4.1).[22] Finally, a fourth-century geographer wrote that one of the most distinguishing features of Corinth was that, *habet et opus praecipuum amphitheatrum*, "it even has a structure of a great amphitheater."[23]

Iconographic and literary sources, inscriptions and comparison with other theaters of Late Antiquity all suggest a broad range of performances, spectacles and competitions were held in the two central arenas of the Theater and Odeum in the third and fourth centuries, even after they were equipped for combat, and perhaps still in the Amphitheater. Events in the games of the *Caesarea*, *Sebastea* or *Asklepia*, festivals for various deities, *munera* staged by local officials, and other public events not held at Isthmia, the Circus or a stadium once filled these buildings with crowds, and encouraged their repair

Figure 4.1 Marble gladiator's tombstone, probably of the third century, Corinth Museum inv. no. I-2664.

and remodeling into the early fifth century. If a letter attributed to the emperor Julian is genuine, the city of Corinth gained control over the finances of neighboring Argos in the middle of the fourth century, and came to the attention of Julian as a result of a protest by the Argives against taxes levied on that city to finance Corinthian beast hunts.[24] Julian referred to Corinth in other writings as well. In his panegyric of Eusebia he called Corinth a center for training in philosophy.[25] He also addressed another one of his letters to the city, and praised its citizens for receiving his father.[26] Regulations were passed for the restoration of the Theater at Sparta in 359, and a statue of the Governor of Achaia, Anatolius, was put up there a little after 375, thanking him for restoration help at Sparta (perhaps after the earthquake); in this era the Theater at Corinth was probably still actively in use by the governor as a venue to entertain crowds of Corinthians too.[27]

Public festivals were celebrated not only with beast hunts and gladiatorial combat, but also with drama, pantomime dance performances, mimes, and oratory. Already at the dedication of the Theater of Pompey in 55 BCE, the first stone theater in Rome, Greek tragedy competed for attention alongside "athletic contests, music, gladiators, races, and the hunting of wild beasts."[28] The last entirely new plays at Athens' City Dionysia festival seem to have been presented in the first century, but the festival continued to be held far into Late Antiquity mounting new productions of old plays.[29] Meanwhile, a second- or third-century re-interpreter of Euripides, Sophocles and Timotheos was in competition at Isthmia, and perhaps Corinth too.[30] Pantomime did away with actors and dialogue, presenting the story by means of a solo dancer and accompanying musician and chorus; the mime was an unmasked show presented by a troupe of male and female actors, with a selection of dramatic excerpts, animal shows, music and farce.[31] Most mimes incorporated elements of Classical drama, but eschewed the masks, boots and stylized gestures of traditional performances. Rhetoricians (like St Augustine) also presented speeches or scenes from tragedy and history in competitions, as did singers and lyre-players.

However, the upkeep of theaters and the production of public spectacles required money, official interest and social will, and perhaps the most compelling evidence for decline in public assembly in the fourth century concerns the details of financing of these spectacles and competitions. Evidence from outside Corinth, especially from Aphrodisias and Antioch, reveals a pattern for festivals: their growth and early support by foundations and public offices, their adoption by imperial officials in Late Antiquity, and their gradual decline as fewer public and private patrons paid for them.[32] In Carthage, in the later fourth century, St Augustine famously berated himself for his devotion to the theater, describing not only his love of theater as a boy, but also the respect given to the citizens who put on the shows.[33] Consular diptychs through the reign of the emperor Anastasius feature tragic actors alongside mimes, jugglers, acrobats, hunters and charioteers in performance spaces entertaining crowds at the consuls' expense.[34] Yet dwindling funds and the disapproval of Christian clergy for festivals turned more and more of these events into extensions of imperial cult in the fifth century, or reduced them to productions in private homes rather than traditional monumental public venues.

Gymnasia, Stadium and Circus (Hippodrome)

Besides the Theater, Odeum and Amphitheater, however, a number of other spaces for civic assembly, entertainment and culture were located along the northern edge of Corinth's lower city terrace, where the drop to the plains below formed the natural northern boundary of the city (Figures 3, 7). Somewhere between the Theater and the Asklepieion on the very edge of the terrace, Pausanias located two temples of Zeus, the Lerna Fountain and the Old Gymnasium.[35] Combining his description with the archaeological reports on material culture of this area shows its shifting use as public space throughout Late Antiquity. James Wiseman referred to his decade of excavations in this area by reference to the Old Gymnasium, which Pausanias placed near the Theater.[36] Pausanias' description, however, leaves it unclear whether he is referring to "old" as in pre-Roman, or "old" in contrast to some more recently constructed Gymnasium elsewhere in the city, or even if he means a specific complex of buildings rather than a neighborhood. Pre-Roman Corinth had *gymnasia* at the north of the city at a place called Sura, and to the east in the Kraneion neighborhood (see Chapter 7 below). Conclusions are elusive for the identity or era of the many ancient buildings in the northern area, perhaps Sura, which was partially uncovered by

Wiseman's excavations. By comparison with Ancient Messene or Athens, the Corinthian gymnasium of Late Antiquity should have still included facilities for young men of the city to exercise and train both their bodies and minds: a bath, palestra, running track, lecture halls and stoas.[37] The unexcavated brick ruins standing in the field just north of the Theater may be a bath, perhaps even the Baths of Hadrian that Pausanias referred to in passing, but they are more likely from the third or even fourth century based on the brickwork, and thus added on to a nearby gymnasium in Late Antiquity.[38]

Just to the north, there is a short stretch of what appears to be one end of a circus *spina*, where a monumental marble truncated cone, interpreted by David Romano as a *meta* (turning post) was found, along with a marble egg that might belong with the *meta*. Romano proposed that this was the site of the Roman Circus (Hippodrome), near the Old Gymnasium's stoa. Sanders argues that the area for a track around the excavated *spina* is too narrow and short for the circus which Romano places there, although Romano offers persuasive parallels for small circuses in the Eastern Empire.[39] Some sort of running track, stadium or racetrack for athletes once stood nearby, since a starting-block for running was found reused in the proposed *spina*, and an inscribed herm with a victors' list of the athletic contests of the year 57 was found in the Fountain of the Lamps swimming pool nearby.[40]

Shear's tombs on the northwest hillock of Cheliotomylos near the edge of the lower city terrace are largely fourth to seventh century in date according to their lamps, while the Asklepieion and adjacent Lerna Fountain were also the site for extensive burials, some with epitaphs, in the same era.[41] Mary E. Hoskins Walbank and Michael B. Walbank argue that Euplous, identified in an epitaph as a ἡνίοχος, could be a "charioteer" (rather than Kent's "teamster"), employed in the Circus at Corinth, maybe along with Korinthas the ἱπποιατρός ("horse doctor"), who is known from another early sixth-century epitaph.[42] The Circus was certainly located nearby, either at Romano's site, or on the plain below, and thus chariot racing, as well as the beast hunts noted above, and maybe even athletics, might still have been enjoyed by Corinthians into the sixth century at the city center.

In the sixth century, Procopius claimed that in the name of Justinian and the preservation of security in the Peloponnesus, the official Alexander the so-called Snips transferred all the civic and spectacle funds of cities in Greece to the Imperial Treasury, for the support of 2000 troops at Thermopylae (see below, Chapter 8).[43] Thereafter in all Greece, and specifically Athens, "no public building was restored." Procopius more generally accused Justinian elsewhere of stripping other cities all over the Empire of their civic and spectacle funds, thus depriving them of public servants like teachers and doctors, public services like street lamps and, most dramatically, public spectacles:

> For the theaters and hippodromes and circuses were all closed for the most part – the places in which, as it happened, his wife had been born and reared and educated. And later he ordered these spectacles to close down altogether, even in Byzantium, so that the Treasury might not have to supply the usual sums to the numerous and almost countless persons who derived their living from them. And there was both in private and in public sorrow and dejection, as though still another affliction from Heaven had smitten them, and there was no laughter in life for anyone.[44]

The evidence for closure of theaters all over the empire is patchy, and Justinian issued at least one *Novel* supporting theatrical professionals. However, one looks almost in vain for evidence of civic funds or spectacles in Corinth, or southern Greece, in the sixth century; from the evidence of the disassembly of the structure of the Theater and Odeum, most public spectacles ceased at Corinth in the fifth century, with only chariot racing continuing into the age of Justinian.

Isthmia and the Isthmian Festival

The highest honor of service in civic government at Corinth into the fourth century was still to serve as *agonothetes*, or games-giver, of the Isthmian Festival in honor of Poseidon, though far more than these Panhellenic biennial *agones* (games) were still celebrated and presented to the public.[45] Evidence for the primacy of the Isthmian Festival in Corinthian civic life comes from the Forum as well as the site of the Sanctuary of Poseidon on the Isthmus (Isthmia) itself (Figures 2, 5, 9). Alongside the other public spectacles of beast hunts, gladiators, chariot-racing, athletics, music, dance and theater at Corinth outlined above, and the spaces to train for these performances and hold them, the Isthmian Festival probably persisted as a place and time for Corinthian public assembly to watch athletics into the fourth century. In an eastern shop of the South Stoa, a mosaic was laid *c.*200 of a male athlete with the personified Goddess of Good Fortune, identified from her shield reading Ἐυτυ]χία (*Eutychia*, Good Fortune). The iconography of this mosaic suggested to Broneer that the office for the Isthmian *agonothetes* could plausibly be placed there.[46] More recently, B.A. Robinson has outlined the range of meanings that this mosaic image could have had for third-century viewers, and how it was repaired as a public space continuously over the next 200 years.[47]

Broneer also identified a built round base supporting a central column at the east end of the Central Shops as the base for a Corinthian statue of an emperor (or deity) holding a scepter flanked by horses known from a coin of Lucius Verus.[48] The horses could indicate an imperial victory monument for the Isthmian games, placed appropriately close to the office of the Isthmian *agonothetes*. More than half of all the inscriptions referring to the Isthmian *agonothetes* found at Corinth came from this southeast corner of the Forum.[49] Notably, a long second-century decree honoring the *archiereus* (high priest) P. Licinius Priscus Iuventianus was found here, which thanks him for building a stoa with 50 *oikoi* for housing athletes, probably at Isthmia, and repairing eight altars and temples there.[50] Nearby, there was also a base for the statue of an equestrian *agonothetes* named Cornelius, honoring his patronage of the *Isthmia, Caesarea, Sebastea and Asklepia* in about the middle of the third century (dated by the script), our latest epigraphic evidence that the celebration of all those festivals continued until then at Corinth.[51]

On a plateau at the eastern side of the Isthmus, commanding the approach to Corinth from the north or east by land or by sea, and easily accessible from Corinth itself, lay the ancient Panhellenic Sanctuary of Poseidon on the Isthmus, modern Kyras Vrysi, where the *Isthmia* were held (Figure 9).[52] The sanctuary centered on the Classical Temple of Poseidon, with bronze Tritons on the roof, and numerous statues of Poseidon, his wife Amphitrite and their marine entourage inside, including a valuable chryselephantine group dedicated by Herodes Atticus and described at length by Pausanias.[53] The Roman sanctuary also contained an important shrine for the heroized child god known as Melicertes or Palaemon, protector of mariners, which Pausanias described as follows:

> within the enclosure on the left is a Temple of Palaemon, with images in it of Poseidon, Leucothea and Palaemon himself. There is also what is called his *adyton*, and an underground descent to it, where they say that Palaemon is concealed. Whosoever, whether Corinthian or stranger, swears falsely here, can by no means escape from his oath. There is also an ancient sanctuary called the Altar of the Cyclopes, and they sacrifice to the Cyclopes upon it.[54]

The excavated shrine of Palaemon includes ruins of two small round temples, an *adyton* probably identified in Antiquity with his tomb, and a number of sacrificial pits with evidence of nocturnal mystery rites. Gebhard proposes that Palaemon initially had a small temple to the east of the Temple of Poseidon, with the *adyton* (sacred chamber) to the south, and that the eastern temple was replaced by the one visible today to the south, which was built over the *adyton* when the east stoa replaced the eastern temple.[55] Mary E. Hoskins Walbank proposes that the temple for Palaemon to the south of the Temple of Poseidon was built *c.*161–5, with the support of the *archiereus* mentioned above, P. Licinius Priscus Iuventianus.[56] A stadium, a theater, the Roman bath complex mentioned before and monumental stoas filled the remainder of the slopes leading down to the seaside of the Saronic Gulf east of these temples.[57]

A monumental Arch (or Propylaia) covered the road which ran into the Sanctuary of Poseidon from the northeast, the route from Athens, Megara and Theseus' Scironian cliffs.[58] Pausanias presented the Sanctuary of Poseidon at the Isthmus at the beginning of his Book 2 on the Corinthia, viewing its monuments and mythology from the perspective of a traveler arriving along this road. Gebhard points out that he sets the scene and shows his interests by ending his first book with an account of the tomb of Ino, mother of Melicertes, at Megara, and the Molourian Rock on the Scironian Cliffs from which she leapt with her son, transforming them into the protectors of sailors, Leucothea (the White Goddess) and Palaemon.[59] Pausanias (2.1.3) thus starts his account of the Corinthia by connecting himself, the landscape and the second-century Isthmian festival directly with ancient Greek mythology: "the pine still grew by the shore at the time of my visit," he wrote, "and there was an altar of Melicertes. At this place, they say, the boy was brought ashore by a dolphin; Sisyphus found him lying and gave him burial on the Isthmus, establishing the Isthmian Games in his honor." He continues the description by pointing out the theater, the stadium "of white stone," and then the road up to the Sanctuary of Poseidon (and Melicertes/Palaemon) flanked by cypresses and statues of Isthmian victors.[60]

Pausanias thus highlighted the sacred, sculptural and festival aspects of the Sanctuary of Poseidon in the middle of the second century, when still every two years the Corinthians held the Panhellenic Isthmian festival, in which contestants from all over the Mediterranean competed.[61] Roman coins of Corinth depict runners, wrestlers and boxers, some with the palm of victory, as well as the the Temple of Poseidon, and the shrine of Palaemon, where Corinthians and visitors from abroad sought protection from Palaemon through nocturnal mystery rites.[62] Evidence for victors in the *Isthmia* stretches into the late third century, and for *agonothetes* into the middle of the fourth century, after which the Isthmian festival was apparently no longer celebrated, although the Roman bath continued in use for several more centuries.[63] Besides the third-century inscription mentioned before from the Corinthian Forum, a tetrarchic-style male head from Corinth wears the characteristic pine wreath of an Isthmian victor, and two victor monuments from Isthmia are possibly third-century in date.[64]

Another intriguing portrait head, and literary testimonia outlined in the next chapter, suggest activity still related to devotion to Poseidon and public gatherings in the fourth century at the Isthmus. A bearded portrait head from the foundations of a Byzantine house in the Hexamilion's Eastern Fortress at Isthmia belongs to a notable group of at least nine copies of this same late third- or fourth-century man from Greece, the so-called Iamblichus portrait.[65] Whether a notable philosopher like Iamblichus, a benefactor or perhaps even the famously bearded but never securely identified emperor Julian, this man was clearly widely honored all around Greece, especially at ancient Panhellenic sanctuaries like Isthmia, Delphi or Epidauros. The discovery of this same portrait head at these other shrines means that the portrait was almost certainly originally erected at Isthmia in the Sanctuary of Poseidon itself to reward benefactions of the fourth century related to the Panhellenic cult of Poseidon at the Isthmus and its Corinthian festival.

CHAPTER 5

CREATION AND DESTRUCTION OF PUBLIC SCULPTURE

Corinth had a vast and ancient collection of public sculpture at the start of Late Antiquity. Arrayed around the Forum on inscribed bases, and standing in the stoas, fountains, baths and other public spaces were hundreds of carved or cast statues: portraits of local grandees, governors of Achaia and emperors, venerable cult statues and pedimental groups atop temples (see cover image, Figures 11–12, 2.1, 5.1–5.12, 6.1–6.2). However, from about the fifth century onwards, most of this sculpture was deliberately and systematically destroyed or discarded: statues of men, women, gods and animals beheaded, buried, cut up for walls or melted down to make lime mortar (or bronze). A decline in the quantity and quality of production of new public sculpture stretched from the third into the early fifth century at Corinth, and then production of new sculptures in the round probably ended with marble public portraits of the governor, imperial officials and emperors in the fifth century. Yet epigraphic texts of Late Antiquity still warmly praise the naturalism and value of the new portraits, even as their proportions appear more awkward, and their material of manufacture much more *ad hoc* than under the high empire. Physical destruction of statuary could even coexist with creation in the fifth century at Corinth.

Whether Christian iconoclasm, economic imperatives or new fortification wall building were most to blame, some basic change in civic and aesthetic values came over the Corinthians in the later fifth and sixth centuries, in relation to the manufacture as well as the appreciation of public sculpture in the round. Both new portraits and old divine images were cut up and reused side by side by builders in construction of the fifth and sixth centuries, and heads were particularly singled out for removal from bodies, and sometimes for separate disposal in drains. All sculpture in the round was taken down, whether in wood, bronze or stone, centuries old or brand new, religious or secular. While cult statues bear the brunt of Christian fervour in literary texts, there are just as many public portraits as divine images marked with crosses at Corinth, and both were beheaded, reused or melted down, in the Corinthian version of the wider dramatic change in attitudes towards public sculpture happening all over the Roman Empire.[1] In Byzantine Corinth, as in the other Christianized cities of the Eastern Roman Empire, new sculpture was carved mainly for churches: architectural elements like column capitals, lintels and relief slabs carved from reused marble with Christian, animal or vegetal imagery. In this chapter, I outline the sculptural and epigraphic evidence for the last public sculpture erected at Corinth, put it in context, and draw conclusions about the patrons of its creation, and the agents of its destruction.[2]

Most fragments of ancient marble sculptures (and the few small bits of bronze ones) were excavated at Corinth from around the Forum Area, with a few found farther afield (e.g. at the Sanctuary of Demeter and Kore, or Isthmia). The majority of extant marble bodies are headless, and were found in walls or pavements reused alongside architectural *spolia* and statue bases. Far fewer heads were found than bodies or body fragments; most heads were in drains or other watery filled-up underground spaces. Stratigraphy, coins and pottery analysis have allowed scholars to date some of these medieval walls, pavements or fills, and hence the disposal of the sculpture in them, to the later fifth to ninth century. Marble statuary is hard and heavy, and hence difficult to break or move long distances. Therefore most statues were intentionally, not accidentally, broken into pieces. Pieces which one person cannot easily lift today probably didn't travel too far from their original display context, and were moved by an organized building crew, using specialized equipment, and with a planned destination. Thus we can say with some certainty that the preferred areas for public display of honorific portraits in Late Antiquity were near the older portraits and divine statuary: ringing the Forum, along the upper Lechaion Road, in front of the stoas, shops and temples, and around the Fountain of Peirene, the Peribolos of Apollo and the Theater.[3] On either side of the Lechaion Road, and around the Forum, portrait statues of civic benefactors looked down from their high bases upon the traffic, markets and court cases, while texts on their bases announced the identity of the images to all who could read the Greek or Latin language. When the Governor of Achaia made his *adventus* coming up the long, straight road from the harbor at Lechaion, he was flanked by his predecessors set in stone. Some images of gods, heroes and mortals stood out in the open air, while others stared out from the shadowy depths of temples, shopfront shrines or fountain niches.

As noted in Chapter 3, Betsey Robinson has made a close and well-researched study of the centuries long history of the Fountain of Peirene, including its many important late antique phases and varied sculptural assemblage.[4] Peirene's imperial Roman statuary display included a Scylla water spout, Tritons and nude figures of Nymphs (or Aphrodite), as appropriate to a fountain. It is predictable that these were targeted for disposal or reuse in the sixth century as emblems of pagan culture and the nude female body, both beheaded and, in the case of one Nymph, dumped in Peirene's west supply tunnel still with traces of the drill marks around her waist from being cut down into manageable pieces of marble (Figure 5.1).[5] Other sections of her body, and especially her head, must have been melted down in one of the many adjacent lime kilns. However, there were also many portraits of mortal benefactors standing in and around Peirene in the last monumental phases of the fourth to sixth century outlined in Chapter 3, and many of their heads were spared destruction, but also deliberately deposited in dark, watery underground places.

The three male heads of the Introduction were found deposited together in "Early Byzantine fill of the approach to the Cyclopean Fountain," an ancient section of Peirene closed off and filled in during sixth-century renovation of the Spring Façade and access routes to the fountain's waters (Figures. 11–12).[6] The bearded man from the cover is wearing a laurel wreath over a *strophion* (headband), and thus likely represents a public portrait of a Greco-Roman priest wearing his wreath of office, perhaps a priest of Apollo (from the laurel).[7] His head shows the finest carving of the three, both in the hairstyle and the pensive eyes, which may mean he is earlier than the others, and that the portrait was more expensive. The shallow pecked section with small holes cut away from the wreath may be an ancient repair to this

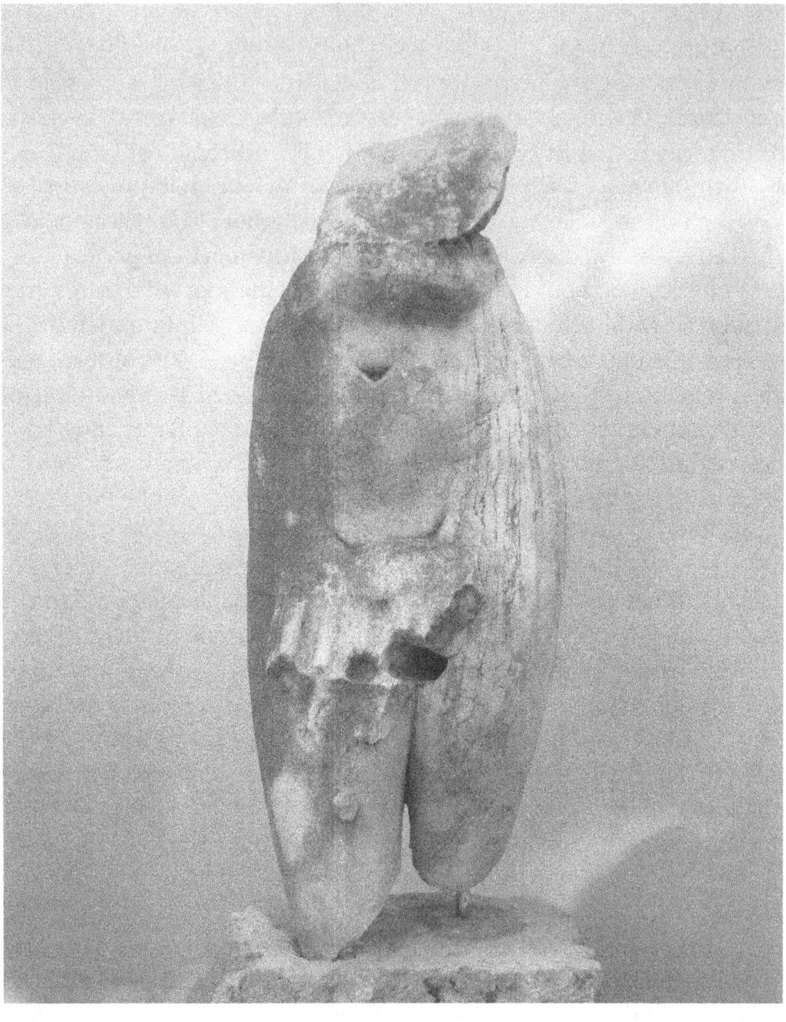

Figure 5.1 Marble torso of a Nymph, with drill marks at waist, Corinth Museum inv. no. S-1024.

head, or evidence of a metal attachment, showing what value the portrait had when on display. Catherine de Grazia Vanderpool assigns him a stylistic and historical date of *c*.361–91, with the end date aligned with Theodosius' legislation against pagan religion. Priests of so-called pagan cults in the third and fourth century often held multiple civic and religious offices in and outside their home cities, for example, also serving as *agonothetes* or imperial cult priests.[8]

Vanderpool judges that the other two men's heads were carved about a century later, *c.*450–500, due to their hairstyles and shallower carving. The man with his face smashed has swept-forward hair, and a beard that looks like a coral, all squiggly lines on a bulbous mass; he is the latest in date if we date by quality and naturalism (Figure 11).[9] Finally, the fellow marked on his forehead with a small Christian cross also has swept-forward hair but a shorter beard (Figure 12).[10] Was he neutralized or converted with the cross, remembered as an opponent of Christianity? Was he on display with the cross visible? The closest parallels for this type of cross on the forehead come from portraits from Ephesus and the East, both long-standing Julio-Claudians and newer imperial or civic honorands, marked in Late Antiquity with a small and carefully cut cross at the center of the forehead.[11] Divine heads more often have the eyes, mouth or limbs targeted; for more on the symbolism of cross marking, and other examples from Corinth. These three men, as I argued in the Introduction, were distinguished imperial or civic honorands of fourth- and fifth-century Corinth, representatives of the old authorities and religion, with their portraits commissioned and paid for by those same authorities: the City Council, priests and other officials drawn from the *curiales*, or the Governor of Achaia. They stood upon marble bodies and inscribed bases celebrating their lineage and honoring their service for all to see in a prominent location, alongside divine statuary and earlier honorands.

A number of other newly carved portrait heads of third- to fifth-century style were excavated from the subterranean network of drains and tunnels between the Southwest Forum, Peirene and the Great Bath on the Lechaion Road.[12] A bearded shaggy-haired head found in a Peirene drain near the Great Bath on the Lechaion Road is also of high quality, and to Vanderpool possibly represented an imperial official of barbarian origin of the late fourth century, given his resemblance to figures on the obelisk base of Theodosius in Constantinople (Figure 5.2).[13] A single fragment of the front of a face from the Southwest Forum is the only late antique portrait from Corinth copied elsewhere. He could represent a Praetorian Prefect (or *Magister Militum*) of Illyricum, perhaps even one who served during Theodosius' tenure in Thessalonike, since a very well-preserved portrait bust of the same man was found in western Macedonia, along with a bust of his wife bearing a later fourth-century hairstyle.[14]

Figure 5.2 Corinth Excavations photograph from 1919 of Niko holding a newly excavated marble male head, probably of the fourth century, Corinth Museum inv. no. S-1199.

There were also female benefactors at Corinth in Late Antiquity, especially around Peirene Fountain. A woman's head, with her hair covered in a scarf or snood except for two small locks in front, in the modest style of Late Antiquity, was probably carved *c*.400, with neck shaped for insertion into a separate female portrait body or bust (Figure 5.3).[15] Regilla had a base in Peirene, many times reused and possibly inscribed in Late Antiquity. Robinson suggests a draped Little Herculaneum female portrait body, found alongside another Nymph (or Aphrodite) body and two monumental draped bodies (Demeter and Kore?) near the northeastern entry to Peirene,

Figure 5.3 Marble female head, *c.*400, Corinth Museum inv. no. S-986.

might have borne this head as a late antique replica of Regilla (Figure 5.4 on the left).[16] Whether this late antique lady was meant to represent Regilla, or was a female benefactor active in the late fourth or early fifth century at Corinth, her marble head was found deposited together with a bearded head of the god Dionysos in the drain just north of Peirene (Figure 5.5).

Charles Edwards restored an Antonine group of Demeter and Kore with Dionysos and Ariadne to the Peribolos of Apollo just north of Peirene, putting together the extant marble bodies of gods with the head of Dionysos found together with the late antique lady's head.[17] The triconch court of Peirene, the Peribolos of Apollo, and the Roman Baths to the north, as well as the Great Bath on the Lechaion Road, were clearly crowded with honorific portrait statues in Late Antiquity, alongside the mythological statuary. Mortal and divine sculpture was then disposed of together in the sixth to seventh centuries, near where it had been displayed together in the fourth or fifth centuries.

Pausanias singled out a few statues of gods for special mention near Peirene: "there is also a statue of Apollo beside Peirene and a *peribolos*, in which the exploit of Odysseus against the suitors is painted. Then on the straight road to Lechaion a seated Hermes of bronze, and a ram beside him ... then Poseidon and Leucothea and there is Palaemon on the dolphin."[18] As noted above in Chapter 3, Pausanias (2.3.5) then digressed about baths and *krenai* (springs/fountains) at Corinth, praising the baths given by Hadrian and especially those of Eurykles "close to Poseidon," perhaps the so-called Baths of Eurykles just north of the Peribolos of Apollo. Pausanias' Baths of Eurykles had further statues of Poseidon and a hunting Artemis at the left of the entry, and a fountain "most worthy to see beside the statue of Artemis, and upon it Bellerophon, and the water runs through the hoof of the horse Pegasus." None of these images have been excavated, although a marble head of Hermes was found in the Room 2 Plunge Bath of the Roman Baths.[19] Pausanias' Apollo and Hermes may have been cult statues, yet all divine images by the later second century were also subject to admiration as famous works of art of an earlier age. The Asklepieion complex at Messene provides a paralell, where cult statues for various deities, and mortal portraits, were placed in a series of small chambers along the west side of the *peribolos* of the Temple of Asklepios and Messene.[20] As there, at Corinth, or in the Stoa Poikile in Athens,

Figure 5.4 Two female portrait bodies, both possibly representing Regilla, Corinth Museum inv. nos. S-55 and S-813.

Figure 5.5 Marble head of Dionysos, Corinth Museum inv. no. S-987.

the display of paintings and divine sculptural groups together was a symbol of ancient Hellenic culture to Pausanias, and still to fourth-century viewers; yet whether in *periboloi* or baths, all these statue groups did not survive the sixth century on display, but were cut up, hidden in drains, or built into new walls right alongside the human portraits.[21]

Honorific portrait heads with surviving necks are almost all cut for insertion into separate portrait bodies or busts, while most marble *togatus* and *palliatus* (*himation*-wearing) bodies found in the Lechaion Road and Forum Area also show signs of recutting to take new heads.[22] Some *togati* and *palliati* have been dated to Late Antiquity by their small size or schematic carving, but many Roman Imperial bodies were doubtless reused many times in Late Antiquity. A Large Herculaneum female portrait body was even recut as a male *palliatus* (a *himation*- or cloak-wearing male portrait body), and found by the *Bouleuterion* (Council House) chamber of the South Stoa, probably its last place of dedication, with a newly carved head (could we call him "the last of the decurions"?) (Figure 5.6).[23]

At least seven marble bodies of men were newly carved along with their attached (now missing) heads in Late Antiquity, wearing the *chlamys*, crossbow fibula, long-sleeved tunic and belt: the uniform of military and civil imperial office after the tetrarchic reforms.[24] More of these *chlamydati* were excavated at Corinth than any other city, apparently a reflection of Corinthian enthusiasm for erecting public portraits of the Governor of Achaia or other imperial magistrates in the fourth and early fifth century. Four of these bodies were found cut down and reused in the western Forum, with one each from the upper Lechaion Road, Theater and Kraneion Basilica. Most are carved from previously worked marble, but they all once had new portrait heads carved in one piece, and the Lechaion Road and Theater officials even display a lively naturalism. The Lechaion Road official had a scroll bundle carved as a support beside his foot, probably advertising his excellence as a bureaucrat, man of letters, or both (Figure 5.7).[25] The Theater official was likely carved before *c*.425–50, if erected in the Theater originally, and he is the most naturalistic, so could even be early fourth century (he is on display in the Corinth Museum).[26] A hand fragment with the cuff of a long sleeve holding a staff or scroll shows that another late antique portrait of an official once stood in the Theater too.[27]

The other four *chlamydati* (chlamys-wearing portrait bodies) from the Forum, and the one built into the Kraneion Basilica, are all stiffer in execution, but also newly carved in Late Antiquity, and once conspicuously marked out from older portrait bodies by their contemporary official costume (Figures 5.9, 5.11). One is only the right side of an official, and cut across the back, probably to support a

Figure 5.6 Marble male portrait body, recarved from a female portrait body, Corinth Museum inv. no. S-2224.

Figure 5.7 Marble male portrait body wearing a chlamys, probably a late antique imperial official, Corinth Museum inv. no. S-314.

roof beam in its reuse.[28] The preserved lower half of another was carved out of a small epistyle block, and then became a portrait with a uniquely ankle-length tunic, suggesting it might represent either a man or a woman, as both were portrayed wearing long tunics and chlamyses in late antique art (for example, the mosaics of Justinian and Theodora in Ravenna).[29] The two best preserved officials, exhibited together in the Corinth Museum, were found built into *spolia* walls which extended the line of the Northwest Shops westwards, along with the bodies of monumental marble statues of Artemis and the Dioscuri, possibly once cult statues (Figures 5.8, 5.10). An official holding a balled-up *mappa*, or handkerchief, to his chest was recarved out of a monumental female body, dubbed "the horror" by the excavators, and even at first thought to be a portrait of a Christian priest rather than a late antique imperial official (Figure 5.9).[30] He could well have served as a priest, but more likely of the pagan than the Christian variety, holding the *mappa* as an *agonothetes* to start the races, and as a mark of proconsular *imperium*, if this statue represented a Governor of Achaia. The other official, whose torso alone is preserved, seems to hold a scroll to his

Figure 5.8 Corinth Excavations photograph from 1905 of a wall at the west end of the Northwest Shops which was built using marble bodies of late antique imperial officials and divine statuary (Imperial official S-819 and Artemis S-820 are visible).

Figure 5.9 Marble male portrait body wearing a chlamys, probably a late antique imperial official, recarved from a female body, perhaps Demeter, Corinth Museum inv. no. S-819.

chest with his right hand, probably again as a symbol of erudition, office and trustworthiness.[31] The varied contents of these walls show again clearly that late antique portraits and pagan statuary were accessible and reused together, in the sixth century, or at least before the ninth century, and both alike beheaded before their reuse as building material.

Finally, the Kraneion Basilica is a three-aisled cemetery church built in the first half of the sixth century in Corinth's eastern extramural Kraneion neighborhood, with an attached triconch mausoleum (or less likely a martyrium) and a baptistry (Figures 3, 8). A large number of inscribed epitaphs for sixth-century Corinthian deacons, soldiers and other Christian worthies were found there, for the more well to do of those once buried in the church and adjacent extensive cemetery (for more detail, see Chapter 7). The northern door of the narthex of this church was cut down from a *chlamydatus* official's portrait statue, whose back now forms the doorsill, apparently an unpopular man with the Church, or at least a potent example of the treatment of statuary by bishops or other Christian benefactors in the early sixth century (Figure 5.11).[32] He may represent a fourth- or fifth-century honorific portrait of an imperial official or Governor of Achaia carried out from the Forum, or he may have been set up as a benefactor by the late antique city gate nearby, which was built in the fifth century. There is also even the possibility that he was a tomb marker before being cut down for a door threshold, since the Kraneion Basilica stood in a centuries-old cemetery. The *Palatine Anthology* (*AnthPal* 7.672) gives the epitaph of a Praetorian Prefect of Illyricum once inscribed in Corinth, probably a Christian, who might even be this man: "The earth holds the good flesh, heaven holds the glorious spirit/of Andreas, who while administering justice to the Danaans and Illyrians,/guarded his clean hands from unholy gain."[33]

Further clues to the identity of these portraits, and their significance in late antique Corinth, comes from extant inscribed statue bases. Honorific statues erected by the city of Corinth (as *Boule*, City Council, or *Polis*, City) are generally inscribed in verse poetry, and in Greek, while the Governors of Achaia more often used prose, and sometimes Latin, for dedications made in the name(s) of the ruling emperor(s). Local Corinthian benefactors, Governors of Achaia and emperors are the people who receive statues most often.[34] The statue base for Parnasius, for example, is one of the best texts for

Figure 5.10 Marble body of Artemis, Corinth Museum inv. no. S-820.

showing the key role which local *archontes* played as patrons in late antique Corinth alongside imperial officials (Figure 5.12). Memmius Pontius Ptolemaeus Parnasius, *vir clarissimus*, was honored with a statue as "patron of the *clarissima* city of the Corinthians" by a certain

Figure 5.11 Marble male portrait body wearing a chlamys, probably a late antique imperial official, turned over from his reuse as a narthex door threshold in the Kraneion Basilica, Corinth Museum inv. no. S-3788. (Photo by author.)

Figure 5.12 Marble statue base for Parnasius, Corinth Museum inv. no. I-1115.

Aur(elius) Eutychianus, *apostra(tegos?, praetorius?)*, *ps(ephismati) b(oules)* (i.e. passed by a vote of the City Council, albeit with the two-letter abbreviation for the latter, *psi beta,* left over from a previous use of the base).[35] This may be the Parnasius of Patras who was prefect of Egypt under Constantius (*c.*357–9), and exiled from that post along with his colleague, the sophist Aristophanes of Corinth, son of Menander, a minor imperial official of the *agentes in rebus,* for consulting an astrologer. Aristophanes of Corinth, at least, was reinstated under Julian through the good offices of Libanius in 362, and both Parnasius and Aristophanes returned to Corinth later in life.[36]

As imperial officials of senatorial status, they were likely exempt from curial duties at Corinth, and thus among those criticized by Libanius for shirking local responsibilities, so this statue base and the next two from the Lechaion Road may represent recognition of benefactions performed above and beyond any official responsibilities at Corinth.[37]

Two tall marble bases with mouldings from the Lechaion Road ramp bear Greek verses with letter-forms of the third or fourth century, and reveal some further characteristics of the civic honors granted with a statue in that era, many of which Corinth shared with other cities, especially provincial capitals like Aphrodisias and Ephesus.[38] The new dedications inscribed over older erased texts on the front of each base celebrate the honorand and his new marble portrait but, unlike the Parnasius base, these texts are written in hexameter Greek poetry.

> Who has captured the pleasing figure of the proconsul Junior, who has carved his form in stone? The stone cutter has imitated his form with his craft, freely bestowing the whole ornament on mother Greece, and blameless Eutychianus, admiring him, set him up, administering Ephyra well in the place of his relative. *Passed by a vote of the City Council.*[39]
>
> I am the man allotted a portion of Periclean blood from an Attic father, the son of Hermolaus, by name Diogenes; Secun[dinus?] set me up in Ephyra ne[ar the spring?] of Peirene as a shining image. *Passed by a vote of the City Council.*[40]

The proconsul *Iounoros* (Junior) was set up by his brother, and successor as Governor of Achaia, Eutychianus, in Ephyra (Corinth). His marble statue is praised in traditional terms for its naturalism and resemblance to him, captured by the skill of the stone cutter (*laotomos*), pride of mother Greece (*Hellas*). The second base also makes reference to a marble statue, a shining image (εἰκόνι λαμπομένῃ), a common trope among honorific epigrams of this era at Corinth and elsewhere.[41] Diogenes, son of Hermolaus, was set up by an otherwise unknown Secun[dinus?] alongside the Fountain of Peirene in Ephyra (Corinth), and praised for his descent from an Athenian father and hence the Classical general Pericles. The text thus combines claims to Athenian ancestry stretching back to the Classical era with precise instructions for placement of the statue at Corinth, but with the epic name for Corinth and without any reason for the statue, or even office. This could possibly be the fourth-century philosopher Diogenes, who was the uncle of the Aristophanes of Corinth mentioned above.[42] Both inscriptions are engraved over erased, earlier texts (removed except for the *psi beta*, which was apparently left to show the continued approval of the City Council).

The upper surfaces of these bases reveal cuttings showing that at least one of the earlier statues was bronze (and set into the base), but both the men honored in the late antique inscriptions were carved from marble, as celebrated in both texts (with the new marble statue's base then clamped down on top of the reused base). The Archaic poet Eumelus' use of the Homeric Ephyra, home of Bellerophon, as a poetic name for Corinth was revived in earnest in the second century, along with the use of Greek for public inscriptions. Ephyra, together with the simple Κόρινθος (Corinth), then quickly supplanted *Colonia Laus Iulia Corinthiensis* in the epigraphic record. A Roman and Latin city name emphasizing Corinth's colonial status thus became one evoking the archaic and epic past of the city, intelligible to those educated in epic and archaic poetry.[43] An otherwise unknown Hesychius, for example, set up a statue of a governor in the fourth century, praising him on the statue base with a Greek poetic text in the name "of the Ephyreans."[44] Rather than praising an honorand's local record, or *cursus honorum*, as texts in the first and second century had done, these texts, like those in other Greek cities of the eastern Empire, moved to glorifying and evoking the Hellenic past, the poetic tradition and especially the carving of naturalistic sculpture in marble.[45] In this way, third- and fourth-century Corinthian officials, benefactors, honorands and all who read the bases and viewed the statues took part in connecting their contemporary city with its Greek past as a center of epic poetry, mythology and the carving of marble sculpture.

Some other bases and revetment plaques honoring governors, local officials, emperors or other benefactors are more fragmentary, but also dated on the basis of their script to the third to sixth centuries, and largely found in secondary contexts in the northwestern or southern Forum areas.[46] For example, a column of gray marble, probably reused as a statue base in Late Antiquity, was recovered from the medieval monastery church of St John (which once stood beside the Northwest

Shops), and honors the otherwise unknown "Fl(avius) Genethlid(ius) Justus ... proconsul of Hellas" with fourth- or fifth-century Greek script and abbreviations.[47] The latest of these public honorific texts, perhaps with an associated statue, are the dedication to the emperor Justin and the acclamation of Justin II and Tiberius the New Constantine, both discussed below, along with a few other texts from the Forum or farther afield dated by letter forms to the sixth century. The latter include an elegiac poem in honor of the Praetorian Prefect of the East from the Forum, and the building inscription honoring the imperial officials Januarius and Paul from the area of the Kraneion Basilica and Pallas' Basilica (see Chapter 7).[48]

Honors for emperors appear sporadically from the third to sixth centuries at Corinth, though it is not always clear if the inscriptions once accompanied statues, or who made the dedication. Trebonianus Gallus in the third century, and then Constans (337–350), as noted above, were the last two emperors known with certainty to have been honored with statues, on statue bases inscribed in Greek from the city of Corinth.[49] The base for Constans was made out of a garland altar reused as a statue base upside down, though comparison with similar garland altars reused in Greece in the second to fourth century shows that an anti-pagan message is not certain, and reasons of economy are more likely.[50] Constans was honored in Greek by "the city of the Corinthians," that is, by the City Council using public funds, and the statue was probably put up in the southern area of the Forum where the base was found, between the *Bouleuterion* (Council House) and the *Bema*.[51]

Three matching marble plaques, on the other hand, were dedicated in Latin by the *praeses* (an equestrian *vir perfectissimus*) of the province of Achaia, Lucius Sul. Paulus, to the tetrarchs Diocletian, Maximian and Galerius (293–305), in the area of the Northwest Shops, where they were found in fragments.[52] Theodosius I, with his sons Arcadius and Honorius, almost a century later, were the last emperors honored in Latin at Corinth, probably by the Governor of Achaia.[53] In the short span from January 393 to Theodosius' death in January of 395, on the eve of Alaric's invasion of Greece, two thick marble plaques were carved and set up, probably with statues, "for the restorer of the Roman Republic, founder of eternal peace, originator of the human race, our lord Flavius Theodosius Augustus, most fortunate father, and his sons our lords the Flavii Arcadius and Honorius, emperors."[54]

This text now seems ironic, in light of Theodosius' autocratic style of rule, and the warfare which would soon ensue (and culminate in the sack of Rome by Alaric in 410). One wonders why Latin was still used, and who was the audience, when honors for emperors, governors and local elites had been for almost a century in Greek, and poetic in content as well.

An important but fragmentary text in Greek on a stele from the area of the quarries outside of Kenchreai was restored as an acclamation by quarrymen, masons and marble workers for "Theodosius, renovator of the city of Corinth." This probably represents publicly posted appreciation for payment provided to these workers in stone for public building projects from emperor Theodosius I or II; the cross and bird on the top of the stele make Theodosius II more likely, and thus a date in the first half of the fifth century, and a possible connection with construction of the Hexamilion and the late antique city wall of Corinth.[55] It is unclear if inscribed marble plaques were once attached to bases, and hence supported statues, or were affixed to walls of public buildings around the Forum. The difference beween use of Latin and Greek in imperial dedications, however, seems to correlate with the Governor and the Corinthian City Council as the authority putting up the inscription, and probably any associated statue.

The last texts from Late Antiquity in honor of emperors are a dedication to a sixth-century Justin, either I or II, and then an acclamation for Justin II and Tiberius the New Constantine, both in Greek on plaques. The first text is neatly carved on a white marble plaque, and preserves only the center of the last three lines, but with formal sixth-century letter forms and abbreviations that allow Sironen to reconstruct: "Justin our Most August (*Eusebestatos*) Emperor."[56] The plaque fragment was found south of Temple E, probably on the east-west *Decumanus Maximus*, near where it may have been posted as a public document. The dedication would date to 518–27, if to Justin I (who sent earthquake relief to Corinth), or 565–78, if to Justin II. The second text, an acclamation for Justin II and Tiberius the New Constantine, is of a very different character. It was carved in small letters inside a *tabula ansata* on an old marble pavement slab, and found reused and reinscribed with a medieval epitaph (to a certain "Pharismanis ... the Corinthian"), to the east of St John's monastery by the Northwest Shops.[57] The use of the pavement slab, the style and the date associate this text with the group of so-called prison inscriptions described above in Chapter 1. Justin is invoked as *basileus* (king), and both emperors are addressed by the text as *despotes orthodoxoi* (orthodox lords); they ruled together from 574 to 578. The text thus shows awareness of imperial power at Corinth, and addresses the emperors, but does not have the public or monumental character of the earlier texts. There are big gaps in date, monumentality and style of honors, first between the Latin dedication to Theodosius from the Governor of Achaia of 393–5, and the Greek dedication to Justin, probably 518–27, and then from Justin to this last acclamation for Justin II and Tiberius the New Constantine (574–8). All these honorific texts might be connected with concrete benefactions, such as earthquake repairs and rebuilding in the later fourth century, and earthquake repair in the early sixth century, under Justin, but this is not certain (see above, Chapter 1).

Besides the emperors, then, only governors, civic benefactors and certain local officials warranted statue bases from the third to sixth centuries, in most cases from the City Council or fellow officials, with an apparent decline in numbers of honors in the fifth century. This tells us much about who was in charge in late antique Corinth, or at least who wanted to look like they were in charge to those who could read (and whose bases have survived the lime kilns). These men, Governors of Achaia along with a small circle of Corinthian elite office-holders, still maintained enough culture and authority over the civic topography, sculptors and letter cutters to commission portraits and put them up. The fourth-century emperors commemorated in inscriptions are more likely to have worn the toga, while fifth- to sixth-century emperors would have been in military costume, or the chlamys with a more elaborate circular brooch (if they received a statue at all). There was a very high turnover of Governors of Achaia, as of other provinces, in Late Antiquity, with the same man rarely serving more than a few years at most, so the *chlamydatus* statues and late antique portrait heads, though numerous, may belong to a relatively short period of time.[58] In light of the Corinthian *chlamydati* known to him, Clive Foss suggested that the Governor of Achaia was depicted in the chlamys rather than the toga since he was subordinate to both the Vicar of Macedonia and the Praetorian Prefect of Illyricum.[59] The latter more often wore the toga in depictions; the sole full length late antique portrait from the Ancient Agora in Athens to survive most likely depicts the patron of the Palace of the Giants, in which it was found, either Praetorian Prefect of Illyricum Herculius (*c*.407–12), or, less likely, the emperor Theodosius II, both honored in nearby inscriptions.[60] Corinthian portraits and their texts in Late Antiquity thus tell us about preferred placement of these honors (in the western Forum and upper Lechaion Road); the honorands and dedicants (mostly Governors of Achaia or locals in imperial service, but also a few women and military figures); and the persistence of statue carving and erecting even in the face of a clear decline in access to new marble.

On the basis of the finished heads, and the *chlamydati*, Catherine de Grazia Vanderpool characterizes Corinthian sculptural style by the late fifth century as "an idiosyncratic, highly localized version of a debased Greco-Roman tradition, often using marble cannibalized from other works."[61] From a peak in manufacturing in the early third century, the number of new portraits and bases decreased sharply in the late third and fourth centuries, then ended in the late fifth century (although dating largely by hairstyle and carving technique means portraits sometimes shift in date, and the most accessible and hence newest portraits may have been first to be melted down).[62] Unfinished portrait heads with hairstyles dated to the second half of the fifth century found in the Corinthian Forum securely represent the continued production of new marble portrait sculpture in Corinth into that era, but probably not long afterwards.[63]

One of the unfinished heads was in fact found oddly placed in a much too small *palliatus* body, and marked on top with a cross, with the whole ensemble then built into a medieval wall at the west end of the Forum; if head and body represent a serious dedication, then it appears to be a very poor one indeed by comparison with finished fifth-century heads and the *chlamydati*.[64] Do we have here a snapshot of the moment when production stopped, and cross-marking and wall-building began, with the memory still alive as to how the newly-carved heads used to be placed into the older bodies? The position of the cross atop the head is matched by two finished portraits from Aphrodisias, one with *chi mu gamma* (a Greek acronym for "Christ to Mary born") atop his head and thus invisible from the ground: the chlamys-wearing provincial Governor of Caria, Oecumenius, was put up *c*.400 on a high base with a poetic inscription.[65] But was this done as a blessing, or a secret signature by the stone-carver? The display contexts, honorands and reuse of material for other late antique portraits at Aphrodisas also correlate closely with Corinth: stoas around the Agora/Forum, the *Bouleuterion* (as Oecumenius), baths and the Theater.[66]

Crosses were marked on three other pieces of statuary at Corinth known to me besides the two portrait heads already noted. A crude Latin cross was cut into the outside of the left arm of the battered remains of a *togatus* portrait body set under a so-called late wall by the *Bouleuterion*.[67] There are also two examples of crosses on divine figures: a marble herm handed in to the Corinth Museum broken at back, neck, and just below the genitals (which are quite abraded), and a striding Artemis Rospigliosi missing head, arms and legs, marked with a neat Greek cross on her thigh sometime before she was built into a Byzantine wall in the western Forum.[68] In context with other mortal and divine examples (notably from Ephesus (cited above), Sparta and Rhodes), Kristensen argues that the cross was marked on sculpture in Late Antiquity to defeat, or convert to Christianity, the power in the statue, which was thought to reside especially in the head and eyes.[69] One constant through all the cross-marked pieces, as well as most of the sculpture at Corinth, is the separation of heads from bodies, and the disposal of most surviving heads in watery underground contexts, largely closed-up drains containing sixth-century coins and pottery. The placement of heads in watery underground contexts recalls Roman attitudes to averting pollution by burial or drowning, as well as a parallel stream of Christian thought on Hell as a watery rather than fiery place.[70]

The earliest case at Corinth seems to be also one of the most well dated: the disposal of smashed up divine and human heads together in the late fourth or early fifth century in a well at the Sanctuary of Demeter and Kore (and the Fates, *Moirai*) south of the city center of Corinth on the slopes of Acrocorinth. Here, the excavation of Well 1961–11 (Q:19) yielded at least three female heads along with many other fragments of sculpture, including hands, feet, and marble tusks (for more on the sanctuary, see Chapter 7).[71] The heads had been roughly chopped from bodies or busts; two represented girls, probably priestesses, with their mouths and noses smashed, and the third female head undoubtedly came from a cult statue, probably an acrolithic Demeter (or Kore Persephone), with her nose and mouth battered, and inset eyes roughly removed. Further sections of this head's hair and neck were found outside the well in Building A and in the West Temple (probably the Temple of Demeter), testament to the deliberate chopping up of the neck before disposal of the head in the well. While the well might indeed have served for 'cleanup' after the raid of Alaric in the late fourth century, as the excavators suggest, and defacement is clear, it also seems likely that either the raiders, or those conducting the cleanup, or both, targeted the heads of the statues, both mortal and divine, for destruction and permanent (perhaps even ritual) disposal down the well.

Eunapius of Sardis recalled Alaric's march into Greece with his army of Goths in 395 just afterwards, blaming the governor of Achaia and Christian monks:

> Alaric with his barbarians invaded Greece by the pass of Thermopylae, as easily as though he were traversing an open stadium or a plain suitable for cavalry. For this gateway of Greece was thrown open to him by the impiety of the men clad in *black raiment* (τὰ φαιὰ ἱμάτια, the monks), who entered Greece unhindered along with him, and by the fact that the laws and restrictions of the hierophantic ordinances had been rescinded.[72]

For Eunapius, this event was significant as the beginning of an era prophesied by the Eleusinian hierophant Nestorius, an era of "the overthrow of the temples and the ruin of the whole of Greece," when "the sacred temples would be razed to the ground and laid waste," and "the worship of the Goddesses (Demeter and Kore) would come to an end."[73] Eunapius also adds that in "the general misfortunes" (τῆς κοινῆς συμφορᾶς) that followed Alaric's advance into and occupation of Greece over the next year or two, his friend the painter Hilarios was staying near Corinth when he and his servants were captured and killed by barbarians.[74] For Eunapius, at least, Alaric's men had a specific antipathy towards the goddesses Demeter and Kore, and though his time in Greece seems to have been authorized, to some extent, by Eastern authorities, it was actively opposed by Western authorities, perhaps even to the extent of open warfare in the Peloponnesus, and certainly to the detriment of civic order, economic prosperity and traditional religion in late fourth-century Corinth. See below, in Appendix I on literary sources for late antique Corinth, for more detail of the background to Alaric's advance into southern Greece, and retreat northwards about two years later.

From display and collection, to disposal or reuse, some literary testimonia and further archaeological parallels from outside of Corinth help us to understand some of the short- and long-term causes of statue destruction in fifth- and sixth-century Corinth. The two especially famous and violent destructions of pagan sanctuaries and their cult statues are the Serapeum at Alexandria in 392, and the Sanctuary of Zeus Marnas at Gaza in 402.[75] A long and complicated history of conflict among locals, civic and imperial officials and Christian bishops led to the violence in each case. In the case of Gaza, where there are literary sources, the Emperor's unwillingness to offend the pagan majority seems clear, and it was the Empress Eudocia who provided the funds and persuasion for the persistent Bishop Porphyry to accomplish his goals. His biographer Mark the Deacon said Porphyry then deliberately paved the atrium in front of his new church with *spolia* from the torn-down temple, "so that they would be trodden on by women and dogs and pigs and other animals. This pained the idolators more than the burning of the temple."[76]

Just prior to his death in 485, the Neoplatonist Proclus dreamt that Athena Parthenos asked for a place in his house, after "her statue seated hitherto in the Parthenon was transferred by those who move unmovable things."[77] Proclus lived on the slopes below the Parthenon, in the vicinity of the Omega House, where about 50 years later a relief of Hermes and the Nymphs was reused facedown, with heads of all the figures chopped off, and in proximity to a beheaded Athena used as a door threshold. A number of other statues, including imperial portrait heads, were thrown down the well of the Omega House (sculpture was treated similarly in houses excavated under the New Acropolis Museum in Athens).[78] For the destruction of imperial portrait statues, there is the important evidence of the Riot of the Statues in Antioch in spring of 387: statues of the emperor Theodosius and his family were destroyed by a mob, John Chrysostom sought to calm the situation with some 22 sermons on the topic leading up to Easter, and Antioch's Archbishop Flavian sought forgiveness from the emperor himself in Constantinople.[79] Eastern practices of statue iconoclasm likely came to Corinth with the so-called barbarians and Christian monks of Alaric about 395, but the end of portrait sculpture followed only in the middle of the fifth century, with active disposal or reuse of most mortal and divine statuary on display following in the sixth century.

Most sculpture found at Corinth went into the construction of walls, which were given late antique, dark age, Middle Byzantine, medieval, early modern or just late dates of construction by the early excavators. Sometimes whole portrait bodies were cut down and used alongside cult statues, but the lime mortar used to hold them together was also likely made from marble statuary melted down in lime kilns. New walls of *spolia* were built to renovate public buildings like the Northwest Shops and the Peribolos of Apollo, to construct new houses or churches, or to erect fortification walls. At Rome, such walls have largely been dated to the fifth to seventh century, and there is evidence that at Corinth this date range (or slightly later) is appropriate too.[80] Furthermore, Sanders has pointed to the extensive new defensive walls built around the city of Corinth and across the Isthmus in the fifth and early sixth centuries as probably *the* major destination for sculpture and ancient architecture in the form of *spolia* and lime mortar.[81] The pro-Christian and anti-pagan bias of the builder (or at least finisher) of the Hexamilion Wall for Justinian is confirmed by the two Victorinus inscriptions which were once set into it. The standing parts of the Hexamilion Wall, and its Eastern Fortress, are indeed built of architectural *spolia*, and though the city wall of Corinth itself is not well preserved, the example of the post-Herulian wall and newly excavated gate in Athens shows statue bases and *spolia* employed already in later third-century fortification wall building (for more on fortification walls, see Chapter 8).[82]

In conclusion, Corinth was clearly still a city where the City Council, Governor or local benefactors could pay to create and erect bespoke marble statuary around the Forum for imperial and local benefactors into the fifth century (even if the quality of material and carving was clearly declining). Then, in the late fifth and sixth century, all statuary was suddenly fair game for disposal, though of several different and distinctive kinds. The only new sculpture was in the form of architectural elements or Christian reliefs for church decoration, while other statuary of religious or political significance alike was occasionally marked with crosses, and all defaced, beheaded, cut up, reused, melted down or consigned to the depths of the earth. Yet the stylistic dating of portraits and the large number of *chlamydati* suggest that the Corinthian authorities possibly even used statues as building material, while still erecting new portraits of the Governors of Achaia and emperors in the fifth and even the sixth century (in the unlikely case that Justin I, Justin II or Tiberius received portraits).

This is part of the central paradox of Late Antiquity: how could some create statues while others tore them down? As answer to this question, one fact remains clear: the creation or destruction of statues was a deliberate action undertaken by civic authorities and organized labor, not random individuals, in the context of protecting and renovating a civic center with functioning monumental public spaces: a Forum, stoas, shops, roads, water fountains, baths and churches. Statues were clearly made with intent, in a long tradition of civic patronage and benefaction, by the old authorities (many of whom were among the honorands). However, destruction of statuary was similarly intentional and organized and, whether for anti-pagan or anti-demon reasons, for building of new shops, churches or fortification walls, or both, this fundamentalist and fundamentally different iconoclastic attitude to public sculpture was steadily on the rise from the later fourth century onwards.

CHAPTER 6

SACRED SPACES AROUND THE FORUM

In the center of the South Stoa, just adjacent to the *Bouleuterion* (Council House), the room called Shop XX by the early excavators was probably a public shrine of Serapis, guardian of urban wealth: a marble bust of Serapis with a gilded face was found there, with a built altar and a reused statue base with a dedication to the *Colonia* of Corinth.[1] This is one of the best-preserved polytheistic sacred assemblages excavated at Corinth: a statue, altar and associated architecture. Much more common are single fragments of sculpture in later construction or fills, or suggestive pairs, like the small busts of Serapis and Isis from the rooms behind the Hemicycle on the Lechaion Road.[2] The occurrence of these finds among the offices, shops, baths and fountains of the Forum brings us to the monuments and complex traditions of Greco-Roman polytheism and Christianity at late antique Corinth, especially the prominent temple ruins.

Most scholarly efforts related to religion at Roman Corinth have been aimed at reconciling Pausanias with archaeology, or connecting Roman cults with their Greek predecessors, while Rothaus studied the Christianization of Corinth in his monograph.[3] The following two chapters focus first on late antique evidence for cults and Christianization in the Central Area, then the broader city of Corinth, and finally the Corinthia. Continuities in sacred space seem to be present along routes to the north and east of Corinth, at the harbors, and atop Acrocorinth. Important ruptures, on the other hand, are visible around the Forum, and especially to its west and south.

Pausanias gives the only extant description of the sacred spaces and *hiera* (sacred or holy things) on the Forum (his Agora) at Corinth in the middle of the second century, also revealing his interests:

> Worthy of mention in the city [of Corinth] are first the things still left of the ancients, though most of these were made after their acme. There are then on the Agora- for that is where most of the sacred (*hiera*) objects are- wooden statues (*xoana*) of Artemis, titled *Ephesia*, and Dionysos, gilded except for their faces. Also their faces are decorated with red varnish. They name one [Dionysos] Lysios, the other Baccheios. And what is said about the *xoana* I also write … [Pausanias tells myth of Pentheus]. And later, as the Corinthians say, the Pythia prophesied to them to find and worship that tree equal to the god. And from the same [tree] therefore they have made these images. And also there is a Temple of Tyche, [with an] upright statue of Parian marble. And next to this there is a *hieron* for all gods. And nearby is built a fountain, and a bronze Poseidon atop it and there is a dolphin under the feet of Poseidon spouting water. And there is a bronze Apollo called Clarios and a statue of Aphrodite made by Hermogenes of Cythera. And of Hermes there are statues of bronze, both standing, and for one also a temple has been made. The [statues] of Zeus, also these are in the open air, [and] the one did not have a title, the other of these they call Chthonios and the third Hypsistos. In the middle of the Agora there is a bronze Athena, and on her base there are carved statues of Muses. And over (*hyper*) the Agora there is a Temple (*naos*) of Octavia, sister of Augustus, ruler of the Romans after Caesar founder of contemporary Corinth.[4]

Thus, for Pausanias, the most important things were the monuments and statues "still left of the ancients," i.e. made by the ancient Corinthians, the Greeks of the pre-Roman city, though what was visible was mostly "made after their acme," therefore of Hellenistic rather than Archaic or Classical date. Pausanias starts, as usual when describing a city, with the Forum (his Agora), and with the *hiera* (sacred things): wooden statues (*xoana*) of Artemis *Ephesia* and Dionysos, then a Temple of Tyche, and adjacent sanctuary of all the gods, and then a fountain of Poseidon. He continues through statues of Apollo, Aphrodite, Hermes, Zeus and finally Athena. A Temple of Octavia "over" (or beyond, *hyper*) the Forum is the last thing he mentions, before moving via the Propylaia in the northeastern corner of the Forum onto a description of the monuments along the Lechaion Road. Statues of gods, as elsewhere in his work, are the clear focus of his attention, along with sanctuaries, mythology and local Corinthian lore. Gods are given their Greek names, and sometimes their material of manufacture, artist, and what the Corinthians said about them. Only *two* statues are specified as standing in temples, Tyche and Hermes, although the three wooden statues of Artemis and Dionysos must have been inside as well, for protection from the elements, and their placement by Pausanias first signals their venerable nature, and probably veneration in a shrine or temple as cult statues.

All of the eight Roman temples discovered to date on the Forum at Corinth stand on its western side (Figure 5). Small temples H and J sit side by side, and are the latest, ascribed epigraphically to the patronage of the emperor Commodus in 191, after Pausanias' visit. Scranton suggested that they were dedicated to Commodus as Herakles (Temple H) and as Poseidon or Helios (Temple J).[5] The latter, Temple J, was built right on top of Pausanias' Fountain of Poseidon with a dolphin, making Poseidon more likely than Helios.[6] The connection of Temple H with Herakles is bolstered by the discovery in a nearby drain of a bearded male nude torso identified by Sturgeon as Herakles, and the hero was quite popular in Roman Corinth.[7] The Babbius Monument, which stood alongside the Fountain of Poseidon, may have been dedicated to Palaemon, as a sacred pair with Poseidon. These shrines would thus form a counterpart to the sanctuary at Isthmia on the refounded Forum of Corinth (even more so with the addition of Herakles, by some accounts founder of the Isthmian games).[8]

Before the reign of Commodus, however, when Pausanias visited, there were just three or four small temples, the Fountain of Poseidon and the Babbius Monument on the west side of the Forum, and then two larger temples inside *periboloi* behind them to the west, Temple E behind the West Shops and Temple C beside it, just outside the Northwest Arch (Figures 4–5).[9] Of the two small temples right on the Forum itself, at its southwest corner, the southernmost Temple F is the only one identifiable from epigraphic evidence. The dedication on the pediment *to Venus* (V]ENERI) indicated to Mr Williams that Pausanias' statue of Aphrodite by Hermogenes of Cythera should be located inside, rather than Scranton's suggestion of Tyche.[10] The immediately adjacent Temple G would then be dedicated to Apollo Clarius, as the site of his statue.[11] These two temples to Augustus' patron deities of Venus and Apollo could then be related to his role as developer of the colony for Caesar.[12] These bronze statues of Aphrodite and Apollo might have also stood outside, however, making Scranton's identification of this pair of temples as Tyche and the sanctuary for all the gods still possible.

The foundations of the small Temples D and K stand slightly elevated in the northwest corner of the Forum. Millis placed Temple D for stratigraphic reasons in the early third century, arguing it was a replacement for Temple K, just adjacent, which he argued was demolished.[13] Thus Temple K, and then later Temple D, should house Pausanias' bronze statue of Hermes (Roman Mercury), the second statue Pausanias explicitly places in a temple, and the god of the marketplace and commerce.[14] This may also be the statue of Hermes in a temple depicted on Corinthian coins (whether Temple K, or more likely D), and the origin of a number of marble statues of the god found in the vicinity.[15] A pedimental relief bearing a medallion portrait of a bearded man wearing a wreath and *strophion*, symbols of a pagan priest, probably represents the benefactor of the temple (Figure 6.1); it was also found near Temple D, could come from it (or one of the other small temples), and has been dated by hairstyle and drilled pupils to the fourth century, thus representing Corinth's latest temple renovation (or construction).[16] Fragments of two other medallion portraits which might also come from construction or renovation of the small temples were found in the immediate area.[17] Mr Williams argues for Dionysos as the dedicant of Temple D, and some sculptural finds related to the worship of Dionysos came from the northwest of the Forum.[18]

However, the three-apsed north-facing chamber at the west end of the Central Shops also likely served as a shrine; it had an altar outside in front of it, marble paving and a number of tables, altars or statue bases along its back wall.[19] Scranton placed Pausanias' *xoana* of Dionysos here, while Mr Williams preferred it as the location for the bronze statue of Hermes in a temple. However, since this is not a traditional temple like the small Temples K or D, I would prefer to put

Figure 6.1 Marble temple pediment with a male portrait bust, probably a pagan priest, Corinth Museum inv. no. S-890.

Hermes there, and leave this apsidal chamber along with other chambers in the South Stoa, Central Shops and Northwest Shops available for some of Pausanias' other statues, particularly the wooden ones of Artemis and Dionysos, which must have been kept under shelter.[20] Pausanias started his account, after all, with the *xoanon* of Artemis *Ephesia*, which he must have thought especially venerable.

As Scranton argued, Pausanias seems to have started at the southwest of the Forum, since he ended in the northeast with the statue of Athena. A monumental headless and armless Artemis was found in the so-called Byzantine Circuit Wall over the west end of the Northwest Shops, along with other pagan statuary and the two *chlamydati* portraits, discussed in Chapter 5, while the half lifesize striding Artemis Rospigliosi, also already mentioned, was found over the Central Shops marked with a cross (Figures 5.8–5.10). These images of Artemis were perhaps once accompanied by other statues of the goddess found scattered about the Forum, in a shrine to Artemis referenced by coins, and by more widely dispersed statuettes at Corinth.[21] Artemis, Apollo and Dionysos were worshipped together at Delphi, after all, as they may have been also at Corinth in the tripartite shrine of the Central Shops.

When we turn from these small temples and chambers to the two larger temples in *periboloi* behind them on the west, however, it becomes highly relevant that Pausanias only mentions a few actual buildings in his account of shrines on the Corinthian Forum, and only *one* clear pair, the Temple (*naos*) of Tyche with the sanctuary (*hieron*) of all the gods beside (*para*) it.[22] If we accept that by *naos* and *hieron* Pausanias was indicating two structures side by side, *and* we rule out Temples F and G (on the epigraphic evidence for Venus/Aphrodite in Temple F), then only Temples E and C are left as a pair of identifiable religious structures on the Forum side by side. Temple E thus could be Pausanias' Temple of Tyche (as Fortuna, Roma or Aphrodite of Corinth), with Temple C the subsidiary *hieron* of all the gods (or Pantheon) beside it. Though there were the small temples, the Fountain of Poseidon, the Babbius Monument, a road and the West Shops between Temple E and the Forum, it was entered from the east, faced eastwards towards the Forum, and formed its western axis.

Temple E, from its prominent placement above the central western side of the Forum, could have been built originally as the Capitolium of Corinth, as Mary E. Hoskins Walbank argues, or as a sanctuary for Fortuna (Greek *Tyche*), Roma, Venus (Greek Aphrodite), the imperial cult, or some combination of these figures. It was largely rebuilt in the Flavian era, after the earthquake.[23] By the era of Pausanias' visit, Temple E had been decorated with idiosyncratic marble pedimental sculpture including a River God, a draped goddess (Aphrodite?), a young man, a seated Roma, an Omphalos Apollo and other figures.[24]

Most scholars identify Temple E as a temple of the imperial cult at Corinth, and thus as what Pausanias called the Temple of Octavia beyond (or over) the Forum.[25] However, there are very few imperial portraits and dedications from the western side of the Forum, and the mention of that temple last in Pausanias' account of the Forum suggests a different explanation.[26] From its position next to Temple C, pediment sculpture, and associated finds, Temple E is most likely for Pausanias his Temple of Tyche. It is the first temple he mentions on the Forum, and certainly the most prominent in the landscape today after the Archaic Temple of Apollo (on which more below). Coins of Corinth show female figures with the rudder of commerce and wearing a city-wall crown, emblems both of Tyche (Fortuna) and Aphrodite Euploia, patrons of the city.[27] A concentration of finds related to the cult of Tyche/Fortuna come from late contexts in the west of the Forum: a standing Tyche or Nemesis with a wheel, the intact head of a mural-crowned female Tyche (Figure 6.2, which might belong to Temple E's pediment), and a more monumental but more fragmentary mural-crowned head as well, possibly a cult statue.[28] Also relevant may be a base inscribed VICTORIAI SACRUM (sacred to Victory), and a monumental female marble torso once fitted with wings, identified as Roma Victrix or Athena Nike.[29] The type of a city Tyche as helmeted goddess with mural crown was invented in Roman Greece in association with the imperial cult, influenced by Roma, Minerva (Athena) or Venus Victrix (Armed Aphrodite, Figure 2.1).[30] Sanctuaries of Tyche were often prominent in late antique cities, as the goddess yielded easily to a civic rather than polytheistic interpretation.[31] Though Temple E may not have started as a Tychaion, I would argue that it was interpreted as such by Pausanias in the middle of the second century.

A base for a statue of Herodes Atticus' wife Regilla was also found in the western Forum; according to the inscribed text, she was depicted as Tyche, and the *Boule* (City Council) of Corinth commanded the statue to be erected in Tyche's *temenos* (temple enclosure), apparently ruling out any of the small temples on the Forum.[32] Regilla's portrait might also survive, as a female portrait body of the second century was found near the west end of the Northwest Shops (Figure 5.4).[33] This statue of Regilla might have been placed by Temple E, Temple C or the Archaic Temple of Apollo, the only enclosures around temples. By comparison with Athens, and Herodes' placement of a Tyche

Figure 6.2 Marble head of Tyche, personification of the Fortune of Corinth, Corinth Museum inv. no. S-1540.

temple above the Panathenaic Stadium there, we may connect this base in honor of Regilla placed in the *temenos* of Tyche with the enclosure of Temple E, and even speculate that she (or her husband) had some role in Temple E's second-century renovations or cult.[34]

The second-century pedimental sculpture of Temple E could even evoke that of Hadrian's Temple of Venus (Aphrodite) and Roma (Tyche) in Rome; the Roma in the pediment is said to be based on the statue there, the Tyche head echoes Aphrodite-Venus, and the temple in Rome was referred to as the temple of Tyche in Late Antiquity.[35] Thus the original dedication of Temple E may have been to Roma and Augustus, as at Athens or Caesarea, which Pausanias could later interpret as Tyche.[36] A blue marble statue base found in the South Stoa by the *Bouleuterion* bears similar lettering to Regilla's base in the fragmentary text of a four-line honorific poem; Kent postulated that the "shining statue" for "the servant of the Muses" put up by the City Council "with the permission of the proconsul" in the text was for Herodes Atticus, but Sironen now argues that the statue and poem were for an early fourth-century honorand, and not the husband of Regilla.[37]

Temple C was built in the middle of the first century just adjacent to and north of Temple E, on the west side of the road leading out of the northwest corner of the Forum (with its entry just outside the Roman Northwest Arch).[38] I suggest it represents Pausanias' sanctuary of all the gods, or Pantheon. Williams notes that the Pantheon should be close (*plesion*) to the Poseidon fountain, which was between Temple C and the Forum (Temple K was closer to Poseidon, as was the Babbius Monument, but the latter cannot, in my opinion, fit the description of a *hieron* to all the gods).[39] A pair of Archaizing piers with multiple deities in relief were discovered in the Southwest Forum/Agora, and seem suited to a Pantheon, though they could derive from nearly any structure in the western Forum Area, according to the excavators.[40] Any other identification of Temples E and C other than Tyche and Pantheon requires us to accept Temples F and G as that pair (not Venus/Aphrodite and Apollo?), or Temples K and D (if contemporary, and then whither Hermes or Dionysos?). Whichever temples we assign the various statues to, at least Pausanias' identified deities correlate fairly closely with the types of statuary found in the western Forum Area, and the devotions of the Corinthian benefactors of the first to fourth centuries: Poseidon, Aphrodite (Venus), Apollo, Artemis (Diana), Dionysos, Hermes (Mercury), Herakles and Tyche (Fortuna).

The central sacred landscape of Roman Corinth also extended westwards beyond these temples, outside the Roman arch over the

Road to Sikyon, to the north and west of the Forum. Just above the Odeum and the Theater were a number of sacred monuments described by Pausanias as along the Road to Sikyon or near the Theater, only one of which has been located.[41] The Glauce Fountainhouse was carved from the living bedrock there, and has always been visible. Pausanias says a fountainhouse in this area bore the name of Glauce, the princess who threw herself in a fountain when poisoned by Medea, and this seems to be the monument visible today, cut from the living rock just northwest of the Temple C precinct and southeast of the Odeum.[42]

Pausanias locates the Tomb of Medea's children here too, and a statue of Terror probably associated with it, making a cluster of monuments tied to the Corinthian myth of Medea. Pausanias denies that the cult of Medea's children continued in his day, though his contemporary Aelian wrote that "up until now the Corinthians make sacrifices to the children."[43] The venerable sanctuary dedicated to Hera Akraia at Perachora (or Peraia), at the tip of the peninsula across from Lechaion, would have been prominently visible from that harbor as well as from Corinth, especially from the area of the Glauce Fountain.[44] In Late Antiquity, however, as in the Roman era, the cove seems to have been visited only occasionally, and no longer for a major festival or prominent dedications, though there were houses, industry and a long building constructed in the area, and the connection of the sanctuary with the myth of Medea was remembered in texts.[45]

This concentration of monuments above the Theater and Odeum devoted to Corinth's mythical history, and overlooking the Gulf of Corinth, continued with the Sanctuary of Athena *Chalinitis* (the Bridler), as the goddess who assisted Bellerophon in taming Pegasus by giving him a bridle, and whose sanctuary at Corinth was mentioned as early as the poems of Pindar.[46] Aileen Ajootian suggests that this particularly local, and possibly venerable, Sanctuary of Athena seen by Pausanias should be above and south of the Odeum, beyond the Temple E precinct.[47] She points in support of this to a colossal third-century Archaizing Athena, and a fragment of a second, found in the Odeum ruins, but not necessarily part of that building, as well as another statue of Athena found to its south.[48] Yet excavations in this area south of Hill House yielded mainly quarries, filled in under Claudius, and an enigmatic Roman building with an atrium attached to (and possibly adjoining) the Temple E precinct, with many fragmentary elements of colossal sculptures.[49] Mr Williams places the Sanctuary of Athena *Chalinitis* in the area of Hill House, or farther north in unexcavated fields to the west or northwest of the Theater, but it might even have been up the road towards Anaploga.[50]

Athena was once connected with the ruins of the frescoed Terraced Building or Buildings 5 and 7 to the east of the Odeum, but these hillside rooms on East Theater Road should rather be identified in the Roman period with worship of the Egyptian gods and domestic cults, on the basis of finds and frescoes.[51] A rectangular building, with its entrance on the short north side, and which was built in the early years of the colony, Building 5 was maintained until late in the fourth century.[52] Mr Williams properly argued for a cultic function there, but not for Athena, as the preponderance of finds link Building 5 with the worship of the Egyptian gods, who were otherwise present in the South Stoa shrine mentioned above, in the Hemicycle, on the slope of Acrocorinth south of the Forum, and at the harbor of Kenchreai.[53] Building 7's Room 2 was decorated with frescoes of deities, including Herakles, Hera (Juno), Zeus (Jupiter), Athena (Minerva) and Corinth's own Armed Aphrodite (Venus), whose statue stood in her temple atop Acrocorinth (see Chapter 7, and the statuette of the same image, Figure 2.1, in Chapter 2).[54]

The start of the Sikyon Road was dominated in Late Antiquity, as for centuries before, by the Archaic Temple on Temple Hill.[55] Though only the preserved southwest end of the Temple now looms over the Forum and is visible from afar on all sides, in Antiquity the complete temple would have been slightly less visible from the Forum, with its lower half hidden behind the intact colonnade of the Northwest Shops and the second storey of the Northwest Stoa, but very much more imposing to those approaching upwards from west, north or east, or looking down from the south (Figures 1.1, 1.3, 1.4). Several pieces of evidence support its identification as a Temple of Apollo, beyond Pausanias placing a statue of Apollo on his right when leaving the Forum towards Sikyon.[56] The current structure of the later sixth century BCE replaced a seventh-century BCE temple, one of the earliest monumental buildings of Corinth (or indeed Greece).[57] Apollo was the patron god of the Greek Corinthians' political life and adjacent racetrack, and the placement at the center of the city has parallels in Corinthian colonies like Syracuse and Dorian cities like Argos.[58] Though Corinth was refounded by

Caesar, its actual redevelopment happened under Augustus, a well-known patron of Apollo; he, and his colonists, are as likely to have revived a pre-existing cult of Apollo in the Archaic Temple as elsewhere in Corinth. But the prominence of this temple at Corinth also suggests that the Julio-Claudian Corinthian coins which bear a temple labeled CAESAR, AUGUSTUS or GENT IULI could be identified with this building, rededicated by Augustus (or the Corinthians) to the *Gens Julia* (Julian Family) or their founder the divine Caesar.[59] Ziskowski has argued for the association of Athena Chalinitis as the inhabitant of the Archaic Temple before the Roman sack of Corinth, and the temple could have been shared as well, for example, between Athena and Apollo (before or after the sack), Artemis and Apollo, or Apollo and the divine Julius Caesar in Roman Corinth, since its interior divisions remain unclear.[60]

Finally, Pausanias' last-named and most mysterious temple "above (or beyond) the Agora" has not been surely identified. This "temple (*naos*) of Octavia, sister of Augustus, ruler of the Romans after Caesar founder of current Corinth" could be identified with Temple E, or with the Archaic Temple of Apollo, or could even be unexcavated, perhaps somewhere on the heights east of the Forum (Pausanias' Agora), south of the modern village *Plateia* and the modern Panayia Church (which stands atop the ruins of an early modern mosque), as suggested by Torelli.[61] No temple specifically dedicated to Augustus' sister Octavia is known from any other ancient city, so scholars have cast around for a more traditional dedication hidden in this, either to imperial cult, Roma or a goddess depicted as Octavia. The numismatists Imhoof-Blumer and Gardner, before excavations began, suggested that a temple of the *Gens Julia* (Julian Family), known from Corinthian coins, could have had a cult statue of the *Gens* (Family) depicted as Octavia inside.[62] Temple E, and the Archaic Temple of Apollo, could both be described as over the Agora, as could any building east of the Forum, since it lies in a valley. If Temple E was the Tychaion, then perhaps the Archaic Temple of Apollo was Pausanias' Temple of Octavia, and had a statue of Apollo by its western entrance. However, with all our excavated temples accounted for in my interpretation of Pausanias' itinerary so far, the unexcavated area of the village on the heights to the east of the Forum must remain a possibility for Pausanias' Temple of Octavia. After his statue-stuffed tour of the west side of the Forum, Pausanias mentions a statue of

Athena in the middle of the Forum, and then the Temple of Octavia. He next immediately moves on to a description of the Propylaia, and then, outside it, the monuments on the Road to Lechaion to the north. Now, if you pass the bases in the middle of the Forum, and stand by the Propylaia ruins today, the only things you can see which are over the Agora are the Archaic Temple columns to your left, and the modern Panayia Church of Ancient Corinth to your right (Figures 1.3–1.4). It is thus possible to locate in Pausanias' itinerary the Temple of Octavia on this commanding ridge east of the Forum, beyond the Julian Basilica, on the heights south of, and above, the medieval and modern *Plateia*, where Corinth's central mosque once stood, and where an Early Christian church may have been built before the mosque.[63]

Among the finds from the early excavations are many Early Christian and Byzantine marble architectural elements and liturgical materials, which seem neither to belong to the Middle Byzantine churches on Temple Hill, in Peirene and atop the *Bema*, nor to any converted Greek or Roman building, as most of this evidence came from north of the Peribolos of Apollo, towards the modern village *Plateia*.[64] One capital was unearthed recently by the Greek Archaeological Service in roadworks southeast of the *Plateia*.[65] Many of the architectural elements found in the early ASCSA Corinth Excavations are now built into Carpenter's Folly, a Byzantine (tenth- to twelfth-century) house located between Peirene and the eastern edge of the excavations, which ASCSA Corinth Excavations Director Rhys Carpenter rebuilt as a Byzantine Museum in the 1930s.[66]

This material may signal the presence of an unexcavated sixth-century Early Christian basilica church somewhere north or more likely east of the Forum, perhaps near where the modern village's Panayia Church now stands (in the place of the early modern mosque), or to its south, near the now demolished Panayia Church.[67] Such an Early Christian church in the city center would almost certainly have served as the cathedral of Corinth. Support for the construction of an Early Christian church in the Forum Area comes from the construction of the Hemicycle Market in Late Antiquity on the Lechaion Road, which has a close parallel in the shape and location of the so-called Sigma Square laid out on the main road at Stobi, which was a market built just acros the road from the new Episcopal Basilica.[68] Also, beside the small sixth-century bath in

Panayia Field, just southeast and above the Forum, one aisle of a monumental Long Building of isodomic masonry running east-west was excavated (Figure 2.3). Its dating in the sixth century, fish scratched on the wall plaster (as at the Lechaion Basilica) and finds from inside, like a glass hanging lamp, all show it could have formed part of a sixth-century Christian basilica complex, either as an ecclesiastical building, like a warehouse for bread and wine, or part of an episcopal residence (perhaps along with the Panayia Bath).[69] A similar structure of three to five chambers placed end to end was built in the Roman or late antique era on the so-called Agora of the harbor at Perachora near the Sanctuary of Hera Akraia.[70]

Christians at Corinth apparently met for services in house churches throughout the fourth and early fifth centuries, as they had done in the era of persecution beforehand for centuries.[71] A *trapezophoros* (table support) of Christ as the Good Shepherd now in Athens, dated *c.*400 from style alone, could have been the altar support from a house church, but it has no provenance beyond Corinth, so such house churches as must have once existed are so far indistinguishable among the excavated late antique houses discussed in Chapter 2, except for the villa above Loutraki which contained Christian lamps.[72] Everyday items like lamps marked during manufacture, or afterwards, with Christian symbols begin to appear in Athens *c.*425, and elsewhere in Greece too.[73] Kimberley Bowes has pointed to the widespread use of house churches around the Mediterranean into the fifth century, and also the construction of private chapels at aristocratic rural villas (like the villa above Loutraki), and the problems it caused for some bishops in exerting their authority (at least in Gaul).[74] Some public buildings near the Forum like the Hemicycle, the Peribolos of Apollo or even the Roman Baths on the Lechaion Road may have been modified for domestic uses, including Christian worship in the fifth or sixth centuries. Sigma or *agape* tables of white and red marble, possibly for celebration of the Eucharist rather than elite dining, were found in the ruins of the Hemicycle and the Peribolos of Apollo, as well as in a Byzantine building west of the Kraneion Basilica.[75]

Three purpose-built Middle Byzantine or more likely Frankish Christian churches were excavated in the Forum Area at Corinth: one just northeast of the Archaic Temple of Apollo, one at the west end of the Forum (St John's Monastery) and another in the Frankish Area to the west of the West Shops, with small chapels also built atop the *Bema* and inside the Fountain of Peirene, and a church possibly located inside the Southeast Building (Figure 6). Suprisingly, though, no temple of Corinth's civic center seems to have been converted into a church in Late Antiquity.[76] The Archaic Temple of Apollo, and possibly Temple E, were certainly large enough to house a church, yet the Corinthians apparently did not follow the route of the Athenians, or the bishop of Aphrodisias, in continuing to worship at a central civic temple (unless there was one under the modern village which was converted). Whether because the Archaic Temple of Apollo was not in good shape, or considered too tied up with polytheism (or imperial cult) to use as a church, the Corinthians built a new church alongside it on the high ground at the center of the city only in about the twelfth century. There is sadly no evidence that this church adjacent to the Archaic Temple of Apollo had an earlier predecessor atop Temple Hill; we also don't know what happened to the many missing monolithic columns from the east end of the Temple.

None of the western temples were converted to churches; all were stripped down to bare concrete foundations for the lime kilns in the sixth to eighth centuries. They were all fairly small Roman-style podium temples in any case, except for Temple E, unsuited for gatherings of more than a few people inside. None was apparently a building which inspired strong feelings of civic identity, or Christian devotion, and none was preserved as the nucleus of a Corinthian Christian urban community, or housed a strong cult which was taken over by a Christian saint. This is very different from Athens, where the central Asklepieion was replaced with a church, perhaps dedicated to the doctor saints Cosmas and Damian (or St Andrew), on the same site, and the Parthenon converted and redecorated, to remain the house of the chief female protector of Athens, from about the sixth century. The only western temple large enough to house a church, Temple E, was thoroughly demolished, with most of its architectural elements and pediment sculpture buried, melted down or cut down for building material, just like most of the other sculpture (secular and religious) from the Forum. The result around the western end of the Forum in Late Antiquity seems a paradox, with functioning shops and civic spaces in the Northwest Shops, West Shops and South Stoa, and an open Forum, but also featureless lumps of concrete left behind where once stood the Roman temples, drains blocked with broken statuary, and a thick layer of marble chips underfoot.

This transition from polytheistic to Christian religious space was not, however, the whole story of sacred space around the Forum of late antique Corinth. Near the Forum in Late Antiquity there was a Jewish synagogue as well, which survived into the Byzantine era. A Jewish community, and probably a gathering place for them, had existed at Corinth at least since the early first century. Philo attested to Jews at Corinth under the emperor Gaius Caligula, and the expulsion of Jews from Rome by the emperor Claudius brought St Paul's hosts in *Acts* 18 to the city.[77] In the early fourth century, John Chrysostom refers to Jews at Corinth during St Paul's visit burning 5,000 magical books in order to cast out a demon, but the origin of his information is unclear.[78] The Corinthian Jewish community of St Paul's correspondence, and that depicted in the biblical book of *Acts*, was supplemented by 6,000 Jews brought by Vespasian from Tarichaeae in the Galilee to dig the Corinth canal in the 70s.[79] Corinthian Jews in Late Antiquity are only attested by fragmentary material evidence, all difficult to date or associate with a specific building, but they were certainly present.

The evidence for Jews at Corinth in Late Antiquity was recovered from the Forum, the Lechaion Road or north of Temple Hill, suggesting that there was a Jewish synagogue north of the Forum, near the Hemicycle or near the Theater north of Temple Hill. A single pillar capital from the Theater excavations bears menorahs (*menorot*) and other Jewish symbols in relief, and has been dated by style to the fifth century.[80] A fragment of a *tabula ansata* with the Jewish name Sara in script of *c*.300 came up nearby.[81] The much-reused central block of a door lintel was found in the 1898 excavation of the Lechaion Road's Byzantine ramp, with the Greek text Συν]αγωγὴ Ἑβρ[αίων, Syn]agogue of the Hebr[ews.[82] This lintel has been dated to the late third century at the earliest, on the basis of the lank lettering and occurrence of the term Ἑβραῖοι (Hebrews).[83] From the Central Area, there are also six fragmentary texts of late antique or Middle Byzantine date: four Hebrew inscriptions on stone, a bilingual Greek/Hebrew epitaph for a certain Anna (or Sus]anna), and a bronze Samaritan amulet.[84] But in the absence of any architecture, evidence from elsewhere in Greece and the Balkans must fill in the picture of what the late antique synagogue of Corinth looked like: probably a large hall with a niche at one end, decorated with marble revetment, mosaics and frescoes.[85]

CHAPTER 7

SACRED SPACES IN THE CITY AND CORINTHIA

Roads ran out of the city center and Forum Area of Corinth in all directions: to the harbors, Acrocorinth, Sikyon, Argos, the Isthmus and beyond. In the third century, each of these routes through the Corinthian landscape held polytheistic temples or sanctuaries at prominent transitional locations. Many of these sacred spaces were established before the Roman colonization of Corinth, and refurbished in the first or second centuries, while others were recent foundations in honor of Roman or Eastern gods. The northern and eastern routes running in and out of the city of Corinth had venerable shrines to Zeus and Asklepios (on the north), and Bellerophon and Aphrodite (on the east), and gained Christian basilicas by the early sixth century, in part to serve as cemetery churches. The harbors at Lechaion and Kenchreai likewise had churches built adjacent to the ruins of pagan shrines. On the other hand, on the southern route leading up to Acrocorinth, the Sanctuary of Demeter and Kore (and the Fates) was destroyed and largely abandoned in the early fifth century. Atop Acrocorinth, the Corinthian patron goddess Aphrodite had her temple entirely torn down and replaced by a church at the summit of the acropolis, but the date of this change is unclear. In this chapter, I explore the details and the dating for late antique transitions in sacred space along the major routes running in and out of the Forum and the city of Corinth, and at the watery and airy boundaries of the Corinthia where land met sea and sky (see Figures 2, 3, 8–10).

North of the Forum: Northern Terrace Edge and Lechaion Harbor

To the northwest of the Forum, along the road to Sikyon, Pausanias mentions a temple of Zeus *Kapetolios* or *Koryphaios* (Jupiter *Capitolinus*), *hyper* (over or beyond) the Theater.[1] Pausanias seems to be describing the route towards Sikyon past the Glauce Fountain, and past the Odeum too, so he is not likely referring to Temple E, with its main entrance on the Forum facing east. This Zeus temple was likely west or north of the Forum, perhaps the origin of a fragmentary altar to Jupiter Optimus Maximus found at the Odeum.[2] However, Pausanias also describes a temple of Zeus *Olympios* in this direction, and so elements of a Doric temple built into the so-called Epistyle Wall have been attributed to one or the other of his temples of Zeus on this northern side of Corinth. The so-called Largest Temple in the Peloponnese (actually second-largest after Olympia) is a temple reassembled entirely on paper by Dinsmoor, and more recently by Christopher Pfaff, from drawings and measurements of the architectural *spolia* still built into the Epistyle Wall at the northern edge of the lower terrace of the city of Corinth (Figure 7).[3] These massive Doric architectural elements carved of local limestone likely did not travel far in order to be built into the Epistyle Wall, but no foundation to fit them has yet been found. The monumental stoa excavated to the east may be a temple *peribolos*; its columns still project from the earth, though it was partially excavated by Wiseman, who also discovered further architectural elements from this temple.[4] The monumental scale and Archaic date of this stoa suggest an association of both stoa and temple with Pausanias' Temple of Olympian Zeus with a bronze statue inside, perhaps the pre-Roman temple known from Theophrastus as the Olympieion at Corinth. Christopher Pfaff dates the temple on stylistic grounds to the late sixth century BCE.[5]

Alongside a Temple of Olympian Zeus, Pausanias also described the Lerna Fountain on the north side of Corinth, which was first identified by some with the Asklepieion Fountain, and then by others with the complex known as the Fountain of the Lamps to its west, which does better suit Pausanias' description of a pool surrounded by columns and seats (Figures 3, 7).[6] In the third and fourth centuries, the Fountain of the Lamps was still accessed by a courtyard with a portico around a swimming pool, set into the northern terrace's rocky edge and fed by a natural spring; three rock cut chambers along the southern side of the courtyard directed the spring waters, into a reservoir, a nymphaeum and a bathing chamber dating back to the Hellenistic era.[7] However, in the fifth to sixth centuries, Wiseman argues that the exterior areas of this Fountain were not maintained, while some 4,000 lamps were deposited in the Fountain in the practice of nocturnal rituals, many inscribed with Christian invocations. Jordan and Avraméa followed Wiseman in interpreting these practices at the Fountain of the Lamps in Late Antiquity as connected with baptism or other aspects of Christian cult, and linked closely with the Christian burials marked by epitaphs which took place from the fifth to seventh centuries all around, and especially between the Fountain of the Lamps and the Asklepieion.[8]

East of the Fountain of the Lamps, directly north of the Forum and probably near a temple of Zeus, Corinth's sanctuary of the healing god Asklepios was sited at the very edge of the northern city terrace (Figures 3, 7).[9] The pre-Roman cult was revived at the same location and with the same major deity, with the temple standing above a courtyard with a natural spring. Marble cult statues of Asklepios and Hygieia were located inside the temple, and Roman marble dedicatory statuettes found there include Aphrodite.[10] Besides the elaborated natural springs at the Fountain of the Lamps and the Asklepieion, with baths and fountains, Landon has identified several other natural springs along the terrace edge which were tapped in the Roman era, for irrigation of agriculture on the plain below, domestic and industrial use as well.[11] A bronze casting pit was uncovered in Wiseman's excavations near the Old Gymnasium, and other messy and water-intensive industries may have been located here too.[12] Among these public buildings, temples, fountains and forges were more houses too; the edge of the lower terrace where it drops down to the plain has a fine view of the sea which has attracted wealthy Corinthians throughout history (including the Bey of Ottoman Corinth, whose ruined palace still stands above the spring called the Baths of Aphrodite, to the east of the Asklepieion).[13]

The development and the use of this whole northern Old Gymnasium area in the late fourth century is unclear beyond the growing Christian cemetery. Most civic buildings were suppposedly destroyed in the 375 earthquake, or by Alaric's Goths, but the argument is largely based on coin evidence.[14] The temples of Asklepios, and perhaps of Zeus, were probably in use through the late fourth century, until the materials of the latter were taken for the Epistyle Wall, and the former probably for other fortification walls.[15] There are several clear exceptions to this pattern of fifth century destruction, however. A large centrally planned building of fourth-century style lay south of the Gymnasium stoa, which might once have formed the *peribolos* of the Temple of Olympian Zeus.[16] As noted above, lamps from the Fountain of the Lamps date from the fifth and sixth centuries, and sometimes have inscriptions invoking angels, identifying the fountain as a place of baptism, or at least Christian ritual.[17] In the fifth century, almost immediately after the end of worship of Asklepios at his centuries-old sanctuary, and while worship of the god was still alive in Athens, Christian burials intruded into his sanctuary. They continued into the seventh century, and many epitaphs reveal the Christian identity of the dead and their families, and their civic professions, as noted above in Chapter 2.[18] About 500 meters to the east of these Asklepieion burials, at the base of the terrace, and probably in honor of a local martyr and his spring, a large Christian basilica was constructed in the early sixth century.

The St Quadratus (or Agios Kodratos) Basilica is located at the northern side of the largest of the depressions or bays which corrugate the northern edge of the lower city terrace, and thus alongside what was once the main northeastern road running in and out of Ancient Corinth (Figures 3, 8). Skias suggested that this low-lying area sloping down to the northern plain was once used as the city's stadium, but it was certainly a cemetery, at least from the second century BCE, below a natural spring, and between roads running north to Lechaion and northeast to the Isthmus.[19] The floor of this bay has never been fully excavated or explored, except for the St Quadratus Basilica itself and surrounding tombs at its north end, and around the St Quadratus Spring at its south end, which emerges from a (partly human-made) cavern in the terrrace edge. Though the current size and shape of the cavern probably dates from the Byzantine era, the collecting tunnels behind the cavern are ancient, and the spring was certainly used in Late Antiquity, both before and after the construction of the Basilica, probably to supply farmers, travelers and funerary rites.[20]

The St Quadratus Basilica, and some of the immediately surrounding graves, were excavated in 1961–2 by Stikas for the

Greek Archaeological Service.[21] The church is a three-aisled basilica with high parapets between the nave and aisles, and with a later narthex and atrium added on to the original building. Masses of graves fill the nave, aisles, adjacent chambers to north and south, and the later narthex. A large tower by the west side of the church is probably an earlier mausoleum, and perhaps served the church later on as a bell tower, watch tower or both. While the construction of the excavated church was initially dated by Stikas to the fourth or fifth century, Pallas corrected this to "no earlier than the beginning of the sixth century," and this date has been followed by later scholars.[22] The name of the church was assigned on the basis of an inscription honoring St Quadratus on a marble door lintel, which was found reused in a grave within the church, but which Stikas assigned to an earlier architectural phase.[23] The inscription was certainly originally quite prominent and visible along the top edge of the doorway, and is reconstructed to read: [Ἅγι]ε *vac.* Κοδρᾶτε, μνήσθ[ητι] τῶ δούλου σο[υ] ("St Quadratus, remember your servant/slave"). The inscription prays that St Quadratus will help the builder of the doorway, who was probably also the builder of wherever the doorway once led, either into the sixth-century church, or into a fifth-century shrine of the saint which the church replaced. Stikas associated this inscription, and hence the original dedication of the Basilica, with the martyr and mountain sage St Quadratus (also spelled Codratus or Κοδράτος (Kodratos)) and his students. They were supposedly decapitated at Corinth under the emperor Valerian on 10 March 258, which became their feast day, celebrated both inside and outside of Corinth.[24]

Support for the identification of this excavated church as dedicated to St Quadratus is found in the pre-Christian cemetery at the site, where he and his followers may have been buried (or at least thought to lie buried in the fourth or fifth century), and the adjacent natural spring. From at least the ninth to eleventh centuries, a spring and adjoining church is known to have attracted pilgrims to Corinth to honor the memory of St Quadratus and to seek healing waters, almost certainly at this excavated Basilica.[25] The spring was certainly already there in Late Antiquity, and though the literary and archaeological evidence for its use as a healing shrine is Byzantine, these practices almost certainly started in Late Antiquity. There is an inscription with a list of locally honored saints from Sikyon which features the feast of St Quadratus in March.[26] At some point during the Frankish or

Ottoman era at Corinth, however, the basilica fell into ruins, and the current much smaller cemetery church dedicated to St Anna was built just to the south, still by the modern road running into Ancient Corinth from the northeast.

On the west side of Corinth, it is worth noting that there may have been another Early Christian basilica on the site of the modern St Paraskeve cemetery church, today the western edge of the village of Ancient Corinth, and certainly the site of a church by the twelfth century.[27] Farther west still, the existence of another Roman temple is based only on a fragment of marble tympanum with relief medallion found just above the Vrysoula spring, one of several natural water sources in the western ravines leading down to the Longopotamos river gorge.[28]

Therefore, the northern side of Corinth and the edge of the lower terrace retained its status as a center of healing cult, water and burial throughout Late Antiquity. The polytheistic cults disappeared, as at least two large temples, and probably more, were torn down to build fortification walls. Graves came closer to the city center, and moved towards Christian orientation and burial rites, but were still outside the settled urban area of the Corinthian city center in the fifth century. Athletic games, and whatever sort of athletic training went on in the Old Gymnasium, clearly either ceased, or lost an architectural framework, by the sixth century. The main road descending from the terrace towards Lechaion did not shift, however. A traveler towards the harbor of Lechaion once passed the Temple of Asklepios on the left, and then in Late Antiquity passed the new St Quadratus Basilica on the right. Thus a religious building still marked the passage from the lower city terrace and urban space down onto the northern plain and rural space.

On the northern plain, two or possibly three Christian basilicas were constructed in Late Antiquity along two major roads, probably to serve as cemetery churches for the inhabitants of Lechaion, Corinth or villages on the plain. The sixth-century Skoutela Basilica is located northwest of Corinth on a road which now passes straight through the church, but originally ran beside it, and on to the coast and Sikyon (Figures 3, 8). Pausanias noted a burnt-out temple, perhaps dedicated to Apollo or Olympian Zeus, on this road to Sikyon, which may possibly precede the church, but no trace of it has ever been found.[29]

Directly north of Corinth, on the line of the Lechaion Road which began in the Forum, there was at least one other church on the plain. Little is known today about a building discovered and partially dug by Carl Blegen in 1916.[30] The owner of a modern house, which was apparently built over the south aisle of a ruined Early Christian basilica, called Blegen when he hit upon some sculpture. Blegen then dug enough of an eastern-oriented single apse, a nave, a north aisle and some external tile graves to conclude that it was "a big church," in his words, and roughly 16 m. wide, to judge from his plan, which sat atop a destruction level containing headless statues of Dionysos and a Striding Poet (Alcaeus?), probably the ruins of a second- to fourth-century *villa rustica*.[31] Blegen does not specify the exact location of the modern house, but Nancy Bookidis concluded that it was in the region of Bourneri, east of the line of the ancient Lechaion Road, between Corinth and Lechaion, though she found no trace of a building there in 1996 (I also looked without success).[32] A modern chapel on the west side of the ancient Lechaion Road, just south of this general area, may be the successor of this Early Christian basilica.[33]

By far the largest Christian basilica ever built in Corinth lay at the end of the Lechaion Road, on the sandy spit between Lechaion Harbor and the Gulf of Corinth: the Lechaion Basilica (Figures 3, 8, 1.1–1.3, with apse in 1.2). It has two aisles on either side of the nave, separated off by colonnades with parapets, a central ambo, a single apse at the east, a transept, a narthex and two atria, adding up to 180 m. of church complex from east to west. The inner atrium also has a large fountain, and an extensive baptistry with a similar ground plan to the Panayia Bath is attached to the north aisle.[34] Several buildings with apsidal dining rooms just south of the inner atrium likely represent episcopal quarters. After the construction of this complex, visitors to Corinth from the west could certainly not avoid encountering the church when arriving or leaving by sea.

Demetrios Pallas, the excavator of the Lechaion basilica, connected its dedication with Leonidas and the seven virgin deaconesses who were martyred at Corinth, and indeed they are the only Corinthian martyrs explicitly connected with Lechaion, so it is an attractive identification. Leonidas and his seven (or more) female followers were honored on 16 April for their execution by the procurator Venustus (*c.*240).[35] Four versions of their martyrdom exist, ranging in date from the fifth to the tenth centuries, of unclear relation to one another.[36]

Leonidas and the women are said to have fasted, prayed, and preached in Corinth; they were then arrested, separated, interrogated and asked to sacrifice. Once they had given fairly stock philosophical and Christian answers and refused, Leonidas was tortured, then hung, while the ladies were flogged, chained, weighted down with rocks and dropped in the Gulf of Corinth. Upon washing up at Lechaion, Leonidas and the ladies were then buried by fellow Christians together under a shrine which later displayed healing powers, and which would have been replaced by the Lechaion Basilica and its baptistry. This is an appropriate association for a church with a large and prominent baptistry, just on the shore of the Gulf, as the deaconesses were said to have undergone a so-called second baptism when they were drowned.[37]

Pallas first dated the construction of the Lechaion Basilica to *c.*450–500 from coins in the foundations; coins under the floors extending through 518 perhaps indicate repairs or new pavements, while coins in the nonbonding outer atrium date to 527. Thus the Lechaion Basilica may have been built in the middle to late fifth century, and was likely refurbished, and expanded, as Sanders suggests, in 522–30 by Justin and Justinian, as part of restoration at Corinth after the 520/1 earthquake.[38] The church was used into the early seventh century in its monumental form, as collapsed sections of the apse masonry fell on top of the tomb of the presbyter Thomas, whose grave goods date to *c.*600.[39] Thus for over a century, and certainly for many generations of Corinthians, the Lechaion Basilica was a prominent Christian landmark of Corinth on the shores of its western Gulf, just at the mouth of the harbor. It would have dwarfed the other buildings of the port, even large warehouses or the famous bath. It was not just monumental, but also lavishly decorated with polychrome mosaics and opus sectile marble floors, as well as custom-made marble columns and capitals. The column capitals, of the Theodosian fine-toothed acanthus type, appear to be original products of an imperial workshop which supplied the Studios Basilica in Constantinople (453/4), the Acheiropoeitos Basilica in Thessalonike and Basilica B at Philippi, and which were widely imitated in the early sixth century.[40]

Given its scale, and imperial patronage, it seems likely that the Lechaion Basilica was a Martyrion for Leonidas and possibly even the seat of the Archbishop of Corinth in the sixth century, the cathedral of the city. As almost the only excavated church not in a cemetery, it also provides intriguing glimpses of Christian liturgy in the early sixth century. Certainly the scale of the baptistry and font, for full body immersion and with subsidiary chambers, suggests to Sanders a population undergoing adult mass baptism. Besides baptism, such a large basilica located in an urban environment would have witnessed the preaching of homilies and sermons, celebration of the Eucharist (Communion), the singing of hymns, choral odes and *kontakia* (like those of Romanos), celebrations of local and foreign Saints with readings from their miracle stories and veneration of their relics, and other regular feasts, pilgrimages, healing or problem-solving of other kinds, incubation, veneration of icons and processions. The opulence and materials of the Lechaion basilica certainly suggest imperial sponsorship, maybe even over multiple reigns, for example by Anastasius and then Justin and Justinian. The imperial connection is supported by the centrally placed ambo and solea, and the screens between aisle columns, fitted for an eastern Constantinopolitan rather than a western liturgy.[41]

East of the Forum: Kraneion to Kenchreai

Kraneion, or the place of the skull, was the eastern region of Corinth famed in literature for its expensive residences, market, Gymnasium and connection with the life and death of Diogenes the Cynic. In Roman Corinth, the neighborhood certainly preserved ancient Greek grave monuments and sanctuaries, along with notable new houses, burials and then churches at the city limits on the route to Kenchreai and the Isthmus (Figures 2–3).[42]

Among a number of texts which highlight the connection between Diogenes the Cynic and the Kraneion, the early third-century biography by Diogenes Laërtius provides the most detail. He places the main Gymnasium of Greek Corinth at the Kraneion (rather than on the north side of the city), near the Gate to the Isthmus, and he describes how Diogenes lived, died, and was buried there, with his grave marked by a column bearing a marble dog, and bronze statues with the inscription:

> Even bronze ages with time, but in no way will
> all eternity destroy your glory, Diogenes;

> since you alone showed to mortals the path to
> swiftest glory, independence of life and livelihood.[43]

Pausanias includes Diogenes' tomb in his description of the monuments visible in the Kraneion neighborhood of the second century:

> As you go up to Corinth, there are other monuments on the road and by the gate is buried Diogenes of Sinope, whom the Greeks nickname Dog (*Kyna*, hence Cynic). In front of the city is a grove of cypresses called *Kraneion*. Herein are a *temenos* of Bellerophon and a temple of Aphrodite *Melainis* (Black) and the grave of Laïs [the elder], on which as a marker is a lioness gripping a ram in her front feet.[44]

Neither of these famed graves has been located at Corinth, but excavated burials clearly mark the eastern edge of the Roman city, and the late antique city, with the lines of the ancient Greek and the Late Antique Wall (Figure 3).[45] The *temenos* of Bellerophon may have been in origin a royal or noble grave monument or enclosure from Archaic Corinth.

The Temple of Aphrodite *Melainis* also had associations with death and burial through the epithet, Black. Strong suggests some dedications and activities of Classical and Hellenistic Greek courtesans more often linked with Aphrodite on Acrocorinth could, on the basis of this epithet, and the grove, be placed here.[46] A delicate column base with reliefs of doves, and an Aphrodite statuette, are thought to come from this temple, which like the *temenos* of Bellerophon has not been located.[47] This is also perhaps the place Ampelius praised in the third century as "a shrine of Venus in which is the marble basin of Laïs," given her grave's location nearby.[48] However, as with the monuments and references collected by Strong, we really have no clear way of telling whether this temple or the Sanctuary on Acrocorinth is meant in these literary sources.

In the later fifth or early sixth century, the cults of Aphrodite *Melainis* and Bellerophon, both associated with care for the dead, were themselves supplanted by at least two large Christian churches. One was located just southwest of the Amphitheater, in an area where a small Byzantine chapel (today ruined) with cypresses around it is visible in a drawing by Gell. Though visible as masonry on the surface, the presumed Early Christian church has only been surveyed to date, and is referred to as Pallas' Basilica (from its discoverer), or the Amphitheater Church. Two large centrally planned linked structures, it was likely a martyrium or baptistry with an attached domed church.[49] This large church complex was certainly inside the Late Antique Wall, which makes a deliberate eastward jog just to its south, to keep it inside the fortified area.[50]

South of this unexcavated church, also on the main road leading east from the ancient city towards Kenchreai, and just outside a gate in the Late Antique Wall, the Kraneion or Cenchrean Gate Basilica was first discovered in 1928 (see Figures 3, 8, 5.11).[51] This three-aisled cemetery church is filled with graves, like St Quadratus, but also features an attached baptistry and a brick triconch mausoleum, perhaps for the family of the builder of the church (or, less likely, a martyrium).[52] The pottery, lamps and coins in the graves, embedded in the masonry of the building and under its floors yield a firm date of construction in the first half of the sixth century.[53] Like St Quadratus, this church survived into the medieval era (and perhaps even the early modern era), constantly acquiring new graves, and serving, like the pagan shrines before, as a marker of the eastern border of Corinth, the road to Kenchreai and the passage between the worlds of the living and dead. The wider area of Kraneion to north and south outside the Late Antique city wall contained an extensive cemetery which continued in use into the Middle Byzantine era.[54]

At the eastern end of this road across the Corinthia was Isthmian Sanctuary of Poseidon discussed in Chapter 4, and the town and harbor of Kenchreai (Figures 2, 10). On the Isthmian side of Kenchreai, to the north, were so far unexcavated temples of Artemis and Aphrodite, and on the south were sanctuaries of Asklepios and Isis, all likely catering to the needs of seafarers, to whom these gods were particular patrons; as at Lechaion there was also a bronze statue of Poseidon. Pausanias gave a very brief account of the sacred topography: "on the road running to Kenchreai from the Isthmus there is a temple (*naos*) of Artemis and an ancient wooden statue (*xoanon archaion*). Then in Kenchreai there is a temple (*naos*) of Aphrodite and a marble statue, and after this, upon the mole running into the sea, a bronze [statue] of Poseidon, and on the other side of the harbor sanctuaries (*hiera*) of Asklepios and Isis."[55] Apuleius' narrator-turned-ass in the later second century described a festive procession in honor of Isis descending to her seaside sanctuary in Kenchreai from the city center of Corinth.[56] The Sanctuary of Isis at Kenchreai has been identified within the partially submerged complex excavated on the southern mole of the harbor, where warehouses, fish-tanks and two apsidal rooms said to be shrines were crowded together on top of a long pier. Scranton suggested that the pier was damaged in the 365 quake, spurring the ordering of glass panels with Nilotic motifs, which were found in their crates not yet installed when the whole complex was destroyed in the 375 earthquake, based on coins of 364–75 found in the debris.[57] Now, however, Rothaus has argued the quake which sunk the pier, and destroyed the glass panels, occurred *c.*400, but was still certainly a catastrophic and sudden seismic event.[58] The central apsidal buildings of the pier were quickly rebuilt upon the ruins, however, and then the Kenchreai Christian Basilica was built in the fifth or sixth century atop the landward end of the southern mole, probably installing the Christian religion in a similar location to Isis for the devotions of travelers coming and going.[59] Coin finds from excavations along the harbor range from the third into the early seventh centuries, bearing witness to intense mercantile activity in Late Antiquity.[60]

On the northern headland, near where the Aphrodite temple should have stood, a large building complex of the Roman and late antique era was excavated along the shore.[61] This domestic and perhaps religious complex of buildings was used throughout the fourth century, supposedly repaired after 365–375, and destroyed *c.*400.[62] Above Kenchreai to the north and west, Roman-era family tombs reused in Late Antiquity have been excavated on the ridge above the sea, and along the roads leading into Kenchreai from Corinth and from the Isthmus.[63] Kenchreai harbor, then, like Lechaion, included domestic, mercantile and religious activity side by side throughout Late Antiquity.

South of the Forum: Egyptian Gods, Cybele and Demeter and Kore (and the Fates)

South of the Forum was the route up to Acrocorinth, either on the *Cardo Maximus*, the southwards extension of the Lechaion Road running through the middle of the South Stoa under the rebuilt colonnade, or on the parallel road to the west, which ran south through the arch between the western end of the South Stoa and the *peribolos* of Temple E. These southern routes out of the Forum went up through housing onto rocky slopes, instead of down into agricultural land. Yet here, as in the other directions out of the Forum, the passage out of the city center went through a mix of public and private spaces on a grid of roads, with the transition out of the city marked in the landscape by the religious shrines known to us mainly from Pausanias, and later by the line of the Late Antique Wall (Figure 3).

The Egyptian gods Isis and Serapis had sanctuaries under various epithets just south of the Forum on the way up to Acrocorinth.[64] A small marble tripod base from this area bearing a Hellenistic dedication by Philotis, daughter of Philonidas, to Isis and Serapis shows that their pre-Roman sanctuary was here as well.[65] Stroud points out that this location was well-watered by the Hadji Mustafa Fountain spring, and that access to water was an important part of most sanctuaries of the Egyptian gods.[66] Though these divinities and many details of their cult originated in Egypt, by the third century they had been worshipped in Greece alongside the Greco-Roman pantheon for centuries, and at Corinth at the harbor of Kenchreai as well as near the center of the city. At late antique Corinth, it is anachronistic to speak of them as in any way foreign to the Corinthians, or to Greece, despite the Egyptian elements of their cult which remained distinctive.[67]

The excavated urban sanctuary of the Egyptian gods in Thessalonike aids in reconstructing the undiscovered sanctuaries of Isis and Serapis at Corinth. Their cult was particularly patronized by merchants, mariners, freedmen and those in search of healing.[68] At Thessalonike, the Serapeum was also just above the Agora (under the modern Ptolemaion and Antigonidon Streets). In the third through fourth centuries it consisted of a peristyle enclosing a temple with naos and pronaos; in the naos an apsidal niche and altar were built into the rear wall. An underground chamber below this held a centrally placed altar and a very worn Herm still in a niche; a 10 meter tunnel led down into this chamber.[69] From this tunnel, the site and neighboring properties, came almost one hundred Hellenistic and Roman statues and inscriptions: Serapis, Isis and Harpocrates are represented along with Priapus, Aphrodite Homonia, Aphrodite of Aphrodisias, a Frejus Aphrodite, a small Egyptian basalt sphinx and portraits of cult personnel.[70]

The bust of a priest of Isis at both Thessalonike and Philippi, L. Titonius Primus, was recut in the third century from an earlier portrait.[71] Among the dedications, one for Osiris *Mystes* testifies to mystery cult held at the sanctuary already in the Hellenistic era, and the appearance of his cult statue, a beardless man leaning on his left arm, wearing a *himation* wrapped around his waist and left arm.[72] Other inscriptions record poems in honor of Osiris and Isis, dedications to Serapis, Isis, Anubis, Hypsistos Theos and Dionysos (especially by cult personnel, donating parts of the sanctuary), and decrees of Macedonian kings and local city officials.[73] A burial association of Anubis is also known from the western cemetery at Thessalonike.[74] Of particular interest for comparison with Corinth is the dedication at Thessalonike of a pair of feet carved on a marble block, which finds a parallel at Corinth with the mosaic of feet in the central Roman temple attributed to Kore in the Sanctuary of Demeter and Kore, and the Fates, which lay just above Corinth's Egyptian sanctuaries.[75] Thus architecture, sculpture and epigraphy all display elements which, if found separately, would be classified as Greek, Roman or Eastern, yet coexisted quite happily for the third- and fourth-century Thessalonicans using this sanctuary. Especially notable is the strong connection with Aphrodite, and the enduring continuity of the cult at the same urban location.

After the sanctuaries of the Egyptian Gods at Corinth, Pausanias also described a number of other cults and monuments as he proceeded southwards up the slopes of Acrocorinth. The altars of Helios the sun god were appropriately just beneath Acrocorinth, which, according to myth, Helios had won from Poseidon, and then bestowed on Aphrodite.[76] There was next a Sanctuary (*hieron*) of the personified goddesses Ἀνάγκη (Necessity) and Βία (Force), "against the law to enter," and then a Temple of Cybele, Mother of the Gods, with a stone statue and throne.[77] These shrines were likely all on a single road up Acrocorinth, above the Forum but below the Sanctuary of Demeter and Kore, and the Fates, the only place located archaeologically so far.

After Cybele's temple, Pausanias next lists temples of the Fates (*Moirai*), Demeter and Kore, which he says had concealed statues.[78] Thus, like the entire Sanctuary of Necessity and Force, and the rites practiced at the Temple of Cybele, there was a secret aspect to this Sanctuary on the slopes of Acrocorinth.[79] Pausanias' temples are probably the three small Roman prostyle Ionic temples, set side by side on a terrace overlooking the Gulf of Corinth, and excavated above several Roman cult buildings and a monumental approach, including stairs and a propylon (gate).[80] The worship of these goddesses in this rocky liminal area overlooking Ancient Corinth and the Corinthian Gulf below was another element of continuity from the Greek to the Roman city of Corinth.[81] The Greco-Roman cult practiced here in the second, third and fourth centuries seems to have centered on these three temples, one each from west to east for Demeter, Kore and the Fates, with women's as well as men's concerns about agriculture and fertility pursued in formal festivals, informal devotion, and even nocturnal magic rituals in the lowermost Building of the Tablets.[82]

The authorities of the cult and its devotees are known mainly from epigraphic and sculptural sources. About the year 200, the *Neokoros* (Temple Steward) Octavius Agathopous recorded his gift of a mosaic floor for the central temple in a *tabula ansata* laid in the mosaic just inside the doorway, "when Chara was priestess of Neotera."[83] Stroud and Bookidis persuasively identify Neotera, whose name literally means the younger goddess, with Kore (as also at Eleusis), and place her in the central temple.[84] Above the mosaic text were depicted a pair of feet pointing towards the outside, probably symbolizing the presence of the goddess, between two mystic *cistae* (baskets) encircled by snakes. Other Roman benefactors are attested in tiny inscribed fragments of marble revetment; the longest contains the name Sex(tus or -tia) A[-] / Eutych[-], possibly an ancestor of the Eutychianus mentioned in Chapter 5, who honored his brother and predecessor as Governor of Achaia, Junior, as well as Parnasius, in the middle of the fourth century.[85]

The elegantly delicate marble portrait heads of young priestesses from the well, also mentioned above in Chapter 5, certainly suggest a civic cult important to upper-class Corinthian young women and their parents throughout the third century, and into the fourth century. This sort of cult can be paralleled in the dedications of portraits of young female priestesses of the imperial Roman era to Artemis at Brauron near Athens, and especially at Messene in the shrine by the Asklepieion.[86] Other devotees and authorities of the cult and sanctuary are attested by 18 inscribed lead curse tablets of the first to fourth century, most in Greek and found along with lamps, incense burners and other evidence of nocturnal rituals in the Building of the Tablets, at the lower area of the Sanctuary by the stairs.[87]

The Sanctuary of Demeter and Kore at Corinth was functional and frequented until the late fourth century, and then met the violent end described above in Chapter 5: portraits and divine sculpture were smashed and thrown down a well, while roof collapse sealed destruction debris, coins, pottery and other artifacts on the floor of the central temple (probably the temple of Kore), and the other two temples of Demeter and the Fates were pillaged.[88] This is the clearest example of anti-pagan action at Corinth, and most closely datable, to the late fourth or early fifth century. The end of the Sanctuary was final, and was not replaced by any formal Christian worship in the area, although a small number of Christian graves were dug by the road in the lower part of the former Sanctuary, probably in the fifth to sixth centuries.[89]

Acrocorinth

Just before he reached Acrocorinth, as Pausanias climbed up the hill, he noted a *hieron* of Hera *Bounaia*, Hera of the Mountain.[90] This was a pre-Roman cult place, known at least from the Hellenistic period as a fortified sanctuary above Corinth. Then, on the saddle west of the citadel itself, Pausanias mentions the southern city gate leading to the town of Tenea in the southern Corinthia, and an adjacent sanctuary of Eileithyia, the goddess of childbirth.[91] The Sisypheum or Sanctuary of Sisyphus possibly also stood on this saddle between Acrocorinth and Penteskouphi, or to the east higher up on Acrocorinth, an appropriate locale for this famous first king of Corinth, who spent eternity pushing a boulder uphill.[92]

The Sanctuary of Corinth's patron goddess Aphrodite, the Roman Venus, lay above the Upper Peirene spring near the summit of Acrocorinth, and though apparently revived by the Romans at its previous location, both sanctuary and cult are as difficult to describe in Late Antiquity as beforehand.[93] Coin images show a schematic small tetrastyle, prostyle temple atop Acrocorinth, sometimes with the famous statue of Armed Aphrodite inside, nude to the waist and holding a shield (Figure 2.1).[94] Pausanias mentions only three statues standing in the temple: Armed Aphrodite, Eros with his bow and Helios the sun god.[95] Roman statuettes, frescoes and coins of this cult statue of

Armed Aphrodite are found at Corinth, and she has also been linked by scholars with other Hellenistic (Venus di Milo) and Roman (Capua, Arles) images of Aphrodite, but it is unclear whether the statue seen by Pausanias was an original late Classical or Hellenistic cult statue, or a Roman replacement or copy of some sort.[96] Such debates are based partly on assumptions about the thoroughness of Mummius's sack, and partly on the continuing scholarly debate about Greek originals and Roman copies. Armed Aphrodite was accompanied by Eros with his bow as her son and Helios as the winner of Acrocorinth in his contest with Poseidon, who then gave the citadel to her to protect (hence her shield, spear and perhaps helmet).[97]

Excavations in 1926 at the highest peak of Acrocorinth turned up only meager architectural fragments of any sort of sanctuary: the corner of a small building of the late seventh century BCE, and poros architectural members of a fifth-century BCE Doric temple, without a clear temple foundation.[98] The corner of the small building was dated from pottery; the temple members, none in situ, were placed by Blegen either on a destroyed foundation under the church, or south of it on a smoothed-down rectangular area about 16 m. long and 10 m. wide, which could have held an amphiprostyle or prostyle temple, or its forecourt. Mr Williams summarized Blegen's discoveries of pottery at the site as mainly third century BCE, with a scattering going back to late Mycenaean, and a mere seven fragments of terracotta figurines, one Mycenaean, the others Archaic through Hellenistic. He thus concluded the dedications were largely perishable, money or kept in the lower city. I think it likely that the sanctuary was large, but the temple small, as Strabo called it a *naidion* (a little temple). The revived Roman Sanctuary probably included a largely open air *temenos*, with this small temple inside it for just the statues and most valuable dedications, like the temple for the maritime city goddess Aphrodite *Euploia* at Cnidus.[99]

Beyond the three statues, it is a great mystery what else this Sanctuary of Aphrodite still contained in Roman times. The marble vase of Laïs noted above was more likely in the Sanctuary of Aphrodite *Melainis* near her monument.[100] A fragmentary inscription is possibly a late antique epigram honoring Sisyphus, who received the Fountain of Upper Peirene from the River Asopus, and as noted had his sanctuary on the way up Acrocorinth.[101] Athenaeus, in his compilation of quotations set at a banquet of learned men at Rome *c*.200, portrays the character Myrtilus asserting not only that he had been a sophist at Corinth, but also that a certain epigram of Simonides and a *pinax* (painting) were still to be found in the Sanctuary of Aphrodite there, honoring courtesans who prayed to Aphrodite for the salvation of the Greeks after the Persian invasion of 480 BCE.[102] Yet the assertion of survival of these dedications comes in a passage citing, and perhaps quoting, Chamaeleon's lost third-century BCE biography of Pindar, who gives as his sources the Classical historians Theopompus and Timaeus. A *scholion* to Pindar confirms that Theopompus cited a version of the epigram, and that he claimed to have seen it on the left as he entered the temple in the fourth century BCE; however, Theopompus omitted the name of Simonides, and gave the honorands only as women of Corinth.[103] The third attestation of the epigram, Plutarch's *Malice of Herodotus*, must use Theopompus too, from similarities of phrasing and his interpretation of the epigram as referring to women.[104] But Plutarch, like Athenaeus, ascribes the epigram to Simonides, gives a different text from Theopompus, and adds bronze *eikones* (images) which accompanied the epigram. Thus the possibility remains that Athenaeus and Plutarch were referring to actual surviving, or renewed, dedications of Roman times in a Corinthian temple of Aphrodite representing women praying to Aphrodite.[105] Yet again, the further question remains as to whether the sanctuary of Aphrodite on Acrocorinth or that of Aphrodite *Melainis* in the Kraneion is under discussion.[106] Finally, while one of these Greek sanctuaries of Aphrodite also accepted the dedication of sacred slaves (*hierodouloi*) and owned their income, some of which was earned by acting as *hetairai* (courtesans), that is in a sense, sacred prostitution, we know nothing of any corresponding practice in the Roman sanctuary, and it would be unlikely to have been revived by the colonists.[107]

There can be no doubt that the Temple of Aphrodite on Acrocorinth was replaced by a Christian church, though the manner and date when this happened is open to debate.[108] Built almost completely of temple spolia, the first phase of the Christian basilica was roughly 20 by 10 meters with a central nave, single apse and side aisles separated by colonnades. The latter were constructed of temple blocks and Doric columns cut down to make Ionic-style column bases and new columns.[109] A date in the sixth or seventh century seems likely for the construction of this first Christian basilica on

Acrocorinth, when Corinthians mustered the manpower to demolish the Temple of Aphrodite and were present on Acrocorinth in large enough numbers to maintain the church throughout the Middle Ages. Another church may have been built on Acrocorinth just inside the fortification walls, by the main western inner gate, perhaps even by the end of the sixth century. I have observed a marble basilica window-mullion and column fragments where MacKay (from Christian and Muslim graffiti) placed Evliya Çelebi's "Fetihye (Conqueror's) Mosque in a converted church" of 1668.[110]

The urban periphery, harbors and citadel of Corinth thus form an important contrast to the Central Area in Christianization (though this may be an aspect of excavation as much as history). There were at least eight large, new sixth-century churches built, all adjacent to earlier pagan sanctuaries; the only excavated peripheral sanctuary not replaced by a church, that of Demeter and Kore, and the Fates, was probably thoroughly destroyed by Christians in the late fourth or early fifth century. Traditional polytheistic worship practices probably ceased about that time, or were thoroughly transformed as the relevant buildings were torn down for fortifications, and political and social pressures made the old ways untenable, while the consecrated spaces marking the northern and eastern boundaries of Corinth yielded to Christian graves, and then, in the sixth century, Christian basilicas. The boundary between urban and rural space, the world of the living and the dead first remained prominently marked, and major communication routes remained open and trafficked.[111] Christian churches marked routes and borders as the pagan religious buildings preceeding them had done.

Construction of monumental new churches in late antique Corinth on the edges of the city, adjacent to former pagan sanctuaries and atop cemeteries, follows a widespread pattern across Greece and the Balkans, for example, at Athens or Nikopolis (although at both these cities there is far clearer data for temple-conversions and new churches in the civic center too).[112] Moreover, these peripheral churches in cemeteries on major communication routes, like the St Quadratus and Kraneion basilicas, lasted in use long beyond Late Antiquity, while harbor churches like the Lechaion and Kenchreai basilicas did not survive the seventh century. Corinthians apparently held fast to these churches at their cemeteries, which marked the locations for funerary rites, martyrs' festivals and processions.

The new Corinthian churches built in the later fifth or early sixth century were doubtless financed, as elsewhere, by a combination of private individuals, clergy and imperial officials, and supported sporadically by the state, especially by the transfer of funds and land from religious organizations deemed polytheist or heretical in nature.[113] Justinian passed legislation aimed at directing potential church founders to the repair of existing churches, and the construction of new churches only if there was also money set aside in endowment for maintenance of the church.[114] West of Corinth, the Archpriest Dometios recorded his construction of Nikopolis Basilica A in flowery poetry on its floor, while to the north the basilica at Daphnousia near the Lamian coast of Locris was financed to bless the *illustris* Evgeneios, his wife Dionyseia and their children.[115]

A few epigraphic texts from Corinth can be tentatively linked with church construction, notably those found north and east of the city center, besides the inscriptions mentioned in Chapter 1 related to Christian bishops. A very fragmentary text in large letters beginning with a Christian *chi rho*, the abbreviation for Chr(ist) was found on three plaques of white marble in Shear's excavations just north of the Theater in 1928; it probably belongs to the dedication of a Christian church of the fifth or sixth century north of the Forum Area.[116] The second text was on a column fragment (or round statue base?), which was found north of the Amphitheater in the eastern Kraneion region of Corinth much battered in 1931, but was once at the house of Notaras in the village of Ancient Corinth east of the Forum Area, where it was copied in 1785. The text read at that time: "It was built under Januarius, the *gloriosissimus patricius*, and Paulus, the *clarissimus domesticus*."[117] These men may have held civil or military offices in the imperial bureaucracy, but their high rank (*illustris* and *clarissimus*) and activity at Corinth makes military office and involvement with fortification walls likely, according to Feissel. The script and the titles suggest a fifth- or sixth-century date for their oversight of a building project in the northeastern neighborhood of Corinth, either a church such as Pallas' Basilica, or a military project like the late antique city wall (see Chapter 8). Corinth thus had its own elite Christian benefactors, whether among the clergy, imperial officials or local landowners, who had the resources to fund the many churches and the fortification walls constructed across the Corinthia in the sixth century.

The placement and patronage of these newly built churches has been discussed, but it is worth enquiring here into their purpose and use. Distinction is drawn in scholarship between the cathedral of a city, almost certainly the Lechaion Basilica (from its scale) or a newly-built church in the city center, neighborhood parish churches and cemetery churches. Bishops were more often the patrons of the cathedral, and non-clergy the patrons of the other types. In modern Greece, services are held at the cathedral and parish churches weekly and more often during festivals, while cemetery churches only see activity during services for the dead. Besides services, Corinth's sixth-century churches must also have acted as nodes for processions, and the celebration of *panegyreis*, Christian festivals featuring markets and communal open-air feasting along with church services.[118] The transition from temples to churches was thus accompanied by larger transitions in the schedule of festivals, but there were likely continuities in communal feasting as an element of public festivals.

CHAPTER 8

FORTIFICATION WALLS: ISTHMUS, CITY AND ACROCORINTH

An extensive system of fortification walls was the largest new infrastructure built at Corinth in Late Antiquity, apparently an imperial response to insecurity in Illyricum (the southern Balkans) as a whole, created by the barbarian invasions of the third and especially the late fourth centuries.[1] The construction of the Hexamilion (Six Mile) Wall across the Isthmus, its fortresses at each coast, fortification walls around Corinth's city center and the *enceinte* of Acrocorinth all involved the extensive demolition of older urban public buildings, and probably extended from the fifth into the middle of the sixth century (Figures 2, 3, 10). After the reign of Justinian, these three sets of fortification walls then had very different fates, which affects our ability to date their construction and appreciate their impact today. The Hexamilion and its fortresses were sporadically repaired through the fifteenth century, then replaced by an ambitious but unfinished new system of walls to the south by the Venetians in the late seventeenth century. The Hexamilion is still prominent in the landscape across the Isthmus, and parts of its eastern fortress are excavated, while its western fortress is largely destroyed. Around the city center of Ancient Corinth, the late antique city wall of Corinth itself is almost totally gone today, excavated only in two short stretches on the east. Important questions remain as to its date and exact line, especially on the western side of Corinth (Figure 3).[2] However, what remains of it does give us the chance to reflect on the functions of various neighborhoods, cemeteries and religious spaces, as well as dramatic changes to the urban structure of Corinth, and the role of imperial patronage in the fifth and sixth centuries. There were probably at least two late antique phases of construction of the fortifications across the Isthmus and around the city center of Corinth. The first phase in the middle to late fifth century is established on the basis of archaeology, and hard to dismiss given the demolition of so many important structures in this era, like the Theater at Corinth and the Temple of Poseidon at Isthmia, the appearance of fourth-century material under walls and fifth-century material up against them, and the existence of earlier phases in the sixth-century walls.[3] The second phase, in the middle of the sixth century, is attested epigraphically and in Procopius' laudatory literary praise of Justinian's building program, as well as by archaeology. Finally, Acrocorinth's walls were well-maintained in the medieval and early modern era all the way up until Greek Independence in the early nineteenth century, making any late antique repairs to the Hellenistic circuit wall difficult to determine today. The existence of this mountain refuge, however, is important in any survey of defensive structures at Corinth. The construction of new fortification walls is a characteristic of cities in Late Antiquity all around the Roman Empire. Corinth is a useful example of the phenomenon, since we can track which public buildings as well as sculptures were selected deliberately for reuse in wall building, and since the epigraphic and literary testimonia are unusually explicit about the justifications and imperial patronage behind the wall building, at least under Justinian.

Hexamilion Wall across the Isthmus and Fortresses

Across the Isthmus and in Isthmia a significant and permanent change certainly occurred in the landscape between the early fifth and the middle of the sixth century: the building of the Hexamilion Wall and its Eastern Fortress. Procopius credited Justinian with the Hexamilion Wall, and an official of that emperor, Victorinus, claimed responsibility in the name of Justinian in two large inscriptions once set into the Hexamilion Wall, for protecting those who dwell according to God in Corinth and Greece, worshipping Jesus Christ and Mary the *Theotokos* (Bearer of God).[4] The massive Hexamilion trans-Isthmian Wall, and its twin fortresses, undeniably obliterated the Isthmian Sanctuary of Poseidon, its performance facilities and many other ancient monuments from the landscape, and ensured that travelers would henceforth traverse the Isthmus only through certain selected gateways at east or west. The construction of both the Hexamilion Wall and its fortresses thus caused a clear rupture with the past history of the Isthmus, and particularly with its centuries-long connection with the worship of Poseidon and other maritime deities on the eastern side, where the Eastern Fortress was constructed next to, and out of, the Sanctuary of Poseidon. There were at least two previous trans-Isthmian walls, both of which had respected the Sanctuary.[5]

The Hexamilion Wall itself was about 3 meters thick and constructed, just like Corinth's city wall, of two faces of squared off spolia blocks filled in between with rubble and mortar. A number of square towers projected from its northern side, in front of which were once a lower *proteichisma* (a wall in front of the wall), a ditch and an earthen *antiteichisma* (a low wall).[6] It replaced earlier trans-Isthmian Walls, which had been repaired as recently as the middle of the third century, under Valerian. However, near the eastern end of the Hexamilion Wall at the coast (and probably on the western end as well), an all-new rectangular Eastern Fortress of similar construction, but narrower wall-width, and also with external square towers, was attached to the inner southern face of the Wall, just east of, and below, the Sanctuary of Poseidon.[7] The entire Hexamilion Wall and particularly this Eastern Fortress incorporated so much *spolia* from the Sanctuary of Poseidon, including almost all of the Temple of Poseidon down to the foundations, that the construction of both the Hexamilion Wall and this fortress must have necessitated the demolition of every stone building in the vicinity, and beyond, down below foundation levels (and the melting of all marble statuary for mortar).

As Jon Frey has demonstrated, practically all of these old architectural members were then carefully cut into trapezoidal headers and stretchers, and laid in regular courses with the smoothed face out; visible *spolia*, mortar and tile were kept largely underground in the foundations; on the west side, mortar was used to smooth the outher face, while on the south side, a claw-chisel was used, testifying to at least two teams of workmen.[8] Graffiti in the wet mortar made by these workmen include fish like those at the Lechaion Basilica and on the

Panayia Field Long Building, as well as crosses, palm branches and a scene of ships with a woman near Tower 15.[9] Such images surely sacralized the Hexamilion Wall and the Eastern Fortress, and, combined with the Victorinus inscriptions, they confirm that the workmen were Christians, and they even suggest that this military construction project also was intended on some level to replace Poseidon's Sanctuary in the religious landscape of the Isthmus. But the *spolia* were not triumphally displayed; rather the old temple elements were cut down and shaped to resemble the grand fortification walls of the Hellenic past, and possibly to intimidate the enemy, like the Theodosian Walls of Constantinople. Indeed, the Roman Arch which once led into the Sanctuary of Poseidon was now completely encased in new towers, replacing its past history of triumphal entrance to the Sanctuary with a statement of purely military might.[10]

Some form of wall across the Isthmus was likely still standing in Late Antiquity, and the Hexamilion visible today might date from as early as the middle of the fifth century, but surviving epigraphic and literary texts all credit the emperor Justinian with funding the construction of the trans-Isthmian Hexamilion Wall, the series of forts (*phrouria*) and the 153 bastions (or towers, *phylakteria*). The latter number is given in connection with the emperor Manuel Palaeologus' repairs to the Hexamilion Wall, and its Eastern Fortress, undertaken in 1415.[11] Comparison with other fortification projects in the fifth to sixth centuries suggests that the Hexamilion itself would not have taken more than ten years to build.[12] Certainly placed alongside the Lechaion Basilica, the inscibed texts placed on the wall indicate a powerful interest on the part of Justinian's government in taking credit for fortifying the Corinthians both spiritually and militarily.[13]

There is no denying that Justinian took the credit for the Hexamilion Wall in Late Antiquity in a prominent way: he had his name and his Christian ideology writ large upon the two large blocks of stone which survive, and which were probably once placed above gateways.[14] One block echoes the Nicene Creed:

> Φῶς ἐκ φωτός, Θεὸς\ ἀληθινὸς ἐκ Θεοῦ ἀληθινοῦ,\ φυλάξη τὸν Αὐτοκράτορα\ Ἰουστινιανὸν καὶ τὸν\ πιστὸν αὐτοῦ δοῦλον\ Βικτορῖνον, ἅμα τοῖς\ οἰκοῦσειν ἐν Ἑλάδι τοὺς κ(α)τ(ὰ) Θεὼν\ ζῶντας.

> Light from Light, True God from True God, guard the emperor Justinian and his faithful slave Victorinus, along with those who dwell in Greece living according to God.

The other block adds:

> Ἁγ(ία) Μαρία Θεοτόκε, φύλαξον\ τὴν βασιλείαν τοῦ\ φιλοχρίστου Ἰουστινιανοῦ\ καὶ τὸν γνησίως\ δουλεύοντα αὐτῷ\ Βικτωρῖνον σὺν τοῖς\ οἰκοῦσιν ἐν Κορίνθῳ κ(ατὰ) Θεὼν\ ζῶντας.
>
> Holy Mary, *Theotokos*, guard the empire of Christ-loving Justinian and Victorinus who serves him wisely, along with those who dwell in Corinth living according to God.

Thus between the death of Theodora in 548, and the writing of Procopius' *Buildings* in the later 550s, Justinian made his blessing clear: only the inhabitants of Corinth and Hellas who accepted his God, his Mary *Theotokos* and his Creed would be blessed by protection from his Wall. And whether or not Justinian's official Victorinus, or even a previous emperor, really built the wall, Justinian got the credit for all time. When Procopius groused in the *Secret History* that Justinian and Theodora referred to their high officials as their slaves (*Anek*. 30.26), he clearly wasn't making it up.[15]

Procopius' longest references to Greece in all his works concern fortification walls, and especially the fortification of the strategic pass of Thermopylae at the northern boundary of Achaia (Figure 1).[16] In his *Buildings*, Procopius devotes all of his chapter on Greece to fortifications, and about a third of it to Thermopylae, where he claims Justinian walled high passes, repaired the fort at the main pass, and installed cisterns, granaries and a 2,000 man garrison. He says this was a great improvement on the peasants' efforts, whom he blames for allowing previous barbarian incursions (rather than imperial officials), and who: "when the enemy came down, would suddenly change their mode of life, and becoming makeshift soldiers for the occasion, would keep guard there in turn; and because of their inexperience in the business they, together with Greece itself, proved an easy prey to the enemy."[17] South of Thermopylae, he specifically mentions repairs only to the circuit walls of Athens, Plataea and Corinth, and the construction of the Hexamilion, which he calls a new fortification wall across the Isthmus of Corinth, with forts and garrisons.[18]

In the *Secret History*, Thermopylae also gets the most attention, but for a completely different reason. Indeed, there Procopius credits the hapless peasants of his own *Buildings* with completely capable service in times of war, and condemns Justinian for approving his own official's wasteful decision to station 2,000 troops there, and even more terrible, pay for it not from the imperial treasury, but rather from "the entire civic funds and the funds for the spectacles of all the cities of Greece, on the pretext that these soldiers were to be maintained therefrom, and consequently in all Greece, and not least in Athens itself, no public building was restored nor could any other needful thing be done."[19] Thus the clever construction of walls and concern for his subjects shown by Justinian in the *Buildings* is overshadowed by the lack of need for the garrison and disastrous misallocation of funds. Funds and spectacles tied to traditional religion mostly had disappeared in the early fifth century, though, while those for civic or imperial festivals do not survive the early sixth, as discussed above in Chapter 4. However there are hundreds of new churches constructed all over Greece under Justinian, and repairs to public stoas, fountains and baths, as well as fortifications. Surely not all the public funds of every city in Greece could have been taken for the support of one garrison? Even if they were, it was a very short-lived commitment, for these are most likely the same troops sent to Croton from Thermopylae just a few years later to help with the war against the Goths in Italy.[20] The Eastern Fortress at Corinth, at least, was garrisoned throughout the sixth century, and grew into a small town by the later sixth century.

Late Antique City Walls of Corinth

Up in the city center of Corinth, however, two very different kinds of late antique fortification wall have been excavated, and their connection to one another, and to Procopius' claim that Justinian also rebuilt Corinth's circuit wall, remains under discussion (Figure 3).[21] As noted in Chapter 1, a very fragmentary text found in the South Stoa seems to record orders about wall construction in the sixth century sent to a proconsular Governor of *Hellas* in Corinth by the Praetorian Prefect of Illyricum.[22] However, earlier initiatives in the late third and/or early fifth century could certainly have been made by governors or the City Council to fortify the city center of Corinth against barbarian attack (as at Athens with the Post-Herulian Wall in the late third century).[23] The first kind of fortification wall in the urban center of Corinth is represented by short stretches built of uncut *spolia* down on the plain by the Old Gymnasium, northwest of the Forum; of these, only the so-called Epistyle Wall has been documented in any detail (Figure 3, 7). Along with a further stretch of *spolia* wall just to its west, with a round tower and a gate, the Epistyle Wall sits just back from the northern edge of the lower city terrace, west of the Asklepieion, aligned roughly east-west, and composed of uncut Archaic temple *spolia* and thick mortar.[24] These *spolia* likely originated in an Archaic temple, perhaps that of Olympian Zeus which once stood near this area (see Chapter 7). A monumental epistyle block is prominent among the visible elements of the wall, hence the name of the wall. Parts of this set of *spolia* walls have always been visible; Shear called them "the mediaeval fortifications."[25] Yet a concreted mass of late fourth-century coins was found "associated" with the Epistyle Wall, and was interpreted as dating it, though questions have since been raised about the connection between hoard and wall.[26] There remains the possibility that these walls belong to a detached bastion or gate complex, even one renovated as late as the Ottoman or Venetian era, as old maps and images of Corinth show fortifications there (Figure 1.1).[27]

Another short stretch of uncut *spolia* wall runs on an east-west line north of the Theater, incorporating stage-building *spolia* set in mortar, and then, according to Mr Williams, the north and west walls of the Theater's North Peristyle court. He argues it dates to *c.*500–50 on pottery and stratigraphic evidence, but it is difficult to connect it up into an *enceinte* enclosing the city of Corinth.[28] These *spolia* stretches of wall are thus all of similar construction, but they are difficult to connect with one another, or with any other walls. The only potential links on this northwestern side of Corinth are the east-west Terrace wall above the Theater, which replaced the Terraced Building and Buildings 5–7 in the early fifth century, and masses of concrete and masonry in the scarp above and to the east of the Julian Basilica.[29] Some sort of fortification was likely made in Late Antiquity on this side of Corinth, therefore, but it remains unclear whether the Forum was inside or outside of it, and what its precise line was.

On the eastern side of Corinth, however, a completely different north-south running wall has been traced for some 800 m., which is built of cut-down *spolia* limestone blocks, set in two faces with rubble and mortar in between, about 3m thick, just like the Hexamilion (Figure 3).[30] Numerous burials along its outer face place it in the middle of the fifth or the early sixth century, but unlike the northwestern segments of wall it is continuous, features exterior square or triangular towers, and closely matches the careful construction techniques of the Hexamilion. Greek Archaeological Service excavations (1985), and a resistivity survey conducted by Michael Boyd (2000–5), revealed the northeast and southeast corners of this late antique fortification wall around the city of Corinth, along with potential gates on the east and south sides. Gregory linked this eastern late antique wall with the Epistyle Wall to create a large Late Roman circuit wall, and dated the whole construction in the early fifth century, on the basis of the hoard already mentioned from the Epistyle Wall, and fourth-century material from under an eastern tower.[31]

Sanders, alternatively, leaves out the Epistyle Wall as not late antique, and links this eastern wall with traces of wall above and east of the Julian Basilica, to make a small circuit wall only for Corinth's population, and perhaps an ecclesiastical center, of the middle of the sixth century. This smaller circuit, a dotted line in Figure 3, excludes the Forum Area to its west, as well as the stretches of wall by the Theater. Sanders estimates the length of his entire wall as three km., and its height as five m., thus enclosing 16–20 hectares, and demanding some 30,000 square meters of *spolia* blocks and 30,000 cubic meters of cement, largely melted down from marble and hard limestone. Here he sees the destination for the sculpture, epigraphy and architecture of the Forum Area and Theater in the eary sixth century, with most of those blocks then robbed out in turn to serve for medieval, Frankish, Venetian, Ottoman and early modern construction in the village of Ancient Corinth (where they still remain). Images of early modern Ancient Corinth clearly show standing fortification walls around this domestic, commercial and religious center below Acrocorinth, where Evliya Çelebi tells us most Corinthians lived in the seventeenth century (Figure 1.1).[32]

Acrocorinth

Towering above the city of Corinth, and commanding views of the rest of the Corinthia and the two gulfs, the citadel of Acrocorinth has always been the natural acropolis of Corinth. It was inhabited as recently as the early nineteenth century, though ravaged in the Greek Revolution and War of Independence. Yet archaeology there has been limited to excavation around Upper Peirene Fountain and on the peak itself, along with some study of the monumental surviving circuit walls.[33] In Late Antiquity, the monumental Hellenistic circuit was still standing at least to the height which remains today, prominent especially at the inner western gate and its flanking towers. There were once five gates in the circuit wall leading out to roads, with the main gate always on the west, where the Hellenistic wall and towers are best preserved, and the approach easiest. Repairs in Late Antiquity are likely, but difficult to demonstrate. Certainly the construction of a church at the peak and the continued use of Upper Peirene Fountain in the medieval era demonstrate circuit wall maintenance in the Middle Byzantine era.

In conclusion, it seems clear that the eastern, Saronic Gulf shoreline of Isthmia and Kenchreai was, from the late third century, more susceptible to pirates and raiders than the Corinthian Gulf. Whether invaders came by land or sea, they arrived first at the Isthmus, and this was the spot which seems to have suffered the most under Alaric's Gothic army. The major investment in infrastructure at Corinth in the fifth and sixth centuries was firstly a monumental wall with fortresses across the Isthmus, a much smaller scale circuit wall around the city of Corinth itself, and perhaps repairs up on Acrocorinth. Secondly, though, Corinthians built churches out on the coasts and in the cemeteries, not just behind these new walls. Both Corinthian harbor towns demonstrate remarkable religious continuity in Late Antiquity. The biggest church ever built at Corinth was established at Lechaion. Though the construction of the Lechaion Basilica destroyed the previous buildings on the site, we know from texts that sanctuaries once stood by the harbor. At Kenchreai, a Christian basilica was built at the base of the southern mole, in the area which probably once held sanctuaries of Isis and Asklepios. Recent surveys at the northern pier, near Pausanias' Aphrodite Temple, may yet reveal a church. Thucydides' ancient observations on Greek retreat from the coast in times of trouble seems to take hold at Corinth only in the later sixth and seventh centuries, when both Kenchreai and then Lechaion lost much of their population, and settlement in the Corinthia shifted up to Acrocorinth, inside the new circuit wall into the city center of Corinth, and into the Hexamilion's Eastern Fortress at Isthmia. In each case it was behind high fortification walls, but with the identity and inhabitants of the city of Corinth preserved in the Byzantine and then Frankish eras.[34] The Ottoman traveler of the later seventeenth century, Evliya Çelebi, tells us that the Corinthia supplied 3,000 Ottoman troops in his day, and that most Corinthians then lived in the suburb below Acrocorinth at the ancient city center (i.e. Ancient Corinth), around the ancient Forum and the standing columns of the Archaic Temple of Apollo.[35] Though the practicalities and actual maintenance of the Hexamilion have been widely debated, it is a fact that Acrocorinth remained a heavily fortified and strategic citadel throughout the middle ages, with maintenance and rebuilding of both the Acrocorinth *enceinte* and the Hexamilion Wall and its fortresses, and less enduring but still occasional attention paid to circuit walls around Ancient Corinth.

CONCLUSION

CORINTH AT THE END OF LATE ANTIQUITY

In the fifth century, Corinthian civic officials and public buildings decreased sharply in visibility, and probably in actuality. Local civic authorities were dissolved by law in the later fifth century, but replaced by new less formal administrative bodies affiliated with the Christian Church, and staffed by many of the same men. The imperial civil and military hierarchy as reformed by Diocletian continued to exist through the sixth century, yet few actual officials of this hierarchy are clearly recognizable at Corinth after the later fifth century, due to decreasing documentation. Victorinus under Justinian is given no title other than slave of the Emperor.

Yet surely there continued to be a Governor of Achaia, who then was replaced by a *Strategos* of Hellas, this imperial representative is just far less visible than before from the fifth century. Where did he live and what did he do? Fine houses are numerous at Corinth, both in the city and the Corinthia, and used into the sixth century. The most secure evidence for the presence of a Governor in fifth- or sixth-century Corinth consists of the *chlamydati* and fragmentary inscriptions. In the sixth to eighth centuries, the system was reformed again, and the imperial official at Corinth was given the title of *Strategos*, General of the *theme* of Hellas. Both local and imperial traditional authorities had to make do with less funding in Late Antiquity, but also produced fewer monumental buildings, sculpture and inscriptions. The imperial officials at Corinth shifted clearly in focus from Rome to Constantinople and the East after Alaric's invasion and Theodosius' division of the Empire in 395. However, the concerted effort to tear down the Theater, Odeum, statues, inscriptions and especially temples in the fifth and sixth centuries and build fortification walls was certainly directed by imperial officials, and probably managed in practice by the wealthy local landowners and former decurions.

The rise of a Christian hierarchy alongside the local and imperial one is recognizable in literary sources from the first century onwards, with presbyters (or elders) of an *ekklesia* (church assembly, or community), and then a bishop with deacons, deaconesses and other clergy. The responsibilities and organization of these ecclesiastical officials grew slowly in some eras, and faster in others, though our evidence is sporadic. The legalization of Christianity in Achaia in 313 probably brought them out into public life more visibly, as they benefited from fourth- and then fifth-century imperial legislation. The criminalization of most other religious practices, besides Judaism, in the later fourth century left them (along with Jewish leaders) as the only legal religious authorities. Then, in the fifth and sixth centuries they took on the construction of churches, as well as some tasks previously overseen by local or imperial authorities, such as fountain repair or commissioning of architectural sculpture. Christianity thus both streamlined and localized authority in Corinth. The leaders of the church in Corinth took part in setting up an empire-wide second hierarchy alongside the imperial one, but they also basically replaced certain functions of local government and let others disappear. The elites of Corinth probably shifted from City Council leadership to Christian leadership, though in truth we do not have the evidence at Corinth to say much about the family background of bishops. It is significant that Corinth had enough clergy to supply other places in Achaia too, like Athens and then Patras. Direct literary and artistic evidence for this shift comes in some detail from Thessalonike, but from Corinth it is present only in the form of churches, references to the holding of synods and the travel of clergy to church councils. Therefore, they were men of some means, particularly in the sixth century.

Clearly Christianity became part of Corinthian civic identity in Late Antiquity, but inhabitants of Corinth remained Corinthians. The name of the city and its people was never lost; bishops representing them continue to appear in literary sources throughout the seventh century. A few traditional elements of civic identity also did not shift until after Late Antiquity. A continuous water supply was maintained to the Forum and Central Area, flowing from natural springs into architecturally elaborated fountains. Public baths completed the shift from large-scale to small-scale bathing and continued to be built in the city center. Substantial fortifications for the protection of "those who dwell in Corinth" went up in the fifth or sixth centuries. Though it is unclear how long those around the lower city were maintained, those on Acrocorinth and at the Isthmus became long-lasting features of the landscape.

From a modern perspective, the most recognizable role of all ancient civic officials, whether local, imperial or ecclesiastical, was the collection of taxes (or tithes), the provision of services, and the exercise of authority. But what sort of services? Imperial taxes paid the Roman army and bureaucracy, local benefactions and liturgies maintained the city, and Christian offerings supported their gatherings, clergy, and good works. But the relative authority and funds available to all officials shifted throughout Late Antiquity, as did their degree of intervention in Corinthian urban life, and the rewards they expected to receive for their work. Continued maintenance of some urban institutions in Late Antiquity and the abandonment of others is apparent, but the most basic solution to the issues is, as always, to follow the money and discover under whose authority it was spent for urban infrastructure.

After the late fourth century, there were no more athletic or artistic competitions in honor of the old gods at Corinth or Isthmia, and the buildings which accomodated these activities also fell into ruins or were completely removed. Temples, sanctuaries and pagan divine sculpture suffered a similar fate. Monumental construction, sculpture, epigraphy: all of these things became confined to the the context of the Church, except for the fortifications on the Isthmus, marked with the last monumental inscriptions of late antique Corinth, in the form of Christian prayers. Parts of the urban center of Corinth became steadily less monumental in the fifth and sixth centuries, but damaged public buildings besides civic basilicas or temples were usually rebuilt with cut *spolia*, less often with uncut *spolia*, or, on a much smaller scale. There is very little evidence at Corinth for the abandonment of any public buildings; building stone, sculpture and epigraphy was carried off for reuse by organized groups of workmen, or, in the case mainly of portrait heads, placed out of reach in watery underground spaces.

Certainly the city center by the late sixth century was far less monumental, adorned by fewer remaining old sculptures and almost no new ones, characterized by the skeletons of old buildings hiding under more recent constructions built mainly of *spolia*. Most of this *spolia* was very well-cut so as to appear new, however, like the cladding of the Hexamilion Wall or the outriders façade of Peirene. The former site of the Theater was apparently partly a quarry and partly a large ruin, right below the Forum Area. The many temples of the West Terrace were in a similar state, concrete rubble cores stripped of all architectural elements. Graves were even starting to be set into the ruins of the temples, and the Julian Basilica.[1] Yet the Forum and Lechaion Road featured stoas, shops, fountains and bath complexes still in use.

It is hard to believe that church services and festivals offered the range and depth of culture available in the third century from Greco-Roman traditional religious festivals, artistic and athletic competitions, and even gladiatorial or hunting spectacles. Though they were more humane by our standards than some previous events, and probably provided more public charity, Christian civic events were also more limiting to creativity and human expression. And with the loss of these very obvious buildings and events went all sorts of less visible aspects of civic life, like public education, or professions dependant on polytheism, like performers, portrait carvers or garland weavers. This change was not entirely or even primarily the fault of the Church: there were important economic and political factors too, like the collapse of the frontiers or the instability in imperial officeholders in Constantinople.

Regret on the passing of ancient Greek and Roman civic culture is not just a modern sentiment. Procopius expressed real concerns when he criticized Justinian in his *Secret History* for "destroying the marks of distinction and all the things which confer honour and beauty both in Byzantium and in every other city," diverting provincial civic funds for public services, teachers, doctors, building repair and spectacles to Constantinople, so, "there was both in private and in public sorrow and dejection, as though still another affliction from Heaven had smitten them, and there was no laughter in life for anyone."[2] It is still very hard to discern, however, who was driving these changes (besides Justinian in Procopius' opinion), the people or the authorities, or pressure alternately from above and below. Some changes, for example to imperial laws or Christian doctrines, were clearly initiated by emperors, patriarchs in Constantinople or popes in Rome, or by their intimate officials, while others seem to have come from the local level. At Corinth, the trend from the fifth into the sixth centuries is less monumental buildings, more local products, less travel, fewer imports and the attenuation of people and products from Rome, Italy, Gaul, Hispania or North Africa. It is also clear that power in the city was shifting from the traditional authorities to the Christian ones. Yet it is unclear if the same families were taking on the new positions, as the old were abolished or ceased to exist.[3]

The evidence at Corinth in Late Antiquity contributes to showing widespread Christianization, with continuity in some areas of civic life and notable decline in others. There was decline in certain urban institutions, primarily those connected to Greco-Roman traditional religion and public assembly outide the Church. There were fewer new public buildings constructed, and sloppier repairs than in the past to what still stood. However, the Forum was still at the city center into the sixth century, and there were not just public streets with stoas, markets, fountains and baths, but also new public portraits into the fifth century. At the same time, some sculpture was used as *spolia* in new Christian basilicas rising on all sides of the city; along with fortifications, they represent most of the monumental construction of the fifth and sixth centuries.

Christianity caused some changes to civic life at Corinth, but it also emerged in a diverse urban environment of Roman colonists, freedmen, veterans, Jews and Greeks all bound together under local and imperial Roman authorities. Christianity expanded there, as elsewhere, and then became visible in the landscape largely through the actions of authorities with communities large enough to build and use new basilica churches.[4] Imperial officials administered the demolition of old public buildings for the construction of new fortification walls to protect the cities under their authority. Individuals like emperors, imperial governors and Christian bishops all took actions to change their cities, as did communities of people like the Corinthians themselves. At the end of the sixth century, Corinth was still a city, but one defined in different terms, lacking much of what had made it a city 200 years before, but in possession of new buildings and frames of reference moulded by shifts in Roman authority, economic realities and Christian religion.

APPENDIX I

EPIGRAPHIC AND LITERARY SOURCES FOR LATE ANTIQUE CORINTH

The inscriptions of Corinth are the only texts to survive from Late Antiquity written by the Corinthians themselves, and also the only ones unmodified since their composition, at least in their textual content (since almost all are broken, many profoundly so). The late antique inscriptions recovered from Corinth itself are relatively and absolutely large in number, though weighted heavily towards Christian epitaphs. They form the most significant data set for the history of Corinth in Late Antiquity, and I have only hinted at their potential in this book. There are over 638 texts written on stone, or in a few cases other media like mosaic or lead, composed in Corinth between the third and sixth centuries, and surviving to the present day (for numbers of inscriptions, see Sironen's 2016 edition of *IG* IV^2 3). A few inscriptions have been known for centuries, or are recent finds, but the majority were recovered in the American School's Corinth Excavations in the early twentieth century, in the Forum or the Christian cemeteries north and east of the city center. A minority were in their original location; most had been reused as building material or smashed into small pieces, and carried an unknown distance from their original site of creation and display (though the larger the inscription, the closer it is likely to be).[1]

Despite these limitations, a strength of the collection is its large size and thorough study and publication. Texts recovered in the American School excavations through 1950 (or collected beforehand) are published in three volumes of the *Corinth* series (VIII.1, 2, 3), while many of those found since, or restudied, are published in short articles, excavation reports or the *SEG*.[2] Corinth's Christian inscriptions were collected in the *CG-CIH* 1.1 in 1941, and, much more recently, edited along with the non-Christian inscriptions of the fourth to sixth centuries by Erkki Sironen as *IG* IV^2 3. His research, along with that of Sterling Dow, Louis Robert, Denis Feissel, Ronald Stroud and Michael B. Walbank means that Corinth's late antique epigraphic record has received unparalleled scholarly attention.[3]

In genre, the inscriptions consist of a few public texts, and hundreds of private ones, mainly Christian epitaphs. Though the public inscriptions are small in number, fewer than survive from Early Roman times, they are still a rich source for public life in the third- to fourth-century city, after which they become rare (e.g. the Victorinus inscriptions from the Hexamilion). The public inscriptions include at least five edicts or regulations, some twenty statue bases or plaques honoring emperors, imperial officials and local grandees, and six building inscriptions. Though few, these public documents show the government of the city and province at work, and the people involved, particularly the Governor of Achaia and the *Boule* (or City Council). Many of the statue bases are very well preserved, and were recovered from reuse contexts in close proximity to marble portrait heads and bodies on the Forum or along the upper Lechaion Road. Yet, unfortunately, exact joins and dates are rare, established only for a few texts by emperors' regnal years or names known from outside Corinth.

The majority of the late antique inscriptions from Corinth are private and memorial: twelve traditional and at least 372 Early Christian epitaphs, ranging from a few letters to many whole gravestones, most often slabs of schist. This material, the letter forms and the formulae of the epitaphs are all distinctive; their concentration north and east of the city provides a clear indication of the sites of Early Christian cemeteries, mostly continuing pagan ones. They yield many names, a remarkable range of professions, and details on the business of burial.[4] The lack of dates on most enables dating only broadly by style, before or after the indiction became usual on epitaphs, so in the fifth or sixth centuries. By contrast, the traditional epitaphs are few, though they were uncommon at Corinth in Early Roman times too. The remainder of the private inscriptions consist of some 28 Christian acclamations or invocations, two dedications to pagan gods, and miscellaneous graffiti, curse tablets and incerta.[5] Almost all the Corinthian inscriptions have been classified and edited in print, and many have been studied in very great detail.

Many ancient or medieval literary authors mention aspects of life in late antique Corinth, but there is no narrative history of the city for any era. The context and genre of authors is vital for understanding their attitudes towards Corinth, the use they made of the city and its citizens, and their strengths and weaknesses in historical narrative. Most literary texts are dated, and some are contemporary with events they describe, though no preserved author was a native Corinthian. It is often hard to determine if references to Corinth are about the contemporary city, or the Classical Greek one. All these texts found an appreciative audience who distributed and copied them widely enough to ensure they survived in manuscripts and then passed into print.

Pausanias takes first place among ancient authors of literary sources for late antique Corinth. His detailed description of the city and Corinthia at the start of book 2 of his *Description of Greece* is a fundamental text for Corinthian topography at the height of the Roman Empire, and the last detailed description of Corinth before early modern travelers.[6] Pausanias hailed from Ionia but traveled widely, writing down his *Description* of the regions of Greece in the province of Achaia in ten books, *c.*155–75.[7] Like the geographer Strabo, some 200 years before, Pausanias must have visited Corinth often, if only to pass through to the Peloponnese, or across the Isthmus. His description of Corinth follows his usual pattern in a city: monuments of interest (mainly sanctuaries and statues) are described in sequence as they could be seen, interspersed with mythology and (mainly Classical and Hellenistic) history associated with them. He begins his description of the Corinthia by crossing the border from Megara into the Corinthia north of the Isthmus, and then describes the monuments along routes in, around and out of the Forum (his Agora) and city center. He comments on the contemporary city, and even notes some entirely Roman buildings like the Odeum.[8] His description of Corinth is short, both because it was so well-known and easily accessible in his day, and because he considered that, "worthy of mention in the city are the things still left of the ancients, and most of these were made later than their acme."[9] Thus he highlights Corinthian monuments from before the Roman sack, and judges most of these to be post-Archaic. Recent scholarship on Pausanias has re-emphasized that he had access to many histories which no longer survive, actually visited most places he describes, and was careful, if selective, in his presentation of his contemporary topography.

Other Second Sophistic authors made reference to Corinth too, but most often to the city of the past. Those who refer to contemporary Corinth do so in literary fashion for their own wider purposes within genre conventions. The unique character of Corinth as both Greek and Roman city attracted notice, and some writers resisted the tendency to elide difference between ancient and contemporary. Dio Chrysostom, his student Favorinus, Aelius Aristides and other orators contrasted Corinth's Roman character with its glorious Greek past, or with (more Greek so morally superior) Athens.[10] Corinth's festival of Isis figures prominently in Apuleius' *Metamorphoses*; this adventure of a man who becomes an ass in Thessaly and is saved by Isis in Corinth is comic fiction, drawing on lost earlier Greek novels, but the action is situated in the author's own era, and seems designed not to contradict audience assumptions about contemporary Greece.[11] With the *Learned Banqueters* (*Deipnosophistae*) of Athenaeus, we find a similar situation: the banquet in question is set in Rome *c.*200, and contemporary Corinth is explicitly mentioned, but the style imitates earlier Symposia, and the majority of the dialogue consists of quotations from Classical Greek literature.[12] The philosopher biographies of Diogenes Laërtius, including that of Diogenes the Cynic, were written around the year 200, but were largely set in the Classical past and drew on sources from that era.[13] More contemporary in focus may be Ampelius, who praised the baths and temples of Corinth *c.*230 in his didactic *Liber memorialis*, a primer for his ten-year-old son assembled from sources of unknown age.[14]

Among authors of Late Antiquity to mention Corinth, there are only a few extant narrative histories like those of Zosimus or Procopius, and many more of the so-called fragments, that is quotations made for literary, political or other content, as well as Christian literature such as epistles, sermons, commentaries and hagiography. Christian texts made much use of their own bible books relevant to Corinth, such as the letters of St Paul and *Acts of the Apostles*, but did not often engage with the contemporary city. Modern Christian clerics and New Testament scholars remain interested in the early Christian presence in Roman, late antique and medieval Corinth.[15] This interest has been recognized by archaeologists at Corinth, notably Broneer.[16] While most scholars of Early Christianity focus closely on the mid-first century, they often expand their focus to Corinth in earlier and later periods if there is relevance for St Paul and his ministry and the growth of the Early Church. Eusebius' groundbreaking work of Christian history set the standard for focusing on Church Fathers and emperors, so for Corinth he includes only the visit of Paul, a few early bishops like Dionysius, and the emperor Constantine's sculpture-acquiring agents.[17]

The most important third-century historian of Greece was P. Herennius Dexippus, Athenian archon, orator and historian.[18] Dexippus came from a wealthy and well-connected family, endowed the Panathenaia, and wrote two lost works of history in the 250s–70s which concerned contemporary Greece.[19] Photius summarizes them as "a *History* covering the chief imperial deeds up through Claudius (II Gothicus, 268–70), ... and the *Scythica*, in which the battles between the Romans and the Scythians and worthy deeds are written down by him."[20] Evagrius specifies further that the *Scythica* focused on "Karpoi and other barbarian tribes fighting against Hellas, Thrace and Ionia," probably from Maximus and Balbinus to Aurelian (*c.*238–75).[21] Dexippus' works were widely used by late antique historians, and along with elements of his Thucydidean and annalistic style, they preserve episodes from third-century Greece and Corinth related to the so-called Herulian Invasion of 267/8.[22] Millar argues that Dexippus represents the first of a new generation of Greek historians who present what he calls "a 'Byzantine' viewpoint," that is, history told from the point of view of Greeks, "embattled against the barbarian threat."[23] Dexippus' literary scenarios were repeated by writers covering Greece to characterize interactions with invading barbarians from the Balkans throughout Late Antiquity.[24]

The orators Libanius and Themistius, and the emperor Julian, then make important references to Corinth and to Corinthians in fourth-century imperial service.[25] Ammianus Marcellinus is the most important historian to set alongside them for fourth-century Greece: first on the staff of general Ursicinus under Constantius II, he was with Julian in 360–3, and after the latter's death he returned to his home in Antioch, writing his *History* (*Res gestae*) there and at Rome in the 380s. It was published in parts, the last section after 391, covering Roman history from the acession of Nerva to the death of Valens at the Battle of Adrianople (378). Though he chose to write in Latin, Ammianus certainly visited Greece, and drew on his own experiences there.[26] Other imperial annalists of the fourth century have little to say about Greece.[27] Controversies remain about the relationship of all these writers to putative lost works, and to the enigmatic *Historia Augusta* on the emperors up to Diocletian, compiled *c*.400.[28]

In 395, southern Greece and Corinth suddenly figured prominently again in imperial events, with the descent and then departure two years later of the Goth Alaric and his army, supposedly assisted by the Governor of Achaia. This episode was described at the time in both West and East but, as with the Herulians, the surviving accounts must be carefully assessed as sources for actual events at Corinth.[29] In the west, the poet Claudian at the court of Honorius at Milan composed, performed and published intricate Latin poems, many in honor of this young Emperor of the West and his regent, the Vandal general Stilicho. Claudian wrote panegyrics, invectives, verse histories and other forms, responding directly to events as they happened and pitching them to his audience for the benefit of his patrons and his own glory. He consistently lionized Stilicho and celebrated his military engagements, including his two campaigns against Alaric in Greece: Thessaly in 395 and the western Peloponnesus in 397. A pagan according to Augustine and Orosius, Claudian also wrote on Christian subjects like Easter.[30] He received a statue in Rome, and his poems were widely read, but their historical content must always be read in the context of his poetic and political goals.[31]

These same years of 395–7 in Greece were also treated in the east by Eunapius of Sardis, who left his native city to study in Athens with the sophist Prohaeresius the Armenian, probably in 362–7, then returned home to write and teach with the sophist Chrysanthius until after 414.[32] He wrote the extant biographies *Lives of the Sophists* (*VSoph*) after 395, and a lost continuation of Dexippus' *History* covering the years 270 through 404, excerpted by Zosimus, the *Suda* and the Constantinian collections.[33] This work ended with the exile of John Chrysostom and the death of the Empress Eudoxia, but there was at least one earlier edition ending in 378, and a third as well, with the frequent attacks on Christianity removed.[34] Eunapius was interested in Athens and Attica, the place of his schooling and the venerable Hellenic monuments and traditions which he celebrated and mourned as they passed away; he mentioned Corinth as events there touched on the lives of his sophists, on the events of his political history, and on his particular concern with the decline of Hellenic culture in the face of increasingly militant Christianity in the early fifth century.

Zosimus, *comes* and lawyer for the *fisc*, shared the concerns of Eunapius, one of the main sources for his *New History* covering mythical times down to 410.[35] He seems to have written *c*.500; the latest works he refers to are by authors who wrote *c*.430, and some of his *New History* was published before Eustathius of Epiphania used it *c*.503.[36] Zosimus is our most extensive surviving historical narrative for the years 238–70, relying on Dexippus, and then for 378–410, relying on Eunapius and then Olympiodorus of Thebes. He adapted the accounts of these lost historians to fit his own Polybian style and anti-Christian agenda, but otherwise seems to have preserved much of their content and historical conclusions, though the degree of his dependence remains debated.[37] He is thus essential for the history of Corinth from the 3rd century through 410, after which we have only ecclesiastical sources until the works of Procopius.

In the fifth century, for the first time most authors who mention Corinth are Christians writing in literary genres shaped to its service, genres which persisted for centuries.[38] The commentaries of John Chrysostom on St Paul's *Letters to the Corinthians*, like those of most subsequent writers on St Paul, focused on theology and exegesis, but rarely on contemporary Corinth. Ecclesiastical historians after Eusebius continued to have little interest in Greece, focusing rather on the top of the ecclesiastical and imperial hierarchy. However, surviving clerical letters and *Acts* of Church Councils do reveal the bishops of Corinth as key players in power struggles between the Archbishops of Rome and Constantinople, from the fifth century extending continuously into the middle ages.[39] Christian hagiography may have been written on martyrs from Corinth's Christian community in Late Antiquity, but the texts we have today are largely Byzantine, and of limited historical value for the third or fourth centuries, though their stories seem known to the sixth-century builders of basilica churches at Corinth.[40] There are divisions between Latin and Greek *vitae* and, within the latter, between accounts from before and after the late tenth-century work of Symeon Metaphrastes. His *Menologion* of saints' lives and *martyria* arranged according to the calendar and rewritten in purified high style Greek was influential, and either displaced earlier hagiographies or led to their rewriting.[41]

Procopius was certainly the last historian critical of Christianity, and he is also the last of relevance to this book who mentioned contemporary Corinth, though the historicity of his assertions on Greece as on other matters is hotly debated. It is fair to say that we must constantly choose whether to accept his account of the reasons for the end of many ancient urban institutions at Corinth (and other Greek cities), or come up with an alternative account.[42] He came from Caesarea to Constantinople as a young man, and by 527 was on the staff of Justinian's general Belisarius, with whom he traveled extensively on campaigns to the East (527–31), North Africa (533–4), and Italy (534–40), before settling down in Constantinople, where he probably died in the early 560s. He was, during his lifetime and afterwards, the most widely read historian of the reign of Justinian, for Greece as for the rest of his empire. Procopius first published in 551/2 a *History of the Wars* (*Bell.*), describing the context and conduct of Justinian's contemporary wars against the Persians (two books), Vandals in Africa (two books) and Goths in Italy (three books); then in a final one-book summary written some years later he brought political events up to 552/3.

But besides this traditional history, and apparently as a supplement to it, he composed the *Anekdota* (*Unpublished* or *Secret History*, *Anek.*), a catalogue of the sins he had omitted, both of his boss Belisarius and his wife Antonina, and especially the emperor Justinian and the empress Theodora. The similarity of the start of the *Anekdota* and the eighth book of the *Wars*, and many references back to the events of the *Wars* in the *Anekdota*, clearly link their composition. Procopius also tells us four times near the very end of the *Anekdota* that 32 years have passed since Justinian took up power and certain abuses began, so I agree with the minority opinion that he was then writing in 558/9, and that he began the *Anekdota* around the same time or just after Book 8 of his *Wars*, that is *c*.554–7.[43] He certainly meant to keep it unpublished until the death of Justinian, and it was transmitted in a separate tradition.[44] Beside this combination of history and invective, he turned his hand to panegyric later in life, and his final surviving work is *On the Buildings* (*Aed.*), a flattering enumeration of Justinian's building program throughout the empire in six books, written in 554 or *c*.560.[45] Like many of his predecessors,

Procopius made use of a style of Greek which Atticized, and was deeply indebted to the language, sentiments and style of Herodotus, Plato and especially Thucydides. The lost *History of Philip of Macedon* of Theopompus has been proposed as a precedent for the *Secret History*, but the more recent tradition of rhetorical invective demonstrated by Claudian, for example, is a better basis for comparison.[46] Procopius also points out contemporary Christian or Latinate words like *monachos*, monk, and makes extensive credited and uncredited quotations.[47]

Procopius mentions Corinth and Greece rarely, since his focus is on the wars, the politics of the capital and buildings elsewhere. What he does write is important for its specific content and its wider significance. He is aware of the emerging double meaning of Hellene as both resident of Greece and polytheist (or pagan), and refers to problems associated with this.[48] Cities in Greece including Corinth appear when he enumerates fortifications in his survey of Justinian's building program, and in direct or indirect quotations from ancient authors.[49] Corinth also figures, like other provincial cities, when subject to some notable disaster (in the case of Corinth earthquake and plague) which Procopius can seize upon to indicate divine disapproval for Justinian, and fulfill his goals of invective.[50] In this way he is poised between ancient historians, in his focus on disasters, and Byzantine ones, in crediting them alternatively to Tyche (Fortune) or the Christian God.

The texts of Byzantium itself span historical and literary texts, *ekphraseis* (descriptions) and military manuals, saints' lives and official documents, with registers of Greek style and allusions to both Classical and Christian authors.[51] The focus of most Byzantine texts is Constantinople and its vicinity, but several chronicles and hagiographies incorporate unique information relevant to late antique Corinth. Most important of the *Chronicles* are those of Syncellus and Theophanes. George (the) Syncellus, an advisor (literally cellmate, *synkellos*) of the Patriarch Tarasios (784–806), worked on his *Chronicle* in Constantinople from 808 until his death sometime after 810, writing from the creation of the world up to the reign of Diocletian (284).[52] After his death, the *Chronicle* was carried up through the ninth century by his successor Theophanes Confessor, and then translated into Latin by Anastasius Bibliothecarius.[53] For the third century, Syncellus drew on Eusebius, Dexippus and others; from the fourth to sixth century, Theophanes consulted a range of sources.[54] Later Byzantine chroniclers like Zonaras occasionally include information on Greece not present in earlier sources.[55]

From the Crusades until the arrival of academics and archaeologists at Corinth in the late nineteenth century, there are also Ottoman or Western documentary records and travelogues. From the locals of Corinth themselves we have almost nothing, typical of Greece as a whole in that era. Some Ottoman and Venetian documentary records are published or translated, but their potential contribution to late antique history is mainly beyond my reach.[56] Almost 300 travelogues touching on Corinth exist, most published in the nineteenth century, but a few earlier.[57] The lone published Ottoman traveler, Evliya Çelebi, visited Morea (the Peloponnesus) on his way to Crete in 1668, then *c.*1680 wrote up his *Travel Journal* for an audience back in Constantinople (Istanbul).[58] For Corinth, as elsewhere, he offers a combination of geographic, practical, exotic and antiquarian information, describing (generally favorably) the roads, castle and town, along with the authorities, magnates and general population, with their public and private buildings, agriculture, dialects, clothing and slaves. He copies down Ottoman inscriptions, recounts colorful stories like the attempted ancient cutting of the Corinth canal, and has a passion for numbers and personal detail common to other Islamic travel literature. He gives a unique though brief snapshot of the political, economic and cultural details of everyday life in the Peloponnesus and Corinth just before the late seventeenth-century Venetian invasion.

In contrast to Evliya Çelebi's fulsome praise for the land and people of Corinth, a critique of present Corinth in comparison with its past glories was a persistent trope of western writers from the Grand Tour travelers onwards.[59] Most other travel accounts were composed for Western Europeans, and are often brief, picturesque, and lacking in long-term observation. However, they do preserve evidence about monuments long vanished today, and continuities of urban life at Corinth, though the interests of most European travelers followed their education in searching for the Corinth of Pausanias, or before.[60] Spon and Wheler, Gell, and the detailed observations of Colonel Leake, are particularly helpful for seventeenth- to nineteenth-century Corinthian topography, culture and standing ancient buildings.[61]

APPENDIX II

CORINTH EXCAVATIONS OF THE AMERICAN SCHOOL OF CLASSICAL STUDIES AND LATE ANTIQUITY

The history of archaeological excavation in and around Ancient Corinth includes the extensive Corinth Excavations of the American School of Classical Studies at Athens, the excavations of the Greek Archaeological Service, the Archaeological Society of Athens, and a few other institutions. The areas excavated, methods used and interests of the archaeologists have all changed significantly over the last century, and this is crucial in order to understand the strengths and weaknesses of material culture for charting the history of late antique Corinth.[1] Scholarship on late antique material culture at Corinth has undergone important shifts in emphasis and understanding: from marginalization, to fundamental early work, to equal (or even preferred) study with other periods. Corinth has always been, and remains, an exceptional place in Greece, and the world, for archaeological research. Most excavated material of all periods was catalogued from the very beginning, and is still accessible to scholars; excavation has occurred in almost every region of the ancient city; and, since the directorships of Mr Morgan and particularly Mr Robinson, the post-Roman eras have received significant attention in their own right. All of these factors which influence the course of archaeological research and its use for history of any period are rare at other sites in Greece. In this Appendix, I offer an in-depth account of how material was excavated by the Corinth Excavations under the auspices of the American School of Classical Studies at Athens, with reference also to Greek and other excavations, and a special focus on Late Antiquity.

While the seven standing columns of the Doric Archaic Temple of Apollo on Temple Hill and other scattered remains to the north of the village of Ancient Corinth were always visible, formal archaeological excavation began only in the late nineteenth century. In 1886, Wilhelm Dörpfeld of the German Archaeological Institute (DAI) sunk the first scholarly trenches below the standing columns of the Archaic Temple, and published an account of this work with a history of the Archaic Temple and a plan (noting also the elements of a second monumental Doric temple built into the Roman or Byzantine walls along the northern edge of the city's lower terrace, the Epistyle Wall).[2] He hesitated to assign a deity to the Archaic Temple, though Athena Chalinitis had been suggested by travelers in the past (based on Pausanias), and he mentioned Apollo in connection with the monumental Doric Temple on the lower terrace, which came to be known from Pausanias as the Old Gymnasium area. Dörpfeld suggested further walls there belonged to a church, also seen by Leake and Curtius, perhaps the St Quadratus basilica? Another as yet unexcavated church might have been associated with the Asklepieion and Lerna burials, and near an athletic facility like the stadium or circus by the Old Gymnasium to honor an early martyr. Dörpfeld was followed in 1892 by A.N. Skias of the Archaeological Society of Athens, who dug a number of trenches east of the village center, exposing walls but not the Roman Agora he had sought with the guidance of Pausanias and the early travelers documented above.[3]

The American Excavations at Corinth, begun in 1896 by R. B. Richardson for the American School of Classical Studies at Athens, represent the greatest contribution to archaeology at Corinth. The American Excavations, which continue today, have revealed an unprecedented area of ancient Corinth, and have catalogued by far the majority of the material accessible to scholars today.[4] The history of the American School Excavations at Corinth falls roughly into five eras, based on areas under investigation, methods used, and expertise of the directors and archaeologists involved: Discovery (1896–1924), Interwar (1925–45), War/Postwar (1946–64), Mr Williams (1965–97) and Guy D.R. Sanders (1997–2017).

The first era of discovery included a decade of well-documented annual excavation campaigns (1896–1905), a decade of more sporadic excavation and sparse publication (1906–16) and a series of study seasons devoted largely to non-archaeological issues (1917–24), before excavation began again in 1925 under changed direction, and with new expectation of publication.[5] The American School of Classical Studies at Athens (ASCSA, or the American School) was established in the early 1880s with the assistance of the Archaeological Institute of America (AIA) as a center for American students and faculty of the Classics to study on site in Greece.[6] At first individual directors, students and faculty ran independent excavations at ancient sites during their time at the School's headquarters in Athens, but by 1896 the School was ready to initiate a long-term excavation, for the first two years with the financial support of the AIA, and then later with sporadic funding from private donors and the archaeologists themselves. Richardson, Director of the School, was also from 1896 the Director of the Corinth Excavations, which became the usual pattern until 1966. He was replaced as director in Athens and Corinth first briefly by T.W. Heermance (1903–5), and then after the latter's sudden death by Bert Hodge Hill (1906–26).

In the first decade of the dig (1896–1905), Richardson and then Heermance sought and indeed promptly found ancient buildings which they could relate to Pausanias' itinerary and thus back to the Greek city of Corinth, or at least to the Roman city of St Paul.[7] Their primary professional interest as Classicists was in the Greek city before the Roman sack of 146 BCE, but important secondary interests included the refounded Roman city in its first two centuries, early Christianity, and ancient Art History. In the first season of 1896 they identified the Theater, then in the next years Pausanias' Agora and Road to Lechaion extending north from its northeast corner, with the expected Propylaia in between, Peirene Fountainhouse to the east, and Glauce Fountainhouse to the west. The Archaic Temple's standing columns were assigned to Pausanias' Temple of Apollo in 1896 (not without later doubts), while bare foundations of other temples were identified only by letters as they were found. Temples were only the most easily categorized of the many other ruins emerging from the ground which could not easily be matched up with the account of Pausanias or that of any other ancient author, and so building names were assigned on the basis of location and architecture, usually with reference to the Forum, and not without some confusion and later changes. By the time Heermance died of typhoid in 1905, the Lechaion Road Basilica and Shops, Captives' Façade, Northwest Shops, Northwest Stoa and West Shops had all been partially uncovered and named (Figures 4–6).

The excavation of all these buildings followed the same basic methodology. For a few months each spring a network of long, narrow exploratory trenches was excavated, reaching outwards from around the Archaic Temple, or, later on, farther afield. These trenches were widened only if a physically solid and recognizably ancient monument was encountered. The monuments were then cleared of earth, and sometimes masonry deemed post-Roman, and identified as to age, use and ancient name on the basis of Pausanias, their architecture and the artifacts found around them. The emphasis was on discovery, and the archaeologists were generally quick to assign a title to buildings associated with their function and first use. Actual digging was done by large (100 +) teams of local diggers working with picks and shovels, supervised by one archaeologist per trench. He (or sometimes she) recorded in greater or lesser detail the area and progress of the digging along with notable sculpture, coins, whole ceramics and other obvious artifacts in a numbered notebook. Artifacts from Neolithic pottery to Byzantine inscriptions were numbered separately according to genre, with most sent to the museum built by the Greek state early in the twentieth century (now the Old Museum).[8] Then the earth and stone removed from the trenches was taken away in railroad cars along narrow-gauge track and dumped in a rented beanfield to the north of the Archaic Temple (where it remains today). Many walls and artifacts were drawn, and specific relationships between items described, but recording style varied enormously at the beginning, from bare weekly lists to detailed diaries of daily discoveries.[9]

Richardson and the other early excavators were generally professional Classicists and, along with their students, interested in specific ancient historical eras, authors and art. The explicit goal for most was the recovery of buildings and artifacts from the Greek city of Corinth, the city before its destruction and refounding, with remains from the Roman colony and later periods inevitable, more easily identifiable and still of interest, but less preferable for most. This attitude was (and to a large extent still is) tied in with wider issues in Classical Archaeology, and a whole range of Enlightenment attitudes about the relative value of Greek, Roman and Byzantine literature, philosophy, architecture, art, politics and ethics, as well as the perceived loss of dominance in these fields by the Greeks under the influence of Rome, Christianity and autocratic rule.[10]

Though Hill was director from 1906–26, actual seasons of excavation took place only in 1907–11 and 1914–16, and several Roman buildings were added then to the map: Philostratus' Odeum above the Theater, and Pausanias' Peribolos of Apollo and Roman Baths (of Eurykles?) just north of Peirene. There were many more non-Pausanian buildings too, like the Julian Basilica and Southeast Building on the east side of the Forum. Archaeological progress was first slowed and then stopped, however, by a combination of factors: the perennial problems of funding and publication, and the more specific challenges of wars and water. Specifically, the latter flowed constantly and often copiously out from Peirene spring, but its interruption by archaeology led to flooding and pestilence, only stopped at great cost.[11] No digging at all took place at Corinth from 1917 to 1924, but Hill continued to study what had been found, and to enlist others to assist as well. He is credited with introducing more modern excavation methods to Corinth at the end of this era, and remained working at the site and contributing to its study long after his replacement as director.[12]

A few early scholars, like E.H. Swift, were interested in Byzantine Corinth, which for them (as for the modern Greek state) began with Constantine, but their ability to differentiate Byzantine archaeological remains from Roman or even post-Byzantine ones was not yet well developed.[13] There was at first little dating by stratigraphy or seriation; instead, readable coins, generalizations about construction methods and broad categories of ceramic decoration helped locate the excavators in time, at Corinth as elsewhere in that era. Thus Byzantine coins, glazed pottery and Christian symbols betrayed late levels; rubble masonry, vaulting and *spolia* late architecture, but the transition between Roman and Byzantine was never well defined. Almost all so-called late artifacts were catalogued and kept, regardless of their Antiquity, but some late architecture, like walls, graves, roadways, churches or parts of standing buildings, was demolished, albeit with considerably more documentation than at other contemporary excavations in Greece, particularly after Hill assumed the directorship.

Thus the results of this first era of excavation for Late Antiquity were mixed. Hundreds of inscriptions and works of sculpture from the second to sixth centuries were uncovered and catalogued, though many could not be securely linked to a specific building or stratum; the situation was similar for late antique coins, pottery and other small finds, many of which came from much later levels.[14] As for the buildings themselves, much Roman and late antique masonry vanished into the beanfields along with that from Byzantine or later eras. Most notably gone today are the phases of the Peirene fountainhouse from the fifth century on, and the third-century vaults of the north section of the West Shops. The emphasis during excavation season was to clear ancient buildings of overlying dirt, and sometimes post-Classical modifications or phases were cleared as well. Architectural plans of the building in its first phase were then drawn, subsequent phases noted, and catalogues of artifacts compiled, but stratigraphic sequences or complex histories of use were not yet possible.

In 1925, the second era of the excavations was inaugurated, with several important changes. Hill was replaced as American School and Corinth director, first by his student Carl W. Blegen (1927), then by Rhys C. Carpenter (1928–31), Richard Stillwell (1932–5) and Charles H. Morgan II (1936–8). In the Forum Area, buildings partly uncovered were exposed by intensive clearance excavations up to the outbreak of World War II, some (like the South Stoa) were named, and most Byzantine levels were recorded before removal.[15] But while the director usually supervised the main excavations, other archaeologists like T. Leslie Shear and Oscar Broneer began to work semi-independently on the site under American School auspices, and the area under exploration thus widened significantly, leading to the discovery of many late antique buildings outside the Forum Area.[16]

Just to its west, Broneer (under Benjamin D. Meritt's direction) began uncovering the Odeum in 1928; Shear had already started on the Theater in 1925, moving from the *skene* (stage building) and orchestra to the *cavea*.[17] Shear also uncovered part of a Roman villa at the northwest corner of the lower terrace at Kokkinovrysi in 1925, and a series of Roman and earlier tombs further north (the first of hundreds).[18] Blegen also branched out with his own team, conducting excavations up on Acrocorinth in 1926 which yielded much medieval material which was carefully studied. In 1928,

Carpenter found the first late antique church of the excavations, the Cenchrean Gate (or Kraneion) Basilica, while looking for the East Gate of the Classical city walls (Figures 3, 8). On the northern edge of the lower terrace, de Waele dug the Sanctuary of Asklepios, along with its numerous late antique burials, and the fountain court to its west which was associated with Pausanias' Lerna (Figures 3, 7). An urban plan of Corinth thus began to take shape, and it was primarily the city as it was at the end of Late Antiquity, with one large excavated area still widening out from around the Archaic Temple, and many smaller areas, or windows down into the ancient city, opening up all around it. Corinth thus became one of the most extensively excavated cities in all of Greece.

Methods remained massive in scale, with five to ten archaeologists overseeing over 100 workmen most seasons, and dirt carried away by the railroad carload. There were institutional and financial pressures to remove Byzantine remains, to publish the Classical and Roman periods of the Forum/Agora or Central Area, and then make it accessible and intelligible to visitors. But recording became more scrupulous too in these years, as Hill, Blegen and then Carpenter introduced and advanced Dörpfeld's and Wheeler's methods of recording all that was recovered by stratigraphic excavation.[19]

But while the area under excavation was quick to expand and deepen in the Interwar era, scholarly interests and publications were slower to follow suit. Carpenter emphasized in his excavations, directorship, scholarship and publications "things Greek," and it is clear that he saw these as anterior to the Roman sack of Corinth. But he still devoted considerable attention to his excavation of a Christian basilica and much of the Byzantine city center, built what he planned as a Byzantine Museum in the excavated shell of a tenth-century house found on the far eastern side of the Central Area by Peirene, and supervised the publication of Byzantine landmarks elsewhere in Greece.[20] Long time Corinthians also left in this era: Shear had the unique opportunity to initiate excavations in the Athenian Agora in 1931, while in 1927 Blegen followed his interest in prehistory to Troy and then Pylos, and in 1952 Broneer shifted focus to nearby Isthmia.

Yet in this second era of excavation, Corinth also began to attract attention from scholars specifically for its Roman and Byzantine monuments and well organized artifacts. Recently, Kostis Kourelis has argued that scholarship on these eras emerged at Corinth between

1925 and 1940 as part of a "modernist aesthetic" which Byzantine art historians shared with modernist artists and writers in the US and Greece.[21] The most important of the scholars working at Corinth on Byzantine archaeology in this era, through 1953, was Mr Morgan. Though a specialist in Classical art, he pioneered the rigorous analysis of Corinth's Byzantine pottery, creating a unique, original typology which was impossible at other sites, and then publishing his study of that pottery in what immediately became a standard reference work.[22] Edward Capps Jr. studied late antique ivories before moving to work at Corinth, then published on the Hellenistic and Roman city and its sculpture, sadly leaving the catalogue of sculpture found at Corinth since 1923 unfinished and unpublished at his death in 1969.[23]

This second era also brought the first articles on late antique Corinth in *AJA*, and in the ASCSA's own new journal, *Hesperia*.[24] Beyond renewed excavation, comprehensive publication of the work already done at Corinth was a major priority for Edward Capps, Chair of the Managing Committee of the ASCSA, and he pursued it by removing Hill from his directorship in 1926, getting his replacement Carpenter to bring out a guidebook to Corinth in 1928, and assigning Harold North Fowler to organize publication of the finds from Corinth in the first of the *Corinth* volumes.[25] Carpenter's guidebook was subsequently revised by Broneer and then Henry Robinson, but no new version has appeared since the 1960s, leaving tourists at the site largely cut off from progressing scholarship since then.[26] A new Corinth guidebook was announced by the American School in 2004; with a change of authorship, it is now due to be published in 2017, bringing the results of academic study of the site to a wider public.[27] The *Corinth* volumes were originally intended to form a complete record of the American excavations, but in practice they represent an impressive yet partial publication of masses of material filtered through frameworks of topograpy, artifact typology and scholarly interest. Several include brief sketches of Corinthian history, but the emphasis throughout is on the description and analysis of specific buildings (mainly of the Forum/Agora) and types of material (pottery, lamps, inscriptions, sculpture).

The first generation of *Corinth* volumes issued up to and through World War II was largely focused on the publication of the Early Excavations, those of Richardson, Heermance and Hill until 1926.

Among the general architectural volumes, late antique Corinth frequently appeared in the phases as the last use of a building or area being described; but almost all of the corpora of artifacts included late antique material, a substantial amount in the case of Mr Morgan's Byzantine pottery volume, as well as the inscription and lamp volumes.[28] The coin volume unusually contained all coins from the excavations, through the Byzantine and even Ottoman issues, and was soon supplemented by regular reports which have made Corinth one of the only sites in the world with extensive numismatic publication.[29] Two volumes of this first generation focused exclusively on Roman buildings, though the general preference in publication remained Greek rather than Roman, typology rather than narrative.[30]

In the 1940s many scholars devoted more time to publication because excavation in Greece was curtailed by the War; some material from after 1926 crept in to the *Corinth* volumes, and closer dating became possible. The fruit of this wartime work was thus a second generation of *Corinth* volumes which appeared in the two decades after the end of the War; these filled out the architectural publications so that almost every building dug was now represented in print. However, they brought only two sets of artifacts up to the War itself: minor finds and inscriptions.[31]

In 1957, Scranton devoted an entire volume to the architecture of late antique, Byzantine and medieval Corinth. This volume did not appear until sixty years after excavation began, but there was more than enough architectural material to fill it, primarily from the early excavations alongside short historical summaries drawn from Bon and Finley's works of the 1930s.[32] The dating of the various phases was very loose, and largely based on readable coins, but Scranton's volume was also unique for its era, and represented a desire to see all the excavated architecture of Corinth's center published at a time when this was still not typical for sites in Greece. He also collected almost all of the clearly post-Antonine and pre-Ottoman architecture from the city center in one volume, at the cost of considerable effort on his part (see Figure 6). Most of the Byzantine walls he described were long gone by then, but a huge mass of artifacts, especially sculpture, was presented systematically.[33]

Besides publication, some digging resumed at Ancient Corinth after World War II under Broneer (to 1952) and Morgan (to 1953); excavations resumed on a large scale only in 1959 under Director

Henry S. Robinson.[34] Broneer returned with much of the pre-war Corinth crew in 1946 to clean up the site, restore the old and current museums, complete publication of the Central Area and the Asklepieion, and continue excavation on a necessarily smaller scale (first under Scranton in the area north of the old Panayia Church (now north of Panayia Field)).[35] Yet between 1950–8, the new American School Director Caskey chose to pursue excavation at prehistoric Lerna near Argos, rather than at Corinth as previous directors had done. Broneer moved to Isthmia (see below), and work by those at Corinth concentrated on publication. When new director Henry S. Robinson reopened excavations in the Corinthian Forum/ Agora in 1959, it was with an unprecedented goal: the excavation and recording of Byzantine Corinth in its previously unexcavated southwest corner.[36] Robinson's tenure as director also saw the excavation of parts of the Great Bath on the Lechaion Road, the Roman market south of Hill House, the Anaploga Villa or Sanctuary, Roman tombs and the underground water systems of Corinth. He also revived the pre-war tradition of separate excavations outside the city center, under American School auspices but led by other directors.

Thus on the slopes of Acrocorinth south of the Central Area, Ronald S. Stroud began a small excavation in 1961 where ancient material had previously turned up. This quickly proved to be the Sanctuary of Demeter and Kore (and the Fates) as mentioned by Pausanias, and excavation continued through 1975, with a final clean up in 1994, first directed by Stroud and then also Corinth Assistant Director Nancy Bookidis.[37] The modern excavation methods, prompt publication and interest of the excavators in the Roman phases of the sanctuary lend this small area of the city of Corinth extra weight in the archaeological record of Late Antiquity. The *Corinth* volumes and articles devoted to the Sanctuary of Demeter and Kore admirably take architecture and artifacts from the site up and into Late Antiquity, although the exact dating and preferred interpretation of these remains debated.[38]

Although work continued in the Sanctuary of Demeter and Kore, the later 1960s otherwise witnessed major changes in areas, goals and methods for the American School Excavations at Corinth. American universities were invited to open up new areas of the city, and the main excavation in the city center was for the first time under its own director, Charles K. Williams, II, who first held this position separate from the director of the American School of Classical Studies at Athens, until his retirement in 1997. He trained many fellows of the ASCSA in archaeology yearly, with some invited to stay on and work on material from the site.[39] In the city center, he sought again the Greek levels of the city below the level of the early excavations, excavated Greek and Roman phases East of the Theater, and opened up an important medieval 'Frankish' area southwest of the Forum.[40]

Mr Williams excavated and published on all eras of the city, Late Antiquity included, and also worked to make the Corinth Museum and Hill House Library suitable for scholarship on all eras.[41] Though his own scholarly interests lay initially in the Greek city, its architecture and cults, he studied the Roman and medieval city extensively too, especially its religion and architecture. He published preliminary reports of his work yearly in *Hesperia*, and introduced School members every year to modern excavation methods, the long span of Corinthian history and the detailed system of Corinth notebooks as developed by himself and Bookidis. He also designed and built new facilities for the Corinth Excavations, and encouraged a new generation of scholars to take on dissertations and publication projects of every era left unfinished by the pre-war generation, now largely deceased or no longer on-site.

This was also an era of renewed expansion of excavation, for the first time under separate University sponsorship and School auspices. In 1965 John K. Anderson brought a team from U.C. Berkeley to the north side of the temenos of Temple E, while James R. Wiseman of U.T. Austin opened up excavations north of the Theater at the edge of the lower terrace, where Pausanias had located the ancient Gymnasium.[42] While Anderson chose not to return, Wiseman dug in this northern Gymnasium area yearly through the summer of 1970, generating a mass of late antique buildings and artifacts, published up until now mainly in preliminary reports, and on which his own work and that of his students and others is ongoing.[43] The uneven publication of this northern area of Corinth remains a challenge for understanding the urban landscape between the Theater and the Asklepieion (Figures 3, 7).

Mr Robinson continued working at Corinth, conducting salvage excavations along the north edge of the lower terrace, in advance of the construction of an aqueduct, while still director (early 1960s), and then as emeritus director bringing a team from Case Western

University to dig on Temple Hill, where he discovered a Middle Byzantine church (1968–78).[44] In this era two more churches were investigated on the north side of the city by E.G. Stikas of the Archaeological Society of Athens, both cemetery basilicas originating in the sixth century. Stikas named one Skoutela from its area, down on the plain to the north of Ancient Corinth, and the other St Quadratus/Agios Kodratos from its likely dedicatee, and he published plans and general descriptions of both of them (Figures 3, 8).[45]

Mr Williams passed the torch in 1997 to current Director Guy D.R. Sanders, inaugurating the fifth and current chapter in the ASCSA Corinth Excavations. In the Corinth Museum, Assistant Director Ioulia Tzonou-Herbst replaced Assistant Director Emerita Nancy Bookidis in 2003, and welcomed a new generation of scholars alongside the old to work on research and publication at Corinth. In 1995, Sanders reopened excavation in the area of the Panayia Field where the Greek Service had hit ruins. This area is southeast of the Forum, south of the ruined Panayia Church area (now under the basketball court), just south of where Broneer and Scranton excavated in 1946–7. In regular seasons of excavation there from 1998 to 2007, he excavated (among monuments of many other eras) several of the important Late Roman buildings and contexts hinted at by the earlier American School trench and Greek Service excavations, in particular a third- to fourth-century domus (or urban villa), a small sixth-century bath and a monumental sixth-century structure, perhaps part of a Christian basilica or other ecclesiastical building (the Long Building) (Figures 2.2–2.3).[46] He has pursued modified open-area single-context excavation to bring unity to excavation of whole buildings and contexts, and analyzed stratigraphy and assigned dates on the basis of pottery chronologies established by the latest research.[47] These excavations were carried out by ten to fifteen local professional excavators alongside five to ten American School members working on a volunteer basis and at first recording baskets and finds in traditional numbered Corinth notebooks. This yielded a slower and smaller scale area of excavation, with much more recovery of small and delicate finds, and a deeper understanding of specific questions of stratigraphy and chronology.

Although Sanders' own research interests lie in the fields of geography, archaeological science and post-Roman pottery, he has strongly promoted research into material from all eras of archaeology at Corinth, the use of Corinthian material for historical writing, and the digital publication of Corinthian excavation data.[48] It was due to our common interests in Late Antiquity that my Ph.D. advisor, epigraphist and former Corinth excavator Ronald S. Stroud, suggested I work with Sanders at Corinth. I was a Regular Member of the American School in 2003–4, and excavated in the Panayia Field in 2004 and 2005 before pursuing the Ph.D. research that led to this work as an Associate Member from 2005–8. Though my time at Corinth means I worked closely with Sanders, Tzonou-Herbst and architect James Herbst in the Museum, I also met and became familiar with the work of their predecessors Mr Williams and Nancy Bookidis. They have all provided important feedback on the ideas developed here, and their eras of activity at Corinth have shaped my own approaches as well as my knowledge of past work at the site. In the spring of 2007, Sanders closed excavation at Panayia Field, and from 2007–13 he directed excavations south of the South Stoa and South Basilica, in another area with great potential for late antique, Byzantine and medieval discoveries (mainly domestic, but also including the intersection of the Lechaion Road with the *Decumanus Maximus*). From 2014–17, he directed further excavations in the Frankish Area and the New Apotheke site west of the Theater. He has also modernized recording methods and initiated larger-scale use of sieving, flotation and soil analysis. The excavation methods currently employed at Corinth are available in print in the new *Corinth Excavations Archaeological Manual*.[49]

Finally, there is one last other source of archaeological data in the Ancient Corinth, the salvage excavations in advance of construction, notably along the aqueduct (1960s), the new Athens-Patras railway line (2000s) and the new highway line (2010s), all running just to the north of the lower city terrace edge. Construction in the village of Ancient Corinth also necessitates yearly salvage work. These salvage excavations were conducted by the American School for the Nauplion Ephoreia until the late 1960s or early 1970s. Since that time, the Archaeological Service has employed excavators under both the 37th (Lambda Zeta) Prehistoric and Classical Ephoreia and the 25th Byzantine Ephoreia, uncovering artifacts, graves and many, many ancient walls around the city, some apparently belonging to late antique villas.[50] Some of this material is still visible in open trenches, and published in newspapers, the *Deltion*, or surveys of the archaeology of the Corinthia as a whole.[51] Since 2014, the Corinth Museum has had a formal program of educational outreach, with lesson plans available online.[52]

A third generation of *Corinth* volumes has appeared in smaller numbers from the second half of the 1970s onwards. The sole architectural volume (aside from the results of the Sanctuary of Demeter and Kore mentioned above) is the Great Bath on the Lechaion Road; the two sculpture volumes devoted to the Theater finds included late antique sculpture.[53] Most Roman or late antique artifacts found up to the 1920s were published in the first generation volumes, with publication coverage much more uneven since then. The articles in the Corinth Centenary volume, along with the Work in Progress list on the Corinth website, give an idea of those areas related to Late Antiquity where work is ongoing and where there are gaps.[54]

The Corinthia outside the ancient city has also been explored by survey or excavation under archaeologists representing the American School, the Archaeological Society of Athens, or the Archaeological Service of the Hellenic Ministry of Culture. These efforts have provided important evidence for the late antique landscape which supported the city. Overviews of the ancient topography of the whole Corinthia relevant to Late Antiquity include those by Nikolaos Faraklas, made in 1971 for Doxiadis' project at the Athens Center of Ekistics, and James Wiseman, published in 1978 but based on his own walks and those of American School colleagues, especially Ron Stroud, in the 1960s.[55] Gregory and colleagues have conducted intensive survey projects: on islands in the eastern Corinthian Gulf (1981–4), along the Saronic Gulf coast between Isthmia and Kenchreai (1982–3), on islands in the western Saronic Gulf (1986–92), at a number of locations in the Eastern Corinthia with the Eastern Korinthia Archaeological Survey (EKAS, 1997–2003), and in the southeastern Corinthia with the Saronic Harbors Archaeological Research Project (SHARP, 2007–9).[56]

Short and long excavation campaigns guided by literary sources, historical significance and standing remains have reached out of the ancient city of Corinth to Acrocorinth, onto the Isthmus, and into the ancient harbor areas of Kenchreai and Lechaion. The most intensive excavations in the Corinthia, outside of the ancient city center, lie on the eastern side of the Isthmus, at the ancient sites of Isthmia and Kenchreai (Figures 9–10). The general area of ancient Isthmia (modern Kyras Vrysi) was identified early on from standing stretches of the eastern end of the late antique Hexamilion Wall and its prominent tetragonal eastern fortress.[57] But the Sanctuary of Poseidon, site of the Isthmian games, was only disconnected from the fortress when the latter was recognized as late antique in 1932–3 by R.J.H. Jenkins and H. Megaw, digging there for the British School at Athens.[58] The Sanctuary itself was discovered when Broneer famously hit the foundations of the Temple of Poseidon with his very first trench for the University of Chicago excavations there in 1952.[59] He thus initiated the first postwar excavation in the Corinthia under the auspices of the American School, combining short excavation campaigns with long-term study and publication by a large team of scholars. Between 1952 and 1967, Broneer uncovered the Temple of Poseidon and adjacent religious, athletic and domestic buildings, confronting the challenges of a site largely leveled by construction of the Hexamilion Wall and its Eastern Fortress.[60] He initiated a numbered series of final volumes like the *Corinth* series for Isthmia divided by building and type of artifact, and published on late antique lamps, Roman buildings and St Paul.[61] Broneer's successor Elizabeth R. Gebhard assembled a team of scholars to work on the material from Isthmia, directed its publication, and continued excavation in the Sanctuary, in 1989 co-directing a dig with F.P. Hemans which focused on the Late Roman phases of the Sanctuary.[62] She published on the Theater at Isthmia, brought John Hayes to the site to study the Roman and late antique pottery, and continues to interpret the excavation of the area around the Temple of Poseidon and direct its publication with the assistance of Jennifer Palinkas.[63]

From 1967, a second team began work by the Eastern Fortress alongside Broneer (and later Gebhard), at first under Paul Clement of UCLA (a wartime colleague of Broneer at the Institute for Advanced Study in Princeton), and since 1987 under Timothy E. Gregory of The Ohio State University. These scholars had an interest in the Hexamilion Wall and its Eastern Fortress, and the periphery of the Sanctuary; especially under Gregory, they excavated and published with an emphasis on the late antique period.[64] Their work exposed and elucidated Roman to Byzantine aspects of Isthmia in the area around the Roman Bath and Hexamilion Wall and Fortress. Both Gebhard's and Clement's teams co-operated in the construction of the museum at the site which opened in 1978, and which has recently been renovated, while Gebhard and Gregory edited papers together from a conference about Isthmia.[65]

American excavation expanded south from Isthmia in 1962 when Robert L. Scranton and E.S. Ramage began joint University of Chicago and University of Indiana excavations at the ancient harbor of Kenchreai (1962–9), digging mainly around masses of Roman masonry on the moles on the northeast and southwest sides of the natural cove, into shallow water, and making finds both spectacular and ordinary, which they published in a series of popular and scholarly articles, and five excavation volumes.[66] Work continued to the north of the harbor under Scranton, and was renewed by Joseph L. Rife and Elena Korka in the Roman-era cemetery on the Koutsongila Ridge just to the north (2002–).[67] The mostly Roman and late antique archaeological material from Kenchreai was analyzed to a certain extent by the excavators, who had research interests in the Roman period, but the identifications of the buildings uncovered and their historical and religious significance remains under discussion, as does the topography of Kenchreai in Late Antiquity.

American projects at Isthmia and Kenchreai have thus been relatively constant since the 1950s, and have uncovered extensive Late Roman settlements and monuments. Yet excavation at Corinth's ancient western port of Lechaion has been much more sporadic, though almost entirely late antique. Greek, American and European archaeologists have exposed only small parts of the artificial harbor and its town outside of the Lechaion Basilica.[68] The most extensive excavations, by Demetrios Pallas for the Archaeological Society of Athens, exposed the foundations of this largest Christian basilica in all of Greece, but these excavations were published only in preliminary reports before his death.[69] Mr Pallas also conducted other small but important Late Antique investigations all over the Corinthia in the 1950s–70s, including further work on the Kraneion Basilica.[70] His work is now being published and continued by scholars from the Greek Archaeological Service, the Archaeological Society, Aristotle University of Thessalonike and the local Corinthian authorities.[71] Since 2014, Dimitris Kourkoumelis of the Underwater Ephoreia and Bjørn Lovén of the Danish Institute at Athens have led the Lechaion Harbour Project, exploring the undersea moles and harbor areas. Since 2016, Paul Scotton has directed archaeological exploration for the Lechaion Harbor and Settlement Land Project on behalf of the American School of Classical Studies at Athens.

NOTES

Introduction Significance, Scholarship and Structure

1. Corinth Museum inv. nos. S-920 (priest's head), S-909 (bearded head) and S-919 (cross-marked head). For further images and excavation data on these and other finds listed below from the ASCSA Corinth Excavations, see the website ascsa.net and enter the inventory number (inv. no. or Corinth Excavations Notebook (NB) number). For public sculpture and its disposal in Corinth in Late Antiquity see Chapter 5, Amelia R. Brown 2012a, 2016a, 2016b; Betsey Ann Robinson 2011, 281–92.
2. Late Antiquity here corresponds with an era of ancient history variously called Late Roman, Early Christian, Early Byzantine or early medieval, extending in *political* terms from the end of the Severan Dynasty of Roman emperors in 235 to the murder of the usurper emperor Phocas in 610. The subsequent emperor Heraclius founded a new dynasty and lost political control over much of his Eastern Roman (Early Byzantine) Empire to invading Avars, Slavs and Muslim Arabs. These political markers, along with changes in material culture, signal a shift to Late Antiquity from the Roman Empire of the early third century, and then to the Middle Byzantine or medieval era of the early seventh century. Late antique Corinth was always officially a city of the Roman Empire, ruled from Rome, and then from Constantinople, by Roman emperors. This was still the case until the Crusader (or at Corinth the Frankish) era of the thirteenth century, and then the Venetian and Ottoman conquests which preceded the foundation of the modern Greek state in the nineteenth century. The history of Corinth in Late Antiquity starts in the later second and early third century, with the high Roman Empire, with Corinth near the geographic center of the Empire, and contributes our greatest concentration of literary and monumental

evidence. Since much of the ancient (especially archaeological) evidence can be dated only within a century, the scope of this study is from that era to roughly the later sixth and early seventh century, before the Avar and Slav invasions and Arab raids.

3. Pausanias 10.5.3. Only in the middle of the nineteenth century was Corinth's civic center transferred northwards down to the shore of the Corinthian gulf, between the ancient western harbors of Lechaion and Poseidonia. When many Corinthians moved there, new settlers from the hills in the southern Corinthia resettled the village of Ancient Corinth, atop the ruins of the ancient, late antique, Byzantine, Frankish, Venetian and Ottoman civic center, and welcomed the archaeologists.
4. John Chrysostom, *Homily on the First Epistle to the Corinthians* Argument 1–2 (*PG* 61, 9), ed. Schaff 1898 (*NPNF* 12).
5. For Byzantine Corinth, and the Peloponnese, see Avraméa 1997; Anagnostakis and Kaldellis 2014.
6. Cameron 1991; Brown 1992; Horden and Purcell 2000.
7. Gibbon 1788 (1994); Jones 1964; Brown 1971; Heather 2005; Ward-Perkins 2005.
8. Avraméa 1997, 72–9; Sanders 2003b.
9. Morgan 1942 (*Corinth* XI); Hayes 1972; Slane and Sanders 2005.
10. Alcock 1989, 1994.
11. Scranton 1957 (*Corinth* XVI).
12. Carpenter 1928; Finley 1932; Fowler and Stillwell 1932 (*Corinth* I); Davidson 1937; Davidson 1940; Weinberg and Weinberg 1946; Charanis 1952; Davidson Weinberg 1974, 1975. See further details in Appendix II.
13. Slane 1987, 1990 (*Corinth* XVIII.2), 1994, 2000, 2003, 2004, 2012, 2015, 2017 (*Corinth* XXI).
14. Pallas 1954 (1957), 1957, 1967, 1979 (1981), 1990; Pallas and Dantis 1977 (1979).
15. Avraméa and Kyrkou 1988; Avraméa 1997; Athanasoulis 2013; Athanasoulis and Manolessou 2013; Kissas 2013.
16. Sanders 2002a, 2003b, 2004, 2005, 2014; Slane and Sanders 2005.
17. Besides his excavations and surveys focusing particularly on Roman and late antique material at and around Isthmia (see Appendix II), Gregory has published extensively on late antique Greece and Corinth, for example on popular violence (Gregory 1983, 1984), fortifications (Gregory 1979, 1982), the Slavic invasions (Gregory 1992, 1994), and the Christianization of Greece (Gregory 1986, 2013a). He has recently moved forward into the study of the early modern Corinthia: Gregory 2007, 2013b.
18. Rothaus 1992, 1994, 1995, 1996, 2000; Rothaus et al. 2008; Kardulias 1995, 2005; Kardulias et al. 1995; Moore 2000; Caraher 2003, 2014, 2015; Caraher and Gregory 2006; Caraher et al. 2006;

Frey 2006, 2008, 2015a, 2015b, 2016; Frey and Gregory 2016; Pettegrew 2006, 2007, 2008, 2011, 2014, 2015, 2016. The festschrift for Tim Gregory (Caraher et al. 2008) has important articles on late antique Corinth.

19. Histories of Greek Corinth which usefully employ Pausanias and the Corinthian landscape include O'Neill 1930; Will 1955; Salmon 1984; Dubbini 2011; Dixon 2014; Pettegrew 2016. Unpublished Ph.D. theses on Roman Corinth include Darrow 1906 (to Herodes Atticus); Bagdikian 1953; Mary E. Hoskins Walbank 1986a (to the death of Commodus).
20. Amandry 1988 (Corinthian administration through its coinage, updated by Mary E. Hoskins Walbank 2003, 2010a, 2015); Williams 1989; Mary E. Hoskins Walbank 1989, 1996, 1997, 2010a, 2010b; Rizakis and Zoumbaki 2001; Rizakis and Lepenioti 2010; Romano 1993b, 1994, 1996, 1998a, 2000, 2003, 2010; Romano and Schoenbrun 1993; Romano and Tolba 1995; Romano and Stapp 1998.
21. Appendix II.
22. Appendix I.
23. Williams and Bookidis 2003 (*Corinth* XX).
24. Schowalter and Friesen 2005; Friesen et al. 2010; Friesen et al. 2014.
25. Gebhard and Gregory 2015.
26. Kissas and Niemeier 2013.
27. Rothaus 2000; Scotton 2002. See also Brown 2016b for revisions to Rothaus' data and assertions about sculpture in late antique Corinth.
28. Engels 1990, extending unevenly into the third and fourth centuries.
29. Pettegrew 2016.
30. Recent scholarship on late antique cities: Lavan 2001a. Byzantine cities in Greece: Bouras 2013.
31. For an archaeological-style report on a late antique city describing buildings and linking them with short historical summaries, such as Scranton wrote for Corinth, see for Athens: Frantz 1988 (*Agora* XXIV). For forced links between such reports and historical events: Snodgrass 1987.
32. Conference volumes on late antique urbanism: Lavan 2001c; Lavan & Bowden 2003; Bowden et al. 2006; Krause & Witschel 2006; Dally and Ratté 2011 (Asia Minor).
33. Synthetic studies of specific cities in Late Antiquity include Di Branco 2006 (Athens); Spieser 1984 (Thessalonike); Curran 2000; Lançon 2000 (Rome); Haas 1997 (Alexandria); Downey 1961; Liebeschuetz 1972; De Georgi 2015 (Antioch), Poulter and Blagg 1995 (Nicopolis ad Istrum); Hattersley-Smith 1996 (five Macedonian cities).
34. The ancient Greek city through Late Antiquity: Jones 1940 (1988); Tomlinson 1992.

35. Spieser 1982 (Greece); Liebeschuetz 2001; Saradi 2006 (sixth century); Zavagno 2009 (sixth to ninth century); Leone 2007, 2013 (North Africa); Jacobs 2013 (Asia Minor).
36. Mango 2008. Different views on the role of the Mediterranean Sea for civic change: Braudel 1995, 2001a, 2001b (early modern); Horden and Purcell 2000 (Antiquity). See now Abulafia 2011 (ancient to modern); Broodbank 2013 (prehistoric).
37. Saradi 2006; Dey 2015, 19.
38. Caraher 2010.
39. History of late antique archaeology: Lavan 2003a.
40. See the articles in Friesen et al. 2014 for the application of these interests to Corinth.
41. Hansen and Nielsen 2004; Hansen 2006a.
42. Lavan 2001c.
43. Lightfoot 2012; Osland 2016; López Quiroga 2016.
44. Pausanias 10.4.1, cited by Wycherley 1962, xix–xxi; Alcock 1995; Crow 2016. For ideal civic institutions at the transition from Hellenistic to Roman eras of writing about architecture, see also Vitruvius 1.3.1. For inscriptions and archaeology of ancient Panopeus, modern Agios Vlasios, see Rousset et al. 2015.
45. For late antique urban "activity areas" see Lavan 2003b, 2003c.
46. For the recovery of processes (and post-processes) not just spaces and objects in Greece see Pettegrew 2007.
47. Late antique urban political life and administration: Jones 1964; Matthews 1985; Avraméa 1997; Lavan 2006; Lenski 2006.
48. Late antique urban economy: Jones 1964, 1974; Whittaker 1983; Wickham 1988; Hendy 1985, 1989; Reynolds 1995; Fulford 1996; Hodges and Bowden 1998; Parkins 1997; Moore 2000; Kingsley and Decker 2001; Ward-Perkins 2001; Cartledge et al. 2002; Kingsley 2003, 120–5.
49. Late antique urban religion: Lane Fox 1987; Trombley 1993; Lieu 2004; Frakes and Digeser 2006; Busine 2015. Late antique urban culture and society: Jones 1964; Storey 1999; Wickham 2001.

Chapter 1 Landscape and Civic Authorities in Late Antique Corinth

1. Topography of Corinth: Thucydides 1.13.2–6; Strabo 8.6.20–22 (378–80); Pausanias 2.1–5; Miliarakis 1886; Fowler and Stillwell 1932 (*Corinth* I), 18–114; Sakellariou and Faraklas 1971; Wiseman 1978; Kordoses 1981; Pettegrew 2016. For landscape's significance for the writing of history, see Avraméa 1997, 41–50 (earthquakes and erosion in the Byzantine Peloponnese); Zangger 1996 (Argolis); Rackham and Moody 1996 (Crete); Rackham 1983 (Boeotia); Cary 1949 (Greece).

2. The Corinthia has been a political and geographic entity since early in Antiquity, always including the Isthmus but varying in its precise borders in the mountains to both north and south. For the borders of the Greek *polis* (city-state) of Corinth, see O'Neill 1930, 1–58; Will 1955; Salmon 1984; Dixon 2014. For Roman Corinth, see Earle Fox 1903; Darrow 1906; Broneer 1941; Wiseman 1979; Mary E. Hoskins Walbank 1986a, 1986b, 1997; Engels 1990; Romano 2000, 2003; Pettegrew 2016. For Byzantine Corinth, see Avraméa and Kyrkou 1988; Sanders 2002a. For Ottoman Korintos or Kordos, see Beldiceanu and Beldiceanu-Steinherr 1986; MacKay 1968; Shariat-Panahi 2015. For the modern Greek *nomos* of the Corinthia, see Miliarakis 1886; Kordoses 1981.
3. The Corinthian Gulf north of Corinth is split by the Perachora (or Peraean) peninsula into the Halcyonian (Livadostra) Bay to the north and the Lechaion (Corinthian) Bay to the south; Lechaion and modern Corinth border on the latter, along with the small harbor of the Heraion west of Loutraki (ancient Thermai).
4. Strabo 8.6.21–2, 9.1.8; Pausanias 1.1.3, 1.44.4–10, 2.1.1–5; Scylax *Periplus* 55. See Wallace (1969, 496) on the accuracy and organizing principles of Strabo's description of the Corinthia based on the view from Acrocorinth, with the text extended by Aly 1956. See Wiseman (1978, 20–2) on the Corinthia north of the Isthmus.
5. On Mt Oneion and Stanotopi to the south of the Isthmus see Xenophon *Hell.* 4.4.5; Stroud 1971; Caraher and Gregory 2006. On the southeastern Corinthia see Dixon 2000, 51–122, 273–86.
6. Leake 1830, 3.397; Strabo 8.6.23–5 (382); Pausanias 2.5.4–5.
7. Acrocorinth: Blegen et al. 1930 (*Corinth* III.1); Carpenter and Bon 1936 (*Corinth* III.2); Athanasoulis 2009.
8. On the terraces or tables of Ancient Corinth, and this fertile agricultural plain: Strabo 8.6.21; Aristophanes *Birds* 967–8; Livy 37.31.1; Lucian *Icaromen* 18; Athenaeus 5.219.
9. Lechaion: Georgiades 1907; Paris 1915; Shaw 1969; Rothaus 1995; Stiros et al. 1996.
10. Kenchreai: Thucydides 4.42, 8.20; Ovid *Trist.* 1.10.9; Strabo 8.6.22 (380); *Acts* 18:18, *Rom.* 16:1–2, *Constitutiones Apostolorum* 7.46.10; Pliny *NH* 4.4.10, 4.5.12; [Dio Chrysostom] Favorinus 37.8; Pausanias 2.2.3; Apuleius *Met.* 10.35–11.25; Ptolemy 3.16.13; Ambraseys 1962, 899–900; Hohlfelder 1976; Scranton et al. 1978 (*Kenchreai* 1); Bousquet, Dufaure and Pechoux 1983; Mourtzas and Marinos 1994; Noller et al. 1997; Rife et al. 2007.
11. Geology of the Corinthia: Hayward 2003; Higgins and Higgins 1996, 40–5; Landon 1994, 13–20; Collier and Dart 1991; Collier and Thompson 1991; Collier 1990; Koukis 1990; Keraudren and Sorel 1987; Vita-Finzi and King 1985; von Freyberg 1973; Admiralty 1945, vol. 3:161–6.

12. For Corinthian quarries, see Hayward 2003. Corinthian stone was exported in Antiquity to Delphi (*FD* 3.5 (1970), no. 19.27–8) and Epidauros (Burford 1969, 142–3, 179).
13. Whitbread 2003.
14. H. S. Robinson 1962, 126; Landon 1994, 3–20, 2003; B.A. Robinson 2001, 2011.
15. The gulfs are *Graben* or rift valleys filled with water. Individual earthquakes cause surface deformation along the line of the fault itself; vibrations can travel farther, but are limited by the length of the fault and the composition of the earth around and above it. For tectonics and faulting in the Corinthia and Central Greece, see Ambraseys and Jackson 1997; Ambraseys 1996; Armijo et al. 1996; Roberts and Jackson 1991; Taymaz et al. 1991; Ambraseys and Jackson 1990; Papaphotiou 2002; Stiros and Pirazzoli 1995; Pirazzoli et al. 1994; Guidoboni et al. 1994; Collier et al. 1992; Pirazzoli 1988; Flemming and Webb 1986; Papadopoulos and Chalkis 1984.
16. Ambraseys 1996, 30–2. Range and effects of modern earthquakes in Corinthia: Ambraseys and Jackson 1997; Ambraseys and Jackson 1990; Jackson and White 1989; Stiros 1988.
17. Noller 2001, 143–70; Ambraseys and White 1997; Vogt 1993; Rapp Jr. 1986, 365–79.
18. Miller 1986, with quake data from Drakopoulos (1983, 17–23).
19. Libanius *Or.* 18.292; Zosimus 4.18.
20. Rothaus 1996.
21. Jerome *Comm. Is.* (*PL*) 24.15.168, *Vita Hill.* 29.1, *Chron.* 244c.
22. Ammianus 26.10.15–9.
23. *IG* IV 674; Feissel and Philippidis-Braat 1985, 274–5, no. 9 (with notes and French translation by Feissel); Avraméa 1997, 44.
24. Malalas 17.15 (418), trans. Jeffreys et al. 1986: "In that year (520/1) Corinth in Hellas also suffered; and the emperor graciously gave much there too." For the inscription, Corinth Museum inv. no. I–1987–3, Sironen 2016 (*IG* IV^2 3), no. 1259, see Chapter 5.
25. Procopius *Anek.* 18.41–5.
26. Procopius *Aed.* 4.2.23–4.
27. Procopius *Bell.* 8.25.16–23.
28. For belief in the effects of the climate of Greece on its inhabitants in Antiquity, see Aristotle *Pol.* 1327b29–33; [Hippocrates] *Airs, Waters and Places* 1–24. For the winds of the Corinthia, see Aristotle *Metrologika*; Hesychius s.v. Ἀνεμοκοῖται (*Anemokoitai*).
29. Climate and vegetation of the Corinthia: Dallman 1998, 169–202; Mariolopoulos 1961; Philippson 1948. More detailed studies have been done on Boeotia (Rackham 1983), Crete (Rackham and Moody 1996) and Attica (Thompson and Griswold 1982).
30. Stroud (pers. comm. 2005) recalls "very substantial logs" still being cut from the fir trees east of Perachora village and Bisia in the 1960s.

31. On ancient forestry, and the ship-building timbers of fir, pine and cedar, see Theophrastus *Enquiry into Plants* 5.7–8; Philippson 1892; Watkins 2014.
32. Leake 1830, 1:76–7, 132, 258, 349–50; Forbes 1976; Foxhall et al. in Alcock and Osborne 2007, ch. 3.
33. For the great antiquity and continuity in Greece and the Corinthia of mixed agriculture (or mixed farming, or polyculture) of annual field crops, perennial grove crops and herd animals to reduce risk, see Renfrew 1972; Forbes 1976, 1995; Fotiadis 1985; Halstead and O'Shea 1989; Palmer 2001; Hjohlman 2002 (Berbati Valley); Sanders 2014.
34. Çelebi *Travel Journal* (trans. MacKay 1980, 12).
35. Corinthian cash crops went from radishes in Antiquity (Theophrastus in Athenaeus 2.56) to currants in the Middle Ages. The word currant is derived from the toponym Corinth (Sanders 2002a; Chrysostomides 1995, 497, no. 253, 1402.5.23). For agriculture in the nineteenth- to twentieth-century Corinthia see Leake 1830, vol. 3:262–3; Sanders 2014.
36. Stroud (pers. comm. 2005) points particularly to the area around Penteskouphia village where this sort of earth-moving has created new fields but led to the abandonment of old roads.
37. For Byzantine food and drink, see the papers collected in Brubaker and Lindardou 2007. Ottoman Corinthia: Beldiceanu and Beldiceanu-Steinherr 1986; Shariat-Panahi 2015. Agriculture of neighboring areas since Antiquity: Forbes 1982; Mee and Forbes 1997 (Methana); Forsell 2002; Alcock in Alcock and Osborne 2007, ch. 4 (Argolis); Zarinebaf, Bennet and Davis 2005, 9–48 (eighteenth-century Messenia).
38. Laiou 2002; Laiou and Morrison 2007; Sanders 2014.
39. Sanders 2014, with reference to Salmon (1984, 130) and Engels (1990, 27). Blegen (1920, 13) enumerated the agricultural production of the village of Ancient Corinth in the early twentieth century, while Pouqueville (1805, viii–ix) said the Corinthia provided 18% of Peloponnesian wheat exports *c.*1800. Gallant (1991, 77) gives yields of wheat and barley for the Corinthian *nome* in the twentieth century similar to those for Argolis or Attica (Gallant 1991, 77), while Osborne (1985) collects evidence from Demosthenes and other ancient authors for ancient yields from Attica.
40. Vineyards: Strabo 12.3.36. Harsh wine: Athenaeus 1.30f (Kock 1884 (*CAF*), 2.401) for quotation from Alexis, Middle Comedy playwright, on Corinthian wine, also preserved in Eustathius *Commentarii ad Homeri Iliadem* 2, 180 on 13.664.
41. Engels (1990, 79–84) introduces some questionable figures on urban density and demography to arrive at 100,000 for the Roman Corinthia, and cites the 85,000 of Salmon (1984, 165–9) for the

population of the Classical city. Wiseman (1978, 10–2) argued that the Roman Corinthia had a similar or larger population than the Classical city, and cited the Cyrenean grain distributions of *SEG* 9, no. 2 (Tod 1962 (*GHI*), 2.196) to estimate 130,000 in 330–26 BCE. Sakellariou and Faraklas (1971, 83–7) made an estimate of 66,000–73,000 in 400–390 BCE based on the population in the nineteenth century. Beloch (1886 (1968), 86, 119–23) made an estimate of 80,000–100,000 at the beginning of the Peloponnesian War based on hoplite numbers. For strategies for making estimates of Greek city-state populations, see Hansen 2006b. The 2001 population of the modern Corinthia was about 160,000. Romano (2010, 171) agrees with Mark E. Hoskins Walbank (1997) in positing some 1,500–3,000 adult male colonists arriving in 44 BCE to refound Corinth; if each colonist had one wife, one slave and two children, then about 15,000 came in the first century BCE. Romano also argues persuasively for wider centuriation of new farmland under Vespasian, and population growth, so 30,000 is a rough estimate for the second-century city.

42. For civic administration of Corinth through 267, see Wiseman 1979.
43. Jones 1940, 208–10, notes 104–5, citing *Cod. Just.* 1.4.17, 19 (505) and *Monumenta Asiae Minoris Antiqua* III, no. 197A, an early sixth-century constitution, probably of the emperor Anastasius, on these changes from Korykos (Cilicia).
44. Oliver 1953; Burton 1975; Lintott 1993.
45. The Roman province of Achaia included the Peloponnesus, Attica, Boeotia, Locris and Phocis, the heartland of Hellas, and areas not coincidentally described by Pausanias in his *Guide to Greece*. The name Achaia was taken from the Hellenistic Achaian League, which eventually had Corinth as its capital, although it originated in the region of Achaia, the northwestern shore of the Peloponnesus. According to Pausanias (7.16.10), the name was given to the province because the Romans defeated the Achaian League last of all the southern Greeks.
46. The governors of Achaia were collected by Groag 1939, 1946. For the equestrian governors of Achaia, see Groag 1946, 22; Davenport 2013. Achaia was established as a senatorial province in 27 BCE, then taken away, and finally returned to the Senate by Claudius in 44: Dio 60.24.1; Suetonius *Claud.* 25; Larsen 1933, 437–8. Support for the Governor of Achaia as only a *praeses* under Diocletian is found in the three fragmentary plaques to Diocletian, Maximian and Galerius dedicated by Lucius Sul. Paulus, in the dedication to Diocletian identified as *v(ir) p(erfectissimus) praes(es) pr[ov(inciae) Ach]aiae*. See Chapter 5, and, for the dedication to Diocletian: Dean 1922, 467, no. 48, fig. 13; West 1931 (*Corinth* VIII.2), no. 23; Groag 1946, 15; Jones et al. 1971 (*PLRE*), I.685 s.v. Lucius Sul. Paulus II;

Rizakis and Zoumbaki 2001, 385, COR 578; Sironen 2016 (*IG* IV^2 3), no. 1247.

47. Julian *Panegyric to Constantius* 18D, *Or.* 1.6, 1.8; Millar 1969, 15; Frantz 1988 (*Agora* XXIV), 16–17.
48. See Deligiannakis 2005, 399, for dedications to Constantine and his family from Greece: Tegea: *IG* V.2, no. 139; Feissel and Philippidis-Braat 1985, no. 1, 272, no. 4 (Constans); Thespiae: *AE* 1928, no. 57 (Constantine as Caesar); *IG* VII, nos. 1848–9 (Constantine II, Constantius II); Delphi: Vermeule 1968, 428, nos. 2–3; *AE* 1948 no. 50 (Dalmatius); *SEG* 22, no. 469 (Constans); Aegosthena: Vermeule 1968, 432, no. 1 (with Licinius); *SEG* 23, no. 267 (Constantine II); Gargalianoi: Feissel and Philippidis-Braat 1985, 270, no. 2 (Constantine and Caesars, 323–6); Priniko, Laconia: Feissel and Philippidis-Braat 1985, 272, no. 5a (Constantine with Caesars); Amarynthus, Euboea: *IG* XII.9, no. 146; Athens: Sironen 1994, 26, no. 10, 2001, no. 5 (Constantine?), no. 2 (Dalmatius?), no. 1 (Constantine II), nos. 3–4 (Constantius II, with Julian), nos. 2–4 (Constans); Aidepsus: *SEG* 29, no. 801 (Constantine II).
49. Constans base, for a statue set up 337–50: Corinth Museum inv. no. I-2143, Kent 1950; Scranton 1951 (*Corinth* I.3), 147, pl. 67.3; Kent 1966 (*Corinth* VIII.3), no. 510; Feissel and Philippidis-Braat 1985, no. 3; Sanders 2003; Sironen 2016 (*IG* IV^2 3), no. 1250.
50. Wiseman (1979, 501) says the evidence is "still not conclusive" that Corinth was the capital of Achaia, and he is followed by Haensch (1997, 322–8).
51. Oliver 1968.
52. Apuleius *Met.* 10.18.1: *caput est totius Achaiae provinciae.*
53. Ael. Aristides 46.24: καὶ κοινὸν ἄστυ τῶν Ἑλληνών, οἷον μητρόπολίς τις ἀτεχνῶς καὶ μήτηρ αὐτὸ τοῦτο. Further support for Corinth as capital of Achaia: Dio Chrysostom *Or.* 31.105–6.120–123; Cass. Dio 55.27.6;
54. Corinth Museum inv. no. I-1205, Broneer 1933, 562; *SEG* 11, no. 125; Kent 1966 (*Corinth* VIII.3), no. 269. The base was found at the east end of the Forum, the area outside of the Southeast Building, probably the archives building where Favorinus said his portrait once stood (see Chapter 2).
55. Malalas 10.46 (261), "Corinth, the metropolis of Hellas," under Vespasian, and again thus in Theophanes 168 following Malalas 17.15 (418). The sixth-century geographer Hierocles in his *Synecdemus* 10: Κόρινθος ἡ ποτε Ἐφύρα μητρόπολις πάσης Ἑλλάδος.
56. Corinth Museum inv. no. I-902, Philadelpheus 1918 (1921a), 5, no. 8; *SEG* 1, no. 64; Meritt 1931 (*Corinth* VIII.1), no. 10; *IG* IV, no. 364; *Syll.*^{3} 904; Bees 1941, 13–5, no. 5; *SEG* 11, no. 59a; Groag 1946, 58–9; Jones et al. 1971 (*PLRE*), 1.525 s.v. Fl. Ulpius Macarius (6); Rizakis and Zoumbaki 2001, 318, COR 275; Sironen 2016

(*IG* IV^2 3), no. 1814. This marble stele was recarved into a fountain in the early modern era, and recovered from a house in *Diavatiki* (Korakou) between Lechaion and modern Corinth.

57. Max 1918, 90.
58. Roman procurators, proconsuls (governors) and a quaestor in inscriptions from Corinth: Meritt 1931 (*Corinth* VIII.1), nos. 75–6, 80–3; West 1931 (*Corinth* VIII.2), nos. 64 (quaestor), 53–75 (governors, others of senatorial rank); Kent 1966 (*Corinth* VIII.3), nos. 119–29 (governors, others of senatorial rank up to 267 CE), 130–48 (procurators up to 267 CE). Add also the texts of after 267 CE discussed by Sironen including Corinth Museum inv. no. I-1354, Kent 1966 (*Corinth* VIII.3), no. 118 (Honors for proconsul (governor) Illyrius, late third century).
59. See Michael B. Walbank 2010, 270–5, with full bibliography.
60. See Michael B. Walbank 2010, 271–8, notes 24 (bathhouse keeper, from the Asklepieion, Kent 1966 (*Corinth* VIII.3), no. 534; Feissel and Philippides-Braat 1985, no. 55), 27 (text mentioning an inspector of weights from the Lechaion Road Shops, Meritt 1931 (*Corinth* VIII.1), no. 158; Feissel and Philippides-Braat 1985, no. 16), 41 (muleteer Theodore, first inscription: from Stimanga, *IG* IV, no. 437; Feissel and Philippides-Braat 1985, no. 104), and 56 (muleteer of the bishop Theodore, second inscription: from Kraneion, Pallas and Dantis 1977 (1979), no. 8; *SEG* 29, no. 311; Feissel and Philippides-Braat 1985, no. 99).
61. *NotDig.* 1.21: *Sub dispositone viri spectabilis proconsulis Achaiae provincia infrascripta: Achaia. Officium autem habe ita: Principem de scola agentum in rebus ducenarium, qui adorata clementia principali cum insignibus exit transacto biennio. Cornicularium, Commmentariensem, Quaestorem, Adiutorem, Ab actis, Numerarios, A libellis, Exceptores et ceteros apparitores. Proconsul Achaia IIII,* "Under the control of the *vir spectabilis* the *proconsul* (governor) of Achaia is the following province: Achaia." For the authority and staff of Roman governors, see Mierow 1926; Roueché 1998; Slootjes 2006.
62. Corinth Museum inv. nos. I-817, 1109, 1110, 1275, 1602b, Kent 1966 (*Corinth* VIII.3), nos. 507b-f; Feissel and Philippides-Braat 1985, no. 11.
63. Corinth Museum inv. no. 1602a, Kent 1966 (*Corinth* VIII.3), no. 507a; Feissel and Philippides-Braat 1985, no. 11; Sironen 2016 (*IG* IV^2 3), no. 1241.
64. Corinth Museum inv. no. I-2684, Sironen 1992, 223–6, no. 2; *SEG* 42, no. 262; Sironen 2016 (*IG* IV^2 3), no. 1242.
65. *IG* VII no. 24; *SIG*^{3} 908; Sironen 1992, 225–6; *IG* IV^2 no. 1130B.
66. Corinth Museum inv. no. I-1211, Kent 1966 (*Corinth* VIII.3), no. 514; Feissel and Philippides-Braat 1985, no. 49*; Sironen 2016 (*IG* IV^2 3), no. 1243. The title also occurs in Sironen 2016 (*IG* IV^2 3), no. 1252, for Flavius Genethlidius Justus.

67. *IG* VII, no. 26; *SIG* II^3 909; Groag 1946, 77–8.
68. *IG* II^2 5205. Frantz (1979, pl. 64:f) suggests that it is the *Diogenion* refurbished as a gymnasium *c.*400, and also brings in the inscription Epigraphic Museum no. 1861, of similar lettering, found nearby, and possibly from the same building, or another also restored in the early fifth century.
69. Thompson 1950, 1959; Thompson and Wycherley 1972 (*Agora* XIV), 211; Travlos 1971, 233, fig. 37; Frantz 1965, 1969, 1979 (Herculius as statue, patron of Palace), 1988 (*Agora* XXIV), 21–3 (ceramic and coin evidence for Palace construction).
70. For the early Corinthian Christian community, their martyrs and their bishops, see Delehaye 1907; Max 1918, 51–5; Grégoire 1950; Scranton 1957 (*Corinth* XVI), 3–5; Concannon 2014. The *Acta Sanctorum* April vol. 2, 619, lists the first Corinthia martyr as Timon of Veroia, burned at Corinth by the Jews. There are first-century bishops Apollo, Sosthenes and Silas, the late first-century letter of Clement (trans. Kleist 1961), and most crucially the documents collected in Eusebius *HE* 3.4, 4.21, 4.23, 4.24 and 5.23 on the second-century bishops Apollonius, Primus, Dionysius and Bacchylos, who held the first church synod at Corinth. For the letters of bishop Dionysius collected by Eusebius as evidence for the late second-century Christian community at Corinth, see Concannon forthcoming. For the history of the Christian Church at Corinth, see Gritsopoulos 1972.
71. In the Middle Byzantine era, the sees of Illyricum, including Corinth, were transferred to the authority of the Archbishop of Constantinople (Avraméa 1997, 100–1) and the Corinthian diocese was reduced to the eastern half of the Peloponnese when the bishop of Patras became a Metropolitan (Yannopoulos 1993).
72. Rothaus 1992, 1996, 2000.
73. Limberis 2005.
74. Helikonis: *Acta Sanctorum* March 10, vol. 2, 4; *Acta S. Synaxarum Ecclesiae Constantinopolitanae* 1902 (ninth to tenth century), 435. Victorinus et al.: *Menologion* in *PG* 117, 288.
75. Tymonis, Gaius, Crispus: *Parvum Romanum*, ed. Quentin 1908 (1969) (ninth century).
76. Palladius *Lausiac History* 65, trans. Clarke 1918, 171–3.
77. For trials of Christians in the third century, see Lane Fox 1987.
78. Scranton 1957 (*Corinth* XVI), 1–7.
79. Brown 2011b, 2012b.
80. John Chrysostom *Homily on the First Epistle to the Corinthians* Argument 1–2 (*PG* 61, 9), ed. Schaff 1898 (*NPNF* 12).
81. John Chrysostom *Homily on the First Epistle to the Corinthians* 35.4 (*PG* 61, 302), ed. Schaff 1898 (*NPNF* 12), 212.

82. Millar 2006; Limberis 2005.
83. I thank Nancy Bookidis for this suggestion.
84. Pietri 1976, 2.1106–8 (*NPNF* 14.21, 2nd ed.).
85. Letters: Boniface *Ep.* 13, *PL* 20.770; Pietri 1976, 2.1113.
86. *CTh* 16.2.45 (*CJ* 1.2.6, 11.21.1), trans. Pharr 1952, 449.
87. Boniface *Ep.* 10–1, *PL* 20.769–71; Pietri 1976, 2.1118–9.
88. Carpenter 1929, 359.
89. Bon 1951, 8–9; Letters to Pope Leo VII, trans. Hunt 1957, 149–50.
90. *PG* 115.919–44; Limberis 2005, 455–6.
91. Stikas 1961 (1964), 131–2, fig. 3a; Feissel and Philippidis-Braat 1985, no. 35 (epitaph inscribed in two phases, as two different scripts, the first of the fourth/fifth century, and then the second of the fifth/sixth century); Sironen 2016 (*IG* IV^2 3), no. 1494. Michael B. Walbank (2010, 276–8, note 54) credits Mary E. Hoskins Walbank with the plausible suggestion that "the bishop died and was buried" in the fourth/fifth century, then was moved to the church when it was built in the late fifth or early sixth century, with a new line to the inscription added.
92. Rapp 2005.
93. Corinth Museum inv. no. I-2508, Pallas and Dantis 1977 (1979), no. 7; *SEG* 29, no. 302 (dated *c.*536); Feissel and Philippidis-Braat 1985, no. 36 (text and French translation); Michael B. Walbank 2010, 276, note 55 (sixth or seventh century). The prayer reads: "Grant, Christ, to Photius, who is bishop by grace of his goodness, mercy, peace and remission of his sins. …"
94. Corinth Museum inv. no. I-1970, Bees 1941 (*CG-CIH* I.1), 20–1, no. 7; Kent 1966 (*Corinth* VIII.3), no. 568.
95. Michael B. Walbank 2010, 275–80. But, regarding the subdeacon, *subdiaconus*, Anastasius, in the epitaph of Maria wife of Euplous, Sironen (2016 (*IG* IV^2 3), no. 1785) says that this is not the translation for *hypeerétou*. See Feissel and Philippidis-Braat 1985, no. 34.
96. Michael B. Walbank 2010, 275–80, n. 74; Kent 1966 (*Corinth* VIII.3), no. 563; Robert 1966, 765–7; Feissel and Philippidis-Braat 1985, no. 67; Sironen 2016 (*IG* IV^2 3), no. 1465 (Sironen translates as *olitor*).
97. Letters of Gregory, Ind. 11, nos. 6, 38, 39; Max 1918, 92; Setton 1950, 519. For further on Gregory's emissaries to the Patriarch: Marcus 1970.
98. Letters of Gregory, Ind. 13, nos. 52, 57–8; Setton 1950.
99. Scranton 1957 (*Corinth* XVI), 46, n. 25; Michael B. Walbank 2010, 272–4, notes 33–5 on Meritt 1931 (*Corinth* VIII.1), nos. 208 and 207 (Feissel and Philippidis-Braat 1985, no. 22).
100. Archbishop of Corinth Stephanos was at the 6th Church Council of 680 as representative of the Pope; another Archbishop of Corinth in

689 served on an embassy from the Patriarch of Constantinople to Rome (Bon 1951, 103–4). No Archbishop of Corinth is recorded at the 7th Council of 787, but this may have been due to his attitude to icons.

Chapter 2 The Forum and Spaces of Civic Administration

1. The *Corinth* series of excavation volumes published a description of every ancient building of the Forum found in the early excavations, up to the posthumous Hill 1964 (*Corinth* I.6) on the fountains. H. S. Robinson and then Mr Williams returned to excavating in the Forum in the 1960s. Besides their archaeological reports, see Scotton on the Julian Basilica (1997, 2016a, 2016b, forthcoming) and B. A. Robinson on the fountains (2000, 2001) and especially Peirene (2011).
2. Caesar's refounding: Diodorus 32.27; Crinagoras of Mytilene *AnthPal* 9.284; Strabo 8.4.9, 8.6.23, 17.3.15; Plutarch *Caesar* 57.5; Appian *Punica* 136, *Roman History* 8.20; Pausanias 2.1.2; Dio 43.50.3–5; Zonaras 9.31; Mary E. Hoskins Walbank 1986a, 1986b, 1997, 2003.
3. Under the Flavians, briefly renamed *Colonia Iulia Flavia Augusta Corinthiensis*, probably in gratitude for earthquake relief, perhaps accompanied by expansion of centuriation and agriculture in the Corinthia (Romano 2000, 2003, 2010). Epigraphic evidence in Kent 1966 (*Corinth* VIII.3), nos. 82 (*Flavia*), 96, 130, 314. Earle Fox (1903) favored *Corinthus*, followed by the early excavators, but this was corrected by Broneer (1941) following the excavated inscriptions to *Corinthiensis*.
4. Initial layout of Corinth's colonial Forum: Wiseman 1979, 509–21; Mary E. Hoskins Walbank 1986a, 1986b, 1997. Romano (1998b, 2010) argues that the colony of Corinth was made up of four centuries, each of 32 by 15 *actus*, 240 *iugera*, with the Forum at the center, made up of 6 *actus* from each, for a space of 24 square *actus*, or 12 *iugera*, a fairly small proportion of the urbanized area. As Vitruvius 5.2.1 recommends, the Forum had a 3:2 proportion. Williams and Russell 1981 date the paving of the Forum to the second half of the first century, from Mr Williams' excavations by the racecourse.
5. Racecourses: Morgan 1937, 549–51; Broneer 1942; Williams and Russell 1981; Romano 1993a.
6. These are only the pre-existing Greek buildings that we know about from excavation and Pausanias, but there were likely others, for example, on the heights to the east, south of the South Stoa, west of Glauce and north of the Theater. It is unclear if pre-Roman cults like Athena Chalinitis were revived in their original location, or

relocated. General continuity of cult deities and architecture between Greek and Roman Corinth is demonstrated by Lisle 1955; Bookidis 2005; Melfi 2016. Mary E. Hoskins Walbank (1997, 2010a, 2010b) emphasizes the *romanitas* of the early colony's cults, and questions how much knowledge of the old Greek gods and cults survived, and how. By Late Antiquity, the religious landscape appears re-Hellenized, with connections actively sought with pre-Roman Hellenic religion in the second to fourth century.

7. Among the early excavators, only Skias (1892 (1894)) sought both the Greek Agora and the Roman Forum east of the modern village, while at least from Richardson (1900a, 1900b) through Morgan (1939, 255), American excavators placed the Greek Agora under the Roman Forum.
8. Scranton 1951 (*Corinth* I.3), 74–6, 134; Williams 1970, 32–7, 1987, 474.
9. Donati 2008, 2010. Dubbini 2011 discusses the evidence with reference to the Archaic cults there.
10. Terrain: Hayward 2003.
11. Northwest Stoa, north of the Northwest Shops: Stillwell et al. 1941 (*Corinth* I.2).
12. Pausanias 2.3.2 (Lechaion Road, Propylaia), 2.3.6 (Sikyon Road), 2.4.6 (Acrocorinth Road).
13. Macellum: built by Q. Cornelius Secundus under Augustus or Tiberius, dedicatory inscription in Kent 1966 (*Corinth* VIII.3), no. 321; West 1931 (*Corinth* VIII.2), no. 124. Bronze foundry: Stillwell et al. 1941 (*Corinth* I.2), 27–31.
14. Earthquake of 77/8: Corinth Museum inv. no. I-14, West 1931 (*Corinth* VIII.2), no. 20; Suetonius *Vesp.* 17; Malalas 10.46 (261), trans. E. Jeffreys et al. 1986; Scotton 1997, 192–5 (Julian Basilica cryptoporticus jacked up then reinforced, Forum NE repaved); Williams and Zervos 1984 (resoration of Theater's eastern vomitorium, Terrace Building).
15. Peribolos of Apollo: Pausanias 2.3.3; Stillwell et al. 1941 (*Corinth* I.2), 1–54; Slane 1994.
16. Millis 2004; Bookidis pers. comm. 2008.
17. Northwest Shops: Stillwell et al. 1941 (*Corinth* I.2), possibly built in the first century.
18. Latin to Greek language transition: Kent 1966 (*Corinth* VIII.3), 19; Millis 2010, 2014.
19. Propylaia: Sears 1902, 439–54; Fowler and Stillwell 1932 (*Corinth* I), 159–92; Scranton 1951 (*Corinth* I.3), 151. The most recent study is by Charles Edwards (1994), who argues for an Augustan triple-arch, rebuilt as a single arch and decorated *c.*117, with coins of Hadrian depicting this second phase in honor of Trajan's Parthian campaign (for coins see Edwards 1933 (*Corinth* VI), 30, no. 129).

20. Pausanias 2.3.2. One of many legends connected with the bronze horses of San Marco in Venice has them coming from this Propylaia under Constantine, who demonstrably transported much statuary to Constantinople from other areas of Greece. Enea Vico in 1558 attributed the San Marco horses to Corinth, along with other bronzes in Italy like the doors of the Pantheon (quoted in Perry 1975, 207). For the horses, see also Perry 1977; Perocco 1979; Jacoff 1993; Freeman 2004.
21. Captives Façade: Richardson 1902b; Fowler and Stillwell 1932 (*Corinth* I), 150; Stillwell et al. 1941 (*Corinth* I.2), 55, 88; Scranton 1957 (*Corinth* XVI), 5; Hill 1964 (*Corinth* I.6), 118; Vermeule 1968, 83–8, 1986 (favors Alexander Severus); Ajootian 2008 (favors Lucius Verus). Von Hesberg (1983, 234–6) and Schneider (1986, 130, 1998, 115) argue the relief bases used in this Façade were reused from an Augustan monument linked to the recovery of the Standards from the Parthians (20 BCE), while Rose (2005, 53–4) links it rather with Gaius' campaigns of *c*.10–1 BCE.
22. For the Roma Monument, erected after Hadrian's Roman statue of 136/7, see Kent 1966 (*Corinth* VIII.3), no. 352; H. S. Robinson 1974; Stirling 2008. Possibly to be linked to this Roma Monument's base, or to a second free-standing statue of Roma, is a fragment of bare shoulder with drapery: Corinth Museum inv. no. S-158, Johnson 1931 (*Corinth* IX), 67, no. 116; Ridgway 1981, 443.
23. Broneer 1951a.
24. South Stoa: Broneer 1951; Broneer 1954 (*Corinth* I.4); Weinberg 1960 (*Corinth* I.5); Price 1967; Hayes 1973; Scahill 2012, 2016. Central Shops: Broneer 1935, 57; Broneer 1947; Scranton 1951 (*Corinth* I.3), 1957 (*Corinth* XVI).
25. Broneer 1951a, 1954 (*Corinth* I.4), 114.
26. Sakellariou and Faraklas 1971, 140.
27. Wiseman 1979, partly based on Bagdikian 1953.
28. Scotton 1997, 262–7, with reference to David 1983.
29. *Acts* 18.11–2; Broneer 1951a, 91–2.
30. Julian Basilica, Southeast Building: Weinberg 1960 (*Corinth* I.5); Scotton 1997, 2005, 2015, 2016a, 2016b, forthcoming. South Basilica: Weinberg 1960 (*Corinth* I.5). Lechaion Road Basilica: Fowler and Stillwell 1932 (*Corinth* I), 150; Stillwell et al. 1941 (*Corinth* I.2); Scranton 1957 (*Corinth* XVI), 5; Hill 1964 (*Corinth* I.6), 118.
31. Inscriptions from the Julian Basilica in Scotton 1997, 244–55. Dedications to the imperial family include Corinth Museum inv. nos. I-632 + (West 1931 (*Corinth* VIII.2), no. 13, updated by Scotton 2005 (*Caesares Augusti*)), I-653/689 (Kent 1966 (*Corinth* VIII.3), no. 69 (Augustus)), I-688 (West 1931 (*Corinth* VIII.2), no. 17 (Gemellus, Antonia, *Gens Augusta*)), I-694 + (Kent 1966 (*Corinth* VIII.3), no. 81 (Nero)), I-725 (West 1931 (*Corinth* VIII.2), no. 44 (auGVST)), I-711

(West 1931 (*Corinth* VIII.2), no. 45 (aVGVST)), I-695 (West 1931 (*Corinth* VIII.2), no. 51 (caeSARI)) and I-2259 (Kent 1966 (*Corinth* VIII.3), no. 91 (auguSTO/imPERAtori)). Other deities: Corinth Museum inv. nos. I-585 (West 1931 (*Corinth* VIII.2), no. 4 (Apollo?, Genius of the Colony and colonists)), I-726 (West 1931 (*Corinth* VIII.2), no. 5 (Genius of the Colony)), I-699 (West 1931 (*Corinth* VIII.2), no. 10 (Nemesis)) and I-567 (Kent 1966 (*Corinth* VIII.3), no. 61 (SACRVM)).

32. The recognizable imperial portraits are Augustus (Corinth Museum inv. no. S-1116), his grandsons Gaius and Lucius (Corinth Museum inv. nos. S-1080 and S-1065), and a head which may be Nero (Corinth Museum inv. no. S-1088). Two partially draped heroic nude male torso fragments were found, probably Julius Caesar as Jupiter (Corinth Museum inv. no. S-1098), and perhaps originally Claudius (Corinth Museum inv. no. S-1052), along with many fragments of *togati*, limbs and drapery. In Scotton forthcoming, de Grazia Vanderpool argues that the majority of the sculpture was Julio-Claudian, and a female fragment may represent Julia or Octavia. One cuirassed torso (Corinth Museum inv. no. S-1081) came from the Julian Basilica, while another was found southwest of the SE Building (Corinth Museum inv. no. S-1125); both have deeply recarved neck holes to take multiple later imperial portrait heads. On all this sculpture see Swift 1916, 1921a, 1921b, 1921c, 1922, 1923; Johnson 1931 (*Corinth* IX), 70–85, nos. 134–58; de Grazia 1973, 16–20, 87–121, 302–4, 314–9, 328–33, nos. 10–13, 99, 103, 107–8; Ridgway 1981, 434; Pollini 1987; Scotton 1997, 255–61, 2016a.
33. For the bust see Corinth Museum inv. no. S–1141, Johnson 1931 (*Corinth* IX), no. 322 (fourth-century); de Grazia 1973, 339–40, no. 113, pl. 112 (fifth- or sixth-century); Ridgway 1981, 448, n. 103. The very battered head is Corinth Museum inv. no. S-1118, which de Grazia (1973, 121–2, no. 14) suggested was Julio-Claudian. One other bust from Corinth may be wearing a *chlamys*, Corinth Museum inv. no. S-1991–2, from Forum SW.
34. Weinberg 1960 (*Corinth* I.5), 3–31; Scotton 1997, 140.
35. Weinberg 1960 (*Corinth* I.5), 3–31; Kent 1966 (*Corinth* VIII.3), nos. 323, 327; White 2005. A figure of Cybele (Corinth Museum inv. no. S-1124) came from so-called early medieval levels of the SE Building. Is there a connection with the goddess Mater, the Mother, associated with Cybele as supervisor of archives in Athens?
36. [Dio Chrysostom] Favorinus *Or.* 37; White 2005.
37. Philostratus *Life of Apollonius of Tyana* 4.25.
38. Galen *De anat. admin.* 40, vol. 2, 217; Athenaeus 13.567c for Myrtilus.
39. Sanders et al. forthcoming.
40. Scranton 1957 (*Corinth* XVI), 9–12; Scotton 1997, 67–106, 2015; Kent 1966 (*Corinth* VIII.3), no. 728.

41. Panayia Field and adjacent excavations: Richardson 1896; Broneer 1947, 243–6; Sanders 1999, 2002a, 2002b, 2003a, 2003b, 2004, 2005; Sweetman and Sanders 2005; Pfaff 2007; Stirling 2008; Lepinski 2008, 2014, 2015. Bookidis (pers. comm. 2008) says remains of an earlier villa in the Panayia Field include a single wall in different orientation with a black dado; a sluicing pit with fresco fragments filled in the late second century; and a well that was filled in the late third century.
42. Palinkas and Herbst 2011.
43. Dionysos: Corinth Museum inv. no. S-12, Richardson 1896, 1904, 288 no. 1; Johnson 1931 (*Corinth* IX), 35–6, no. 29. Armed Aphrodite statuette (and other finds): Corinth Museum inv. no. S-2548, Broneer 1947, 243–6, pl. 64, no. 28; Sturgeon 2003; Sanders 2005, 424; Stirling 2008, 133.
44. Sanders 1999, 2004, 2005; Sweetman and Sanders 2005. House dated from coins, pottery in well under walls, water system and particularly the concrete *euripus*.
45. Stirling 2008. For late antique domestic religion, see Bakker 1994; Stirling 2005.
46. Ridgway 1981, 442; Stirling 2008, 133. Statuettes of the so-called Europa (Corinth Museum inv. nos. S-1897 and S-1904/2446) were also found at the Mosaic House along with other small marble statuettes of gods. Other Europa statuettes are Corinth Museum inv. nos. S-1051 and S-3575 (Sturgeon 2004 (*Corinth* IX.3), no. 42).
47. Lepinski 2008, 2014, 2015.
48. Stirling 2008, 127: From coins, pottery in destruction layers and under the next house, broken statuettes partly burned in situ.
49. Sanders 2004. Compare Sardis house: Greenewalt and Rautman 2000.
50. Pallas 1990, 764; Sanders 1999. Compare: Ellis 1988, 1991; Curcic 1993.
51. *Praetoria* (Governors' Palaces): Croke 1981; Lavan 1999, 2001b. The emperor Arcadius in 396–407 ordered repair of imperially funded palaces, and restricted their use for other purposes: *CTh* 15.1.35, 7.10.1–2.
52. House of the Opus Sectile Panel: Williams 1976, pl. 24 (reused pebble mosaic floor); Williams and Zervos 1982, 134, n. 25 (earlier excavations in area), 1983, 13–23, 1987, 28 (used throughout third century); Oliver 2001 (glass panel). The East of Theater third-century fire described by Williams (and Zervos 1983, 23) was forward-dated by Williams (and Zervos 1987, 28), then finally dated by Slane (1994) to *c*.300 (and specifically linked to the destruction of Buildings 5 and 7 in the East of Theater area). Support for this later date was already presented by Williams (and Zervos 1983, 15, 1987, 28), where AfRS dish Corinth Museum inv. no. C-1982–18 was given a parallel from Hayes (1972, 68 type 50:46 fig. 12) of *c*.300–60.

53. E-W Theater-Bath Road: Williams and Zervos 1982, 28, 1983, 8-9, 27–8 (650 m. east of Theater, used into sixth century).
54. See the exhibit from the OSE (Railroad) excavations at the new Corinth train station.
55. Pallas (1957) tells a popular legend behind the name of Anaploga from St Paul catching his breath there after being rolled down Acrocorinth in a barrel by Corinthians "displeased by his preaching," in Landon's words (1994, 164, n. 280). Williams (in Landon) offers an alternate story that Paul was escaping a demon in the barrel.
56. Megaw 1962–3, 11; Daux 1963, 725–6, fig. 10; H.S. Robinson 1963 (1965), 78-9, pl. 92, 1969c; Miller 1972. The marble head was found by farmers in the direction of the Anaploga area, about 500 m. west of the Odeum, and brought in to the ASCSA Corinth Excavations team, who were asked by the Greek Archaeological Service to find out what building it came from. As no body was discovered, it was probably acrolithic, but it remains unclear if it belonged in the excavated building or elsewhere. Excavations in Anaploga from 1962–4 directed by Mr Robinson found part of a Corinthian pilaster, two fragments of an epistyle frieze with a Latin inscription (first century?), and the northern walls of a building, with an atrium and a hall paved with mosaic in the second half of the second century or the third century (Hellenkemper Salies 1986). The excavated walls don't seem able to bear the Corinthian pilaster or the Latin-inscribed epistyle, and a more monumental unexcavated sanctuary should be located in the area, perhaps that of Athena Chalinitis.
57. For the excavations, see note above. For the Roman-era water systems, see H.S. Robinson 1969c. For the mosaic floor, see Miller 1972 (architecture "to be published" by H. S. Robinson but was not); Hellenkemper Salies 1986.
58. Miller 1972, 333 n. 5 (Phase III); Daux 1963, 727; Megaw 1962–3.
59. Miller (1972, 333 n. 6) on pottery and coins of Valentinian, Theodosius and Arcadius in the debris over the floor.
60. See Kopestonsky (2016) for the Greek cult of the Nymphs at Corinth, and this shrine, based on her dissertation research on this area excavated by R.S. Stroud in 1961 and N. Robertson in 1962–3. Though her focus was the Classical roadside stele shrine, which she suggests was dedicated to the Nymphs, she notes pottery of the fifth to sixth century found throughout the area in association with walls along the road and the villa.
61. Shear's Villa: Shear 1925, 1930 (*Corinth* V). Farm buildings to the east of this villa: Corinth NB239, 118–38; H. S. Robinson 1963 (1965); Daux 1963, 722 (wine press and olive oil tank, third century).

62. Daux 1965, 689–90.
63. Bowden 2003.
64. Pallas 1955, 1955 (1960); Wiseman 1978.
65. Gregory 1985; Kardulias, Gregory and Sawmiller 1995.
66. Asae: Theopompus 115 *FGH* 173 in StephByz s.v. Ἀσαί; Miliarakis 1886, 110, 170; Bursian 1862, 93; *RE* II 1896 1514; Sakellariou and Faraklas 1971; Wiseman 1978, 100–5.
67. In the Agios Charalambos (Zevgolatio) Bath, the excavators Charitonidis and Ginouvès (1955) marked two phases, second/third-century construction and then fifth-century renovation, by comparison with the Great Baths of Argos. Wiseman (1978, 100) shifted this forward to construction *c.*300 and renovation *c.*400, while Sanders (1999) pushed this last phase into the sixth century, by comparison with the Panayia Bath.
68. For the site of ancient Oenoe or Skoinos, located through Roman pottery on a hill to the SW of Skoinos Harbor on the Halcyon Gulf, see also Payne 1940 (*Perachora* I), 8; Hope Simpson 1965, 35; Sakellariou and Faraklas 1971, App. II.1 (not ancient Oenoe); Wiseman 1978, 30–4. For Roman pottery and a cistern at Sterna, a hill to the NE of Ktena at the west end of the Asprokambos plain, by the Halcyon Gulf, see Payne 1940 (*Perachora* I), 6. For Roman walls at Agios Vlasios hill 2.5 km. north of Perachora town, on the road to Bisia, see Fowler and Stillwell 1932 (*Corinth* I), 38; Payne 1940 (*Perachora* I), 6.
69. Aslamatzidou-Kostourou 2013.
70. Pettegrew 2007.
71. Kosso 2003.
72. Cemeteries on the plain between Corinth and Lechaion: Blegen et al. 1964 (*Corinth* XIII); Eliot and Eliot 1968; Slane 2017 (*Corinth* XXI). Traces of the Long Walls to Lechaion built in 460 BCE doubtless remained in Late Antiquity: Thucydides 1.103.4; Xenophon *Hellenica*. 4.4.7; Diodorus 11.79.1–2; Strabo 380; Plutarch *Kimon* 17.1–2; Pausanias. 2.2.3; Skias 1892 (1894), 112.
73. Caraher et al. 2006; Diakopolos 2006; Tartaron et al. 2006; Tartaron, Pullen and Noller 2006; Pettegrew 2006, 2007.
74. Initial layout of colony of Corinth, countryside and centuriation: Kent 1966 (*Corinth* VIII.3), 20–1; Wiseman 1979, 509–21; Urse 1988; Romano 1993b, 1994, 1996, 1998a, 2000, 2003, 2010; Romano and Schoenbrun 1993; Romano and Tolba 1995; Romano and Stapp 1998; Mary E. Hoskins Walbank 1986a, 1986b, 1997; Doukellis 1994; Rothaus 1994.
75. Engels 1990.
76. Rizakis and Zoumbaki 2001.

Chapter 3 Commerce, Water Supply and Communications

1. López Quiroga 2016.
2. Central Shops: Broneer 1935, 57; Scranton 1957 (*Corinth* XVI).
3. West Shops epistyle inscription (6 blocks preserved): Meritt 1931 (*Corinth* VIII.1), no. 113; Kent 1966 (*Corinth* VIII.3), no. 504; Williams 1977, 63; Feissel and Philippidis-Braat 1985, no. 6; Rizakis and Zoumbaki 2001, 316–7, COR 270.1; Sanders 2003, 395, n. 35; Sironen 2016 (*IG* IV^2 3), no. 1260.
4. South Stoa epistyle inscription (2 blocks preserved): Corinth Museum inv. no. I-1499a-b, Broneer 1954 (*Corinth* I.4), 113; Kent 1966 (*Corinth* VIII.3), nos. 505a–b; Rizakis and Zoumbaki 2001, 316–7, COR 270.2; Sironen 2016 (*IG* IV^2 3), no. 1261.
5. Scranton 1957 (*Corinth* XVI), 6–26; Weinberg 1960 (*Corinth* I.5), 57, 76–7, 122; B. A. Robinson 2001, 125; Sanders 2004, 170–2.
6. Broneer 1954 (*Corinth* I.4), 134, 143, 151, 159; Slane 1994.
7. Scranton 1957 (*Corinth* XVI), 9.
8. Lechaion Road colonnades: Sears 1902.
9. Stillwell et al. 1941 (*Corinth* I.2), 55, 88; Williams 1969, 63, n. 30.
10. Dey 2015; Mango 2001; Segal 1997, 5–10; Lyttelton 1974, 214–6; Crawford 1990, 107–25; Ward-Perkins 1951, 297–8, n. 24 (in the West, stoas were attached to buildings rather than roads); Downey 1937; Foss 1979, 65, n. 39; Welles in Kraeling 1938. For primary sources, see Libanius *Or.* 11: *The Antiochikos*; Festugière 1959, 33–5, 56–8; and the inscriptions in Le Bas and Waddington 1870, 3.1878.
11. Crawford 1990.
12. Stillwell 1932 (*Corinth* I), 159, 191–2; Scranton 1957 (*Corinth* XVI), 37–8.
13. Dey 2015, 191–6 (he appears to conflate the Great Bath on the Lechaion Road and the Roman Baths just north of the Peribolos of Apollo).
14. Pausanias 2.3.3 (for the association with Apollo, from a statue he saw there); Stillwell et al. 1941 (*Corinth* I.2), 1–54, especially 33–5; Kent 1966 (*Corinth* VIII.3), no. 124.
15. North Market: de Waele 1930; Scranton 1951 (*Cor.* I.3), 180–92.
16. Broneer 1926.
17. East of Theater was excavated 1981–8; for preliminary reports, see Williams and Zervos 1982, 1983, 1984, 1985, 1986, 1987, 1988, 1989; Zervos 1988 (coins); Slane 1987; Slane and Sanders 2005 (pottery); Gadbery 1993, Lepinski 2014 (frescoes).
18. See Chapter 2, note 53.
19. Buildings 1–3, butcher's shop in second century, rebuilt partly in third century: Williams and Zervos 1986, 1987. Glassmaking:

Williams and Zervos 1984, 90, 107–8. Forge (crucibles, furnace): Williams and Zervos 1983, 12–3. Fuller (a built trough and basins containing decaying wood): Williams and Zervos 1983, 12–3, ref. Pietrogrande 1977, Figs. 2, 11; Mau and Kelsey 1902, 393–7, Fig. 227.

20. West Shops: Scranton 1951 (*Corinth* I.3), 131; H.S. Robinson 1965, 23; Williams, MacIntosh, and Fisher 1974, 8–9 (construction of building and drain in SW Forum over part of West Shops); Williams and Fisher 1975, 14, 1976, 132–3; Williams 1977, 62–3; Rothaus 1996, 2000, 19–21. Northwest Shops and Stoa: Stillwell et al. 1941 (*Corinth* I.2). Lechaion Road: Sears 1902.
21. Weinberg 1960 (*Corinth* I.5), 109.
22. Williams 1993.
23. Corinth Museum inv. no. I-1970-13, Wiseman 1972, 40–1, no. 29; Sironen 1992, 223–6, no. 1; Sironen 2016 (*IG* IV^2 3), no. 1240.
24. For urban occupations in Egyptian cities, compare Alston 1998, 83–4.
25. Sironen 2016 (*IG* IV^2 3); Bees 1941, 56; Avraméa 1997, 134–5; Michael B. Walbank 2010, 270–96.
26. Michael B. Walbank 2010, 270–91.
27. Ierardi pers. comm. 2016.
28. Edwards 1933 (*Corinth* VI); Harris 1941.
29. Sanders 2003b.
30. Waagé 1935.
31. Davidson 1940; Matson 1948; Weinberg 1975; Whitehouse 1991, 1993; Slane 1994, 164.
32. Mattusch 1977.
33. See Chapter 5, and Sturgeon 2003.
34. For locally manufactured pottery and lamps of the third century: Slane 1994, 2000, 2003, 2004; Slane and Sanders 2005. For local production and export of amphoras and their products; Koehler 1978a, 1978b, 1981, 2004; Vandiver and Koehler 1986; Newton et al. 1988.
35. Slane 1994, 164.
36. Stillwell et al. 1941 (*Corinth* I.2), 54; Scranton 1951 (*Corinth* I.3), 180–92.
37. Choricius *Laud. Marc.* 1.83.
38. Corinth Museum inv. no. I-732/740, Meritt 1931 (*Corinth* VIII.1), no. 294; Hiller von Gärtringen 1932, 364; Feissel and Philippidis-Braat 1985, no. 25*; Sironen 2016 (*IG* IV^2 3), no. 1256.
39. Landon 1994; Lolos 1997; B.A. Robinson 2000, 2001, 2011. For the geology and sacred aspects of water in Greek Corinth, see Kopestonsky 2016. For monumental civic fountains in Roman Corinth and Greece after Hadrian, see Longfellow 2009.
40. Landon 1994, 247–80.

41. Peirene: Pindar *Ol.* 13.61,63–6; Euripides *Medea* 67–9, *Trojan Women* 205–6; Plautus *Aulularia* 557–9 (3.6.21–3); Ovid *Epist. ex Pont.* 1.3.75, *Metamorphoses* 2.240, 7.391; Alexander Aetol. in Parthenios *Narr. Amat.* 14.3; Cicero *Epist. ad Atticum* 12.5; Dio Chrysostom *Or.* 36.46 (Pegasus creates Peirene with hoof); Pausanias 2.3.2–3; Athenaeus 2.43b (Peirene good water to drink), 13.588c (Apelles and Laïs); Herodian 5.92.2; Alciphron *Epist. Paras.* 3.15.1; Richardson 1900; Stevens 1934; Hill 1964 (*Corinth* I.6), 1–115; B.A. Robinson 2000, 2001, 2011.
42. B.A. Robinson 2011, 206–50.
43. B.A. Robinson 2011, 217–9. Balustrade and latticework screen: Corinth Museum inv. nos. I-335/831, 534, 554, 735, 844/1001, 2495, Meritt 1931 (*Corinth* VIII.1), nos. 121–4; Kent 1966 (*Corinth* VIII.3), no. 343.
44. B.A. Robinson 2011, 252–84 (Robinson 4th, Hill 2nd marble phase), dated from destruction debris in rooms to the east, and the architectural style of the triconch court.
45. Corinth Museum inv. no. I-62, Richardson 1900b, 235–7; *AnnÉpigr* 1901, 1; *IG* IV, no. 1599; Powell 1903, no. 21; Meritt 1931 (*Corinth* VIII.1), no. 86; Hill 1964 (*Corinth* I.6), 103; Kent 1966 (*Corinth* VIII.3), no. 15; Tobin 1997, 78–9; Rizakis and Zoumbaki 2001, 374–5, COR 528; B. A. Robinson 2001, 61–2, n. 4–5, 2011, 281–4.
46. B.A. Robinson 2011, 216: Corinth Museum inv. nos. S-55 (female portrait body with repairs, shown in my Figure 5.4, B. A. Robinson 2011, Fig. 114, maybe reused for Regilla); S-1023 (plinth with foot); S-54 (Aphrodite or nymph with repairs, Fig. 115); S-1024 (Nymph with shell, Fig. 116).
47. Pickett 2017.
48. B.A. Robinson (2011, 275–92) outlines a series of fifth- or sixth-century benefactions for Peirene, beginning with the circular basin and outlooker colonnade. The round basin was found in 1897 and photographed (Scranton 1957 (*Corinth* XVI), pl. 2.2), then its excavator, ASCSA and Corinth Excavations Director Rufus B. Richardson (1902a, 322), remarked that it gave way only under "the constant application of dynamite" to reveal the rectangular lower level of the Fountain court still visible today.
49. Scranton 1957 (*Corinth* XVI), 22–3; B. A. Robinson 2011, 275–81.
50. Corinth Museum inv. no. I-24, Richardson 1899, 683, 1900, 238; *IG* IV, no. 1606; Meritt 1931 (*Corinth* VIII.1), no. 198; Sironen 2016 (*IG* IV^2 3), no. 1262: - - - τὸν ὁρώμενον πάντα κόσμον τῇ Πειρήνῃ πα- - -. B.A. Robinson (2011, 281) dates second half of fifth or early sixth century, and Sironen follows this date.
51. B.A. Robinson 2011, 286–310.
52. Pausanias 2.3.5.

53. Also called the Roman Baths or Baths of Eurykles in publications: Broneer 1926; Fowler and Stillwell 1932 (*Corinth* I), 142; Robinson 1965, 25. For their statuary, see Chapter 5. For the first-century BCE C. Iulius Eurycles, and his eponymous later first/early second-century CE descendant C. Iulius Eurycles Herculanus, who entered the Senate in Rome, built baths in Sparta (Pausanias 3.11.4–5) and died in 136/7, see Steinhauer 2010.
54. Williams 1968, 134–8, 1969, 63; Rothaus 1993, 128 (2000, 25).
55. Great Bath on the Lechaion Road: Biers 1985 (*Corinth* XVII), 2003.
56. Scranton 1957 (*Corinth* XVI), 14–21; Biers 1985 (*Corinth* XVII), 61–2; Ivison 1996, 102; Robinson 2001, 126, n. 69.
57. Temple E Bath: Williams and Zervos 1995, 11; Williams, Barnes and Snyder 1997, 37–40; Ajootian 2000, 501.
58. Sanders 1999, 2004, 2005.
59. Robinson 1965, 29.
60. Broneer 1954 (*Corinth* I.4), 145; Biers 2003; Sanders 2004; Sanders et al. forthcoming.
61. Landon 1994, 2003.
62. Slane 1994; Williams and Zervos 1984, 101.
63. Stillwell 1936, 31–9; Broneer 1942, 154–6; Robinson 2001.
64. Williams et al. 1973, 43.
65. Stobi: Hattersley-Smith 1996, 66–7.
66. Hadji Mustafa Fountain, Kakavi spring: MacKay 1967; Landon 1994, 174–8.
67. Hadrianic Aqueduct: Pausanias 2.3.5; Biers 1978; Landon 1994, 342–65, 419–29; Lolos 1997. Sanders (pers. comm. 2005) suggests the castellum may lie on the eastern side of the north slope of Acrocorinth, where a large ruin is visible in a nineteenth-century drawing by Gell. Much of the aqueduct has been traced by Lolos back to Stymphalos, and a similar one brought water down to Argos.
68. Upper Peirene: Strabo 8.6.21; Pliny *NH* 4.4.11; Pausanias 2.5.1; Stillwell in Blegen et al. 1930 (*Corinth* III.1), 31–49; Landon 1994, 154–62; Robinson 2001.
69. Broneer (in Blegen et al. 1930 (*Corinth* III.1), 50–60) gives texts and dates them to the second century, though the parallels range from the reign of Nero and Plut. *de Curiositate* 11 through sanctuary and cliff-side contexts in Roman Greece and Egypt into the third century.
70. Gregory 1995; Frey and Gregory 2016.
71. Philadelpheus 1918 (1921); Stikas 1957 (1962), 89–94; Daux 1963.
72. Ampelius 8.8: *Corintho ballenae costa est magna secundum mare, quam homo complecti non potest.*
73. Pallas 1965 (1967), 143–55 (= Daux 1966, 767–70): houses, bath south of Lechaion Basilica atrium dug in 1965. Corinth Museum

inv. no. S-3745, Daux 1966, 769–70 Fig. 8; Stefanidou-Tiveriou 1993b, no. 164 (*trapezophoros*).

74. Approval: Socrates 6.22.4; Sozomen 7.1.11; Procopius *'Aed* 5.15.17; Mango 1981a. Disapproval: John Chrysostom *Hom. in Joh.* 118.
75. Hattersley-Smith 1996, 35, 123, 146 (St Demetrios, Acheiropoeitos), 75 (Octagon, Episkopeion), 47 (Central Basilica).
76. Public baths and bathing: Fagan 1999; Biers 2003; DeForest 2013.
77. Excavated urban roads beyond the Forum, Lechaion Road and Theater: Williams (and Zervos 1983, 8, 1987, 1–3, 1988, 95–100) on the east-west road with Ionic *spolia* colonnade excavated in 1973 about 470 m. north of the Forum (Corinth NB565), and, along with an east-west paved road south of the South Stoa running for 400 m. west of Forum, used into the sixth century. Palinkas (2005), and Palinkas and Herbst (2005), describe the north-south Panayia Road along the east side of the Panayia Field, unpaved but with sidewalks on both sides and used through the sixth century along with the drain underneath it.
78. Wiseman 1978; Sanders and Whitbread 1990.
79. Pritchett 1969, ch. 6, 1980, ch. 5; Hammond 1954; Wiseman 1978, 17–27, 113–26; Sanders and Whitbread 1990.
80. Sakellariou and Faraklas 1971; Wiseman 1978.
81. Carpenter and Bon 1936 (*Corinth* III.2); Wiseman 1978, 93, n. 3; Pritchett 1980, 243; Marchand 2003, 2013. The road south to Kleonai from Acrocorinth appears in Pausanias 2.15, and on the Peutinger Map (Talbert 2010).
82. Sakellariou and Faraklas (1971, 32) identify a site just south of modern Chiliomodion village with a theater, walls, houses and Roman graves as "certainly" Pausanias' Tenea, and also (25, Appendix II) cite Papachatzis 1963, pers. comm. of Epimelete Papachristodoulou, and the reasoning that Athikia (Agios Nikolaos) has much less arable land, and Klenia B is much smaller. For a third-century portrait head found between Chiliomodion and Moni Phaneromeni, and thus likely from a grave or villa of Tenea, see Corinth Museum inv. no. S-2605 (de Grazia 1973, no. 44).
83. Sakellariou and Faraklas (1971) identify Klenia B as the Archaic to Roman town, while their Klenia A is the Bronze Age site. Modern Klenia was long associated with Pausanias' Tenea, which is more likely modern Chiliomodion: Frazer 1898, 2.29; Neill 1930, 26–7; Fowler and Stillwell 1932 (*Corinth* I), 96; Roux 1958, 130–1.
84. Wiseman 1978, 121–5.
85. This cave is 60 m. deep, and was first investigated by N. Bertos in 1930: *BCH* 54 (1930) 479; Chatziangelou 2013.
86. For the road to Oenoe, see Wiseman 1974, 1978, 30–4.
87. Simonides *AnthPal* 7.496 is an epitaph for a shipwreck off Geraneia, by the Scironian waves and ravines of snowy Methurias

(Methana?). For Crommyon (modern Agioi Theodoroi), see Thucydides 4.45.1; Xenophon *Hell.* 4.4.13, 5.19; Scylax 55; Strabo 8.6.22 (380, 391); Pliny *HN* 4.23; Eudoxos in Stephanus of Byzantium s.v. Κρομμύων. For the Crommyonian sow (or boar) killed by Theseus, see Pausanias 2.1.3; Plutarch *Theseus* 9; Ovid *Metamorphoses* 7.435. Crommyon is an *emporion* in Hierocles *Synecdemus* 10. Many ruins were seen by the early travelers, though most are now gone, except around the church: Leake 1830, 3.347; Boblaye 1832, 35; Vischer 1875, 229; Frazer 1898, 2.3; Fowler and Stillwell 1932 (*Corinth* I), 46; Roux 1958, 86–7; Sakellariou and Faraklas 1971. Excavated ruins by the Agioi Theodoroi train station to the north of the track and the west of the platform include the round structure in Alexandri and Verdelis 1961 (1962), perhaps a deme theater. For Sidous (probably modern Sousaki), see Boblaye 1832, 35 (walls now gone under the national highway); Leake 1846, 397; Sakellariou and Faraklas 1971, App. II, 10 (Roman sherds 500 m. higher up to NE of Agia Theodora church); Xenophon *Hell.* 4.4.13, 4.5.19; Scylax 55; Rianus 265 *FGH* 47 in Athen. 3.82b, Apollodorus 244 *FGH* 159 in Athen. 3.82b; Pliny *HN* 4.23; Stephanus Byz. s.v. Σιδοῦς, Hesychius s.v. Σιδουντιάς.

88. Walls and sherds seen *c.*1970 by Faraklas, in Sakellariou and Faraklas 1971, App. II, 9–10. For Schoinous, which probably means something like *diolkos*, the drag across place, see Strabo 8.6.4, 22, and 9.1.2; Pomponius 2.48; Ptolemy 3.16.13; Pliny *NH* 4.7; *IG* IV^2 no. 71, lines 23–4; Fowler and Stillwell 1932 (*Corinth* I), 49.
89. Lechaion: Simonides 545 (Campbell 1991, 3.440–1); Dionysius *Descr. Gr.* 108 (Müller *FHG* 1855, 1.242); Xenophon *Hell.* 4.4.12 (shipsheds); Polybius 5.2.4; Diodorus Siculus 14.86–15.68; Propertius 3.21; Strabo 8.6.22; Pliny *NH* 4.4.10, 4.5.12; Plutarch *Aratus* 24; Plutarch *Moralia* 146B–64D *Dinner of the Seven Wise Men* (set in the age of Periander, but perhaps featuring details of Plutarch's day like a *hieron* of Aphrodite, fine villas, baths, a palestra and a grove by the sea); Pausanias 2.2.3.
90. Gerster 1884, 226; Georgiades 1907; Paris 1915; Fowler and Stillwell 1932 (*Corinth* I), 95; Carpenter and Bon 1936 (*Corinth* III.2), 29; Roux 1958, 103; Pallas 1959 (1965), 139, 1960 (1966), 165, 1961–2 (1963), 75, 1965 (1967), 143–55 (= Daux 1966, 767–70: houses, bath south of Basilica atrium); Wiseman 1978; Rothaus 1995; Stiros et al. 1996. Ancient artificial harbors: Shaw 1972; Casson 1994a, 1994b.
91. Pausanias 2.2.3; *SEG* 23, no. 170; Pallas 1958, 132.
92. Georgiades 1907; Shaw 1969.
93. Corinth Museum inv. no. I-1391, Quinet 1830, 288 (read at Lechaion in 1825); Bursian 1862; *IG* no. IV 209; Groag 1946, 36–8; Robert 1958, 33–5; Kent 1966 (*Corinth* VIII.3), no. 503, pl. 42; Shaw 1969; Feissel and Philippidis-Braat 1985, no. 23.

94. See "New underwater discoveries in Greece reveal ancient Roman engineering," *Guardian*, 14 December 2017.
95. *IG* VII, no 24; *SIG* [3] 908; Sironen 1992, 225–6.
96. The foundation was visible inside a deep hole in 2008, and the information came from the owners of the land.
97. Rickman 1971; Cavalier 2007 (Andriace, Patara).
98. Kenchreai: Thucydides 4.42, 8.20; Ovid *Trist.* 1.10.9; Strabo 380; Pliny *NH* 4.4.10, 4.5.12; Ptolemy 3.16.13; Pausanias 2.2.3; Hohlfelder 1970a.
99. Scranton and Ramage 1964, 135–41 (villas); Scranton 1965; Hawthorne 1965; Scranton and Ramage 1967; Shaw 1967b, 1970, 1972; H.S. Robinson 1972; Hohlfelder 1976 (imperial history). Scranton et al. 1978 (*Kenchreai* 1); Adamsheck 1978 (*Kenchreai* 4: Pottery); Hohlfelder 1978 (*Kenchreai* 3: Coins); Williams 1981 (*Kenchreai* 5); Stern and Thimme 2007 (*Kenchreai* 6: Ivory, Bone, Wood); 'Korka and Rife 2013; Heath et al. 2015.
100. Shaw 1967a.
101. Scranton 1967; Ibrahim, Scranton and Brill 1976 (*Kenchreai* 2: Glass Panels).
102. Stroud (1985) in his review of Salmon 1984 gives evidence for heavy traffic through this area based on *IG* IV^2 1, no. 71 l. 17. Gregory is studying this material in connection with SHARP, though the focus of the 2007–8 excavations was the Mycenaean era: Tartaron and Pullen 2008.
103. Canal-cutting endeavors: Diogenes Laertius 1.7.99 (Periander); Eratosthenes in Strabo 1.3.11 (54) (Demetrius Poliorcetes); Suetonius *Caesar* 44.3; Plutarch *Caesar* 58.4; Cassius Dio 44.5 (Caesar's freedman Anienus for Caesar); Suetonius *Gaius Caligula* 21 (Caligula); Pliny *NH* 4.4.10 (Demetrius, Caesar, Caligula, Nero); Suetonius *Nero* 19; Josephus *de Bell. Jud.* 3.10.10; Pseudo-Lucian *Nero s. de fossione Isthmi*; Cassius Dio 63.16–19; Philostratus *Life of Apollonius of Tyana* 4.24 (Nero with 6,000 Jews); Philostratus *Vitae Soph.* 2.1.10, 2.6 (Herodes Atticus); Pausanias 2.15 (Nero or Herodes Atticus?, considered impious); Leake 1830 3.300 (thought he saw Nero's traces, more likely Venetian); Gerster 1884 (also attributes traces visible in 1884 to Nero: two trenches, each varying from 3 to 30 m. deep, 40–50 m. wide and on the west coming in 2000 m. and on the east 1500 m., each then giving way to a series of pits on line of planned canal every 40–5 m.); Pettegrew 2016.
104. *Diolkos* used for warship transport across the Isthmus (besides M. Antonius inscription): Thucyd. 3.15.1, 8.7, 8.8.3; Aristophanes *Thesm.* 647–55, with scholion to 648; Scylax *Periplus* 40 (*diolkos* is 40 stades long); Agathermus 24 (ed. Müller 1882); Polyb. 4.19.7 (318), 5.101.4 (484); Cassius Dio 51.5 (Octavian in 30 BCE after Actium); Strabo 8.2 (335), 9.6 (369), 378; Mela *Geogr.* 2.48; Pliny *NH* 4.4.10, 4.5 (againt Gods, on which see also Tac. *Ann.* 1.79, Hdt. 1.174 for

Cnidians); Hesychius s.v. *diolkos*. For Byzantine examples see Theophanes Continuatus pp. 300–1; Zonaras 4.132; Skylitzes 152–3 (in 873 the Byz. Admiral (droungarios tou ploimou) Niketas Ooryphas or Coryphas takes a fleet from east to west across the Ishmus to attack the Cretan pirate Photius, who is raiding the west Peloponnesus); George Phrantzes 1.33 (*CSHB* 20, ed. Bekker and Niebuhr 1968, 96) (in 883 (the same?) Niketas takes a fleet across the Isthmus to fight the Arabs). Modern Observations and Excavations: O'Neill 1930, 10–13; Fowler and Stillwell 1932 (*Corinth* I.1), 49–51, 55–9; Verdelis 1956, 1956 (1959), 1958, 1960 (1962), 1960 (1966), 1962 (1966) (excavations of 1956, 1958, 1960, 1962); Wiseman 1978, 45–50; Cook 1986; MacDonald 1986; Raepsaet 1993; Papachatzis 1963, on Pausanias 2.22–4; Papaphotiou 2007.

105. Ancient sources for the use of a *diolkos* (the term is Strabo's) across the Isthmus are collected by Fowler and Stillwell 1932 (*Corinth* I.1), 49–51, n. 1; Baladié 1980, 250–63; Pettegrew 2011, 2014, 2016. The road across the Isthmus traditionally referred to as the *diolkos* was partially excavated by Verdelis (1962 (1966), 1960 (1966), 1960 (1962), 1956 (1959), 1958, 1956), and is still clearly visible today at its western end just south of the modern Corinth canal. See also Papaphotiou 2007; Raepsaet 1993; Cook 1986; MacDonald 1986; Wiseman 1978, 45–50. The cutting of the modern Corinth canal was matched by heaping up of excavated earth mainly to its south, deforming the natural landscape and making the Isthmus higher: Gerster 1884.

106. Koutsouba and Nakas 2013; Lohmann 2013; Pettegrew 2014, 2016; Sanders 2014. Among the inscriptions used to pave the Lechaion Road ramp mentioned above was Corinth Museum inv. nos. I-788 to 791, which bears a Greek inscription of the fourth century BCE (Meritt 1931 (*Corinth* VIII.1), no. 31), and which was recut with a poetic inscription in Latin (West 1931 (*Corinth* VIII.2), no. 1), and set up in Isthmia or Corinth in the first century BCE, apparently lauding Marc Antony's grandfather Marcus Antonius for transporting a fleet across the Corithian Isthmus as *praetor pro consule* against the pirates in 102 BCE, with the name ANTONI MARCI erased. The Antonii were removed from the *fasti* in 30 BCE (*CIL* I, 422, 439), probably provoking this erasure, though later they were restored in Rome (Tacitus *Ann.* 3.18; Dio 59.20).

107. Collart 1976.

108. Hjohlman 2002.

109. Procopius *Bell.* 2.22–3, trans. Dewing 1914, 450–73.

110. Justinian *Nov. Ed.* 7 Pref. (542): *mortis enim periculum per omnia loca propagatum*; *CIC Nov.* 118 (543), 122 (544).

111. See now McCormick 2015. Rubini (2008) has made a recent announcement of a Justinianic plague mass grave, near Rome at Castro dei Volsci. A slight rise in dated epitaphs in Palestine between 541 and 544 (Meimaris 1992, 129–30, 236–8), and mass inhumations in Valencia and Cartagena in Spain of early to mid-sixth-century date (Kulikowski 2007), have both been linked with the plague. For comparative material on the economic and social effects of other plagues, see Hope and Marshall 2000 (Peloponnesian War); Duncan-Jones 1996; Scheidel 2002; Bagnall 2002; Greenberg 2003; Bruun 2003 (Antonine second century); Congourdeau 1998 (fourteenth-century Byzantium); Cipolla 1973 (Renaissance Italy), 1979, 1981 (seventeenth-century Italy).
112. Seibel 1857; Russell 1968; Patlagean 1977, 85–91; Allen 1979; Durliat 1989; Sallares 1991, 263–71; Whitby 1995; Conrad 1996; Stathakopoulos 2000, 2004; Meier 2002; Sarris 2002; Little 2007.
113. In Constantinople, the plague recurred in 558 (Malalas 18.127 (489); Agathias *Histories* 5.10) and 573 (John of Biclar *Chronicle* 33, *CCSL* 173A.66; Agapius of Menbidj *Universal History*, ed. Vasiliev 1910 (*PO* 8), 437).
114. Barsanouphius *Correspondance* 569, cited by Peter Brown, *CAH* 14.781.
115. Casanova 1984 (Egypt); Sarris 2002 (economy).

Chapter 4 Spaces of Civic Assembly and Entertainment

1. Robert 1971, 117, no. 60; Shear 1925, 384–5, 1926, 451–3; Stillwell 1952 (*Corinth* II), 97.
2. Beacham 1992; Brown 2012c; Remijsen 2016.
3. See Chapter 2, note 53.
4. Theater: Xenophon *Hell.* 4.3.2–3; Diodorus 14.86.1; Plutarch *Aratus* 17.4 (1034), 23.1–2 (1037); Pausanias 2.4.5; Heermance 1903; Shear 1925, 1926, 1928a, 1928b, 1929, 1931b; Capps Jr. 1949; Stillwell 1952 (*Corinth* II); Sturgeon 1977 (*Corinth* IX.2), 1997, 1998, 2004 (*Corinth* IX.3); Mac Isaac 1987; Williams and Zervos 1985, 1986, 1987, 1988, 1989; Williams 2013a.
5. Stillwell (1952 (*Corinth* II), 84–98, 140) describes the conversion of orchestra to arena; Williams (2013a, 494–5) identifies it as Phase 6, and dates it to "late in the Severan period." Williams (pers. comm. 2007) argues the Corinthians judged their Amphitheater too small, and renovated the Theater as an arena when they abandoned the Amphitheater. Welch (2007, 185) argues the Theater was modified as an arena in the second century from a desire to host gladiatorial games "in the more prestigious civic center, as other Greek cities were now doing." She does not rule out continued use of the old Amphitheater.

6. Sturgeon 1977 (*Corinth* IX.2), 1997, 1998c, 2004 (*Corinth* IX.3).
7. Corinth Museum inv. no. S-2804, Robinson 1969a. For Caracalla as the New Achilles, see Rose 2005. For Theater phases after the third century, see Williams and Zervos 1987; Williams 2013a.
8. Heads: Corinth Museum inv. nos. S-3317 (de Grazia 1973, no. 36; Sturgeon 2004 (*Corinth* IX.3), no. 32), S-3320 (Sturgeon 2004 (*Corinth* IX.3), no. 33). Base: Corinth Museum inv. no. I-2433, Kent 1966 (*Corinth* VIII.3), no. 272; *SEG* 38, no. 1934; Robert 1966, 752–3; *SEG* 41, no. 266; Sturgeon 2004 (*Corinth* IX.3), 183–5, no. 71. For the *chlamydatus* and hand, see Chapter 5, and Brown 2012a, 2016a.
9. Williams 2013a, 495–7 (Phases 7–9), quotation p. 497.
10. For later phases, see Shear 1926, 454; Stillwell 1952 (*Corinth* II), 140–1; Williams and Zervos 1987, 31; Sanders and Slane 2005; Williams 2013a, 494–9, 511–47.
11. Williams 2013a, 497–9, 532–4.
12. Pausanias 2.3.6; Philostratus *Vitae Soph.* 2.1.9 (551); Graindor 1930, 25; Broneer 1932 (*Corinth* X); Ameling 1983; Williams and Zervos 1984; Tobin 1997, 296–302, 311–4.
13. Conversion of Odeum to arena: Broneer 1928, 464; Robert 1971, 117, no. 61. The date of rebuilding as an arena is based on a coin of Alexander Severus (222–35) under an orchestra manhole. Robinson (2001, 122) argues for a conversion 225–50, while Broneer (1928, 1932 (*Corinth* X), 58–9, 65, 96) favored 225. Broneer (1932 (*Corinth* X), 72, 145) also proposed a first-century construction date for the Odeum on stratigraphic grounds, with a renovation by Herodes. A fragmentary cuirassed body of Hadrian may belong to this phase (Corinth Museum inv. no. S-1456; Broneer (1932 (*Corinth* X), 125–33, no. 6); marble coffer/screen fragments with carved masks and other decorations were thought to belong to the stage revetment either of the first (Broneer 1932 (*Corinth* X), 111–16) or second phase, but are disassociated from the building entirely by Ajootian (2008). The screen was destroyed at the end of the 3rd c. and used along with Captives Façade fragments in 4th c. terracing to the east of the Odeum (Williams and Zervos 1984, 92). For further construction and destruction phases, see Broneer 1932 (*Corinth* X), 146–7; Williams and Zervos 1987.
14. Williams pers. comm. 2007.
15. I follow Welch (2007, 181, 1999) that Dio Chrysostom is describing the Corinthian Amphitheater in *Or.* 31.121, trans. Welch 1999: "But as matters now stand, there is no practice current in Athens which would not cause any man to feel ashamed. For instance, in regard to the gladiatorial shows the Athenians have so zealously emulated the Corinthians, or rather, have so surpassed them and all others in their mad infatuation that whereas the Corinthians watch these combats outside the city in a glen, a place that is able to hold a crowd

but otherwise is dirty and is such that no one would even bury a free-born citizen there, the Athenians look on this fine spectacle in their theater under the very walls of the Acropolis ..." (*Rhodian Oration*, written in 70s).

16. Williams pers. comm. 2007; Welch 2007, 178–83, 255–9, no. 18, 1999, 134–40 (Grimani 1701 plan); Golvin 1988, 138; Robert 1971, 33, 117, no. 61; Fowler and Stillwell 1932 (*Corinth* I), 79 (plan), 89–91, Figs. 54–6; de Waele 1928, 25–31 (plan); Friedlaender 1921, 4.230; Lampros 1877, 282–8, Plan 19; Vischer 1875, 264–5; Curtius 1851/2, 2.527; Blouet et al. 1838, 3.36–7, pl. 77, fig. III (plan); Leake 1830, 3.244–5; Dodwell 1819, 2.191.
17. Welch 1999.
18. Lucian *Demonax* 57: "When the Athenians out of rivalry with the Corinthians were thinking of holding a gladiatorial show, [Demonax] came before them and exclaimed, "Don't pass this resolution, men of Athens, without first pulling down the Altar of Pity!"; Philostratus *Life of Apollonius of Tyana* 4.22: "He (Apollonius) also corrected the following abuse at Athens. The Athenians ran in crowds to the theater beneath the Acropolis to witness human slaughter, and the passion for such sports was stronger than it is here in Corinth today; for they would buy for large sums adulterers and fornicators and burglars and cut-purses and kidnappers and such rabble, and then they would take them and arm them and set them to fight one another" (written *c.*230, set in mid- to late first century).
19. Before Augustus, gladiatorial games were only held by Roman citizens in Greece. However, after Augustus, most cities in Greece started to hold them in concert with imperial cult celebrations (Welch 1999). Eastern cities with purpose-built amphitheaters in Robert 1971, 33–4: Gortyn, Antioch, Beirut, Caesarea, Alexandria, Ptolemaïs, Pergamon, Cyzicus, maybe Laodicea of Phrygia. Conversions: Athens' Theater of Dionysos was converted to an arena (Robert 1971, 34), along with those of Philippi, Thasos, Sagalassos, Termessos, Aspendos, Myra, Patara, Aizanoi, Tralles, Magnesia, Priene, Iasos, Miletus, Ephesus, Pergamon, Assos, Troy. Gladiatorial combat, though, was staged in Athens long before the arena conversion, with literary sources collected by Welch 1999. Messene's stadium was also converted into an arena, as were the stadiums of Aphrodisias and Perge.
20. Apuleius *Met.* 10.18–19, 29–35.
21. Kaibel 1878, 885; Dübner and Cougny 1888, 3.1.295; *IG* IV, no/ 365; *CIG* 1106; Robert 1971, 117–18, no. 61. Welch (1999, n. 36) suggests these could be the *carceres* of the *porta triumphalis*.
22. Corinth Museum inv. no. I-2664, Pallas *AE* 1977, 76–7, no. 21.
23. *Expositio totius mundi et gentium* 52 = *Liber iunioris philosophi in quo continetur totius orbis descriptio* 28, Rougé 1966; Di Branco 2005.

24. Julian *Ep.* 28 (or 198) written *c.*360–3, probably to the Governor of Achaia, possibly Praetextatus if genuine (Spawforth 1994 calls it spurious).
25. Julian *Or.* 3.119.
26. Julian *Frag. brev.* 3; Kordoses 1981, 60; Athanassiadi 1992, 86.
27. Feissel and Philippidis-Braat 1985, 285–7, no. 24 (restoration of 359); Feissel and Philippidis-Braat 1985, 288, no. 26 (statue for Governor of Achaia Anatolius, probably restoration a bit after 375 after earthquake).
28. Dio 39.38.1.
29. Pickard-Cambridge 1968, 82.
30. Isthmia statue base: Isthmia Museum inv. no. IS-1, Broneer 1953, 192–3.
31. Beacham 1992, 128.
32. Roueché 1993; Ratté 2000.
33. Augustine *Conf.* 1.
34. Bieber 1961, 251–2.
35. Pausanias 2.4.5.
36. Gymnasium Excavations: Wiseman 1967a, 1967b, 1969a, 1969b, 1970, 1972; Dengate 1981 (coins).
37. Gymnasia in Roman Greece: Delorme 1960; Themelis 2003 (Messene).
38. Williams 2013b.
39. Theater Bath: Robinson 1965b, 29. Possible circus, *spina* and *meta* (Corinth Museum inv. no. A-767): Wiseman 1969b, 64–72; Romano 2005, 2010; Sanders pers. comm. 2006; Wiseman 2015.
40. Corinth Museum inv. no. I-1970-39 is a herm inscribed with the beginning of a victor list for the athletic contests of the year 57 held at Corinth: the *Neronea Claudiea Caesarea Sebastea Germanicea*, the *Isthmia* and the *Caesarea*. For text, translation and commentary see Wiseman 2015. Romano (2005, 587, note 10) notes the herm, and lists the fragmentary sculpture and lead curse-tablets found over his proposed *spina*, the apsidal structure excavated by Wiseman.
41. Shear 1928, 1929, 1930, 1931; Blegen et al. 1964 (*Corinth* XIII), 65–313; Slane 2012, 2015, 2017 (*Corinth* XXI); Mary E. Hoskins Walbank 2014.
42. Euplous: Bees 1941, no. 30; *SEG* 11, no. 154; Feissel and Philippidis-Braat 1985, no. 34; Mary E. Hoskins Walbank and Michael B. Walbank 2006; Michael B. Walbank 2010, 278–80, notes 72, 80. Korinthas: *SEG* 35, no. 256; Michael B. Walbank 2010, 281–2, note 85.
43. Procopius *Anek.* 26.
44. Procopius *Anek.* 26, trans. Dewing 1935.
45. Wiseman 1979, partly based on Bagdikian 1953.

46. Broneer 1962c; Waywell 1979, 297, no. 19. For the date of the mosaic, see Hellenkemper Salies 1986.
47. Robinson 2012.
48. Broneer 1942, 145, 153–4; Scranton 1951 (*Corinth* I.3), 79, 127. Imhoof-Blumer and Gardner (1885, 64) connect this coin and several others which seem to depict the same monument with Pausanias 2.2.2, the Isthmian Games and a stadium or circus at Isthmia.
49. Kent 1966 (*Corinth* VIII.3), 28–31; Scotton 1997, 254–5.
50. Corinth Museum inv. no. I-2194, Isthmia Museum inv. no. IS-261, *IG* IV, no. 203, Broneer 1939, 1955, 124; Robert 1940, 45–53; Broneer 1955, 124; Kent 1966 (*Corinth* VIII.3), no. 306; Geagan 1989, 358–60; Gebhard 2013; Mary E. Hoskins Walbank 2015. A small part of the upper edge of this decree was found in the Hexamilion Fortress at Isthmia, and though Broneer thus thought it came from there, I think it more likely that it traveled to Isthmia with other *spolia*, especially considering that the decree is by the *Boule* and *Demos* of Corinth. It is said to have been read from the Bema (*rostra*) at Corinth, and the majority of it was found in the South Stoa.
51. Corinth Museum inv. no. I-1426, Kent 1966 (*Corinth* VIII.3), no. 230.
52. Diodorus 16.80.6 (340–39 BCE, Timoleon sends booty to be dedicated in the *hieron* of Poseidon).
53. Pausanias 2.1.7–9. Temple of Poseidon: Broneer 1953, 1955, 1958, 1959, 1962, 1971 (*Isthmia* I), 1973 (*Isthmia* II), 1977 (*Isthmia* III).
54. Corinthian Palaimonion and the cult of Melicertes-Palaemon: Pindar fragment 6.5(1) (ed. Snell 1964), with *Scholia* on Euripides *Medea* line 1284, referring to Sisyphus' foundation of the Isthmian games; Pausanias 1.44.7–8 (myth of leap into sea), 2.1.3 (burial by shore), 2.2.1 (shrine); Musti and Torelli 1986, 207 (commentary on Pausanias); Gebhard 2013; Philostratus *Imag.* 2.362.30 (Melicertes-Palaemon buried in a chasm opened by Poseidon); Will 1955, 169–80, 210–2; Burkert 1983, 196–9; West 1997, 58 (Greek and Roman cult); Hawthorne 1958; Koester 1990 (cult is Roman invention); Vikela and Vollkommer 1992, "Melikertes" in *LIMC* 6.1–2:436–44 (iconography); Broneer 1973 (*Isthmia* II), 99–112; Gebhard and Hemans 1992, 12–18, 52–71; Gebhard, Hemans and Hayes 1998, 405–56; Gebhard 1993, 89–93 (excavations); Gebhard and Reese 2005.
55. Gebhard 2013; Gebhard and Dickie 1999 (two temples); Gebhard and Reese 2005.
56. Mary E. Hoskins Walbank 2015 (one temple).
57. Isthmia Sanctuary complex: Peppers 1979 (pottery); Gregory 1995 (Bath); Gebhard 1979, 1993, 2005, 2007, 2013; Gebhard and Reese 2005; Sturgeon 1987 (*Isthmia* IV); Lattimore 1996 (*Isthmia* VI)

(Sculpture); Raubitschek 1998 (*Isthmia* VII) (Metal objects); Rife 2012 (*Isthmia* IX) UCLA 1968–71 excavations of Clement east of the Temple: Clement 1968, 1969, 1970 (1972), 1971 (1974); Megaw 1967–8; Daux 1968; Michaud 1970. UChicago 1989 excavations: Gebhard and Hemans 1992; Gebhard at al. 1998.

58. Roman Arch at Isthmia: Gregory and Mills 1984.
59. Pausanias 1.42.8, 1.44.6–8; Gebhard 2013.
60. Pausanias 2.1.7; Gebhard 2013.
61. Broneer 1962 (Isthmian crown); Geagan 1968 (agonistic institutions), 1975 (synod at Isthmia under Trajan), 2005 (triangular victor monuments); Biers and Geagan 1970 (victor list). See Golden 1998; Potter and Mattingly 1999; Miller 2004; Bell 2004; Futrell 2006; Kyle 2007.
62. Imhoof-Blumer and Gardner 1885, 64; Mary E. Hoskins Walbank 2015.
63. Frey and Gregory 2016.
64. Corinth Museum inv. no. S-340, de Grazia 1973, no. 47, is the male portrait head of an Isthmian victor of tetrarchic style. It was brought in to the Corinth Museum with Corinth Museum inv. no. S-341, de Grazia 1973, no. 41, a female portrait head, perhaps his wife. Victor monuments include: Isthmia Museum inv. no. IS-69–1, Clement 1970 (1972), 166–7, pls. 140–1b; Michaud 1970, 947–9; Clement 1974, 36–9, pls. 2–4; *SEG* 29, no. 340; *SEG* 31, no. 293; *SEG* 33, no. 296; *SEG* 38, no. 1934; *SEG* 41, no. 270; Lattimore 1996, no. 87, pls. 27–8; Isthmia Museum inv. no. IS-69–2, Clement 1970 (1972), 167, pl. 141c; Michaud 1970, 949; *SEG* 29, no. 341. See also Geagan 2005; Wiseman 2015.
65. Corinth Museum inv. no. S-2415, Jenkins and Megaw 1934, 82 Fig. 8; de Grazia 1973, 196–201 no. 46 pl. 60. Epidauros: Katakis 2002, no. 104. For portraits possibly of the emperor Julian, see Kastriotis 1923; Lévêque 1960; Inan and Alföldi-Rosenbaum 1966, 157, no. 108, n. 5; Smith 2001. For the group of heads, called Iamblichus: Rodenwaldt 1913; L'Orange 1933; Harrison 1953 (*Agora* I), pl. 47:b; von Sydow 1969, 105.

Chapter 5 Creation and Destruction of Public Sculpture

1. For literary sources and scholarship of this shift in attitude to sculpture, see Hannestad 1999; Stewart 1999, 2003, 2007; Sauer 2003; Pollini 2007, 2008; Deligiannakis 2008; Smith 2012; Smith and Ward-Perkins 2016; Kristensen and Stirling 2016.
2. See Brown 2012a and 2016a for late antique Corinthian portrait statues, and Brown 2016b for destruction and cross-marking of Corinthian public sculpture in Late Antiquity.

3. For Roman imperial portrait statues and inscriptions also concentrated in these areas see de Grazia 1973; Kent 1966 (*Corinth* VIII.3), 38–100.
4. For the full assemblage of potential Peirene statuary, and its disposal in the course of the sixth- and seventh-century modifications to the Peirene Fountain and use of its waters, see Robinson 2011, 281–92.
5. For Corinth Museum inv. nos. S-54 (Nymph or Aphrodite) and S-1024 (Nymph with shell, drill marks, my Figure 5.1), see Robinson 2011, 215–6 (figs. 115–16), 234–50 (Scylla, fig. 141).
6. Robinson 2011, 282.
7. Corinth Museum inv. no. S-920, Johnson 1931 (*Corinth* IX), 148–9, no. 321; de Grazia 1973, 217–23, no. 53, pls. 69–70; Ridgway 1981, 448, n. 105, pl. 97:d; de Grazia Vanderpool 2003, 380–1, n. 59, fig. 22.14; Robinson 2011, 283, fig. 159; Last Statues of Antiquity (LSA) number LSA-74 (for this and other statues with LSA numbers, see the Last Statues of Antiquity website).
8. For multiple crowns and the significance of each, see the Aizanoi inscription in Wörrle 1992; for a third-century head with a bust-crown from Athens identified as possibly an *agonothetes* of the *Panhellenia*, see Riccardi 2007.
9. Corinth S-909 (LSA-72), Johnson 1931 (*Corinth* IX), 92, no. 183; de Grazia 1973, no. 59 (dates 450–500); Robinson 2011, 283, fig. 160.
10. Corinth S-919 (LSA-73), Johnson 1931 (*Corinth* IX), no. 178; de Grazia 1973, no. 58 (dates 450–500); Robinson 2011, 283, fig. 161; Brown 2016b, 164–6, fig. 5.
11. For engraved forehead crosses, see an Egyptian stone bust of Germanicus in the British Museum (BM inv. no. 1872,0605.1, Fluck et al. 2015, cover and 96); Augustus and Livia from Ephesus (Inan and Alföldi-Rosenbaum 1979; Hjort 1993); two third-century female portraits from Ephesus (Inan and Rosenbaum 1966, 135–6, nos. 164–5, pl. 96); and a tetrarch from Afyon with a cut down nose (Inan and Rosenbaum 1966, 85–6, no. 62, pl. 39:1–2). Johnson compared the Corinth head with the cross-marked head of Aphrodite in the National Archaeological Museum at Athens, though her nose and eyes were smashed, and the forehead cross is quite large and was applied with a point rather than engraved (Kastriotis 1900, 87–90, pl. 5).
12. Third-century male heads: Corinth Museum inv. nos. S-22, de Grazia 1973, 141, no. 25 and S-1470, Ridgway 1981, 445, n. 96. Late antique male heads include Corinth Museum inv. nos. S-1047 (LSA-85), Johnson 1931 (*Corinth* IX), no. 179; de Grazia 1973, 205–6, no. 49 (tetrarchic); S-2496 (LSA-86), de Grazia 1973, 185–7, no. 40, pl. 52 (325–50); S-2749 (LSA-70), de Grazia 1973, 204–5, no. 48 (fourth century); S-1073 (LSA-67), de Grazia 1973, 211–12, no. 51 (late fourth to early fifth century); S-1454 (LSA-75), de Grazia 1973, 223–6, no. 54, pl. 71; Robinson 2011, 284, fig. 163 (fifth century).

For a lost male head, see Tucker 1902, 423, fig. 1, 437–8. Even a portrait identified as Corinth's refounder Julius Caesar (with a short stippled late antique beard added) was pulled from a drain: Corinth Museum inv. no. S-2771, de Grazia 1973, 77–80, no. 7, pls. 10, 11; Datsouli-Stavridi 1970, 109–10, fig. 1D; Ridgway 1981, 430, n. 31; Robinson 2011, 284, fig. 164; de Grazia Vanderpool forthcoming.

13. S-1199 (LSA-71), Johnson 1931 (*Corinth* IX), 88, no. 168; Ridgway 1981, 448, n. 104, pl. 97:c; de Grazia Vanderpool 2003, 381, n. 60–1, fig. 22.15; Brown 2016a, 184, fig. 14.8. For his excavation from the Peirene Fountain drain in the so-called Garden Pit north of the village *Plateia* by the Great Bath on the Lechaion Road, see Blegen 1919, Corinth Excavations NB85A, 55 (July 11, 1919).
14. Corinth Museum inv. no. S-1977-13, de Grazia Vanderpool 2003, 379–80, notes 55–8, fig. 22.13 (dated 350–400). For the busts now in Thessalonike, see Thessalonike Archaeological Museum inv. nos. 1060–1, L'Orange 1961, 68–74, pls. 27.1, 27.3; Kiilerich 1993, 210–11; Stefanidou-Tiveriou 2008, figs. 5–6.
15. Corinth Museum inv. no. S-986 (LSA-77), Johnson 1931 (*Corinth* IX), no. 164; de Grazia 1973, 238–42, no. 63; Ridgway 1981, 448, n. 106; Jesse 1992; Robinson 2011, 284, fig. 162. A fragment of a second lady's head with a similar headscarf came from the Northwest Shops, another late antique female benefactor, or even an empress (Corinth Museum inv. no. S-2474, de Grazia 1973, no. 64).
16. Corinth Museum inv. no. S-55, Robinson 2011, 78–9, 252–3, 281–2, fig. 51; Corinth Museum inv. no. I-62, Kent 1966 (*Corinth* VIII.3), no. 15; Robert 1966, 743. See Robinson 2011, 76, where she quotes from the excavator Dickerman, Corinth Excavations NB7 (May 27, 1898), on four female statues from the area of Peirene's northern exedra, two "mortared into the wall" (Corinth Museum inv. nos. S-67 and S-68?) and two "lying" in the northeast entry of the fountain (Corinth Museum inv. nos. S-54, a Nymph or Aphrodite, and Corinth Museum inv. no. S-55, the female portrait body).
17. Edwards (1993) identified the head of Dionysos (Corinth Museum inv. no. S-987) as belonging to a group with the headless female bodies of Corinth Museum inv. nos. S-67 (as Kore) and S-68 (as Demeter). He brought in also a draped lower body with panther feet beside it, Corinth Museum inv. no. S-69, as an Ariadne Valentini, though this lower body had been previously identified as Apollo or Dionysos. Stewart (2013, 626–7) argues that the so-called Ariadne Valentini statue represented Aphrodite. Tucker (1902) gave the findspot of the statue bodies as the area of the Peribolos of Apollo's southern exedra, where they may have stood, and identified Corinth Museum inv. no. S-69 as Apollo or Dionysos. Johnson (1931 (*Corinth* IX), 34–5, no. 28) linked Corinth Museum inv. no. S-69 with the Dionysos *xoanon* (wooden statue) of Pausanias

2.2.6 on a Hadrianic coin (Imhoof-Blumer and Gardner 1885, E77)), and dubbed the two female bodies, Corinth Museum inv. nos. S-67 and S-68, as Roman matrons of "late work" and poor style.

18. Pausanias 2.3.3–4, modified translation from Jones 1918, 261.
19. Corinth Museum inv. no. S-2755, Daux 1966, 756, fig. 9; Sturgeon 1975, no. 2.
20. Themelis 2003.
21. Brown 2016b.
22. *Palliatus* portrait body Corinth Museum inv. no. S-47 (LSA-78), Johnson 1931 (*Corinth* IX), no. 202; de Grazia 1973, 278, no. 86 (third century, from poor carving). *Togatus* portrait body Corinth Museum inv. no. S-180, Johnson 1931, 94, no. 195; de Grazia 1973, 258–60, no. 73, pl. 85; Havé-Nikolaus 1998, 132–3, no. 23 (Antonine). Marble left hand holding a scroll Corinth Museum inv. no. S-817 (LSA-2359), probably also from a *chlamydatus* portrait. Antonine *togati* from the south end of the Lechaion Road, Corinth Museum inv. nos. S-50 and S-51, with a new head once doweled on and neck slot cut down (Robinson 2011, 282, n. 179).
23. Corinth Museum inv. no. S-2224, de Grazia 1973, 292–4, no. 94, pl. 98; Ridgway 1981, 448; Brown 2012a, 168, fig. 23.
24. For a thorough description of each statue and the significance of the *chlamydatus* costume, see Brown 2012a, 2016a.
25. Corinth Museum inv. no. S-314 (LSA-21), Johnson 1931 (*Corinth* IX), 149, no. 323; de Grazia 1973, 283–4, no. 88 (before join with foot, scrolls); Brown 2012a, 150, figs. 10–12. For scroll supports: Smith 1999.
26. Corinth Museum inv. no. S-903 (LSA-15), Johnson 1924, 253, no. 1, 1931 (*Corinth* IX), 150, no. 325; Kollwitz 1941, 89, no. 13; de Grazia 1973, 282–6, no. 89; Sturgeon 2004 (*Corinth* IX.3), 163–5, no. 54; Brown 2012a, 149, figs. 8–9.
27. Hand: Corinth Museum inv. no. T-863/Sc (LSA-25). 62, Sturgeon 2004 (*Corinth* IX.3), 165–6, no. 55; Brown 2012a, 162, fig. 21.
28. Corinth Museum inv. no. S-2046 'LSA-23), de Grazia 1973, no. 92; Brown 2012a, 153, figs. 17–18.
29. Corinth Museum inv. no. S-925 (LSA-24), Johnson 1924, no. 4, 1931 (*Corinth* IX), no. 328; Kollwitz 1941, 90–1, no. 16; de Grazia 1973, no. 93; Sande 1975, 84; Foss 1979 (1996), 213; Ridgway 1981, 448; Brown 2012a, 154, figs. 19–20.
30. Corinth Museum inv. no. S-819 (LSA-22), Johnson 1924, no. 3, 1931 (*Corinth* IX), no. 327; Kollwitz 1941, 90, no. 15; de Grazia 1973, no. 90; Sande 1975, 84; Foss 1979 (1996), 213; Brown 2012a, 151, figs. 13–14. Ridgway pers. comm. 2011 said that Charles Edwards identified the female statue as a Demeter Mocenigo, the same type as the Demeter statue from the Peribolos of Apollo (Corinth Museum inv. no. S-68).
31. Corinth Museum inv. no. S-822 (LSA-19), Johnson 1924, no. 2, 1931 (*Corinth* IX), no. 326; Kollwitz 1941, 89–90, no. 14; de Grazia 1973,

no. 91; Sande 1975, 84; Foss 1979 (1996), 213; Ridgway 1981, 448; Brown 2012a, 152, figs. 15–6.

32. Corinth Museum inv. no. S-3788 (LSA-80), Pallas 1970 (1972), 98–9, 102–4, 113, fig. 2, pls. 144a, 145b, 157b; Brown 2012a, 142–7, figs. 2–6.
33. *AnthPal* 7.672. Translation adapted from Paton 1917.
34. For honors with third- to fourth-century letter forms from the Lechaion Road see Corinth Museum inv. nos. I-21, Powell 1903, 57–8, no. 35; Meritt 1931 (*Corinth* VIII.1), no. 105; I-388, Smith 1919, no. 97; Meritt 1931 (*Corinth* VIII.1), no. 95; Rizakis and Zoumbaki 2001, 345, COR 382; I-670, Meritt 1931 (*Corinth* VIII.1), no. 87 (from the ramp); I-798/799, Meritt 1931 (*Corinth* VIII.1), no. 106; Rizakis and Zoumbaki 2001, 315, COR 265; I-2760 (ramp); I-2763 (ramp); I-1973-8.
35. Corinth Museum inv. no. I-1115 (LSA-17), Groag 1946, 98, 111; Kent 1966 (*Corinth* VIII.3), no. 502, pl. 42; Feissel and Philippidis-Braat 1985, no. 31 (dates third century); Jones et al. 1971 (*PLRE*), I.667–8 s.v. Parnasius I; Rizakis 1995, 69, no. 20; Rizakis and Zoumbaki 2001, 271–2, COR nos. 102.1, 363, 422 (dates fourth century); Brown 2012a, 166. Kent gives the Greek text.
36. Libanius *Or.* 14, 16, *Ep.* 734, 1228, 1264, 1399 (ed. Foerster 1903–27, 822, 1214); Ammianus 19.12.10; Julian *Ep.* 28, 74 (97 Bidez); Themistius *Or.* 23.295a–296b.
37. Libanius *Or.* 18.135–46, 48.7, 49.19; Jones 1940, 202.
38. Brown 2012a.
39. Corinth Museum inv. no. I-19 (LSA-62), *IG* IV, no. 1603; Powell 1903, no. 23; Wilhelm 1905, 415–6; Meritt 1931 (*Corinth* VIII.1), no. 89; Groag 1946, 97–8, 111; Rizakis 2001, 271–2, COR no. 102.2, 363; Brown 2012a, 164 (Greek text, English translation).
40. Corinth Museum inv. no. I-17/I-18 (LSA-51), *IG* IV, nos 1602, 1604; Powell 1903, nos. 22, 27; *REG* 1904, 247 (I-17 only); Meritt 1931 (*Corinth* VIII.1), no. 88; Dow 1951, 96–100; Robinson 2011, 282; Brown 2012a, 163–4, fig. 22 (corrected Greek text, English translation).
41. Compare the εἰκόνα λαϊνέην, "shining image," in Sironen 2016 (*IG* IV^2 3), no. 1251, a statue base with fourth-century script once associated with Herodes Atticus, and discussed in Chapter 6 with full bibliography, or the [εἰκόν]α Λαμπρίου λαϊν[έην ἔθεσαν], "shining image of Lamprias" restored by Sironen as the last line of a four-line hexameter epigram on a round base with fourth-century script, which may also honor a certain Theodore for his wisdom (Corinth Museum inv. no. I-1768, Kent 1966 (*Corinth* VIII.3), no. 517; Feissel and Philippidis-Braat 1985, no. 51*; Sironen 2016 (*IG* IV^2 3), no. 1255).
42. Libanius *Or.* 14.5–7; Robinson 2011, 63, n. 174, 282, n. 178.

43. Homer *Iliad* 6.152; Eumelus fr. 1b (*Schol.* Apollonius of Rhodes *Argon.* 4.1212); Pausanias 2.1.1; Innes 2001; West 2002; Kopestonsky 2016, 716.
44. Corinth Museum inv. no. I-146, Powell 1903, no. 39; Meritt 1931 (*Corinth* VIII.1), no. 92; Hiller von Gärtringen 1932, 363; *SEG* 11, no. 79; Groag 1946, 62; Feissel and Philippidis-Braat 1985, no. 8*; Sironen 2016 (*IG* IV^2 3), no. 1254.
45. Smith 1999; Stewart 2007.
46. These include, besides the texts I have discussed elsewhere, and in order of discovery, Corinth Museum inv. nos. I-494, Meritt 1931 (*Corinth* VIII.1), no. 96 (dedication to an emperor?, uncertain findspot); I-777, Meritt 1931 (*Corinth* VIII.1), no. 110d (proconsul?, from NW Forum); I-939, Kent 1966 (*Corinth* VIII.3), no. 519; I-1112, Kent 1966 (*Corinth* VIII.3), no. 690; Sironen 2016 (*IG* IV^2 3), no. 1257 (sixth-century honorific poem, from Temple D); I-1381b + , Kent 1966 (*Corinth* VIII.3), no. 274 (third-century dedication to Lucius Veturius Publilianus); I-1471 and 1472, Kent 1966 (*Corinth* VIII.3), no. 273; Rizakis and Zoumbaki 2001, 265, Corinthia no. 73; I-2118/1974-4, Kent 1966 (*Corinth* VIII.3), no. 486 (2118); Martin 1977, 189–95, no. 10, pl. 52 (*cursus honorum*); I-2249, Kent 1966 (*Corinth* VIII.3), no. 501; I-2322, Kent 1966 (*Corinth* VIII.3), no. 518 (G. Ioulius, uncertain findspot).
47. Corinth Museum inv. nos. I-1905/2149, Kent 1966 (*Corinth* VIII.3), no. 516 (just I-2149); Sironen 2016 (*IG* IV^2 3), no. 1252.
48. For an honorific poetic dedication to the Praetorian Prefect of the East in two lines of restored text on a whie marble base from the Forum, see Corinth Museum inv. no. I-2111, Kent 1966 (*Corinth* VIII.3), no. 473; Sironen 2016 (*IG* IV^2 3), no. 1258.
49. Trebonianus Gallus base: Corinth Museum inv. no. I-1751, Kent 1966 (*Corinth* VIII.3), no. 116.
50. Against the Christian triumphal interpretation of Rothaus (2000, 125, n. 64), see a garland altar of 35 BCE reused as a statue base for a statue of Isis in the Thessalonike Serapeum (Thessalonike Archaeological Museum inv. no. 986). Rothaus also follows Kent (1966 (*Corinth* VIII.3), no. 510) in identifying this base as belonging to a statue of Constans II (641–68), which is highly unlikely on the basis of letter forms and historical circumstances.
51. Constans base, for a statue set up 337–50: Corinth Museum inv. no. I-2143, Kent 1950; Scranton 1951 (*Corinth* I.3), 147, pl. 67.3; Kent 1966 (*Corinth* VIII.3), no. 510; Feissel and Philippidis-Braat 1985, no. 3; Sanders 2003; Sironen 2016 (*IG* IV^2 3), no. 1250.
52. Dean 1922, 467, nos. 48–9, figs. 13–14; West 1931 (*Corinth* VIII.2), nos. 23–5; Groag 1946, 15; Jones et al. 1971 (*PLRE*), I.685 s.v. Lucius Sul. Paulus II; Rizakis and Zoumbaki 2001, 385, COR 578; Sironen 2016 (*IG* IV^2 3), nos. 1247–9.

53. Theodosius I, Arcadius and Honorius: Corinth Museum inv. nos. I-228/754 and I-295, West 1931 (*Corinth* VIII.2), no. 26; Kent 1966 (*Corinth* VIII.3), no. 506; Feissel and Philippidis-Braat 1985, no. 10; Rizakis and Zoumbaki 2001, 248, Corinthia no. 4; Sironen 2016 (*IG* IV^2 3), no. 1253. One plaque was found at the east end of the Northwest Shops, the other had been reused as a grindstone in the area of the modern village *Plateia*.
54. The restored Latin text reads: *reparatori R[o]manae rei p[ublicae, fundatori] / aeternae [p]acis, aucto[ri humani] / generis, d(omino) n(ostro) [F]l(avio) Theodos[io Augusto], / felicissimo [p]atri, et fi[liis dd(ominis) nn (ostris) FFll(aviis)] / Arcadio et H[on]orio Im[peratoribus] / –tius Ac––––––*. The fragmentary last line of the inscription should be the name of the dedicator, probably a Governor of Achaia.
55. Corinth Museum inv. no. I-276, Meritt 1931 (*Corinth* VIII.1), no. 245; Feissel and Philippidis-Braat 1985, no. 33; Sanders 2003, 395, note 35.
56. Justin I or II: Corinth Museum inv. no. I-1987-3, Sironen 2016 (*IG* IV^2 3), no. 1259: [Ἰουστ]ῖνον [τὸν]/[εὐσε]β(έστατον) ἡμ[ῶν]/[αὐτ]οκρ(άτορα) - -. Sironen cites Hallof for an alternative restoration of the text to the consulship of Justin in 519 or 524.
57. Emperors Justin II and Tiberius the New Constantine (574–8): Corinth Museum inv. no. I-435, Meritt 1931 (*Corinth* VIII.1), no. 195; Hiller von Gärtringen 1932, 363; Bees 1941, no. 9; Feissel and Philippidis-Braat 1985, no. 18; Sironen 2016 (*IG* IV^2 3), no. 1266.
58. Groag 1946.
59. For identification of these higher officials: Sande 1975, 84; Foss 1979 (1996).
60. This headless statue, now at the north end of the Stoa of Attalos on the Agora in Athens, is the only *togatus* from Greece known to me who wears the late antique toga. For the statue as Herculius: Hattersley-Smith 1996, 201. For Herculius as patron of the Palace: Frantz 1969, 1979, 400. For the Palace: Travlos 1971, 233 fig. 37; Frantz 1988 (*Agora* XXIV), 21–3 (ceramic, coin evidence for Palace construction). Sironen 1995, 1997, 2008 (*IG* II/III^2 5) for the inscriptions. For earlier *togati* from Greece: Havé-Nikolaus 1998.
61. de Grazia Vanderpool 2003, 375.
62. Third-century heads: Corinth Museum inv. nos. S-1155, Johnson 1931, no. 159; de Grazia Vanderpool 1973, 65–9, no. 3; Ridgway 1981, 447, pl. 97:a ("even the Tetrarchic period"); S-1181, de Grazia 1973, 178–83, no. 37; S-1802, de Grazia 1973, no. 45; Ridgway 1981, 447; S-1972-5, de Grazia Vanderpool 2003, 370, fig. 22.4; S-1974-30, Williams and Fisher 1975, 14, n. 28; Ridgway 1981, 438–46; de Grazia Vanderpool 2003, 370, fig. 22.3. For the third or fourth century, no provenance but probably the Forum: Corinth Museum inv. nos. S-72, Tucker 1902, 437–8, fig. 1; Johnson 1931 (*Corinth* IX),

92, no. 181; S-363, Johnson 1931, 92, no. 180; S-1202, Johnson 1931 (*Corinth* IX), no. 182; de Grazia 1973, 207–11, no. 50; Comstock and Vermeule 1976, no. 381; Weitzmann 1979, no. 270; Smith 1990, 144, note 70; Kondoleon 2000, no. 97. Fifth-century heads: Corinth Museum inv. nos. S-2186, de Grazia 1973, 235–6, no. 60; S-2195, de Grazia 1973, 228–9, no. 57.

63. Sturgeon (2003, 362, note 42) mentions unfinished heads Corinth Museum inv. nos. S-697 (Johnson 1931 (*Corinth* IX), 88–9, no. 170; de Grazia 1973, 226–7, no. 55, pl. 72) and S-1610 (de Grazia 1973, 227–8, no. 56, pl. 73). Of unknown provenance, but probably from the Forum, and also unfinished, is Corinth Museum inv. no S-362, de Grazia 1973, no. 62.

64. Corinth Museum inv. no. S-696 (body), Johnson 1931 (*Corinth* IX), 96, no. 198; de Grazia 1973, 279–80, no. 87, pl. 94; Corinth Museum inv. no. S-697 (head), Johnson 1931 (Corinth IX), 88–9, no. 170; de Grazia 1973, 226–7, no. 55, pl. 72. The head was dated by L'Orange (1933, 89) to 450–500, and put with the Vienna group. Sturgeon (2003, 362, note 42) and then de Grazia Vanderpool (2003, 375, note 33, fig. 22.7) both call it an unfinished head, and date it to the second half of the fifth century, but neither mention the cross on top of it, nor regard its matching with the body as original. See now Brown 2016b, 160–4, figs. 4a (head), 4b (top of head) and 4c (body).

65. Roueché 1989, 189–90, no. 31 (Oecumenius base); Smith 1999, 162–5, fig. 6 (Oecumenius statue), 2002, 150–5, fig. 13.1–2 (top of Oecumenius's head); Roueché 1989, no. 145 (second head inscription); Smith 2002, 150–5, fig. 24.2 (top of second head, now in Brussels).

66. Smith 1990, 1999, 2001, 2002, 2007, 2012; Smith et al. 2006.

67. Corinth Museum inv. no. S-3361, de Grazia 1973, 261–2, no. 75, pl. 86; Delivorrias 1991, 112, no. 25, pl. 55B; Kristensen 2012, 42, 60, cat. B19; Rothaus 2000, 120–1, fig. 23 (with reference to *togati* Corinth Museum inv. nos. S-50, S-51 and wreathed male head S-1445a, also found placed under walls); Brown 2016b, 158–60, fig. 3.

68. Herm, not necessarily marked in Late Antiquity with the cross: Corinth Museum inv. no. S-202, Rothaus 2000, 120, fig. 22; Kristensen 2012, 60, cat. B18; Brown 2016b, 154, fig. 1. Artemis: Corinth Museum inv. no. S-2392, Morgan 1939, 266–7, fig. 9; Scranton 1951 (*Corinth* I.3), 70, pl. 27:1; Kahil 1984 (*LIMC* s.v. Artemis), 2.1.646, no. 277, pl. 469; Stirling 2008, 138, note 153; Kristensen 2012, 34–5, 60, fig. 2, cat. B20; Brown 2016b, 154–7, fig. 2. The body of Artemis came from a Byzantine wall of the Central Shops (Corinth Museum inv. no. S-2392, in 1938, Corinth Excavations NB176, 85); her foot was then found in Byzantine wall 13 of Forum SW (Corinth Museum inv. no. S-1997-1 (no. lapsed), in 1997, Corinth Excavations NB898, 114). Morgan (1939,

266–7, fig. 9) dates the statue of Artemis to the late first century, and comments that, "the statue attracted the attention of the Early Christians, who incised a large cross upon the left thigh." Rothaus (2000) doesn't cite her in his examination of statuary defacement.

69. For cross-marking and defacement of statuary see: Delivorrias 1991; Hjort 1993; Kristensen 2012. For a cross-marked head of Hera from Sparta, see Tod and Wace 1906, and for the smashed bronze empress portrait from Sparta now in the Athens National Museum as target of Christian ire see Riccardi 1998 (with Libanius *Ep.* 1518.5 on destruction of statuary at Sparta); for a cross-marked Hera from Rhodes, see Tataki 1994.
70. For Roman attitudes, see Fantham 2012, and for a Christian text on a watery hell, the *Apocalypse of Peter.* I thank Julian Barr for this reference.
71. Stroud 1965, 20–1, pls. 10a–c, 1993; Bookidis and Fisher 1972, pl. 62a; Ridgway 1981, 436; Dunbabin 1990; Bookidis and Stroud 1997 (*Corinth* XVIII.3); Slane 2008. Rothaus (2000, 123, n. 59) calls this cleanup from the sanctuary's destruction, or a ritual deposit. The statues from the well include heads of girl priestesses Corinth Museum inv. nos. S-2666 and S-2667, goddess head Corinth Museum inv. no. S-2668, and marble fragments to be published by Elizabeth Milleker in a future *Corinth* XVIII volume on sculpture from the Sanctuary of Demeter and Kore. However, de Grazia Vanderpool (2003) has referred to the two heads of girls, one with deliberate smashing of nose and mouth by blunt instrument, dating them late Trajanic or early Hadrianic (see also Ridgway 1981, 436; Stroud 1965, 21 pl. 10:b–c). The two girls' heads closely resemble a head in the MFA Boston, inv. no. 96.698 (Caskey 1925, 215–6, n. 127) and one in the Archaeological Museum of Thessalonike, MTh inv. no. 1052 (Despinis et al. 2003, no. 278, pls. 854–5), a portrait of a girl with her hair in a decorated knot, "Unknown provenance, 2nd c." The well was open over the winter between its discovery in 1961 and further digging in 1962, and there is some evidence that sculpture was removed and sold to the art market during this time (Bookidis pers. comm. 2008).
72. Eunapius *VSoph.* 476 (7.3.5), trans. Wright 1921, 439. For the date of composition of the *VSoph.* ca. 399, and Eunapius in Athens 362–7, see Banchich 1987. For Alaric at Corinth see Brown 2011a.
73. Eunapius *VSoph.* 475–6, trans. Wright 1921, 437.
74. Eunapius *VSoph.* 482.
75. Alexandria: Gregory 1983; Chuvin 1990, 57–72; Haas 1997; Watts 2010.
76. Mark the Deacon *Vita Porphyrii* 41 (ed. and trans. Grégoire and Kugener 1930); Fowden 1978, 73.
77. Marinus *Vita Procli* 30.

78. Shear 1973, 161; Camp 1989, 54, Fig. 19; Lawton 2005.
79. van de Paverd 1991.
80. Coates-Stephens 2001, 2004, 2007.
81. Sanders 2003, 2005; Sanders and Boyd 2008.
82. Frey 2016 (for the use of *spolia* in the Hexamilion and other walls in Late Antiquity); Sourlas 2013 (for the abundant use of third-century statue bases in the Post-Herulian Wall at Athens).

Chapter 6 Sacred Spaces around the Forum

1. Serapis bust for insertion into wooden herm: Corinth Museum inv. no. S-2387, Capps Jr. 1938, 548–51, fig. 8; Broneer 1954 (*Corinth* I.4), 132–8. A smashed dedication to the *Genius Augusti* by imperial freedman and treasurer Phileros was recovered from the *Bouleuterion* and this area: Corinth Museum inv. no. I-1835, Kent 1966 (*Corinth* VIII.3), nos. 67, 497. Inside Shop XX, which Broneer interpreted as a domestic context, there was also a hoard of coins (up to Gallienus) in a burned box, the statue head, a built altar and the base with dedication to *Colonia Laus Iulia Corinthiensis*. Redating the burn layer of this shop from the late third to the late fourth centuries: Slane 1994. Another statuette head of a bearded male deity, probably also Serapis, came from Shop XXV just to the west, and possibly was once in shop XX: Corinth Museum inv. no. S-2268, Capps Jr. 1938, 545–7, figs. 5–6. For the Serapis heads in general, see Milleker 1985.
2. Corinth Museum inv. nos. I-1457, I-1458; only Serapis published: Broneer 1926, 56–7; Brady 1941, 64; Smith 1977, 224–5; Milleker 1985, 124–7.
3. Early Roman cults: Mary E. Hoskins Walbank 1986a, 1986b, 1996, 1997, 2010a, 2010b; Bookidis 2005. Christianization of Roman cults at Corinth (with caution as to his presentation of archaeological contexts): Rothaus 2000.
4. Pausanias 2.2.6–2.3.1.
5. Scranton 1944, 1951 (*Corinth* I.3), 51, 67, 70.
6. Robinson 2001, 244–63.
7. Herakles: Corinth Museum inv. no. S-1972-1, Sturgeon 1975, no. 5. The statue lacks head and feet, and was deposited in the drain along with other statues of divinities and a male portrait head in the fifth or sixth century. Examples of Herakles at Roman Corinth include Corinth Museum inv. nos. S-157, Johnson 1931, 57, no. 79 (Herakles Farnese); Lisle 1955, 155; I-83, 838 Kent 1966 (*Corinth* VIII.3), no. 65 (poem for Herakles?); I-240 Meritt 1931 (*Corinth* VIII.1), no. 69 (Herakles dedication); Capps Jr. 1936; Sturgeon 1977 (*Corinth* IX.2) (Theater reliefs, 15 other statues).
8. Robinson 2001.

9. Scranton 1951 (*Corinth* I.3), 65–2; Williams 1989; Torelli 2001; Millis 2004.
10. Temple F for Pausanias' statue of Aphrodite by Hermogenes of Cythera: Williams and Fisher 1975, 25–7. Scranton (1951 (*Corinth* I.3), 61–2), with the same evidence, argued for Temple F once dedicated to Venus Victrix as Pausanias' Tyche. A gilded marble Aphrodite statuette head came from a drain just to the west (Corinth Museum inv. no. S-1972-18, Sturgeon 1975, no. 4, dated middle to second half of the second century). Coin evidence and Hermogenes as a Roman sculptor: Seltman 1928.
11. Corinth Museum inv. nos. S-2704 joined to S-1971-3, Sturgeon 1975, no. 6, belong to a statuette of Apollo (or perhaps Asclepius) with snake and omphalos from just south and east of Temple G.
12. Mary E. Hoskins Walbank 1996.
13. Millis (2004) argued for construction of Temple D as a replacement for Temple K in the early third century. Bookidis (pers. comm. 2008) says there is no evidence for demolition of Temple K this early, and she would like to see more evidence from Millis for the late date of the building of Temple D and the demolition of Temple K. I thank her for pointing out a close parallel for Hermes at the corner of the Forum in the temple at the SW corner of Dougga in Tunisia dedicated to the market god Hermes/Mercury.
14. Pausanias 2.2.8. Scranton (1951 (*Corinth* I.3), 67–72) made this the temple of Hermes too, arguing that Pausanias followed an itinerary from south to north along the west side of the Forum.
15. Imhoof-Blumer and Gardner (1885, 72–3) connect the coins rather with the bronze statue of Hermes with the Ram on the Lechaion Road (Pausanias 2.3.4). For a Severe-style Roman head of Hermes (or Perseus) with winged cap from the Great Drain under Central Shop 5 deposited in fill of the fifth or sixth century, see Corinth Museum inv. no. S-1972-4 (Sturgeon 1975, no. 1, Hadrianic). A head of Hermes (or Perseus) wearing a *petasos* hat came from Forum SW (Corinth Museum inv. no. S-1934A–B, Sturgeon 1975, no. 3, Antonine or later), as did an Archaistic Hermes Kriophoros (Corinth Museum inv. no. S-686).
16. Corinth Museum inv. no. S-890, Johnson 1931 (*Corinth* IX), 90, no. 173 (Trajanic or Hadrianic); de Grazia 1973, no. 21; Ridgway 1981, 436, n. 59 (possibly fourth century, from Trajanic bangs, short beard, drilling of the pupils), citing Winkes 1969, 68–71, 175–6; Delbrueck 1933, pl. 121.
17. Corinth Museum inv. no. S-324, Johnson 1931 (*Corinth* IX), no. 174; S-687, Johnson 1931 (*Corinth* IX), no. 175. Medallion frame fragments: Corinth Museum inv. nos. S-640, 941, 942, 946, 947.
18. For Temple D as the Dionysion, see Williams 2013b. For a *monopteros* over the Sacred Spring at the east end of the Northwest Shops as the

Dionysion, see Williams (and Fisher 1975, 28). For a Roman tripod base see Shoe 1964, 300–3; Williams 1970, 29, fig. 8. For a Maenad base see Corinth Museum inv. no. S-193, Richardson 1904; Johnson 1931 (*Corinth* IX), 131–2, no. 275 (drilled, second- or third-century). For a Maenad relief see Corinth Museum inv. no. S-2597, Broneer 1951, 297–9 (SStoa/NWShops, Antonine). For Dionysos sculpture from the area see Corinth Museum inv. nos. S-194, an overlifesize head of Leaning Dionysos from over the Sacred Spring by the Captives Façade (Richardson 1904; Johnson 1931 (*Corinth* IX), 31–3, no. 25), S-426, an Archaistic "Alkamenes-style" Dionysos head with smashed mouth, from the NW Stoa (Richardson 1904, 296; Johnson 1931 (*Corinth* IX), 37, no. 31) and S-1294, a headless body (Sturgeon 1998).

19. Central Shops Shrine: Scranton 1951 (*Corinth* I.3), 85, 89–90, 125; Roux 1958, 109; Williams and Fisher 1975, 28; Williams 1989; Williams and Zervos 1990, 351–6.
20. Ajootian (2000, 500–2) presents this as one of the possible original locations for a Hermes with the infant Dionysos *trapezophoros* (table support) from Forum SW (Corinth Museum inv. no. S-1993-2), with the others being a predecessor of the Byzantine bath southwest of Temple E, or Temple E.
21. For the standing monumental Artemis, Corinth Museum inv. no. S-220/812/820, see Johnson 1931 (*Corinth* IX), 15-19, no. 8; Ridgway 1981, 440. This wall also yielded a monumental pair of nude youths and a horse head, probably the Dioscuri from a cult group (Johnson 1931, 33, 98, nos. 26, 60–1, 94, 203; Ridgway 1981, 441) and a smaller seated Apollo and Thalia (Johnson 1931, 22–4, nos. 12–3), as well as the two *chlamydati* discussed in Chapter 5. For the striding Artemis Rospigliosi marked with a cross found nearby, Corinth Museum inv. no. S-2392, see also Chapter 5. Other images of Artemis from Corinth include coins in Imhoof-Blumer and Gardner 1885 (1964), 18, no. 12, fig. D:66-7 and Corinth Museum inv. nos. S-1313 (from the Odeum), S-1594 (Ridgway 1981, 446; Kahil 1984 (*LIMC* s.v. Artemis), 2.649, no. 325, pl. 472), S-1628 and S-2408 (Sturgeon 2003, 363; Stirling 2008, nos. 4, 7).
22. Pausanias 2.2.8.
23. See Mary E. Hoskins Walbank 1989 for Temple E as the Capitolium. Temple E excavations and studies: Freeman in Stillwell et al. 1941 (*Corinth* I.2), 210-36; Anderson 1967; Haskell 1980; Williams 1989, 1996; Williams and Zervos 1984, 1987, 1988, 1990, 1991. Bookidis (pers. comm. 2008) notes that among *Capitolia* listed in the *ANRW* she finds that they are never peripteral, nor Doric.
24. Other potential pedimental sculpture includes Corinth Museum inv. nos. S-2335 (Athena) and S-1534, a Nereid riding a dolphin *acroterion* (Lattimore 1976, 67, note 32). The sculpture is under study

by Mary Sturgeon, and has been discussed by Johnson 1931, 21–2, no. 11 (Corinth Museum inv. no. S-827, Roma, but called Enyo or Nike); Stillwell et al. 1941 (*Corinth* I.2), 210-30; Capps Jr. 1950 (a young man, Corinth Museum inv. no. S-1539); Robinson 1974, 482; Loreti 1985, 179 (Corinth Museum inv. no. S-827 recognized as Roma); Ridgway 1981, 441, pl. 95.d (dated Antonine, citing P. Berich Haskell, abstract of AIA Annual Meeting paper in *AJA* 1980, 210–11); Williams 1987, 30–1 (dated pre-Hadrianic); Mary E. Hoskins Walbank 2003, 347 (dated late Hadrianic/Antonine); Stirling 2008, 112–13, 131, 137 (Corinth Museum inv. no. S-827 is Roma, or less likely Virtus, which was copied in a Panayia Villa statuette).

25. Dinsmoor 1949; Roux 1958, 13; Wiseman 1979, 522; Williams 1987, 29.
26. De Grazia (1973, 58–74), nos. 1 (Corinth Museum inv. no. S-1445, a crowned male head), 3 (Corinth Museum inv. no. S-1155, a male head) and 5 (Corinth Museum inv. no. S-706, a female head) come from the western Forum. All likely date from before the third century, and none is an emperor. Fragments of monumental cuirassed figures (and an owl) were found west of the *temenos* (temple enclosure) of Temple E, but their identification and ultimate origin is uncertain. I know of only one non-architectural dedication by or to an emperor from this end of the Forum, that of Faustina from the northwest corner of the *temenos* of Temple E (I thank Nancy Bookidis for this reference).
27. Edwards 1933 (*Corinth* VI), 8, nos. 209, 218; Scranton 1951 (*Corinth* I.3), 68–9, pls. 25.3–26.1.
28. The standing Tyche or Nemesis is Corinth Museum inv. no. S-427, Johnson 1931 (*Corinth* IX), 12–14, no. 6; Scranton 1951 (*Corinth* I.3), 69, note 48, pl. 25.4 (it is carved of Pentelic rather than Pausanias' Parian marble, so not his Tyche cult statue, and found at the west end of the NW Stoa). The head of Tyche now displayed in the Corinth Museum (my Figure 6.2) is Corinth Museum inv. no. S-1540, Stillwell et al. 1941 (*Corinth* I.2), 215, note 5, fig. 171; Vermeule 1968, 36 fig. 14 (it was found in a marble chip layer 3 to 10 m. west of the Temple E podium, and possibly came from the Temple E pediment). The monumental but fragmentary Tyche head is Corinth Museum inv. no. S-802, Johnson 1931 (*Corinth* IX), 46–7, no. 54; Scranton 1951 (*Corinth* I.3), 69, n. 50; Edwards 1990, 531, pl. 83a; Sturgeon 2003, 356, fig. 21.7 (from the western Forum, it does not fit a standing *peplos*-wearing body which Broneer (1935, 67, pl. 20A–B) identified as Tyche). Tyche was previously placed by reference to Pausanias in Temple F by Scranton (1951 (*Corinth* I.3), 68–9), Temple D by Williams (and Fisher 1975, 27) or Temple K by Edwards (1990, 535–7, fig. 2, pl. 86), who identified the fragmentary draped arm from the

southwest Forum, Corinth Museum inv. no. S-1804, as coming from the statue of Regilla-Tyche.

29. For the inscribed base, Corinth Museum inv. no. I-427, see West 1931 (*Corinth* VIII.2), no. 11 (dated reign of Claudius); Scranton 1951 (*Corinth* I.3), 68, note 41, pl. 25.1. For the statue, Corinth Museum inv. no. S-2073, see Stillwell 1936, 41, figs. 18–9; Scranton 1951 (*Corinth* I.3), 68, note 42, pl. 25.2. Stillwell says the statue was found "just north of the Babbius Foundation," with the base about 20 m. farther east.
30. Palagia 2010, 441–3, with example from Sikyon.
31. Noel Lenski pers. comm. 2009, with reference to Libanius *Prog.* 12, desc. 15 on Tychaia in cities in the fourth century.
31. Corinth Museum inv. no. I-1658, Scranton 1951 (*Corinth* I.3), 69; *SEG* 13, no. 226; Bousquet 1964, 609–13; Robert 1966, 369/71, no. 186, 742, no. 177; *SEG* 22, no. 216; *BullÉpigr* 1966, 186; Kent 1966 (*Corinth* VIII.3), no. 128; *SEG* 23, no. 171; *SEG* 35, no. 255; Edwards 1990, 537; *SEG* 40, no. 302; Rizakis and Zoumbaki 2001, 374–5, COR 528.
33. Corinth Museum inv. no. S-813, Johnson 1931 (*Corinth* IX), no. 10; de Grazia 1973, 299, no. 98; Ridgway 1981, 436.
34. Tobin 1993, 1997; Pomeroy (2007) has pointed out how often her own dedications were attributed to Herodes, for example the Nymphaeum at Olympia in Lucian *Peregr.* 19.
35. Rose 2005.
36. For Herod's temple of Roma and Augustus at Caesarea, see Josephus *Ant. Jud.* 15.331–41.
37. Corinth Museum inv. no. I-1752/2264, Kent 1966 (*Corinth* VIII.3), no. 129; Robert *REG* 79 (1966) 742–3 = *OMS* 6, 1989, 560–1; Rizakis and Zoumbaki 2001, 290–1, COR 174.3; Sironen 2016 (*IG* IV^2 3), no. 1251.
38. Temple C: Scranton in Stillwell et al. 1941 (*Corinth* I.2), 131–65; Williams and Zervos 1984, 97–8. Sakellariou and Faraklas (1971) call Temple C the Temple of Hera Akraia, but this should be at Perachora.
39. Williams and Zervos 1984, 97–8.
40. Archaizing Piers: Corinth Museum inv. no. S-1974-27/1935, Williams and Fisher 1975, 23–5, no. 28, pls. 9–10; Williams 1982; Sturgeon 2003, 353, fig. 21.3.
41. NW Arch: Stillwell et al. 1941 (*Corinth* I.2), 109. For relief sculpture of a sacrifice and *fasces* that could have come from this arch, see Edwards 1994, 295–6: a fragmentary Roman sacrifice relief from Forum W and SW (Corinth Museum inv. nos. S-1626, S-2518) and *fasces* from decoration or a procession (Corinth Museum inv. nos. S-3622, A-74-29).
42. Glauce: Pausanias 2.3.6; Richardson 1900; Elderkin 1910, republished with minor modifications in Hill 1964 (*Corinth* I.6), 200–27; B.A. Robinson 2001, 207–33; Pfaff 2003, 133–4. Once considered

Archaic, Williams (and Zervos 1984, 98–101) then suggested a first-century or Hellenistic date. A Hellenistic, or at least Greek, era of first construction was confirmed by Siddall's mortar studies in Sanders 1999, by Christopher Pfaff's research, and by B.A. Robinson's stylistic analysis.

43. Sacrifices to Medea's Children: Pausanias 2.3.6–8; Aelian *Var. Hist.* 5.21: μέχρι τοῦ νῦν ἐναγίζουσι τοῖς παισὶ Κορίνθιοι ("up to now the Corinthians make sacrifices to the children"); Philostratus *Her.* 53.4; Scranton in Stillwell et al. 1941 (*Corinth* I.2), 164.
44. Euripides *Medea* 1378–83; Schol. Euripides *Medea* lines 264 (Didymus quoting Creophylus *FGrH* 417 F3, fourth/fifth century BCE), 273 (Parmeniscus, first to second century BCE), 1379, 1382; Diodorus 4.55.1 ("the Pythian priestess commanded them to bury the children in the sacred precinct of Hera and to pay them the honours which are accorded to heroes"); Apollodorus *Library* 1.145–6 (1.9.28)(Medea killed her children, or Medea left her infant children on the altar of Hera Akraia, and the Corinthians then took them off and killed them). See also Pausanias 2.3.11 (after Eumelus), 2.4.7; Schol. Pindar *Ol.* 13.54 (after Eumelus, that Medea when dwelling in Corinth drove off a plague (*limos*) by sacrificing to Demeter and the Nymphs of the Lakes, perhaps in Perachora where there is a lake).
45. Dunbabin and Payne 1940, 1962 (*Perachora* 1–2); Hammond 1954; Wiseman 1978, 33.
46. Pausanias 2.4.1, 2.4.5. Since the Sanctuary of Athena *Chalinitis* is undiscovered, it is not certain that it was revived at its original Greek location. However, comparison with the Demeter and Kore sanctuary or the Asklepieion at Corinth, or with the Athena *Chalkeoikos* (Bronze House) temple at Sparta above the theater strongly suggests it was. This Athena *Chalinitis* may, given the connection with Pegasos, be the same as the Corinthian Athena *Hippia* (Pindar *Ol.* 13.76–9), and less certainly the Corinthian Athena *Hellotis* (Pindar *Ol.* 13.39; Schol. Pindar *Ol.* 13.56; Ath. *Epit.* 15.22; Athen. 15.678a–b; *Etym. Magn.* s.v. *Hellotis*; Graf *KlPauly* 5.326–7 s.v. *Hellotis*), in whose temple the princess Hellotis was burned during the Dorian sack, provoking a rebuilding of the temple afterwards and a festival with torch races in her honor in Classical Corinth, perhaps held on the race course where the Forum would later be laid out (Herbert 1986). The statue of Athena *Chalinitis* was acrolithic, and held the bridle in her right hand, spear and shield in her left, according to a coin of Hadrian in Imhoof-Blumer and Gardner 1885, 73–4. Stirling (2008, 137) argues that the statue type of Europa-Sosandra could be Hellotis, considering the large number of copies of this rare type from Corinth and neighboring cities: Corinth Museum inv. nos. S-1999-4, Stirling 2008, no. 1 (Panayia Villa); S-1051 (Julian Basilica); S-1904/2446, S-1897, Ridgway 1981,

442 (Mosaic House); S-3575, Sturgeon (*Corinth* IX.3), 151–2, no. 42, pl. 51:a (Theater). Compare figurines from neighbors of Corinth: Katakis 2002, 93, 154, no. 92 (Epidauros); Kritsas 1979, 222–6, pl. 156:a–b (Argos baths).

47. Ajootian 2008.
48. Archaizing Athenas: Corinth Museum inv. nos. S-1368, S-1348, Broneer 1928, 466–8, pl. 6, fig. 8, 1932 (*Corinth* X), 117–24, nos. 1–2; Ridgway 1981, 446; Williams 1982, 177. Athena from south of Odeum, test pit dug near Shear House: Corinth Museum inv. no. S-1436, Broneer 1932 (*Corinth* X), 124, no. 3; Ridgway 1981, 442.
49. Dow's dig of 1933 in this area was unpublished; he was followed by Robinson in 1953 (Robinson 1964, 6–7, fig. 4) and Anderson in 1965 (Anderson 1967), then Williams 1983 (quarries filled in under Claudius).
50. Williams 2013b.
51. For these remains as the Athena Sanctuary, see Shear 1925, 388, 1926, 444, 1928b, 489. For a cult, see Williams 2005. The area of the Terrace Building and Building 5 cultic room yielded much evidence of Egyptian cult. For a gilded head of Serapis, from a separate body or acrolithic statue, see Corinth Museum inv. no. S-2387, Milleker 1985. For a statuette from the Theater identified as Telesphoros, perhaps Harpocrates, see Sturgeon (*Corinth* IX.3), 158–9, no. 49, pl. 52:g. See Williams and Zervos 1985, 67–8, for a bone *pyxis* (box) with an obelisk/pyramid on an altar, a filled basket, and a hand with torch, and compare Marangou 1976, pl. 68, no. 219. From the north entry corridor, probably below the last floor, there is an Egyptian bone revetment plaque with garland-encircled head and nail hole, for which compare Marangou 1976, pl. 65, no. 215–16, dated in the fourth century (though Williams dated end of second century). See Williams and Zervos 1985, 79–80, no. 49, pl. 17 for an Osiris Hydreios steatite jar from a robbing trench of the west wall of building 5, dumped *c.*400, probably mutilated, and compare Wild 1981, 113–28, pls. 16–24. There is a columnar shaft with a dedication to Serapis and Isis from a so-called late wall over the Theater. Williams and Zervos 1986, 148–59, record a terracotta bust of a helmeted Athena (or Armed Aphrodite?, Corinth Museum inv. no. MF-1983-41), terracotta figurines of Aprodite and Artemis, a boat lamp, and frescoes with Hermes, Herakles and Lares from second- and third-century contexts. Bookidis (pers. comm. 2008) adds a Roman statuette of a seated child in the temple boy pose wearing a palm leaf layered wig, probably Harpocrates (Corinth Museum inv. no. T528 TC111), from Shear's Theater excavations.
52. Williams (and Zervos 1984, 89–92) originally gave it a domestic-industrial function; Williams 2005 now suggests a cultic function.
53. Williams 2005.

54. Lepinski 2014.
55. Archaic Temple of Apollo: Dörpfeld 1886; Richardson 1898, 236 (identified from Peirene); Powell 1905 (condition before excavation); Weinberg 1939b (date of construction); Broneer 1954 (*Corinth* I.4), 124; Robinson 1971 (1974); Robinson 1976a, 1976b; Williams 1984 (capitals); Dengate 1988; Bookidis 2000 (terracotta sculpture); Pfaff 2003, 112–15; Bookidis and Stroud 2004 (identification as Temple of Apollo). Capps Jr. (1950) and Bookidis (1970) researched the poros stone sculpture of the temple, remortared in Roman times. See now Frey 2015 on the reuse of the interior colonnade, and Ziskowski 2016 on the suggestion that the temple was dedicated to Athens in the Archaic era and beyond.
56. Pausanias 2.3.6.
57. Rhodes 1984, 1987a, 1987b, 1987c.
58. Apollo of the Agora at Classical and Hellenistic Corinth: Herodotus 3.52; Simonides in *AnthPal* 6.213 (Dedication to Apollo of the Agora: "I pray for your gifts"); Plutarch *Aratus* 40.2–4 (1046)(Aratus avoids an ambush in the Sanctuary of Apollo (*c.*224-3 BCE); Bookidis and Stroud 2004.
59. Imhoof-Blumer and Gardner 1885, 71.
60. Ziskowski 2016.
61. Pausanias 2.3.1; Torelli 2001.
62. Imhoof-Blumer and Gardner 1885, 71. At Mytilene, Augustus' daughter Julia was honored as Thea Aphrodite (*IGR* 4.114), and perhaps his sister Octavia received similar honors at Corinth as another descendent of Venus/Aphrodite.
63. The Mehmet Çavush mosque is briefly described by the seventeenth-century Ottoman traveler Evliya Çelebi (trans. MacKay 1980, 10) as without a lead roof but with many parishioners. It is visible in old engravings of Corinth just west of the standing columns of the Archaic Temple of Apollo (Figure 1.1). Finds from a mosque from north of the Peribolos of Apollo include a marble basin, a painted gravestone (Corinth Museum inv. no. A-739) and a fragment of an Arabic inscription (Corinth Museum inv. no. I-957, Morgan 1929, Corinth Excavations NB103). Some digging was done on this ridge by the ASCSA Corinth Excavations, with trenches 4 and 13, and (in 1946–7) by Scranton under Broneer (see unsigned Corinth Excavations Plan 080 006).
64. See Morgan 1929, Corinth Excavations NB103, for the discovery of Byzantine architectural members (Corinth Museum inv. nos. A-735, A-733, AM-247, AM-280, etc.), late antique lamps (Corinth Museum inv. nos. CL-2070, 2071, 2072, 2079, 2058, 2053), *dipinti* (painted inscriptions) with the word *theou* (of god) on Corinth Museum inv. no. A-741, lead seal Corinth Museum inv. no. MF-2344, and communion bread stamp Corinth Museum inv. no. S-1403.

65. Athanasoulis 2013.
66. Kourelis 2007.
67. Scranton (1957 (*Corinth* XVI), 9), who had excavated in the area, wrote in regards to the search for the cathedral of late antique Corinth: "On the crest of high ground east of the Agora [Forum] remains of a church are known to exist, but the known remains are clearly much later than the sixth century." He dates the Panayia (Dormition of the Virgin) Church still standing then to "around 1840, although the lower parts of the walls may be earlier," connects it tentatively with Wheler's 1676 Panayia Church "at which the Arch-Bishop lives," and concludes, "investigations around the church revealed an unidentified twelfth century complex over late classical remains of obscure character, possibly a hotel of some kind; it is unlikely that there was an early church on the site."
68. Blaksova and Wiseman 1981.
69. Broneer 1947; Sanders 1999, 2002a, 2002b, 2003a, 2003b, 2004, 2005; James 2005.
70. Payne et al. 1940, 15, 22–3, pl. 3. I thank Chris Pfaff for bringing this building to my attention.
71. The visit of St Paul has provoked a lively interest among Biblical historians in house churches at Corinth. Blue (1994, 157–61) surveys four Corinthian houses, but finds evidence of Christianity at none of them (Shear's Villa, the House by Temple E, the Anaploga Villa and the Mosaic House).
72. Byzatine and Christian Museum of Athens inv. nos. BXM 2, BXM 556, T92, Stefanidou-Tiveriou 1987, 249, note 7, 1993b, 21, 25; Sklavou Mavroeidi 1999, 25, no. 12; Ensoli and La Rocca 2000, 343, no. 634; Stirling 2008, 138.
73. Binder pers. comm. 2008, with reference to Karivieri 1996.
74. Bowes 2008.
75. Three sigma tables were published in Scranton 1957 (*Corinth* XVI), 139–40, pls. 36b–d, and are now reconstructed on the walls of the Corinth Museum in the foyer between the Greek, Roman and Prehistoric Galleries. One (or more) sigma tables came from the area of the Peribolos of Apollo just northeast of Peirene, and one each from the L-shaped room west of the Hemicycle and a building west of the Kraneion Basilica.
76. Temples in the center of Athens converted to churches in Late Antiquity include the Parthenon, the Erechtheion, the Asklepieion and the Temple of Hephaestus: Frantz 1988 (*Agora* XXIV); Hattersley-Smith 1996, 210. Basilica building versus conversion: Krautheimer 1986; Macmullen 1986; Nock 1933; Trombley 1993.
77. Jews in Corinth or Greece: Philo *Embassy to Gaius* (*Legat.*) 281–2; *1Maccabees* 15:23. *Acts* 18 mentions an *archisynagogos*, Crispus, and a

god-fearer who lived next door to the synagogue, Justus. Horrell (2004) argues that East of Theater is the sort of neighborhood where the synagogue was probably located; Adams and Horrell (2004) explore at length the question of Corinth's Jews at the time of St Paul's visit.

78. John Chrysostom, *PG* 61, col. 11, quoted in Avraméa 1997, 154.
79. Josephus *de Bell. Jud.* 3.10.10 (540). Noy (et al. 2004, 182) identifies this town with Magdala Nunayya (of the fishes), near Tiberias, modern Migdal.
80. The capital also has other sacred images, *lulavim* or *lulab* (palm fronds) and *etrog* or *ethrog* (citron fruit), and is Corinth Museum inv. no. A-392, Scranton 1957 (*Corinth* XVI), 116, pl. 130a–b; Foerster 1981; Rothaus 2000, 31, n. 79.
81. Sara inscription: Corinth Museum inv. no. I-2283, Kent 1966 (*Corinth* VIII.3), no. 304; Robert 1966, 753–4; Frey 1975 (*CIJ* 1^2), Prol. no. 718a; Lambropoulou 1993, 667; Noy et al. 2004, 184–5, no. Ach48.
82. Lintel: Corinth Museum inv. no. I-123, Richardson 1898, 234; Powell 1903, 60–1, no. 40; Oehler 1909, 538, no. 110a; Krauss 1922, 242–3, no. 42; Meritt 1931 (*Corinth* VIII.1), no. 111; Cadbury and Lake 1933, 5.64, n. 1; Frey 1936 (1975)(*CIJ* 1), no. 718; Bees 1941, 16–9, no. 6; Gabba 1958, 111, no. 34; Barrett 1987, 50, n. 48; Boffo 1994, 361–4, no. 45; Noy et al. 2004, 182–4, no. Ach47.
83. Most recent overview of dating options, and strong arguments for third century as earliest possible date: Noy et al. 2004, 182–4, no. Ach47.
84. Hebrew inscriptions include Corinth Museum inv. nos. I-92, I-1773 (a decree?, from the South Agora); I-257, Starr 1935–6, 42–9 (Epitaph of Eliaqim the Dyer, from the Hemicycle); I-807/808 (a writing exercise, "Moses sent," from the Hemicycle). Noy et al. 2004, 182 says these Hebrew inscriptions are medieval (with I-1773 mislabeled I-957). Bilingual epitaph: Corinth Museum inv. no. I-2483, Pallas and Dantis 1977 (1979), 80–1, no. 29; *BE* 1980, no. 230; *SEG* 29, no. 309; Schürer 1986, 3.1.65–6; Levinskaya 1996, 165–6; Noy et al. 2004, 185–6, no. Ach49 (from the Panayia Church). Samaritan amulet: Davidson 1952 (*Corinth* XII), 260; Pummer 1987, 258–61, no. 4; Lambropoulou 1993, 666, Fig. 5; Rothaus 2000, 31, n. 79; Noy et al. 2004, 186–9, no. Ach50. A fragmentary Roman era inscription in Greek found on Acrocorinth was restored by Pallas (and Dantis 1977, 81, no. 30) to include reference to a synagogue and its leader, but only the reading διδάσ[καλος] καὶ ἀρχ[-?-]ος τῆ[ς] ("teacher and leader of") is certain: Corinth Museum inv. no. I-2506, *BE* 1980, no. 230; *SEG* 29, no. 300; Schürer 1973–86, 3.1.66; Horsley 1987, 213–14, no. 113; Boffo 1994, 364, n. 7; Levinskaya 1996, 166; Noy et al. 2004, 339, no. App18.

85. Compare the first- or second-century synagogue at Delos (Trümper 2004), or the second-century Synagogue I at Stobi endowed by Cl. Tiberius Polycharmus in part of his house, replaced *c.*350–400 with a new mosaic floored building (Synagogue II or church?), then destroyed and rebuilt as a Christian basilica church in the fifth century: Poehlman 1981, 236; Moe 1977, 150–1; Kolarik 1981, 187–97, 1987; Hattersley-Smith 1996, 45–6. For synagogues of the late antique Balkans see Levine 1981, 2005.

Chapter 7 Sacred Spaces in the City and Corinthia

1. Pausanias 2.4.5; Freeman in Stillwell et al. 1941 (*Corinth* I.2), 165, 235–6 (thought equivalent to Temple E); Broneer 1951a, 85; Musti and Torelli 1986, 222.
2. For the altar, see Corinth Museum inv. no. I-886, Broneer 1932 (*Corinth* X), 134, no. 2. For Pausanias' itinerary see Williams 2013b.
3. Pausanias 2.4.5; Dinsmoor 1949; Robinson 1966 (1968), 141; Pfaff 2003, 108, 115–19. The large temple was restored in Roman times, on evidence of stucco, but also taken apart to build the Epistyle Wall near the Old Gymnasium.
4. Williams and Sanders have both suggested that this is a temple *peribolos* rather than part of the Old Gymnasium, though it could really be both, as at Athens' Olympieion, though a temple foundation has not yet been found. Stoa: Wiseman 1967a, 1967b, 409, n. 19, 1970, 1972, 4, 23, 2015.
5. For the Corinthian Olympian Zeus Temple, see Pausanias 2.4.5 (bronze statue inside), 3.9.2 (*c.*398 BCE); Theophrastus *Enquiry into Plants* 5.14.2. The parallelism is clear here between the Kraneion, which we know was in the east, and the Olympieion, which must have been on the north. For a translation, see Hort 1916.
6. Pausanias 2.4.5; Lucian *Historia* 3.29 (Diogenes the Cynic going from Kraneion to Lerna, with Sura in between).
7. Fountain of the Lamps: Wiseman 1967, 31–41, 402–28; 1969, 64–106; 1972, 1–42; Garnett 1975 (lamps); Jordan 1994a (lamps); Rothaus 2000, 126–34; Cline 2011, 105–36 (angels); Wiseman 2015, 196–8 (most recent plan).
8. Jordan 1994a; Avraméa 1997, 151–4. A lamp inscription at first linked with Jews has been proved rather to be a Christian invocation of "Angels who dwell on these waters." See Wiseman 1972, 28–30, no. 21; Lambropoulou 1993, 665–7; Jordan 1994a, 224, no. 1; Rothaus 2000, 128; Noy et al. 2004, 340, no. App18*bis*.
9. de Waele 1933, 1935a, 1935b; Roebuck 1951 (*Corinth* XIV); Wesolowsky 1973 (Lerna cemetery); Lang 1977.
10. Pausanias 2.4.5; Roebuck 1951 (*Corinth* XIV), 144–5, pl. 59, nos. 8–10.

11. Landon 1994, 207–18, no. 12, "Spring of Ayios Kodratos," used in Roman times for "farmers, travelers and burial needs" (quote, p. 215).
12. Mattusch 1991.
13. Robinson 1962, 120–32: trenches revealed possible Roman houses under the Bey's Palace, and those houses were only ruined in the late fifth century, or later, as one had a hoard of late fourth- to early sixth-century coins in it.
14. Wiseman 1967a, 1967b, 409, n. 19, 1970, 1972, 4, 23.
15. See Chapter 8 for more on the Epistyle Wall. Asklepieion: Roebuck 1951 (*Corinth* XIV).
16. Sakellariou and Faraklas (1971, 143) call it domed, probably public and unfinished, and built in the fourth century, but Wiseman (1967b) says it was destroyed by the 375 quake or Alaric, from a coin of Valentinian (367–75) in debris over the floor, and built in the first century.
17. Wiseman 1967a, 31–41, 1967b, 402–28; 1969, 64–106; 1972, 1–42; Garnett 1975; Jordan 1994a.
18. For the North Cemetery, and the epitaphs, see: Slane 2012, 2015, 2017 (*Corinth* XXI); Mary E. Hoskins Walbank and Michael B. Walbank 2006; Michael B. Walbank 2010; Mary E. Hoskins Walbank 2014.
19. Skias 1892 (1894), 114–15, 1906 (1907), 153.
20. Landon 1994, 207–18, no. 12, "Spring of Ayios Kodratos."
21. Stikas 1961, 1961 (1964), 1962, 1962 (1966), 1965; Daux 1963; Pallas 1977, 156–63, 1981 (1979), 105–8, 1990, 778–9; Panagiotide 1970; Rothaus 2000, 97.
22. Stikas 1965, 478; Pallas 1977, 161.
23. Now Lechaion storeroom, with Greek inv. no. KOP 1962/Λ 11, Stikas 1962 (1966), 64, fig. 49:c, 1962, 85, fig. 97, 1965, 478–9, fig. 12; *SEG* 57, no. 318; Feissel and Philippidis-Braat 1985), no. 86*; Sironen 2016 (*IG* IV^2 3), no. 1267. A marble baptismal font with a fragmentary inscribed prayer in fifth-/sixth-century script around the rim was also found in the excavations: Stikas 1961 (1964), 131; *SEG* 57, no. 317; Sironen 2016 (*IG* IV^2 3), no. 1265.
24. Halkin 1957 (*BHG* 3rd ed.), 1.119; *Acta Sanctorum* 10 March, 4–11 (2nd ed. 696–700, 3rd ed. 895–8); *Menologion* in *PG* 117.345–8, for 10 March.
25. Joseph the Hymnographer in the ninth century is the first to mention the basilica and cult; Nikephoros Gregoras, *PG* 149:504–20, is the last source to mention it, and the latest coins from the excavation come from the reign of Manuel I (1143–1180). See Brown 2012b.
26. *SEG* 41, no. 271; Sironen 2016 (*IG* IV^2 3), no. 1825.
27. Corinth Excavations NB346, 11–129; Robinson 1967 (1968); Pallas 1990, 764. Fifth-century or later east-west walls were dated by pottery

built into them; there were twelfth-century burials up against the walls, and a thirteenth-century *osteotheke* (bone compartment).

28. Robinson 1965 (1967), 144; Daux 1965, 693; Sakellariou and Faraklas 1971, 145. For this area, see Newhall 1931.
29. Pausanias 2.5.5; Pallas 1955 (1960); Rothaus 2000, 97 (Skoutela basilica built in early sixth century, damaged in middle of sixth century).
30. Blegen 1916 (Corinth Excavations NB77), 146–50.
31. The Dionysos is Corinth Museum inv. no. S-1294, and the Striding Poet, perhaps Alcaeus, is Corinth Museum inv. no. S-1183 (Johnson 1931 (*Corinth* IX), 93, no. 189; Richter 1965, 1.69, fig. 243, who makes the identification as Alcaeus; Sturgeon 2003, 354–5, fig. 21.5; Dillon 2006, 4, 34, 124, no. A14-1). Blegen also mentions finding a bust, perhaps the unprovenanced Corinth Museum inv. no. S-1210 (Johnson 1931 (*Corinth* IX), 101, no. 215), which was found around the same time.
32. Bookidis 1996, notes made in Blegen 1916 (Corinth Excavations NB77), 146–50.
33. Sanders pers. comm. 2005. This is the chapel at the crossroads near the northwards line of the ancient Lechaion Road, by the modern crossroads of Agiou Dionysiou Road and Kleopatras Road.
34. Pallas 1956 (1961), 1957 (1962), 1958 (1965), 1959, 1959 (1965), 1961–2 (1963a), 1962, 1965 (1967), 1970, 1961 (1964), 141 (his last new plan of the Lechaion Basilica, with coin dates: 450–60 for the church, 518–27 for the atrium), 1957, 1967, 1979 (1981), 1990 (overviews of late antique Corinth in light of his discoveries, particularly the Lechaion Basilica); Krautheimer 1986, 131–4; Rothaus 2000, 96–7.
35. Halkin (1971) argues that Leonidas of Corinth was then conflated with the Archbishop of Athens of the same name and feast on 15 April in the thirteenth century.
36. See Limberis (2005, 450–2) and Delehaye (1933, 262) for the dates. The versions are: Mss Patmos 254, ed. Halkin 1971; *Acta Sanctorum* April 16, 2.399–402 (*de SS. Callisto, Charisio, Leonide, Christiana, Galla, Theodora, Lota, Tertia, Caristo, item Chariessa, Nice, Gallena, Nunechia, Basilissa, Cali. Martyribus Corinthi in Achaia*); *Menologion* in *PG* 117.405; *Parvum Romanum*, ed. Quentin 1908 (1969), 330, Florus of Lyons recension (*apud Corinthum, Calisti et Carisi, cum alius septum, omnium in mare mensorum*).
37. I thank an anonymous reviewer for this point.
38. Sanders 2003b, 2004.
39. Pallas 1956, 177–8, pl. 72b.
40. For these late fifth-century imperial column capitals, and their early sixth-century imitations: Sodini 1984, 226–9; Mango 1978 (1993) (Studios); Hattersley-Smith 1996, 60–2, 146–7, 160.
41. Caraher 2014, 2015.

42. Kraneion: Theophrastus (see above on Olympieion); Xenophon *Hellenica* 4.4.4 (*c*.392 BCE, during Corinthian War, some young men stay there); Athenaeus 13.589b; Plutarch *De exilio* 6 (*Mor.* 601b)(only wealthy Corinthians can live there, like Kollytos in Athens); Lucian *Dialogues of the Dead* 1 (Menippus the Cynic lives there or at the Lyceum in Athens); Themistius *Or.* 2.38.
43. Diogenes Laertius 6.77–8. Further connections between Diogenes the Cynic and the Kraneion in Plutarch *Alexander* 14; Diogenes Laertius 6.38 (Diogenes sunning himself in the Kraneion asks Alexander only to move from his light); Dio Chrysostom *Or.* 4.13–14 (Diogenes fond of the common (*koinoi*) places and shrines, so Alexander the Great found him there when he visited Corinth), *Or.* 6.3–4 (Corinthian appearance, breezes and Kraneion all more beautiful to Diogenes than Ecbatana or Babylon, and compare favorably with the Propylaia and Acropolis of Athens), *Or.* 8.4–5 (Diogenes after the death of Antisthenes goes to Corinth and camps out there), *Or.* 9.4 (Diogenes often seen in Corinth and around there); Lucian *How to Write History* 3, 29 (Diogenes there under Philip II, going from Kraneion to Lerna, with Sura in between); Brown 1949, 24–38; Dudley 1998.
44. Pausanias 2.2.4; Frazer 1913, 2.18–9; Roux 1958, 105–7.
45. Kraneion scholarship and excavations besides the Kraneion Basilica: Skias 1892, 111–12, 1906, 148–9, 165–6; Fowler and Stillwell 1932 (*Corinth* I), 77–80; Elderkin 1945, 4–8; Koutibas 1966, 119–21; Stroud 1972, 210–17, esp. 216, note 42.
46. Strong 1997.
47. Soles (1976, 26) ascribes the column base, now in the Corinth Museum outer courtyard, to this temple on the basis of its decoration and findspot. Corinth Museum inv. no. S-1366 is an unpublished statuette of a nude woman missing head, arms and lower body, a reverse of the Armed Aphrodite statuette (Corinth Museum inv. no. S-2548, Figure 2.1), which was found near the Kakavi spring on the southeast side of Ancient Corinth on 15 March 1927.
48. Ampelius 8.8, on Corinth: *eodem in loco fanum est Veneris, in quo vas marmoreum Laidos*. Arnaud-Lindet (1993, 62) rather improbably connects this basin with the Archaic *perirhanterion* (water basin) in the museum at Isthmia, which has no connection with a shrine of Aphrodite as far as I know.
49. Discovered by Pallas (1959, 1990, 764), and mentioned with reference to him by Scranton (1957, 9), and Sanders 2005. Rothaus (2000, 95) chose instead to call it the Amphitheater Church, and with Timothy Gregory observed late fifth- to seventh-century fine and coarse ware pottery, two impost capitals, and an inscription in the area, which they turned in to the Corinth Museum (Corinth

Museum inv. no. I-1990-3). The material recovered so far and the ground plan seem comparable to the Octagon Church in Philippi, or the three octagonal late antique buildings in Thessalonike: the Rotunda of St George (originally Galerius' mausoleum or a temple, converted to a church in the fourth century), Galerius' Palace Octagon (probably an audience hall) and the Octagon church by the Vardar west gate, perhaps originally a martyrium church dedicated to St Nestor: Grabar 1972; Mango 1972 (1993), 1975 (1993); Spieser 1984, 117, 1998 (2001); Hattersley-Smith 1996, 135–9, 163–5.

50. Gregory 1979; Sanders and Boyd 2008.
51. Pease 1928 (Corinth Excavations NB98); de Waele 1928 (Corinth Excavations NB99); Carpenter 1929, 345–60.
52. Shelley 1943; Scranton 1957 (*Corinth* XVI), 7; Pallas 1959, 204–5, 1962 (1964), 1970 (1972), 1972 (1974), 1976 (1978), 1977 (1979), 1977 (1980), 1990. The triconch mausoleum is convincingly interpreted as a family mausoleum and not a martyrium by Snively (1984, 117–24). Though Rothaus (2000, 98) says (note 25) that Snively argues unsuccessfully that "the Kraneion basilica was not a martyrium," she was just discussing the triconch mausoleum, not the whole basilica. He also has it built in the early sixth century and "damaged and abandoned" in the middle of the sixth century, though evidence from the church shows it was used long into the Byzantine era.
53. Date established by Pallas (1970 (1972), 109–10), and reaffirmed in his subsequent reports and posthumous final summary (Pallas 1990).
54. Athanasoulis and Manolessou 2013, 533–8.
55. Pausanias 2.2.3; Imhoof-Blumer and Gardner 1885, 66–7; Edwards 1933 (*Corinth* VI), no. 149.
56. Apuleius *Met.* 11.8–17.
57. Scranton et al. 1978 (*Kenchreai* 1), 70–1, 75–7; Scranton 1967; Ibrahim et al. 1976 (*Kenchreai* 2: Glass Panels), 264. For Nilotic scenes in Greco-Roman art as emblemmatic of the Good Life, see O'Connell 2002.
58. Rothaus 1996.
59. Pallas 1987–9.
60. Hohlfelder 1970b, 1973, 1975.
61. Rife et al. 2007.
62. Scranton et al. 1978 (*Kenchreai* 1), 87.
63. Cummer 1971; Rife et al. 2007; Ubelaker and Rife 2007. See Morgan (1938, 369–70), for a first-century tomb in the area of modern Hexamilia, on the road from Kenchreai to Corinth, which was robbed in the fourth or fifth century.
64. Pausanias 2.4.6: "On the way up this [mountain] Acrocorinth, there are *temene* (sanctuaries) of Isis, and the one [Isis] they call *Pelagia*

(Marine) and the other Egyptian, and [there are] two [sanctuaries] of Serapis, one of which is called [Serapis] in Canopus." See also Smith 1977; Milleker 1985; Bookidis 2003. Corinth Museum inv. no. S-2268, a bearded head, could represent Serapis.

65. Corinth Museum inv. no. I-2650, Robinson 1966 (1968), 139, 1969b, 2 (findspot in a manhole northwest of Hadji Mustafa Fountain); Daux 1966, 756–7; Vidman 1969, 20, no. 34a; Dunand 1973, 2.18; Smith 1977, 217–8; *SEG* 27, no. 34; Bookidis and Stroud 1997 (*Corinth* XVIII.3), 6.
66. Bookidis and Stroud 1997 (*Corinth* XVIII.3), 4–6. A so-called bath excavated near Hadji Mustafa Fountain may form part of these Egyptian Sanctuaries, for which see Corinth Excavations NB576, 61–7; Biers 1985 (*Corinth* XVII), 1, n. 2, 2003.
67. Griffiths 1975; Millar 1999.
68. For the cult of Isis and Serapis, see Bonnet et al. 2006; Bricault et al. 2007; Roullet 1972 (Rome); Tran 1964 (Pompeii); Sullivan 1975 (Italy).
69. Herm MTh inv. no. 1074. The peristyle and pronaos are also epigraphically attested, as is a Temple of Isis, repaired in an inscription from 14 St Tegoukou Street (MTh inv. no. 8173).
70. In the Thessalonike Archaeological Museum, see MTh inv. nos. 897 (Serapis), MTh 843 (Isis or priestess), MTh 1311 (Isis), MTh 2490 (Isis); MTh 844 (Harpokrates), MTh 1132/1150 (Priapus), MTh 996 (Aphrodite *Homonia*), MTh 831 (Frejus Aphrodite), MTh 1957 (Aphrodite of Aphrodisias), MTh 4922 (sphinx) and MTh 839 (priestess/devotee head).
71. MTh inv. no. 10844.
72. MTh inv. no. 997.
73. Inscriptions from the Serapeum in Thessalonike include MTh inv. nos. 824, 829, 859, 965, 978, 979, 986, 988, 998, 1683.
74. MTh inv. no. 1254, epitaph of Aulus Papius Cheilon. For other Thessalonican second- to third-century burial associations, see MTh inv. nos. 10762, 10771, 21161.
75. MTh inv. no. 841, Dunbabin 1990; *IG* X II.1, 89 (second century), 90, 104, 120.
76. Pausanias 2.4.6; Lucian *Salt.* 42; Philostratus *Life of Apollonius of Tyana* (worship of Helios at Corinth under Domitian). Williams (1986, 17, note 16) links the establishment of these altars with the ejection of the Corinthians by the Macedonians from Acrocorinth during the Hellenistic era.
77. Pausanias 2.4.6. For a second- or third-century curse tablet invoking *Bia Moira Ananke* (*Force Fates Necessity*) from a tomb at Kenchreai, see Faraone and Rife 2007.
78. Pausanias 2.4.7.
79. On the rites of the Mother, see Pausanias' comments at 2.3.4, after seeing the seated bronze statue of Hermes with the ram on

the Lechaion Road: "although I know the story told at the rite of the Mother about Hermes, I do not write it down."

80. Stroud 1965 (excavations of 1961–2), 1968 (excavations of 1964–5), 1993; Bookidis 1969 (excavations of 1968), 1987, 1990, 1993; Bookidis and Fisher 1972 (excavations of 1969–70), 1974 (excavations of 1971–3); Pemberton 1989 (*Corinth* XVIII.1); Slane 1990 (*Corinth* XVIII.2); Bookidis and Stroud 1997 (*Corinth* XVIII.3); Merker 2000 (*Corinth* XVIII.4); Bookidis 2010 (*Corinth* XVIII.5); Stroud 2013 (*Corinth* XVIII.6); Bookidis & Pemberton 2015 (*Corinth* XVIII.7); Bookidis and Stroud 1987; Bookidis et al. 1999; Dunbabin 1990; DeMaris 1995; Pfaff 1999.
81. Bookidis 2013.
82. For the Roman architecture and cult, see Bookidis and Stroud 1997 (*Corinth* XVIII.3), 273–378; Stroud 2013 (*Corinth* XVIII.6), 8–10, 14–16, 81–157. On debates about the identity of the goddesses worshipped here and their cult in the Roman era, see Økland 2004, 2010; Melfi 2016.
83. Corinth Museum inv. no. Mosaic 1973–1, Bookidis and Fisher 1974, 278–85; Dunbabin 1990.
84. Bookidis and Stroud 1997 (*Corinth* XVIII.3), 338–59, 362–70; Stroud 2013 (*Corinth* XVIII.6), 14–16, no. 14. For priestesses of Demeter and Kore in 4th c. BCE Corinth, see Diod. Sic. 16.66.2–5; Plutarch *Timoleon* 8.1–2.
85. Stroud 2013 (*Corinth* XVIII.6), 8–10, nos. 7–9.
86. Themelis 2003.
87. Stroud 2013 (*Corinth* XVIII.6), 81–157. Stroud (pp. 138–53) explores the various deities invoked, the women and men cursing and being cursed, and the literary and archaeological parallels, all of which suggest that specialists in the preparation of tablets and the rituals of cursing, probably women, may have lived as well as worked in the Building of the Tablets.
88. Pemberton 1989 (*Corinth* XVIII.1), 191; Slane 1990 (*Corinth* XVIII.2), 5, note 15; Bookidis and Stroud 1997 (*Corinth* XVIII.3), 378.
89. Bookidis and Stroud 1997 (*Corinth* XVIII.3), 379–91; Slane 2008.
90. Pausanias 4.6.7. This sanctuary of Hera *Bounaia* may be the Archaic sanctuary mentioned in Herodotus 5.92.18–24: the Corinthian tyrant Periander proclaimed a festival of Hera, but then took all the clothes from the women who came and burned them for Melissa. It is probably not the Hellenistic Heraion of Plutarch *Aratus* 21.1 (1036), in which Aratus leads men to a city gate by a Heraion, and 24.1 (1038), where Aratus takes a Heraion and Lechaion first before Corinth. The Hellenistic Heraion mentioned by Plutarch was clearly located on the eastern side of Corinth, and was possibly identical to the sanctuary of Hera Akraia at Perachora.
91. Pausanias 2.5.4.

92. Sisyphus' Sanctuary: Diodorus 20.103.1–4 (walled, used by Cassander's forces 303 BCE); Strabo 8.6.21 (sanctuary below Upper Peirene).
93. Strabo 8.6.20; Pausanias 2.5.1. Cult: Farnell 1896 (1977), 2.653, 734 n. 16, 1911 (1990), 268–83; Nilsson 1972; Will 1955, 225–33.
94. Imhoof-Blumer and Gardner 1885, 74–6; Edwards 1933 (*Corinth* VI), no. 181; Smith 2005.
95. Pausanias 2.5.1. Blegen (1930, 26) lists only three fragments of marble sculpture excavated, a monumental left leg (Helios?), a statuette leg and a piece of drapery.
96. Armed (ὡπλισμένη) Aphrodite: Apollonius of Rhodes *Argonautica* 1.742–6 (Aphrodite with shield); Dio 43.43 (image on ring of Caesar); Imhoof-Blumer and Gardner 1885, 74–6 (image on Corinthian coins, suggest statue dedicated by Caesar); Fürtwangler 1895, 384–8 (a copy of a cult statue by Skopas, late fourth century BCE, referred to by Pliny *NH* 36.25, created for Corinth or elsewhere, also copied in Capua Aphrodite, Naples NM inv. no. 6017, *LIMC* Aphrodite no. 627); Broneer 1930 (image is not Capua Aphrodite, but a nude version of a late fifth-century BCE Nike), 1932 (*Corinth* IV.2), 98–9 (image on lamps, terracotta figurines); Edwards 1933 (*Corinth* VI), 8 (on coins); Bernhart 1936, nos. 164–92 (on coins, Domitian to Commodus); Soles 1976, 41–69 (from a bronze original by Skopas, and the Capua Aphrodite certainly variation of same type, also Venus di Milo, with one or two copies erected on Roman Acrocorinth); Brinkerhoff 1978 (connected with Capua/Arles Aphrodite original of fifth century BCE); Williams 1986, 15–20 (is Hellenistic or Roman); Gadbery 1992, 1993 (copied in statuettes like Corinth Museum inv. no. S-2548, Broneer 1947, 243–6, and Corinth Museum inv. no. S-2608, Soles 1976, 68–9, in a fresco from East of Theater at Corinth, and in the well-preserved Perge dedication of Claudius Peison, Özgür 2008, no. 17, which all clarify connections with Capua Aphrodite, Venus di Milo); Havelock 1995; Smith 1995. There are also suggestive references to an original group of Ares and Aphrodite, perhaps at Corinth, in Ovid *Tris.* 2.296 (unknown temple); Pausanias 5.8.5 (Chest of Cypselus).
97. Pausanias 2.4.6.
98. Hill 1927, 70; Blegen et al. 1930 (*Corinth* III.1), 3–21; Williams 1986, 20.
99. Cnidus: Bankel 1997. Whether or not the round temple held the famous statue of Aphrodite *Euploia* called the Cnidia, there can be little doubt from epigraphy and terracottas that her cult was spread through the small buildings on the ridge above the harbor. Palaipaphos on Cyprus: Herodotus 1.199; Westholme 1933; Iliffe and Mitford 1952; Maier 1979; Budin 2002; Young 2005.

100. Ampelius 8.8.
101. Blegen 1930, 26: [-]ΩΣΚΟΡΕ [-]/[-]ΟΙΣΙΣΥΦ[-], "Greek letters of late Roman date." Pausanias 2.5.
102. Athenaeus 13.573b–e (= Theopompos *FGrH* 115 F285a, Timaeus *FGrH* 566 F10, Chamaeleon *Peri Pindarou* F31 (ed. Wehrli 1957, 56–8; ed. Koepke 1856, F16), with Athenaeus 13.567c for the speaker Myrtilus as a sophist at Corinth in the third century. Epigram texts, translation and commentary: Simonides *Ep.* 14, in Page 1981, 207–11, no. 14; Palumbo Stracca 1985, 58–65; Brown 1991; Kurke 1996; Campbell 1991, 532–3, Simonides 14. The version given by Athenaeus is "These women, both for the Hellenes and their fellow citizens fair in combat, stand praying to divine Kypris; for the goddess Aphrodite did not consider it right to betray the acropolis of the Greeks to the bow-bearing Persians."
103. Schol. Pindar *Ol.* 13.32b (ed. Drachmann 1903, 1.364–5)(=-Theopompos *FGrH* 115 F285b). The scholiast, along with the passage of Plutarch cited below, mentions the foundation of the Sanctuary of Aphrodite by Medea, though the two texts give different stories for her reasons.
104. Plutarch *Mor.* 871A–B *de malig. Herod.* 39. Plutarch's authorship has been questioned, but Pelling (2007) makes a compelling case to accept it as genuine.
105. Athenaeus alone calls the women of Simonides' epigram *hetairai*, courtesans, likely following Chamaeleon (on whom Wendling in *RE* 3, 1899, 2103; Scorza 1934; Nilsson 1957, 376). Wilamowitz (1889) and subsequent commentators joined these *hetairai* with Strabo's Corinthian *hetairai* who are also *hierodouloi* (sacred slaves), on which see note 107. Bergk (1914, 481–2), Boas (1905, 51, note 19) and Page (1981, 207–11) all concluded that the claim of autopsy in Athenaeus is transmitted from Theopompus through Chamaeleon, and that the *pinax* must have been destroyed in the Mummian sack. But was the Temple of Aphrodite actually sacked? Is Athenaeus so clumsy as to transmit impossible autopsy? Page (1981, 207–11) is tempted to allow autopsy for Athenaeus' sophist Myrtilus, and a Roman reality for this, because he thinks it doubtful that Athenaeus' and Plutarch's Simonidean epigrams (and Plutarch's bronze images) can come from Timaeus, or predate the second century BCE. On the other hand, van Groningen (1956) favors the epigram accompanying a *pinax* honoring the wives, and statues honoring the *hetairai*, who all prayed together. Williams (1986, 18) thinks there were sacred prostitutes, *hierodouloi*, and priestesses who prayed recorded on a stele, while Kurke (1996) favors sacred *hetairai* on a bronze tablet, and sees Athenaeus' epigram as the more original. Lanci (2005, 212–13), Budin (2006, 2008) and others (see below) favor just women of Corinth, as part of arguments against the

existence of sacred prostitution, and emphasize the Greekness of Corinth. Keesling (2006, 65) sensibly reasons that, whether a list of female names, a painting or actual statues accompanied the epigram, all were unusual enough in the fifth century BCE that, paired with Corinth's reputation, they might become *hetairai* in stories even by the fourth century BCE, and certainly by Chamaeleon's third century BCE. For *pinakes* as inscribed tablets or panel paintings, she cites Jeffrey 1988, 126, and Löhr 2000, 163, both on the priests of Poseidon *pinax* as a list of names or a painting by Ismenias of Chalcis in the Erechtheion of Athens (see Plutarch *Lycurgus* 843e–f). Faraone (1997, 54–7, 2006, 213) brings attention to the clear verbal and situational connection made by Aristophanes *Lys*. 341–9 to the epigram, which was clearly already familiar in Athens in the late fifth century BCE.

106. Strong 1997.

107. *Hierodouloi* and *hetairai* owned by the Greek temple of Aphrodite: Athenaeus 13.573e–574b, from Chamaeleon, adds Pindar's fragmentary *skolion* F122 (ed. Snell, cf. Athenaeus 5.782d) to Pindar *Ol*. 13 (*hetairai* vowed then dedicated to the sanctuary by victorious athlete Xenophon of Corinth in 464 BCE, on which see Kurke 1996); Athenaeus 13.574b–c (Kock 1884 (*CAF*), 2.389) quotes Alexis, a writer of Middle Comedy (Hellenistic *hetairai* have a separate festival of Aphrodite); Strabo 8.6.20–1 (379) (1000 *hierodouloi* as *hetairai* dedicated to the sanctuary), 12.3.36 (some prostitutes of Black Sea city of Comana are sacred, as at Corinth); Alciphron 3.60 (fourth-century BCE *hetairai* imagined by a late antique author). See Kurke 1996, Strong 1997, and Beard and Henderson 1998, for convincing refutations of the attempts to deny the reality of *any* kind of sacred prostitution at Corinth, even *hetairai* owned by a sanctuary of Aphrodite (as Conzelmann 1967; Calame 1989; Lanci 2005; Budin 2006, 2008). The main point of attack is a denial of Strabo's accuracy: Baladié 1980. For *hetairai* in Greece: Kurke 1997 (Archaic); Neils 2000 (Classical); Keesling 2006 (monuments at sanctuaries). For prostitutes and brothels in late antique cities, see Leontsini 1989; McGinn 2004, 2006. In a rarely cited passage, John Lydus (4.65) in the sixth century says the form of worship at Corinth influenced that at Aphrodite's birthplace sanctuary of Paphos on Cyprus, "the form of worship on Cyprus came from Corinth."

108. Corinth Excavations NB90a, 86–127; Blegen in Blegen et al. 1930 (*Corinth* III.1), 21–8; Pallas 1990, 791–3. Blegen's suggestion of fourth or fifth century seems too early for the demolition of a major temple, extensive recarving of its members, and construction of such a small nave and baptistry. Rothaus (2000, 98–9) pushed the church's construction date forward to "Byzantine or even Frankish times" based on Timothy Gregory's re-examination of pottery

illustrated in the notebooks. It is unclear what dates Rothaus means by Byzantine and Frankish, but I assume seventh to thirteenth century. Blegen found twelfth-century *spolia* in the fifth and final floor of the church, and the modifications for the thirteenth-century tower.

109. Blegen et al. 1930 (*Corinth* III.1), 22–3.
110. MacKay 1968.
111. Rothaus 2000, 99–104.
112. Sweetman 2015. For Athens see the new Ilissos basilica, and then the Temple of Artemis Agrotera converted to a church (Travlos 1971, 112–13), perhaps also the Olympieion and the Temple of Cronus and Rhea (Frantz 1988 (*Agora* XXIV), 335, 403), and the Temple of Eukleia and Eunomia converted to the church of St Agathokleia (Epitaphs: Creaghan and Raubitschek 1947, 4–5, 39; Bradeen 1974 (*Agora* XVII), 188–94 nos. 1063, 1081, 1087, 1091, 1093). Macedonian cities: Hattersley-Smith 1996, 197. Nikopolis and Epirus Vetus: Veikou 2012.
113. Jones 1960; Kaplan 1976, 64–5, no. 43.
114. Justinian *Nov.* 67 (538), 344–7.
115. Spiro 1978, 658 (Nikopolis), 656 (Daphnousia). Other family dedications of mosaics alone come from the basilica at Kallion.
116. Corinth Museum inv. nos. I-2324, 2325, 2326, Sironen 2016 (*IG* IV^2 3), no. 1264.
117. Corinth Museum inv. no. I-1044, *CIG* IV, no. 8824; Kent 1966 (*Corinth* VIII.3), no. 509; Feissel and Philippidis-Braat 1985, no. 34; Sironen 2016 (*IG* IV^2 3), no. 1263: ἐπὶ Ἰανουαρίου | τοῦ ἐνδοξοτάτου | πατρικίου ἐκτίσθη | καὶ Παύλου τοῦ | λαμπροτ(άτου) | δομεστίκου. Michael B. Walbank (2010) also discusses the names and titles.
118. Vryonis 1981.

Chapter 8 Fortification Walls: Isthmus, City and Acrocorinth

1. Gregory 1992.
2. The western stretch proposed by Gregory (1979) has been called into question by Sanders and Boyd (2008). For earlier city walls at Corinth, see Carpenter and Bon 1936 (*Corinth* III.2).
3. Gregory 1993 (*Isthmia* V); Frey 2006.
4. Justinian is directly credited by Procopius with restoring the circuit wall of Corinth (*Aed.* 4.2.23–6) and building the Hexamilion Wall with fortresses across the Isthmus (*Aed.* 4.2.27–8). Victorinus inscriptions: Corinth Museum inv. no. I-1390, *IG* IV, no. 204; Kent 1966 (*Corinth* VIII.3), no. 508; Feissel and Philippidis-Braat 1985, 279–80; Rizakis and Zoumbaki 2001, 397, COR 644; *IG* IV, no. 205, Feissel and Philippidis-Braat 1985, 281. Victorinus as a new kind of imperial official and architect in the Balkans, and his constructions

for Justinian in Greece: Gregory 1982, 1992; Wozniak 1982; Lawrence 1983; Anamali 1987 (Bylis); Feissel 1988; Fowden 1995; Cuomo 2007.

5. Broneer 1966, 1968 (Mycenaean wall proposed, but not widely accepted). Herodotus 7.71, 8.40.2, 8.71–2, 8.74, 9.7–9, 9.10.2–3; Diodorus 11.15–16 (Classical wall, built under the command of Cleombrotus of Sparta in 480–79 BCE); Diodorus 15.68 (temporary fort of 369 BCE); Wiseman 1963, 1978 (Hellenistic wall). Gregory (1993 (*Isthmia* V), 4–6) questions whether any of these walls went across the whole Isthmus before the construction of the Hexamilion.
6. First excavation of the Eastern Fortress in 1883: Monceaux 1884, 1885. Fortress considered the *temenos* wall of the Sanctuary of Poseidon: Leake 1830; Curtius 1851/2; Frazer 1913; O'Neill 1930, 13–19; Fowler and Stillwell 1932 (*Corinth* I), 59. Fortress as Sanctuary questioned first by Fimmen *RE* s.v. Isthmos, and then definitively rejected by Jenkins and Megaw (1934, 69–83), who linked it with Justinian, and excavated sections of both Fortress and Hexamilion Wall. Other excavations in Fortress: Broneer 1953, 182–5, 1955, 124, 1958, 20–2, 1959, 320–1. While Pallas (1961–2 (1963b), 78–83) argued for the completion of the Wall only in the late sixth or even early seventh century, Wiseman (1978, 63–4) followed his 1966 dissertation by suggesting the Hexamilion was begun under Valerian (see below). However, construction of Fortress and Wall was generally credited to Justinian on the basis of epigraphy, literary sources and archaeology until the work of Paul Clement and then Timothy Gregory: Clement 1977b; Gregory and Kardulias 1990; Gregory 1993, and especially Gregory 1993 (*Isthmia* V), 80–3, 97, 101–2, 144–5. They promoted the idea of early fifth-century construction based on pottery, coins, lamps, and burials against the Hexamilion Wall, with Justinianic rebuilding only on the north side of the Fortress, and were followed by Kardulias 1995, 2005; Frey 2006, 271–347, 2015b, 2016. Yet Sanders and Boyd 2008 again favor a sixth-century date for the Hexamilion and Fortress.
7. A similar fortress secured the west end of the Wall, and is visible in drawings of the Venetian fortifications, but was likely destroyed by the construction of New Corinth and the railway line.
8. Frey 2006, 299–347.
9. Gregory 1993 (*Isthmia* V), 98, 100, 113, 120; Frey 2006, 341–3, 2016.
10. The Golden Gate in Constantinople also began as a Roman triumphal arch: Bardill 1999; C. Mango 2000.
11. Procopius *Aed.* 4.2.27–8. Manuel's repairs: Phrantzes in Niebuhr 1968 (*CSHB*), 96–7, 108; Gregory 1993 (*Isthmia* V).
12. Walls of Dara (about 3 km.) built by Anastasius in two to three years in Pseudo-Zachariah of Mytilene *EH* 7.6.

13. Caraher 2015.
14. Monceaux 1884; Fraenkel 1902, 279–81 (nos. 204–5, pl. 2.1); Bees 1941, 1–9 (nos. 1–2); Kent 1966, no. 508; Feissel and Philippidis-Braat 1985, 279–81; Feissel 1988, 136–7; Papaphotiou 2002, 214–16; Cuomo 2007, 139–42.
15. I owe this suggestion to Charles Pazdernik, who discussed these inscriptions and Just. *Nov.* 8, 535, in a paper titled "Ho Gnēsios Doulos: The Master-Slave Metaphor as Evidence of Theological and Political Cross-Pollination in the Early Sixth Century," presented at the 135th Meeting of the American Philological Association in San Francisco in January 2004.
16. MacKay 1963; Gregory 2000; Cherf 2011.
17. Procopius *Aed.* 4.2.2–15, trans. Dewing and Downey 1941.
18. Procopius *Aed.* 4.2.16–28.
19. Procopius *Anek.* 26.31–4, trans. Dewing 1935.
20. Procopius *Bell.* 8.26.1–2.
21. Late antique fortification walls built around the city center of Corinth: Procopius *Aed.* 4.2.23–6; Scranton 1957 (*Corinth* XVI), 8; Gregory 1979; Dengate 1981; Sanders and Boyd 2008.
22. Corinth Museum inv. no. I-1211, Kent 1966 (*Corinth* VIII.3), no. 514; Feissel and Philippides-Braat 1985, no. 49*; Sironen 2016 (*IG* IV^2 3), no. 1243.
23. Gregory 1992.
24. Wiseman 1972.
25. Shear 1925, 382.
26. Dengate 1981; Sanders and Boyd 2008.
27. Venetian walls: Carpenter and Bon 1936 (*Corinth* III.2), 268–71.
28. Williams 2013a, 498 (Phase 10), 546–7.
29. Williams and Zervos 1984, 88, Fig. 5; Sanders and Boyd 2008.
30. Corinth Excavations NB111 (1930); Gregory 1979; Sanders and Boyd 2008.
31. Gregory 1979.
32. MacKay 1980.
33. Acrocorinth: Blegen et al. 1930 (*Corinth* III.1); Carpenter and Bon 1936 (*Corinth* III.2); Athanasoulis 2009.
34. Thucydides 1.2–8.
35. MacKay 1980, 3.

Conclusion Corinth at the End of Late Antiquity

1. Ivison 1996; Ott 2016 (updates dating of Forum burials).
2. Procopius *Anek.* 26, trans. Dewing 1935.
3. Sarris 2004, 2006.
4. Caraher 2003; Sweetman 2015.

Appendix I Epigraphic and Literary Sources for Late Antique Corinth

1. Kent (1966 (*Corinth* VIII.3), 17–8) well describes the almost incredible degree to which all ancient Corinthian inscriptions of every era are smashed and dispersed about the site. I cannot, however, agree with his placing the blame for this on the Herulian and Gothic sacks, as the process of preparation for the lime kilns is more likely to blame.
2. The relevant Corinth volumes are: Meritt 1931 (*Corinth* VIII.1), containing the Greek inscriptions of 1896–1927, West 1931 (*Corinth* VIII.2), Latin inscriptions of 1896–1926, and Kent 1966 (*Corinth* VIII.3), texts of both languages excavated from 1926 to 1950, as well as many from outside the Corinth excavations which came into the collection in those years, and re-readings of many of the older texts. Kent benefitted from the work of many who published significant contributions to the late antique epigraphy of Corinth after the compilations of Meritt and West: Hiller von Gaertringen 1932 (review of Meritt 1931 (*Corinth* VIII.1)); Broneer 1939; Dow 1951. Likewise, important works on Corinthian epigraphy have appeared since Kent 1966 (*Corinth* VIII.3) and his reviews: Clement 1974, 1980; Pallas and Dantis 1977 (1979); Martin 1977; Jordan 1982, 1994a, 1994b; Noy et al. 2004, 181–9 (Jewish inscriptions); Mary E. Hoskins Walbank and Michael B. Walbank 2006; Sironen 1992, 1997. See most recently Sironen 2016 (*IG* IV^2 3).
3. Bees 1941 is *CG-CIH* 1.1, though only *CG-CIH* 10, Bandy 1970, on Crete ever followed; see also Robert 1966 (a supplement more than a review, along with Dow 1967, of Kent 1966 (*Corinth* VIII.3)); Feissel and Philippidis-Braat 1985; Sironen 1992, 1997, 2016 (*IG* IV^2 3); Feissel 2006; Stroud 2013 (*Corinth* XVIII.6), 2014.
4. Michael B. Walbank 2010.
5. Sironen 2016 (*IG* IV^2 3).
6. Pausanias at Corinth: Imhoof-Blumer and Gardner 1885, 59–77; Frazer 1913; Roux 1958; Papachatzis 1963; Hohlfelder 1970a; Jones 1975; Levi 1979; Musti and Torelli 1986; Rocha-Pereira 1989; Mary E. Hoskins Walbank 1989, 2010b. On his more general dates, methods and biases: Habicht 1985; Arafat 1996, 2000; Alcock et al. 2001; Pretzler 2004a, 2004b, 2005a, 2005b, 2007a, 2007b; Akujärvi 2005; Hutton 2005; Georgopoulou et al. 2007.
7. Pausanias' dates in Corinth are estimated narrowly as *c.*152–early 160s by Puech (1983, 32), more broadly by Hutton (2005). Passages which date his overall era of composition include Pausanias 2.26.9, 2.27.6, 5.1.2, 7.5.9, 7.20.6, 8.9.7, 8.43.6, 10.34.5.

8. Strabo, Pliny and Ptolemy are also important sources for the topography of Roman Corinth. Strabo's description has had eight lines of text added since the Loeb translation: Aly 1956; Pettegrew 2016.
9. Pausanias 2.2.6 (for the acme). Pausanias (7.17.1–4) concludes his own account of the sack of Corinth with an explanation for how Greece became weak and subject to Rome from her own people's failings and the *daimon* (spirit), first city by city and then as a whole, running from the Dorian invasion of Argos down to Vespasian's repeal of Nero's freedom of the Greeks.
10. Dio Chrysostom on Roman Greece: Jones 1978; Moles 1995; Whitmarsh 1998. Aelius Aristides on Roman Athens: Oliver 1968; Day 1980. Second Sophistic public oratory and philosophy in Greece: Swain 2000; Whitmarsh 2001.
11. Apuleius *Met.* as a source for Corinth and contemporary provincial life: Birley 1968; Shumate 1996; Millar 1999; Ruebel 2000; Harrison 2000. Collected papers on the context, sources and genre of Apuleius *Met.*: Schmeling 1996, ch. 12G; Harrison 1999, chs. 7–11; Hofmann 1999.
12. Athenaeus' elements of contemporary life: Braund and Wilkins 2000; McClure 2003; Olson 2007.
13. Hicks 1925 (2000); Marcovich 1999; Goulet 2001.
14. Ampelius: Arnaud-Lindet 1993.
15. McDonald 1942; Meeks 1983; Murphy-O'Connor 1983; Furnish 1988; Blue 1994; Gill 1994; Downing 1998; Thiselton 2000, 1–16; Adams and Horrell 2004; Horrell 2004. See also the conferences published as Schowalter and Friesen 2005; Friesen et al. 2010; Friesen et al. 2014.
16. Broneer 1951a, 1962a, 1971, 1976; de Waele 1961.
17. Eusebius: Grant 1980; Cameron and Hall 1999; Maier 1999.
18. Third-century historiography: Millar 1969, 12–16; Mallan and Davenport 2015.
19. *IG* II^2 nos. 3669 (statue from city and children), 3198 (Patron of Panathenaia), 3670 (honors from children); Millar 1969; Jones et al. 1971 (*PLRE* 1), Dexippus 2. See now Mallan and Davenport 2015.
20. Photius *Bibl.* 82 = Jacoby *FGrH* 100 T5.
21. Evagrius *HE* 5.24 = Jacoby *FGrH* 100 T6; Millar 1969, 23–4.
22. Photius *Bibl.* 82; Stein 1957, 10; Millar 1969, 14–6; Brown 2011b.
23. Millar 1969, 25.
24. Millar (1969, 14) cites Plutarch's *Praecepta rei publicae gerendae, Mor.* 814 B–C as an example of peacetime writing.
25. Spawforth 1994, 1995.
26. Matthews 1989; Tritle 1997; Barnes 1998; Drijvers and Hunt 1999.
27. For fourth-century historiography, see recent articles by Averil Cameron (in Cameron and Garnsey 1998, 684–91 (*CAH* 13));

Bowersock et al. 1999, 1–20, and, with caution, papers collected in Rohrbacher (2002) and Marasco (2003).

28. See Barnes (1970) on the *Kaisergeschichte*. For the *Historia Augusta*, see Syme 1971; Barnes 1978; Callu 1992; Chastagnol 1994; Lippold 1998 (favors a date under Constantine in contrast to others). For Dexippus as an important source for the *Historia Augusta*, see *SHA Vita Sev. Alex.* 49.3, *Max. Iun.* 6–7, *Gord.* 2, 9, 19, 23, *Max. et Balb.* 1, 15–6, *Tyr. Trig.* 32, *Claud.* 12; Altheim 1948, 175–92.
29. See Brown 2011b.
30. Augustine and Orosius refer to Claudian's *Panegyric on the Third Consulship of the Emperor Honorius* (*3 Hon.* 1.96) of 395 as evidence for divine aid to Honorius' father Theodosius. Augustine (*De civ. Dei* 5.26) calls him *poeta Claudianus ... a Christi nomine alienus* (the poet Claudian ... foreign to the name of Christ). Orosius (*Adv. pag.* 7.35.21) calls him *paganus pervicacissimus* (a really bad pagan).
31. Besides Augustine and Orosius, Jerome also read Claudian (Levy 1948; Cameron 1965). For Claudian as poet and historical source: Crees 1908; Cameron 1970, 156–88; Hall 1986; Long 1996.
32. Goulet 1980; Blockley 1981; Baldini 1984; Sacks 1986; Banchich 1987; Penella 1990. For Eunapius in Athens: *VS* 493; Goulet 1980 (from 364–9); Banchich 1987 (from 362–7); Fornara 1989; Banchich 1996, 1998.
33. Banchich (1984, 183–92) dates the *Lives* to 399. Summary of Eunapius *History* in Photius *Bibl.* 77, ed. Henry 1959, 1.158–60.
34. Evidence for the publication and authorship of the editions of the Eunapius *History*: Chalmers 1953; Barnes 1978, 114–17; Blockley 1981, 1.1–28; Baker 1988; Banchich 1985, 1988, 1998; Penella 1990, 9–13; Liebeschuetz 2003.
35. Zosimus *NH* 1.1, 2.30; Goffart 1971. Photius (*Bibl.* 98) interpreted *New* as meaning second edition, while Goffart (1971) concludes that Zosimus chose the title *New History* in opposition to *Christian History*.
36. Paschoud (1971–89) prefers 498–520, Cameron (1969) *c.*501, Chastagnol (1964/5) the second half of the reign of Anastasius (*c.*505–18).
37. Goffart 1971; Ridley 1969, 1972, 1982; Paschoud 1975, 1971–89, 2006; Liebeschuetz 2003.
38. For the emergence of Christian literature: Cameron 1991.
39. Brown 2001a. For the importance of Church Councils to historians see Millar 2006, appendix.
40. Martyria: Musurillo 1954; Delehaye 1966. Greek hagiography up to the tenth century: van Uytfanghe 1993; Høgel 2002, 20–60.
41. Sevcenko 1990; Høgel 1996, 2002; Limberis 2005. Appreciation by contemporaries in an *encomium* by Psellos (*Scripta min.* 1.94–107).

42. For Procopius on Greece, and justification of this outline of his career, see Brown 2010b, and also Gregory 2000 (2001).
43. References to 32 years: Procopius *Anek.* 18.33, 23.1, 24.29, 24.33. Justinian's reign began April 1, 527 (Justinian *Nov.* 47 (537)), as Procopius elsewhere accepts and always references (e.g. *Bell.* 1.22.17, 8.15.12). Arguments and support for dating the *Secret History* to 558/9, from Justinian's accession, range from Gibbon 1788 (1994), 4.40.561–2 to Cataudella 2003, 400–4; Croke 2005. Many, however, still follow Haury's arguments for interpreting the 32 years as indicating 550/1, from the accession of Justin: Haury 1891, 9–27; Bury 1923 (1958), 2.422; Dewing 1914; Stein 1949, 2.720–1; Veh 1950/1, 1.9; Rubin 1954, 81, 1960, 1.468; Cameron 1985 (1996), 8–9; Greatrex 1994; Evans 1996; Signes Codoñer 2000, 48–53, 65–7, 2003. Kaldellis (2004, 3, 46) passes over the question of precise and relative dating of the works of Procopius as immaterial to his study. Evans (2000, 4–5), accepting the arguments of Scott 1987 on the date of the *Secret History*, concludes that it is an unpublished "malevolent commentary" on Procopius' own work, begun after Theodora's death in 548, but added to over the years up to the author's own death *c.*561.
44. Procopius states that he waited to write until his main protagonists were gone (*Anek.* 1.2), refers to Justinian, Theodora and Belisarius in the past tense (*Anek.* 8.22), and only at the very end calls Justinian alive and promises truth at his death (*Anek.* 30.34).
45. Those who favor a date of 554/5 point to the unmentioned collapse of St Sophia's first dome in 558, Samaritan revolt of 555 and succesful use of the Chersonnese Long Wall in 559: Stein 1949, 2.837; Cameron 1985 (1996), 9–18, 86; Greatrex 1994, 1995, 2003; Croke 2005. Those who favor *c.*560 follow the reference to the Sangarius bridge under construction: Haury 1891, 27–8; Bury 1923 (1958), 2.428; Downey 1947, 182–3; Whitby 1985 (560/1); Evans 1996, 305–6; Cataudella 2003, 400–4 (558). The Sangarius bridge near Nicomedia, described as under construction in Procopius *Aed.* 5.3.8–10, was begun not much before 559/60 (Theophanes AM 6052, De Boor 1883 (1963), 234, 15–18) and finished by 562 (Agathias in *AnthPal* 9.641; Paul the Silentiary *Ekphrasis* 928.33). Otherwise only the rebuilding of the walls of Topirus in Thrace following a Slav sack of 550 (Procopius *Aed.* 4.11.14–7, *Bell.* 7.38.9–23) and the building of the walls of Chalchis in Syria in 550/1 (Procopius *Aed.* 2.11.1, 8; Prentice 1908, nos. 305–6) can be securely dated after 545. Evans (1969; 1972, 43–4; 1996, 303) prefers to see Procopius *Aed.* 1 as an encomium delivered before 558, and the remainder of the work as finished by 561.

46. Rubin (1960, 1.470) and Angold (1996, 21–2) suggest that the genre of *anecdota* (unpublished histories) was devised by Theopompus, and this is the only surviving example; Kaldellis (2004, 260) rejects both that this was a genre, and that the *Secret History* conforms to any genre at all.
47. Kaldellis (2004) reappraises Procopius' literary style and philosophy as complex, creative and deeply familiar with Classical literature. For signposting of contemporary terms, see Cameron and Cameron 1964.
48. Procopius *Anek.* 24.
49. For example, Procopius (*Bell.* 3.1.17) defines a day's journey as 210 stades, Athens to Megara.
50. Meier 2003, 86–9. See also the provocative arguments of Kaldellis 2004.
51. For style see Sevcenko 1981; Trapp 1993. For Byzantine literature, see Mango 1975; Hunger 1978; Kazhdan 1999; Odorico and Agapitos 2002. For *ekphraseis*, see Webb (1999), and for military handbooks, see Teall (1977).
52. Adler and Tufflin 2002, lxxxii–iii.
53. Mango and Scott (1997, xliii–lxiii) address some of these complex questions of authorship, and give Syncellus much of the credit for the preparation of Theophanes' *Chronicle*, as Theophanes himself did.
54. Adler and Tufflin 2002, xlviii; Mango and Scott 1997.
55. For Zonaras, see DiMaio 1988; Grigoriadis 1998; Banchich 2008.
56. Ottoman and Ventian records: Beldiceanu and Beldiceanu-Steinherr 1986; Shariat-Panahi 2015 (Corinth); Zarinebaf, Bennet and Davis 2005 (Messenia); Kiel 1997 (Boeotia).
57. Early travelers who mention Corinth include: Thompson 1752, 1.364; Le Roy 2004, 431; Quinet 1830, 288; Temple 1836, 1.63; Malherbe 1846, 1.162; Denison 1849, 176; Curtius 1851/2, 2.529; Boullier 1854, 226; Beulé 1855, 454; Baird 1856, 157; Clark 1858, 58; Wyse 1865, 2.322; Schliemann 1869, 83; Jerningham 1873, 83; Vischer 1875, 262; Mahaffy 1878, 369; Belle 1881, 260; Farrer 1882, 453. Lists of travelers to Greece, including Corinth, are collected in Weber 1952, 1953; Simopoulos 1979, 1984–5.
58. Partially translated for Corinth in McKay 1967, 1968; full unpublished translation MacKay 1980.
59. Edward Capps (1896, 233) described the contemporary village of Ancient Corinth as "a little handful of wretched hovels."
60. Analysis of early travelers to Corinth: Kaplan 2001; van der Vin 1980, 615–20. Early travelers to Greece: Kourelis 2004; Eisner 1991; Angelomatis-Tsougarakis 1990; Stoneman 1987; Swinglehurst 1982; Tsigakou 1981.
61. Spon and Wheler 1678 in Carpenter and Bon 1936 (*Corinth* III.2), 146–8; Leake 1830, 3.229–323.

Appendix II Corinth Excavations of the American School of Classical Studies and Late Antiquity

1. The best overview of the history of the Corinth Excavations is Landon 1994, 94–148. The early years were described in print briefly by Seymour (1902) and Wilisch (1908), then by Fowler (1922) from work by B.H. Hill, and finally by Fowler in Fowler and Stillwell (1932 (*Corinth* I), 3–13). The official ASCSA histories of Lord (1947) and Meritt (1984) and the scrapbook of Langridge-Noti (1996) also shed light on the Corinth excavations up to their Centenary in 1986. Preliminary excavation reports are mainly in *AJA*, then from 1932 in the School's annual journal *Hesperia,* while final results are published in the series of *Corinth* volumes. Preliminary reports are generally organized by area(s) under excavation in a given season, including (at least in brief) most archaeological work carried out at Corinth by the American School; *Corinth* volumes are organized either thematically or geographically, publishing catalogues and conclusions for a much more limited number of artifacts and areas of excavation.
2. Dörpfeld (1886, 306) records that the eighteenth-century English antiquarian, architect and artist Stuart had found eleven columns still standing from the Archaic Temple, but by the *Expédition scientifique de Morée* of 1829 there were only the seven still standing to this day.
3. Skias 1892 (1894).
4. Skias (1906 (1907)) mentions his trenches of 1892, the American Excavations of 1896–1905 and their discovery of the Ancient Agora (Forum) following from the identification of Peirene, the Lechaion Road and the Propylaia. In the summer of 1906 his trenches down on the north plain revealed parts of the western Long Wall to Lechaion, and two of the north-south roads running to Lechaion to its east.
5. Origins and first era of the Corinth Excavations: preliminary excavation reports in the *AJA* (Richardson 1897–1902; Heermance 1903–4; Wheeler and Hill 1907–8, 1910), *Carnegie Institution Yearbook* (Wheeler 1909–10), and non-*AJA* ASCSA *Annual Reports* issued by Richardson and Hill. Overviews of this era: Capps 1896; Seymour 1902; Skias 1906 (1907); Wilisch 1908, 414–39; Fowler 1922 (written by Bert Hodge Hill); Fowler and Stillwell 1932 (*Corinth* I), 3–13; Lord 1947, 89–98, 103–6; Langridge-Noti 1996, 1–16.
6. Lord (1947, 92–3) mentions Emerson's Byzantine interests, unusual among the early ASCSA professors. On the tension at the ASCSA from its very beginnings between broad-based archaeology of all periods and professional, narrowly focused Classical archaeology,

with the latter more often practiced: Turner 1999, 315, 369; Kourelis 2007, 394.

7. Shear 1925, 381.
8. Bookidis (pers. comm. 2008) says many portable finds were sent to Athens during the early excavations, with most then returned around 1912, after the Museum at Corinth opened in 1910.
9. Early methods of excavation: Capps 1896, 235.
10. This attitude can be traced to some extent back to ambivalent Roman reactions to Greek culture (e.g. Horace *Ep.* 2.1.157, "Graecia capta ..." with Henrichs 1995, other articles in the same volume), then to Greek response to becoming Roman (Swain 1996; Goldhill 2001), and finally to Byzantine ambivalence about the Greco-Roman heritage (e.g. Mango 1981, and other articles in the same volume). But certainly in modern times the moralizing tension between Greek, Roman and Byzantine, when studying Greece, is present in authors from Gibbon (1994, with Jordan 1971) to Jones (1940) to the dichotomies of current Classical archaeology (Alcock and Osborne 2007).
11. Landon 1994; B.A. Robinson 2001, 2011. For the politics, see also Robinson 2011, 2013.
12. On Hill's modern methods, role as teacher, administration and emphasis on accuracy: Blegen 1959; Blegen's introduction to Hill 1964 (*Corinth* I.6), vii. On his removal for failure to publish: Lord 1947, 190–2; Davis 2007.
13. Swift wrote his dissertation (1921a, 1921b, 1921c, 1922) on the Roman sculpture from the Julian Basilica, taught Roman art at Columbia, then published on St Sophia in Constantinople and other Byzantine topics (1934, 1935, 1940, 1951).
14. Scranton 1957 (*Corinth* XVI).
15. Hill 1926; Weinberg 1939, 1948; Weinberg and Weinberg 1946.
16. For the Corinth Excavations after 1925 up to WWII, see the authorized American School histories of Lord 1947; Meritt 1984 (though this sometimes makes for very dry reading). Unauthorized histories by Oscar Broneer and Dorothy Burr Thompson are said to exist.
17. Broneer 1926, 1928, 1932 (*Corinth* X: Odeum), 1933, 1935; Shear 1925, 1926, 1928a, 1928b, 1929, 1931b.
18. Shear 1925, 1928b, 1929, 1930, 1930 (*Corinth* V: Roman Villa), 1931a; Slane 2012, 2015, 2017 (*Corinth* XXI); Mary E. Hoskins Walbank 2014.
19. Methods: Carpenter 1933, 10, 103; Trigger 1989, 196–200; Dyson 2006, 112–13.
20. Carpenter's Director's Report of 1927–8 in Lord 1947, 208–9; Cullen 2007, 7. The first Early Christian church discovered at Corinth, the Cenchrean Gate (Kraneion) Basilica: Carpenter 1929;

Pease 1928 (Corinth Excavations NB98); de Waele 1928 (Corinth Excavations NB99); de Waele 1930, 442, n. 1. The Byzantine Museum, also called Carpenter's Folly, is a tenth- to twelfth-century house found in 1917, rebuilt with Byzantine *spolia* and re-roofed in 1928–30, unroofed during WWII, with some sculpture now in the West Shops or stuck *in situ*: Scranton 1957 (*Corinth* XVI), 39–41; Kourelis 2007, 403–10. The publication of Hosios Loukas and Daphne monasteries by the ASCSA: Diez and Demus 1931.

21. Kourelis (2007, 393) discusses the famous Paris Byzantine exhibit of 1929 and argues that Byzantine art particularly attracted modernists with its "perceived artistic otherness, abstraction, and spirituality." For an example of the rise of study of Byzantine art in this era, see the dissertation of Weitzmann (Goldschmidt and Weitzmann 1930); for the relatively late emergence of Byzantine art history and archaeology in western scholarship, especially among Classical archaeologists working in Greece: Nelson 1996; Bullen 1999, 2003.
22. Morgan 1936, 1937, 1938, 1939; Thompson 1984. Byzantine Pottery: Morgan 1935, 1942 (*Corinth* XI: Byzantine Pottery). Before Morgan the Byzantine pottery was given to the Greek Society of Christian Archaeology (ChrAE) to publish, apparently out of lack of American interest: Philadelpheus 1924. Minor date changes, importance of the work: Sanders 2000.
23. Capps Jr. was interested in the art of Late Antiquity, e.g. Capps Jr. 1927a, 1927b, and wrote reviews, especially about ivories (Capps Jr. 1942, 1956a, 1956b). His work on Corinth included Capps Jr. 1934, 1936, 1938, 1949, 1950. On his break with his Princeton advisor Morey over the latter's schema of late antique art, see Weitzmann 1986, 14. As he left unfinished *Corinth* IX.2, a planned continuation of the catalogue of Corinth sculpture by Johnson (1931 (*Corinth* IX)), the sculpture from the site found since 1923 has appeared in *Corinth* volumes only in Sturgeon's work on the Theater (Sturgeon 1977, 2004 (*Corinth* IX.2–3)), and otherwise in Catherine de Grazia Vanderpool's unpublished Roman portrait sculpture thesis (de Grazia 1973) and various articles (e.g. Bookidis 1970; Ridgway 1981; Sturgeon 2003; de Grazia Vanderpool 2003; Stirling 2008).
24. For *Hesperia*: Waagé 1934 (whose work was taken up by Morgan); Davidson 1937. But as Cullen (2007, 8) noted, most articles in *Hesperia* (and thus most of the articles published on Corinth) focused on the presentation of primary archaeological data, rather than its analysis or significance for larger historical (or methodological) issues. This tendency is criticized by Dyson 1989, 1993, 204–6; Davis (2007) comments on the founding of *Hesperia* and the impact it has had on the research and image of the American School, in particular its focus on prehistoric to Classical archaeology (see also Snodgrass 1987).

25. On the importance of publications on the excavation of Corinth to Capps from the beginning of his tenure as Chair, see his *Thirty-Ninth Annual Report, 1919–1920*, 14–15, and the circumstances surrounding his removal of Director Bert Hodge Hill in 1926 (Lord 1947, 146, 171–2; Davis 2007, 25–6). After abandoning publication of excavation updates in the *AJA* in 1908, and *Annual Reports* in 1917, Hill next produced a report about his work on Corinth only in 1922, published by Fowler (1922) in the AIA's popular magazine *Art and Archaeology*; no other articles, reports or the desired Corinth guidebook followed, though, and so first H.N. Fowler was made Corinth editor (1925), then Hill was "retired" (1926), then in 1928 the Corinth guidebook and, from 1929 on, Corinth articles and volumes began to appear once again, under Carpenter as both director and general editor.
26. Guidebooks: Carpenter 1928 (first edition); Broneer 1954 (sixth edition); Robinson 1969a. Greek guidebooks have been translated into English more recently: Kasas 1974; Papachatzis 1985.
27. Millis 2004; Sanders et al. forthcoming.
28. Fowler and Stillwell 1932 (*Corinth* I: Architecture); Stillwell, Scranton and Freeman 1941 (*Corinth* I.2); Blegen et al. 1930 (*Corinth* III.1: Acrocorinth); Carpenter and Bon 1936 (*Corinth* III.2); Broneer 1932 (*Corinth* IV.2: TC Lamps); Meritt 1931 (*Corinth* VIII.1: Greek Inscriptions); West 1931 (*Corinth* VIII.2: Latin Inscriptions); Johnson 1931 (*Corinth* IX: Sculpture); Morgan 1942 (*Corinth* XI: Byzantine Pottery).
29. Some 90,000 coins have been excavated at Corinth, and accounts of about 2/3 have been published, according to Michael Ierardi pers. comm. 2007. Publications of coins include: Bellinger 1930; Shear 1931; Edwards 1933 (*Corinth* VI: Coins), 1937; Harris 1941; Price 1967; Dengate 1981; Fisher 1980 (and further addenda to Williams' excavation reports in *Hesperia*); Zervos 1986, 1997 (and further addenda to Williams' excavation reports in *Hesperia*); Mac Isaac 1987; Amandry 1988; Mary E. Hoskins Walbank 2003, 2010a.
30. Shear 1930 (*Corinth* V: Roman Villa); Broneer 1932 (*Corinth* X: Odeum). Broneer often characterized the remains of the the Roman city and its cults as the final stage of a decline (Broneer 1942, 161).
31. Scranton 1951 (*Corinth* I.3); Broneer 1954 (*Corinth* I.4); Weinberg 1960 (*Corinth* I.5); Hill 1964 (*Corinth* I.6: Fountains); Stillwell 1952 (*Corinth* II: Theatre); Blegen et al. 1964 (*Corinth* XIII: North Cemetery); Roebuck 1951 (*Corinth* XIV: Asclepium and Lerna); Davidson 1952 (*Corinth* XII: Minor Finds); Kent 1966 (*Corinth* VIII.3: Inscriptions).
32. Scranton 1957 (*Corinth* XVI: Mediaeval Architecture), in his preface, cites Carpenter and Bon 1936 (*Corinth* III.2) and Finley 1932 as his main modern sources for his account of medieval Corinthian history.

33. Favorable review, some idea of huge challenge he faced: Swift 1958, 352. Additions to his map of Medieval Corinth: Robinson and Weinberg 1960, 229, Figure 2; Robinson 1962, 97, 106, Figures 2, 6; Williams and Bookidis 2003 (*Corinth* XX); Sanders 2005, 427, Figure 16.5.
34. Corinth during WWII: Broneer 1945, 416. On the retreat from modernism and medieval studies in Greece by Americans and a return to hard-core Classicism after WWII as part of a Cold War culture-clash: Saunders 1999.
35. Broneer 1947, 1951b; Weinberg 1949. Vogeikoff-Brogan 2007 reprints the film Broneer made of Greece and the American School in 1947, including the excavations at Corinth.
36. Goals and results: Robinson and Weinberg 1960; Robinson 1962. Robinson's Roman interests: Robinson 1943, 1969a, 1972, 1974. This is the area now known as Frankish south of Temple E, where Directors Williams and Sanders have continued work.
37. Stroud 1965 (excavations of 1961–2), 1968 (excavations of 1964–5), 1993; Bookidis 1969 (excavations of 1968), 1987, 1990, 1993; Bookidis and Fisher 1972 (excavations of 1969–70), 1974 (excavations of 1971–3); Pemberton 1989 (*Corinth* XVIII.1); Slane 1990 (*Corinth* XVIII.2); Bookidis and Stroud 1997 (*Corinth* XVIII.3); Merker 2000 (*Corinth* XVIII.4); Bookidis 2010 (*Corinth* XVIII.5); Stroud 2013 (*Corinth* XVIII.6); Bookidis & Pemberton 2015 (*Corinth* XVIII.7); Bookidis and Stroud 1987; Bookidis et al. 1999; Dunbabin 1990; DeMaris 1995; Pfaff 1999.
38. Late Antiquity at Demeter and Kore: Dunbabin 1990; Slane 1990 (*Corinth* XVIII.2); Stroud 1993; Bookidis and Stroud 1997 (*Corinth* XVIII.3); Merker 2000 (*Corinth* XVIII.4); Bookidis et al. 1999; Stroud 2013 (*Corinth* XVIII.6).
39. Meritt 1984, 162.
40. Forum/Agora SW: Williams 1969 (1970), 1969, 1970, 1971 (1974), 1972 (1976), 1973 (1977), 1978a, 1979, 1980; Williams and Fisher 1971, 1972, 1973, 1975, 1976; Williams et al. 1974; de Grazia and Williams 1977; Williams and Russell 1981; Williams and Zervos 1987, 1988, 1990, 1991. East of Theater: Williams and Zervos 1982, 1983, 1984, 1985, 1986, 1987, 1988, 1989. Frankish Corinth: Williams and Zervos 1990, 1991, 1992, 1993, 1994, 1996; Snyder and Williams 1997; Williams et al. 1998.
41. He has evinced interest in the Greek city (Williams 1981, 1995) and also the Roman one (Williams 1987a, 1987b).
42. Anderson 1967; Wiseman 1967.
43. Wiseman 1967a, 1967b, 1969a, 1969b, 1970, 1972; Dengate 1981.
44. Robinson 1964 (1966), 1965 (1967), 1966 (1968), 1969a, 1971 (1974), 1976a, 1976b.
45. Stikas 1961 (1964), 1962 (1966), 1965.

46. Broneer 1947; Sanders 1999, 2002a, 2002b, 2003a, 2003b, 2004, 2005; James 2005.
47. Slane and Sanders 2005.
48. For example, in the collected papers of Schowalter and Friesen 2005.
49. Sanders et al. 2017.
50. I thank Nancy Bookidis for information about salvage excavations.
51. Athanasoulis 2013; Athanasoulis and Manolessou 2013; Kissas 2013. See also the exhibit from the OSE (Railroad) excavations at the Corinth train station, and articles in the publication of the 2009 Loutraki conference, Kissas and Niemeier 2013.
52. Petrole and Tzonou–Herbst 2016.
53. Biers 1985 (*Corinth* XVII); Sturgeon 1977 (*Corinth* IX.2), 2004 (*Corinth* IX.3).
54. Biers 2003, Landon 2003, Romano 2003, Sanders 2003, Sturgeon 2003, de Grazia Vanderpool 2003, all in Williams and Bookidis 2003 (*Corinth* XX).
55. Sakellariou and Faraklas 1971; Wiseman 1978. For Doxiadis' project at the Athens Center of Ekistics: Doxiadis 1967; Toynbee 1971.
56. Gregory 1985, 2013a, 2013b; Kardulias, Gregory and Sawmiller 1995; Caraher and Gregory 2006; Caraher, Nakassis and Pettegrew 2006; Tartaron et al. 2006; Tartaron et al. 2011.
57. Gerster 1884.
58. Jenkins and Megaw 1931–2 (1934).
59. Broneer 1953.
60. Broneer 1955, 1958, 1959, 1962b. For the history of the University of Chicago Excavations at Isthmia and Broneer: Gebhard 1990, 1992, 2007.
61. Broneer 1962a, 1971, 1976 (St Paul), 1971 (*Isthmia* I: Temple of Poseidon), 1973 (*Isthmia* II: Topography and Architecture), 1977 (*Isthmia* III: TC Lamps).
62. Gebhard 1973, 1979, 1993, 2005, 2013; Gebhard and Dickie 1999; Gebhard and Hemans 1992; Gebhard and Reese 2005; Raubitschek 1998 (*Isthmia* VII: Metal Objects).
63. Gebhard, Hemans and Hayes 1998.
64. Clement 1968 (1969), 1969 (1970), 1970 (1972), 1971 (1973), 1972 (1976), 1973 (1977), 1977a, 1977b, 1980, 1987; Gregory and Mills 1984; Gregory and Kardulias 1990; Gregory 1993, 1993 (*Isthmia* V), 1995, 2013; Gregory and Frey 2016; Lattimore 1996 (*Isthmia* VI).
65. On the opening of the Isthmia Museum: Gebhard 1979. Conference: Gebhard and Gregory 2015.
66. Scranton and Ramage 1964, 1967; Scranton 1965; Shaw 1967a, 1967b, 1970, 1972; Hohlfelder 1970a, 1970b, 1973, 1975, 1976;

Scranton, Shaw and Ibrahim 1978 (*Kenchreai* 1: Topography and Architecture); Hohlfelder 1978 (*Kenchreai* 3: Coins); Adamsheck 1978 (*Kenchreai* 4: Pottery); Williams 1981 (*Kenchreai* 5: Lamps); Stern and Thimme 2007 (*Kenchreai* 6: Ivory, Bone, Wood).

67. Rife et al. 2007; Korka and Rife 2013.
68. Harbor: Shaw 1969, 1972. Villa: Philadelpheus 1918 (1921); Stikas 1957 (1962).
69. Lechaion Excavation reports and dating: Pallas 1956 (1961), 1957 (1962), 1958 (1965), 1959 (1965), 1961–2 (1963a), 1962, 1965 (1967), 1970.
70. Kraneion Excavation reports and dating: Pallas 1970 (1972), 1972 (1974), 1976 (1978), 1977 (1980). Other Late Roman excavations: Pallas 1955 (1960) (third-century villa), 1961–1962 (1963a) (Hexamilion Wall). Summaries of his digs at the basilicas and Corinth between 1956 and 1973: Pallas 1959, 1977.
71. The new study includes Demetrios Athanasoulis, Natalia Poulou-Papadimitriou and A. Papaphotiou.

BIBLIOGRAPHY

Abulafia, D. (2011). *The Great Sea: A Human History of the Mediterranean.* Oxford.

Adams, E. & Horrell, D.G. (eds). (2004). *Christianity at Corinth: The Quest for the Pauline Church.* Louisville and London.

Adamsheck, S. (1978). *The Pottery* (*Kenchreai* 4). Leiden.

Adler, W. & Tufflin, P. (trans.). (2002). *The Chronography of George Synkellos: A Byzantine Chronicle of Universal History from the Creation.* Oxford.

Admiralty (1945). *Greece.* London.

Ajootian, A. (2000). A Roman Table Support at Ancient Corinth. *Hesperia, 69*, 487–507.

———. (2008). The Sculptural Program of the Roman Odeion at Ancient Corinth. *109th Annual Meeting Abstracts*, Vol. 31. Boston.

Akujärvi, J. (2005). *Researcher, Traveller, Narrator: Studies in Pausanias' Periegesis.* Lund.

Alcock, S.E. (1989). Archaeology and Imperialism: Roman Expansion and the Greek City. *JMA, 2*, 87–135.

———. (1994). Minding the Gap in Hellenistic and Roman Greece. In S.E. Alcock & R. Osborne (eds), *Placing the Gods: Sanctuaries and Sacred Space in Ancient Greece.* (pp. 247–62). Oxford.

———. (1995). Pausanias and the *Polis*: Use and Abuse. In M.H. Hansen (ed.), *Sources for the Greek City State, Symposium August 24–27, 1994* (Acts of the Copenhagen Polis Centre). (pp. 326–34). Copenhagen.

Alcock, S.E. & Osborne, R. (eds). (2007). *Classical Archaeology.* Malden, Mass.

Alcock, S.E., Cherry, J.F. & Elsner, J. (eds). (2001). *Pausanias: Travel and Memory in Roman Greece.* Oxford.

Alexandri, O. & Verdelis, N. (1962). Ἅγιοι Θεόδωροι Κορινθίας *ArchDelt, 17B* (1961), 52–4.

Allen, P. (1979). The "Justinianic" Plague. *Byzantion: Revue International des Etudes Byzantines, 49*, 5–20.

Alston, R. (1998). *Aspects of Roman History, AD 14–117.* London.

Altheim, F. (1948). *Literatur und Geschichte im ausgehenden Altertum* (Vol. 1). Halle.

Aly, W. (1956). *De Strabonis codice rescripto, cuius reliquiae in codicibus Vaticanis Vat. gr. 2306 et 2061A servatae sunt.* Vatican City.

Amandry, M. (1988). *Le monnayage des duovirs corinthiens* (BCH Suppl. 15). Paris.

Ambraseys, N.N. (1962). Data for the Investigation of the Seismic Sea-Waves in the Eastern Mediterranean. *Bulletin of the Seismological Society of America, 52,* 895–913.

———. (1996). Material for the Investigation of the Seismicity of Central Greece. In S.C. Stiros & R.E. Jones (eds), *Archaeoseismology.* (pp. 23–36). Athens.

Ambraseys, N.N. & Jackson, J.A. (1990). Seismicity and Associated Strain of Central Greece between 1890 and 1988. *Geophysical Journal International, 101,* 663–708.

———. (1997). Seismicity and Strain in the Gulf of Corinth (Greece) since 1694. *Journal of Earthquake Engineering, 1,* 433–74.

Ambraseys, N.N. & White, D. (1997). The Seismicity of the Eastern Mediterranean Region 550–1 BC: A Re-Appraisal. *Journal of Earthquake Engineering, 1,* 603–32.

Ameling, W. (1983). *Herodes Atticus.* Hildesheim.

Anagnostakis, I. & Kaldellis, A. (2014). The Textual Sources for the Peloponnese, A.D. 582–959: Their Creative Engagement with Ancient Literature. *GRBS, 54,* 105–35.

Anamali, S. (1987). Quatre inscriptions sur la construction des murs d'enceinte de Byllis. *Monumentet, 33,* 70–2.

Anderson, J.K. (1967). Corinth: Temple E Northwest Preliminary Report, 1965. *Hesperia, 36,* 1–12.

Angelomatis-Tsougarakis, H. (1990). *The Eve of the Greek Revival: Travellers' Perceptions of Early Nineteenth Century Greece.* London.

Angold, M. (1996). Procopius' Portrait of Theodora. In C. Constantinides et al. (eds), ΦΙΛΕΛΛΗΝ *Studies in Honour of Robert Browning.* (pp. 21–34). Venice.

Arafat, K.W. (1996). *Pausanias' Greece: Ancient Artists and Roman Rulers.* Cambridge.

———. (2000). The Recalcitrant Mass: Athenaeus and Pausanias. In D. Braund & J. Wilkins (eds), *Athenaeus and His World: Reading Greek Culture in the Roman Empire.* (pp. 191–202). Exeter.

Arjava, A. (2005). The Mystery Cloud of 536 CE in the Mediterranean Sources. *DOP, 59,* 73–94.

Armijo, R. et al. (1996). Quaternary Evaluation of the Corinth Rift and its Implications for the Late Cenozoic Evolution of the Aegean. *Geophysical Journal International, 126,* 11–53.

Arnaud-Lindet, M.-P. (ed.). (1993). *L. Ampelius. Aide-mémoire (Liber memorialis).* Paris.

Aslamatzidou-Kostourou, Z. (2013). Ρωμαϊκή έπαυλη στην Κατούνιστρα Λουτρακίου. In K. Kissas & W.-D. Niemeier (eds), *The Corinthia and the Northeast Peloponnese: Topography and History from Prehistoric Times until the End of Antiquity.* (pp. 179–90). Munich.

Athanasoulis, D. (2009). *The Castle of Acrocorinth and its Enhancement Project (2006–2009).* Ancient Corinth.

———. (2013). Corinth. In J. Albani & E. Chalkia (eds), *Heaven & Earth: Cities and Countryside in Byzantine Greece*. (pp. 192–209). Athens.

Athanasoulis, D. & Manolessou, E.G. (2013). Η μεσαιωνική Κορίνθια. In K. Kissas & W.-D. Niemeier (eds), *The Corinthia and the Northeast Peloponnese: Topography and History from Prehistoric Times until the End of Antiquity*. (pp. 531–50). Munich.

Athanassiadi, P. (1992). *Julian: An Intellectual Biography* (Reprint of *Julian and Hellenism* by Polymnia Athanassiadi-Fowden. Oxford 1981). London.

Avraméa, A. (1997). *Le Péloponnèse du IVe au VIIIe siècle: changements et persistances* (Byzantina Sorbonensia 15). Paris.

Avraméa, A. & Kyrkou, M. (1988). Inventaire topographique de Corinthe et sa region à l'époque chrétienne et byzantine. In H. Ahrweiler (ed.), *Géographie historique du monde méditerranéen* (Byzantina Sorbonensia 7) (pp. 31–45). Paris.

Bagdikian, A. (1953). *Civic Officials of Roman Corinth.* Ph.D. Diss., University of Vermont.

Bagnall, R.S. (2002). The Effects of Plague: Model and Evidence. *JRA, 15*, 114–20.

Baird, H.M. (1856). *Modern Greece: A Narrative of a Residence and Travels in That Country*. New York.

Baker, A. (1988). Eunapius' Nea Ekdosis and Photius. *GRBS, 29*, 389–402.

Bakker, J.T. (1994). *Living and Working with the Gods: Studies of Evidence for Private Religion and its Material Environment in the City of Ostia (100–500 AD)*. Amsterdam.

Baladié, R. (1980). *Le Péloponnèse de Strabon: Étude de géographie historique*. Paris.

Baldini, A. (1984). *Ricerche sulla Storia di Eunapio di Sardi: problemi di storiografia tardopagana*. Bologna.

Banchich, T.M. (1984). The Date of Eunapius' *Vitae Sophistarum*. *GRBS, 25*, 183–92.

———. (1985). *The Historical Fragments of Eunapius of Sardis*. Buffalo.

———. (1987). On Goulet's Chronology of Eunapius' Life and Works. *JHS, 107*, 164–7.

———. (1988). Vit. Sophist. X.2.3 and the Terminus of the First Edition of Eunapius' *History*. *Revista Hispánica Moderna, 131*, 375–80.

———. (1996). Eunapius in Athens. *Phoenix, 50*, 304–11.

———. (1998). Nestorius ἱεροφαντεῖν τεταγμένος. *Historia, 47*, 360–74.

———. (2008). *The History of Zonaras: From Alexander Severus to the death of Theodosius the Great*. New York.

Bankel, H. (1997). Knidos. Der hellenistische Rundtempel und sein Altar. *Archäologischer Anzeiger*, 51–71.

Bardill, J. (1999). The Golden Gate in Constantinople: A Triumphal Arch of Thesodosius I. *AJA, 103*, 671–96.

Barnes, T.D. (1970). The Lost *Kaisergeschichte* and the Latin Historical Tradition. *Bonner Historia-Augusta-Colloquium, 1968/9*, 13–43.

———. (1978). *The Sources of the Historia Augusta* (Collection Latomus 155). Brussels.

———. (1998). *Ammianus Marcellinus and the Representation of Historical Reality*. Ithaca, N.Y.

Barrett, C.K. (1987). *The New Testament Background: Selected Documents* (Rev. ed. Original ed., New York 1956/7). London.
Beacham, R.C. (1992). *The Roman Theatre and its Audience.* Cambridge.
Beard, M. & Henderson, J. (1998). With This Body I Thee Worship: Sacred Prostitution in Antiquity. In M. Wyke (ed.), *Gender and the Body in the Ancient Mediterranean.* (pp. 56–79). Malden, Mass.
Beaton, A.E. & Clement, P.A. (1976). The Date of the Destruction of the Sanctuary of Poseidon on the Isthmus of Corinth. *Hesperia, 45,* 267–79.
Bees, N.A. (ed.). (1941). *Die griechisch-christlichen Inschriften des Peloponnes 1: Isthmos-Korinthos.* Athens.
Bekker, I. & Niebuhr, B.G. (eds). (1968). *Corpus scriptorum historiae byzantinae (CSHB).* (Reprint). Bonn.
Beldiceanu, N. & Beldiceanu-Steinherr, I. (1986). Corinthe et sa région d'après le registre TT 10. *Südost–Forschungen, 45,* 37–61.
Bell, A. (2004). *Spectacular Power in the Greek and Roman City.* Oxford.
Belle, H. (1881). *Trois années en Grèce.* Paris.
Bellinger, A.R. (1930). *Catalogue of the Coins Found at Corinth, 1925.* New Haven.
Beloch, J. (1968). *Die Bevölkerung der griechisch-römischen Welt* (Reprint. Original ed., Leipzig 1886). Rome.
Bergk, T. (ed.). (1914). *Poetae lyrici Graeci 3: Poetae melici.* (Reprint. 4th ed. 1882). Leipzig.
Bernhart, M. (1936). *Aphrodite auf griechischen Münzen: eine numismatische Materialsammlung.* Munich.
Beulé, E. (1855). *Études sur le Péloponnèse.* Paris.
Bieber, M. (1961). *The History of the Greek and Roman Theatre.* Princeton.
Biers, J.C. (1985). *The Great Bath on the Lechaion Road* (*Corinth* XVII). Princeton.
———. (2003). *Lavari est vivere*: Baths in Roman Corinth. In C.K. Williams, II & N. Bookidis (eds), *Corinth, the Centenary: 1896–1996* (*Corinth* XX). (pp. 303–17). Princeton.
Biers, W.R. (1978). Water Supply from Stymphalos. *Hesperia, 47,* 171–84.
Biers, W.R. & Geagan, D.J. (1970). A New List of Victors in the Caesarea at Isthmia. *Hesperia, 39,* 79–93.
Birley, A. (1968). Apuleius: Roman Provincial Life. *History Today, 18,* 629–36.
Blaksova, A. & Wiseman, J.R. (eds). (1981). *Studies in the Antiquities of Stobi 3.* Titov Veles.
Blegen, C.W. (1920). Corinth in Prehistoric Times. *AJA, 24,* 1–13, 274.
———. (1959). Necrology: Bert Hodge Hill. *AJA, 63,* 193–4.
Blegen, C.W., Broneer, O., Stillwell, R. & Bellinger, A.R. (1930). *Acrocorinth: Excavations in 1926* (*Corinth* III.1). Cambridge, Mass.
Blegen, C.W., Palmer, H., & Young, R.S. (1964). *The North Cemetery* (*Corinth* XIII). Princeton.
Blockley, R.C. (1981–3). *The Fragmentary Classicising Historians of the Later Roman Empire: Eunapius, Olympiodorus, Priscus, and Malchus.* Liverpool.
Blouet, A. et al. (1831). *Expédition scientifique de Morée, ordonnée par le gouvernement français.* Paris.

Blue, B. (1994). Acts and the House Church. In D.W.J. Gill & C.H. Gempf (eds), *The Book of Acts in its Graeco-Roman Setting*. (pp. 119–222). Grand Rapids.

Boas, M. (1905). *De epigrammatis Simonideis*. Groningen.

Boblaye, E.P. (1836). *Recherches géographiques sur les ruines de la Morée*. Paris.

Boffo, L. (1994). *Iscrizioni greche e latine per lo studio della Bibbia* (*Biblioteca di storia e storiografia dei tempi biblici* 9). Brescia.

Bon, A. (1951). *Le Péloponnèse byzantin jusqu'en 1204*. Paris.

Bonnet, C., Rüpke, J., & Scarpi, P. (eds). (2006). *Religions orientales – culti misterici: Neue Perspektiven – nouvelles perspectives – prospettive nuove*. Stuttgart.

Bookidis, N. (1969). The Sanctuary of Demeter and Kore on Acrocorinth, Preliminary Report III: 1968. *Hesperia*, *38*, 297–310.

———. (1970). Archaic Sculptures from Corinth (from Notes of Edward Capps Jr.). *Hesperia*, *39*, 313–25.

———. (1987). The Sanctuary of Demeter and Kore: An Archaeological Approach to Ancient Religion. *AJA*, *91*, 480–1.

———. (1990). Ritual Dining in the Sanctuary of Demeter and Kore at Corinth: Some Questions. In O. Murray (ed.), *Sympotica: A Symposium on the Symposium*. (pp. 86–94). Oxford.

———. (1993). Ritual Dining at Corinth. In N. Marinatos & R. Hägg (eds), *Greek Sanctuaries: New Approaches*. (pp. 45–61). London.

———. (2000). Corinthian Terracotta Sculpture and the Temple of Apollo. *Hesperia*, *69*, 381–452.

———. (2005). Religion in Corinth: 146 B.C.E. to 100 C.E. In D.N. Schowalter & S.J. Friesen (eds), *Urban Religon in Roman Corinth: Interdisciplinary Approaches*. (pp. 141–64). Cambridge, Mass.

———. (2013). Acrocorinth: The North Slope. In K. Kissas & W.-D. Niemeier (eds), *The Corinthia and the Northeast Peloponnese: Topography and History from Prehistoric Times until the End of Antiquity*. (pp. 99–110). Munich.

———. (2010). *The Sanctuary of Demeter and Kore: The Terracotta Sculpture Corinth* XVIII.5. Princeton.

Bookidis, N. & Fisher, J.E. (1972). The Sanctuary of Demeter and Kore on Acrocorinth: Preliminary Report IV: 1969–70. *Hesperia*, *41*, 283–331.

———. (1974). Sanctuary of Demeter and Kore on Acrocorinth: Preliminary Report V: 1971–3. *Hesperia*, *43*, 267–307.

Bookidis, N., Hansen, J., Snyder, L., & Goldberg, P. (1999). Dining in the Sanctuary of Demeter and Kore at Corinth. *Hesperia*, *68*, 1–54.

Bookidis, N. & Pemberton, E.G. (2015). *The Sanctuary of Demeter and Kore: The Greek Lamps and Offering Trays Corinth* XVIII.7. Princeton.

Bookidis, N. & Stroud, R.S. (1987). *Demeter and Persephone in Ancient Corinth* (*Corinth Notes* 2). Princeton.

———. (1997). *The Sanctuary of Demeter and Kore: Topography and Architecture* (*Corinth* XVIII.3). Princeton.

———. (2004). Apollo and the Archaic Temple at Corinth. *Hesperia*, *73*, 401–26.

Boullier, E. (1854). *Lettres d'un pélerin à Jérusalem: Journal d'un voyage en Orient*. Laval.

Bouras, Ch. (2013). Byzantine Cities in Greece. In J. Albani & E. Chalkia (eds), *Heaven & Earth: Cities and Countryside in Byzantine Greece.* (pp. 44–73). Athens.

Bousquet, B., Dufaure, J.J., & Pechoux, P.Y. (1983). Temps historique et évolution des paysages égéens. *Méditerranée, 48*, 3–25.

Bowden, W.A. (2003). *Epirus Vetus: The Archaeology of a Late Antique Province.* London.

Bowden, W.A., Lavan, L. & Machado, C. (eds). (2004). *Recent Research on the Late Antique Countryside.* Leiden.

Bowden, W.A., Gutteridge, A. & Machado, C. (eds). (2006). *Social and Political Life in Late Antiquity* (*Late Antique Archaeology* 3.1). Leiden.

Bowersock, G.W., Brown, P., & Grabar, O. (eds). (1999). *Late Antiquity: A Guide to the Postclassical World.* Cambridge, Mass.

Bowes, K. (2008). *Private Worship, Public Values, and Religious Change in Late Antiquity.* New York.

Bradeen, D.W. (1974). *Inscriptions: The Funerary Monuments (Agora* XVII) Princeton.

Brady, T.A. (1941). A Head of Sarapis from Corinth. *HSCP, 51*, 61–9.

Braudel, F. (1995). *The Mediterranean and the Mediterranean World in the Age of Philip II.* Berkeley.

———. (2001a). *The Mediterranean in the Ancient World.* Ayala, R. & Braudel, P. (eds). London.

———. (2001b). *Memory and the Mediterranean.* Ayala, R. & Braudel, P. (eds). New York.

Braund, D. & Wilkins, J. (eds). (2000). *Athenaeus and His World: Reading Greek Culture in the Roman Empire.* Exeter.

Bricault, L., Versluys, M.J. & Meyboom, P.G.P. (eds). (2007). *Nile into Tiber: Egypt in the Roman World. Papers Presented at the Proceedings of the IIIrd International Conference of Isis Studies, Faculty of Archaeology, Leiden University, May 11–14, 2005.* Leiden.

Brinkerhoff, D.M. (1978). *Hellenistic Statues of Aphrodite: Studies in the history of their stylistic development.* New York.

Broneer, O. (1926). Excavations at Corinth 1925: Area North of Basilica. *AJA, 30*, 49–57.

———. Excavations in the Odeum at Corinth, 1928. *AJA, 32*, 447–73.

———. (1930). *Terracotta Lamps* (*Corinth* IV.2). Cambridge, Mass.

———. (1930). The "Armed Aphrodite" on Acrocorinth and the Aphrodite of Capua. *CPCA, 1*, 65–84.

———. (1932). *The Odeum* (*Corinth* X). Cambridge, Mass.

———. (1933). Excavations in the Agora at Corinth, 1933. *AJA, 37*, 554–72.

———. (1935). Excavations in Corinth, 1934. *AJA, 39*, 53–75.

———. (1939). An Official Rescript from Corinth. *Hesperia, 8*, 181–90.

———. (1941). Colonia Laus Iulia Corinthiensis. *Hesperia, 10*, 388–90.

———. (1942). Hero Cults in the Corinthian Agora. *Hesperia, 11*, 128–61.

———. (1945). Archaeology in Greece Today. *AJA, 49*, 416–19.

———. (1947). Investigations at Corinth, 1946–7. *Hesperia, 16*, 233–47.

———. (1951a). Corinth: Center of Saint Paul's Missionary Work in Greece. *The Biblical Archaeologist, 14*, 77–96.

———. (1951b). Investigations at Corinth, 1950. *Hesperia, 20*, 291–300.

———. (1953). Isthmia Excavations, 1952. *Hesperia, 22*, 182–95.
———. (1954). *Ancient Corinth: A Guide to the Excavations* (6th ed.). Athens.
———. (1954). *The South Stoa and Its Roman Successors* (*Corinth* I.4). Princeton.
———. (1955). Excavations at Isthmia, 1954. *Hesperia, 24*, 110–41.
———. (1958). Excavations at Isthmia: Third Campaign, 1955–6. *Hesperia, 27*, 1–37.
———. (1959). Excavations at Isthmia: Fourth Campaign, 1957–8. *Hesperia, 28*, 298–343.
———. (1962a). The Apostle Paul and the Isthmian Games. *The Biblical Archaeologist, 25*, 1–31.
———. (1962b). Excavations at Isthmia 1959–61. *Hesperia, 31*, 1–25.
———. (1962c). The Isthmian Victory Crown. *AJA, 66*, 259–63.
———. (1966). The Cyclopean Wall on the Isthmus of Corinth and Its Bearing on Late Bronze Age Chronology. *Hesperia, 35*, 346–62.
———. (1968). The Cyclopean Wall on the Isthmus of Corinth, Addendum. *Hesperia, 37*, 25–35.
———. (1971). Paul and the Pagan Cults at Isthmia. *HTR, 64*, 169–87.
———. (1971). *Temple of Poseidon* (*Isthmia* I). Princeton.
———. (1973). *Topography and Architecture* (*Isthmia* II). Princeton.
———. (1976). Twenty-Five Years Ago: Cults at St. Paul's Corinth. *The Biblical Archaeologist, 39*, 158–9.
———. (1977). *Terracotta Lamps* (*Isthmia* III). Princeton.
Broodbank, C. (2013). *The Making of the Middle Sea*. London.
Brown, A.R. (2010a). Islands in a Sea of Change? Continuity and Abandonment in Dark Age Corinth and Thessaloniki. *International Journal of Historical Archaeology, 14*, 230–40.
———. (2010b). Justinian, Procopius, and Deception: Literary Lies, Imperial Politics, and the Archaeology of Sixth-Century Greece. In A.J. Turner, J.H.K.O. Chong-Gossard & F.J. Vervaet (eds), *Private and Public Lies: The Discourse of Despotism and Deceit in the Graeco-Roman World*. (pp. 355–69). Leiden.
———. (2011a). Banditry or Catastrophe?: History, Archaeology, and Barbarian Raids on Roman Greece. In R.W. Mathisen & D. Shanzer (eds). *Romans, Barbarians, and the Transformation of the Roman World: Cultural Interaction and the Creation of Identity in Late Antiquity*. (pp. 79–96). Farnham.
———. (2011b). Archbishops, Generals and Governors between East and West in Early Byzantine Greece. In G. Nathan & L. Garland (eds), Basileia: *Essays on Imperium and Culture in Honour of E.M. and M.J. Jeffreys* (Byzantina Australiensia 17) (pp. 39–43). Brisbane.
———. (2012a). Last Men Standing: Chlamydatus Portraits and Public Life in Late Antique Corinth. *Hesperia, 81*, 141–76.
———. (2012b). Medieval Pilgrimage to Corinth and Southern Greece. In T.M. Kristensen (ed.), *The Material Culture of Roman and Early Christian Pilgrimage*, thematic section of *HEROM. Journal on Hellenistic and Roman Material Culture* 1. (pp. 197–223). Leuven.
———. (2012c). Performance and Reception of Greek Tragedy in the Early Medieval Mediterranean. In S.L. Hathaway & D.W. Kim (eds),

Intercultural Transmission in the Medieval Mediterranean. (pp. 146–62). London.

———. (2016a). Corinth. In R.R.R. Smith and B. Ward-Perkins (eds). *The Last Statues of Antiquity*. (pp. 174–89). Oxford.

———. (2016b). Crosses, Noses, Walls and Wells: Christianity and the Fate of Sculpture in Late Antique Corinth. In T.M. Kristensen and L. Stirling (eds). *The Afterlife of Greek and Roman Sculpture: Late Antique Responses and Practices*. (pp. 150–76). Ann Arbor.

Brown, C. (1991). The Prayers of the Corinthian Women (Simonides, *Ep*. 15 Page, *FGE*). *GRBS, 32*, 5–14.

Brown, P. (1971). *The World of Late Antiquity*. London.

———. (1992). *Power and Persuasion in Late Antiquity*. Madison.

Brown, T.S. (1949). *Onesicritus: A Study in Hellenistic Historiography*. Berkeley.

Brubaker, L., and Lindardou, K. (eds). (2007). *Eat, Drink, and Be Merry (Luke 12:19) –Food and Wine in Byzantium*. Papers of the 37th Annual Spring Symposium of Byzantine Studies in Honour of Professor A.A.M. Bryer. Williston.

Bruun, C. (2003). The Antonine Plague in Rome and Ostia. *JRA, 16*, 426–34.

Budge, E.A.W. (trans.). (2003). *The Chronography of Gregory Abû'l-Faraj, the son of Aaron, the Hebrew physician, commonly known as Bar Hebraeus: Being the first part of his political history of the world*. (Reprint. Original ed. London 1932). Piscataway, NJ.

Budin, S.L. (2002). Creating a Goddess of Sex. In N. Serwint & D. Bolder (eds), *Engendering Aphrodite: Women and Society in Ancient Cyprus*. (pp. 315–24). Boston.

———. (2006). Sacred Prostitution in the First Person. In C.A. Faraone & L.K. McClure (eds), *Prostitutes and Courtesans in the Ancient World*. (pp. 77–92). Madison.

Bullen, J.B. (1999). Byzantinism and Modernism, 1900–14. *Burlington Magazine, 141*, 665–75.

———. (2003). *Byzantium Rediscovered*. London.

———. (2008). *The Myth of Sacred Prostitution in Antiquity*. Cambridge.

Burford, A. (1969). *The Greek Temple Builders at Epidaurus*. Liverpool.

Burkert, W. (1983). *Homo necans: The Anthropology of Ancient Greek Sacrificial Ritual and Myth* (P. Bing, trans.). Berkeley.

Burns, T.S. (1994). *Barbarians within the Gates of Rome: A Study of Roman Military Policy and the Barbarians ca. AD 375–425*. Bloomington.

Bursian, C. (1862). *Geographie von Griechenland*. Leipzig.

Burton, C.P. (1975). Proconsuls, Assizes and the Administration of Justice under the Empire. *JRS, 65*, 92–106.

Bury, J.B. (1923). *History of the Later Roman Empire from the Death of Theodosius I to the Death of Justinian (A.D. 395 to A.D. 565)* (Reprinted New York 1958). London.

Busine, A. (ed.). (2015). *Religious Practices and Christianization of the Late Antique City (4th–7th cent.)* Leiden.

Cadbury, H. & Lake, K. (1933). *The Beginnings of Christianity, Part 1: The Acts of the Apostles 4–5: Additional Notes and Commentary*. London.

Calame, C. & Lloyd, J. (1999). *The Poetics of Eros in Ancient Greece*. Princeton.

Callu, J.-P. (ed.). (1992). *Histoire Auguste*. Paris.
Cameron, Al. (1965). St. Jerome and Claudian. *VigChr, 19*, 111–3.
———. (1969). The Date of Zosimus' New History. *Philologus, 113*, 106–10.
———. (1970). *Claudian: Poetry and Propaganda at the Court of Honorius*. Oxford.
Cameron, Al. & Cameron, Av. (1964). Christianity and Tradition in the Historiography of the Late Empire. *CQ, 14*, 316–28.
Cameron, Av. (1985). *Procopius and the Sixth Century* (Reprinted 1996). London.
———. (1991). *Christianity and the Rhetoric of Empire: The Development of Christian Discourse* (Sather Classical Lectures 55). Berkeley.
Cameron, Av. & Garnsey, P. (eds). (1998). *The Late Empire, A.D. 337–425* (*CAH* 13). Cambridge.
Cameron, Av. & Hall, S.G. (trans.). (1999). *Eusebius: Life of Constantine*. Oxford.
Cameron, Av., Ward-Perkins, B. & Whitby, M. (eds). (2000). *Late Antiquity: Empire and Successors, A.D. 425–600 (CAH* 14*)*. Cambridge.
Camia, F. & Kantiréa, M. (2010). The imperial cult in the Peloponnese. In A.D. Rizakis & Cl. E. Lepenioti (eds), *Roman Peloponnese III: Society, Economy and Culture under the Roman Empire: Continuity and Innovation. Meletemata* 63. (pp. 375–406). Athens.
Camp, J. McK., II. (1989). The Philosophical Schools of Roman Athens. In S. Walker & Av. Cameron (eds), *The Greek Renaissance in the Roman Empire, Papers From the Tenth British Museum Classical Colloquium*. (pp. 50–5). London.
Capps, E. (1896). The Recent Excavations at Corinth. *The Biblical World, 8*, 233–7.
Capps, E., Jr. (1927a). An Ivory Pyxis in the Museo Cristiano and a Plaque from the Sancta Sanctorum. *The Art Bulletin, 9*, 330–40.
———. (1927b). The Style of the Consular Diptychs. *The Art Bulletin, 10*, 60–101.
———. (1934). A Gigantomachy and an Amazonomachy from Corinth. *AJA, 38*, 188–9.
———. (1936). The Labors of Herakles from Corinth. *Classical Studies Presented to Edward Capps on his Seventieth Birthday*. (pp. 46–57). Princeton.
———. (1938). Pergamene Influence at Corinth. *Hesperia, 7*, 539–56.
———. (1942). Review: Morath, G.W. *Die Maximianskathedra in Ravenna. The Art Bulletin, 24*, 99–102.
———. (1949). Observations on the Painted Venatio of the Theatre at Corinth and on the Arrangements of the Arena. *Hesperia* Suppl. 8. 64–70, 444–5.
———. (1950). Gleanings from Old Corinth. *AJA, 54*, 265–6.
———. (1956a). Review: Natanson, J. *Early Christian Ivories. AJA, 60*, 88–9.
———. (1956b). Review: Volbach, W.F. *Elfenbeinarbeiten. AJA, 60*, 82–8.
Caraher, W.R. (2003). *Church, Society, and the Sacred in Early Christian Greece*. Ph.D. Diss., The Ohio State University.
———. (2010). Abandonment, Authority, and Religious Continuity in Post-Classical Greece. *International Journal of Historical Archaeology, 14*, 241–54.

———. (2014). The Ambivalent Landscape of Christian Corinth: The Archaeology of Place, Theology, and Politics in a Late Antique City. In S.J. Friesen, S.A. James & D.N. Schowalter (eds), *Corinth in Contrast: Studies in Inequality*. (pp. 143–65). Leiden.

———. (2015). Epigraphy, Liturgy, and Imperial Policy on the Justinianic Isthmus. In E.R. Gebhard & T.E. Gregory (eds), *Bridge of the Untiring Sea: The Corinthian Isthmus from Prehistory to Late Antiquity. Hesperia* Supplement 48. (pp. 327–40). Princeton.

Caraher, W.R. & Gregory, T.E. (2006). Fortifications of Mount Oneion, Corinthia. *Hesperia*, *75*, 327–56.

Caraher, W.R., Hall, L.J., & Moore, R.S. (eds). (2008). *Archaeology and History in Roman, Medieval and Post-Medieval Greece: Studies on Method and Meaning in Honor of Timothy E. Gregory*. Aldershot.

Caraher, W.R., Nakassis, D., & Pettegrew, D.K. (2006). Siteless Survey and Intensive Data Collection in an Artifact-Rich Environment: Case Studies from the Eastern Corinthia, Greece. *JMA*, *19*, 7–43.

Carpenter, R. (1928). *Ancient Corinth: A Guide to the Excavations and Museum*. Athens.

———. (1929). Researches in the Topography of Ancient Corinth-I. *AJA*, *33*, 345–60.

———. (1933). *The Humanistic Value of Archaeology* (*Martin Classical Lectures* 4). Cambridge.

Carpenter, R. & Bon, A. (1936). *The Defenses of Acrocorinth and the Lower Town* (*Corinth* III.2). Cambridge, Mass.

Cartledge, P., Cohen, E.E., & Foxhall, L. (eds). (2002). *Money, Labour and Land: Approaches to the Economies of Ancient Greece*. London.

Cary, M. (1949). *The Geographic Background of Greek and Roman History*. Oxford.

Casanova, G. (1984). Epidemie e fame nella documentazione greca d'Egitto. *Aegyptus*, *64*, 167.

Caskey, L.D. (1925). *Catalogue of Greek and Roman Sculpture*. Cambridge, Mass.

Casson, L. (1994a). *Ships and Seafaring in Ancient Times*. Austin.

———. (1994b). *Travel in the Ancient World*. Baltimore.

Castrén, P. (1989). The Post-Herulian Revival of Athens. In S. Walker & Av. Cameron (eds), *The Greek Renaissance in the Roman Empire, Papers from the Tenth British Museum Classical Colloquium*. (pp. 69–75). London.

———. (1994). General Aspects of Life in Post-Herulian Athens. In P. Castrén (ed.), *Post-Herulian Athens: Aspects of Life and Culture in Athens, A.D. 267–529*. (pp. 1–15). Helsinki.

———. (1999). Paganism and Christianity in Athens and Vicinity during the Fourth to Sixth Centuries A.D. In G.P. Brogiolo & B. Ward-Perkins (eds), *The Idea and the Ideal of the Town between Late Antiquity and the Early Middle Ages*. (pp. 211–24). Leiden.

Cataudella, M.R. (2003). Historiography in the East. In G. Marasco (ed.), *Greek and Roman Historiography in Late Antiquity, Fourth to Sixth Century A.D.* (pp. 391–447). Leiden.

Cavalier, L. (2007). Horrea d'Andriake et Patara. *REA*, 52–65.

Chabot, J.B. (ed.). (1899). *Chronique de Michel le Syrien, Patriarche Jacobite d'Antioche (1166–1199)*. Paris.

Chalmers, W.R. (1953). The ΝΕΑ ΕΚΔΟΣΙΣ of Eunapius' Histories. *The Cambridge Quarterly, 3*, 165–70.
Charanis, P. (1952). On the Capture of Corinth by the Onogurs and Its Recapture by the Byzantines. *Speculum, 27*, 343–50.
Charitonidis, S. & Ginouvès, R. (1955). Bain romain de Zevgolatio près de Corinthe. *BCH, 79*, 102–20.
Chastagnol, A. (1964). Zosime II, 38 et l'Histoire Auguste. *Bonner Historia-Augusta-Colloquium, 75*.
———. (trans.). (1994). *Histoire Auguste: les empereurs romains des IIe et IIIe siècles*. Paris.
Chatziangelou, D. (2013). Το σπηλαίο της Κλένιας. In K. Kissas & W.-D. Niemeier (eds), *The Corinthia and the Northeast Peloponnese: Topography and History from Prehistoric Times until the End of Antiquity*. (pp. 297–304). Munich.
Cherf, W.J. (2011). Procopius *De Aedificiis* 4.2.1–22 on the Thermopylae Frontier. *Byzantinische Zeitschrift, 104*, 71–113.
Christensen, A.S. (2002). *Cassiodorus, Jordanes and the History of the Goths*. Copenhagen.
Chrysostomides, J. (ed.). (1995). *Monumenta Peloponnesiaca: Documents for the History of the Peloponnese in the 14th and 15th centuries*. Athens.
Chuvin, P. (1990). *A Chronicle of the Last Pagans* (trans. B.A. Archer). Cambridge.
Cipolla, C.M. (1973). *Cristofano and the Plague: A Study in the History of Public Health in the Age of Galileo*. Berkeley.
———. (1979). *Faith, Reason, and the Plague: A Tuscan Story of the Seventeenth Century* (trans. M. Kittel). Brighton.
———. (1981). *Fighting the Plague in Seventeenth-Century Italy*. Madison.
Clark, W.G. (1858). *Peloponnesus: Notes of Study and Travel*. London.
Clarke, W.L. (trans.). (1918). *Palladius. Lausiac History*. London.
Clement, P.A. (1969). Isthmia Excavations. *ArchDelt, 23* (1968), 137–43.
———. (1970). Isthmia Excavations. *ArchDelt, 24* (1969), 116–9.
———.(1972). Isthmia Excavations. *ArchDelt, 25* (1970), 161–7.
———. (1973). Isthmia Excavations. *ArchDelt, 26* (1971), 100–1.
———. (1974). L. Cornelios Korinthos of Corinth. In D.W. Bradeen & M.F. McGregor (eds), *Phoros. Tribute to Benjamin Dean Meritt*. (pp. 36–39). Locust Valley.
———. (1976). Isthmia Excavations. *ArchDelt, 27* (1972), 229.
———. (1977a). Isthmia Excavations. *ArchDelt, 28* (1973), 143–9.
———. (1977b). Alaric and the Fortifications of Greece. *Ancient Macedonia, 2*, 135–7.
———. (1977c). The Date of the Hexamilion. *Essays in Memory of Basil Laourdas*. (pp. 159–64). Thessalonike.
———. (1980). Korinthas, Veterinary. In S.M. Burstein & L.A. Okin (eds), *Panhellenica: Essays in Ancient History and Historiography in Honor of Truesdell S. Brown*. (pp. 187–9). Lawrence, Kans.
———. (1987). Isthmian notes. *Φίλια έπη εις Γεώργιον Ε. Μυλωνάν*. Vol. 2. (pp. 380–383). Athens.
Cline, R. (2011). *Ancient Angels: Conceptualizing Angeloi in the Roman Empire*. Religions in the Graeco-Roman World 172. Leiden.

Coates-Stephens, R. (2001). *Muri dei Bassi Secoli* in Rome: Observations on the Re-Use of Statuary in Walls Found on the Esquiline and Caelian after 1870. *JRA, 14*, 217–38.
———. (2004). *Porta Maggiore: Monument and Landscape: Archaeology and Topography of the Southern Esquiline From the Late Republican Period to the Present*. Supplementi 12, *Bullettino Della Commissione Archeologica Comunale Di Roma*. Rome.
———. (2007). The Reuse of Ancient Statuary in Late Antique Rome and the End of the Statue Habit. In F.A. Bauer & C. Witschel (eds), *Statuen in der Spätantike*. (pp. 171–87). Wiesbaden.
Collart, P. (1976). Les milliaires de la Via Egnatia. *BCH, 100*, 177–200.
Collier, R.E.L. (1990). Eustatic and Tectonic Controls upon Quaternary Coastal Sedimentation in the Corinth Basin, Greece. *Journal of the Geological Society, London, 147*, 301–14.
Collier, R.E.L. & Dart, C.J. (1991). Neogene to Quaternary Rifting, Sedimentation, and Uplift in the Corinth Basin, Greece. *Journal of the Geological Society, London, 148*, 1049–65.
Collier, R.E.L. et al. (1992). Rates of Tectonic Uplift in the Corinth and Megara Basins, Central Greece. *Tectonics, 11*, 1159–67.
Collier, R.E.L. & Thompson, J. (1991). Transverse and Linear Dunes in the Upper Pleistocene Marine Sequence, Corinth Basin, Greece. *Sedimentology, 38*, 1021–40.
Comstock, M.B. & Vermeule, C.C. (1976). *Sculpture in Stone: The Greek, Roman and Etruscan Collections of the Museum of Fine Arts, Boston*. Boston.
Concannon, C.W. (2014). *"When You Were Gentiles": Specters of Ethnicity in Roman Corinth and Paul's Corinthian Correspondence*. New Haven.
———. (forthcoming). *Assembling Early Christianity: Trade, Networks, and the Letters of Dionysios of Corinth*. Cambridge.
Congourdeau, M.-H. (1998). Pour une étude de la peste noire à Byzance. *Ευψυχία: Mélanges offerts à Hélène Ahrweiler*. (pp. 149–63). Paris.
Conrad, L.I. (1996). Die Pest und ihr soziales Umfeld im Nahen Osten des frühen Mittelalters. *Der Islam, 73*, 81–112.
Conzelmann, H. (1967). Korinth und die Mädchen der Aphrodite. *NAkG, 8*, 247–61.
Cook, R.M. (1986). A Further Note on the Diolkos. In J.H. Betts, J.T. Hooker, & J.R. Green (eds), *Studies in Honour of T.B.L. Webster* Vol. 1, (pp. 65–8). Bristol.
Crawford, J.S. (1990). *The Byzantine Shops at Sardis* (*Sardis Monograph* 9). Cambridge, Mass.
Creaghan, J.S. & Raubitscheck, A.E. (1947). Early Christian Epitaphs from Athens. *Hesperia, 16*, 1–52.
Crees, J.H.E. (1908). *Claudian as an Historical Authority*. Cambridge.
Croke, B. (1981). Thessalonika's Early Byzantine Palaces. *Byzantion, 51*, 475–83.
———. (2005). Procopius' *Secret History*: Rethinking the Date. *GRBS, 45*, 405–31.
Crow, J. (2016). Introduction: The Byzantine City and the Archaeology of the Third Millennium. In *Proceedings of the 23rd International Congress*

of Byzantine Studies, Belgrade, 22–27 August 2016, Plenary Papers. (pp. 65–7). Belgrade.
Cullen, T. (2007). Celebrating 75 Years of Hesperia. *Hesperia, 76*, 1–20.
Cummer, W.W. (1971). A Roman Tomb at Corinthian Kenchreai. *Hesperia, 40*, 205–31.
Cuomo, S. (2007). *Technology and Culture in Greek and Roman Antiquity*. Cambridge.
Curcic, S. (1993). Late Antique Palaces: The Meaning of Urban Context. *Ars Orientalis, 23*, 67–90.
Curran, J.R. (2000). *Pagan City and Christian Capital: Rome in the Fourth Century*. Oxford.
Dallman, P.R. (1998). *Plant Life in the World's Mediterranean Climates*. Oxford.
Dally, O. and C. Ratté. (2011). *Archaeology and the Cities of Asia Minor in Late Antiquity*. Kelsey Museum Publications 6. Ann Arbor.
Darrow, F.S. (1906). *The History of Corinth from Mummius to Herodes Atticus*. Ph.D. Diss., Harvard University.
Daux, G. (1963). Chronique des fouilles 1962: Corinthie. *BCH, 87*, 718–36.
———. (1965). Chronique des fouilles 1964: Corinthie. *BCH, 89*, 689–707.
———. (1966). Chronique des fouilles 1965: Léchaion. *BCH, 90*, 767–70.
———. (1968). Chronique des fouilles 1967: Corinthie. *BCH, 92*, 773–86.
Davenport, C. (2013). The Governors of Achaia under Diocletian and Constantine. *ZPE, 184*, 225–34.
David, J.-M. (1983). La tribunal dans la basilique: évolution fonctionelle et symbolique de la république à l'empire. *Architecture et société de l'archaïsme grec à la fin de la Républic romaine*. (pp. 219–41). Paris.
Davidson, G.R. (1937). The Avar Invasion of Corinth. *Hesperia, 6*, 227–40.
———. (1940). A Medieval Glass Factory at Corinth. *AJA, 44*, 297–324.
———. (1952). *The Minor Objects* (*Corinth* XII). Princeton.
Davidson Weinberg, G.R. (1974). A Wandering Soldier's Grave in Corinth. *Hesperia, 43*, 512–21.
———. (1975). A Medieval Mystery: Byzantine Glass Production in Corinth. *JGS, 17*, 127–41.
Davis, J.L. (2007). The Birth of Hesperia: A View from the Archives. *Hesperia, 76*, 21–35.
Day, J.W. (1980). *The Glory of Athens: The Popular Tradition as reflected in the Panathenaicus of Aelius Aristides*. Chicago.
de Boor, C. (ed.). (1903). *Excerpta de Legationibus*. Berlin.
———. (ed.). (1905). *Excerpta de Insidiis*. Berlin.
———. (ed.). (1963). *Theophanis Chronographia*. (Reprint. Original ed., Leipzig: 1883–5). Hildesheim.
de Georgi, A. (2015). *Ancient Antioch: from the Seleucid Era to the Islamic Conquest*. Cambridge.
de Grazia, C.E. (1973). *Excavations of the ASCS at Corinth: The Roman Portrait Sculpture*. Ph.D. Diss., Columbia.
de Grazia, C.E. & Williams, C.K., II. (1977). Corinth 1976: Forum Southwest. *Hesperia, 46*, 40–81.
de Grazia Vanderpool, C. (2003). Roman Portraiture: The Many Faces of Corinth. In C.K. Williams, II & N. Bookidis (eds), *Corinth, the Centenary: 1896–1996* (*Corinth* XX). (pp. 369–84). Princeton.

———. (forthcoming). Julius Caesar and Divus Iulius in Corinth: Man, memory, and cult. In Di Napoli, V., et al. (eds), *What's New in Roman Greece? Recent Work on the Greek Mainland and the Islands in the Roman Period*. Athens.

de Waele, F.J. (1930). The Roman Market North of the Temple at Corinth. *AJA, 34*, 432–54.

———. (1933). The Sanctuary of Asklepios and Hygieia at Corinth. *AJA, 37*, 417–51.

———. (1935a). Asklepios und das Asklepieion von Korinth. *American Anthropologist*, 642–52.

———. (1935b). The Fountain of Lerna and the Early Christian Cemetery at Corinth. *AJA, 39*, 352–9.

———. (1961). *Les antiquités de la Grèce. Corinthe et Saint Paul*. Paris.

Dean, L.R. (1922). Latin Inscriptions from Corinth. *AJA, 26*, 451–76.

DeForest, D. (2013). *Baths and Public Bathing Culture in Late Antiquity: 300–700 A.D.* Ph.D. Diss., The Ohio State University.

Delbrueck, R. (1933). *Spätantike Kaiserporträts von Constantinus Magnus bis zum Ende des Westreichs*. Berlin.

Delehaye, H. (1907). *Les versions grecques des actes des martyrs persans sous Sapor II*. Paris.

———. (1933). *Les origines du culte des martyrs* (2nd, rev. ed.). Brussels.

———. (1966). *Les passions des martyrs et les genres littéraires* (2nd ed.). Brussels.

Deligiannakis, G. (2005). Two Late-Antique Statues from Ancient Messene. *BSA, 100*, 387–406.

———. (2008). Christian Attitudes Towards Pagan Statuary: The Case of Anastasios of Rhodes. *Byzantion: Revue International des Etudes Byzantines 78*, 142–58.

Delivorrias, A. (1991). Interpretatio Christiana: Γύρω από τα όρια του παγανιστικού και του χριστιανικού κοσμου. In *Ευφρόσυνον. Αφιέρωμα στον Μανόλη Χατζιδάκη* (pp. 107--23). Athens.

Delorme, J. (1960). *Gymnasion: étude sur les monuments consacrés à l'éducation en Grèce (des origines à l'Empire Romain)* (Bibliothèque des écoles françaises d'Athènes et de Rome 196). Paris.

DeMaris, R.E. (1995). Demeter in Roman Corinth: Local Development in a Mediterranean Religion. *Numen, 42*, 105–17.

Dengate, C. (1988). *The Sanctuaries of Apollo in the Peloponnese*. Ph.D. Diss., University of Chicago.

Dengate, J.A. (1981). Coin Hoards from the Gymnasium Area at Corinth. *Hesperia, 50*, 147–88.

Denison, A., Lord. (1849). *Wanderings in Search of Health*. London.

Despinis, G., Stefanidou-Tiveriou, T., & Voutyras, E. (1997). *Catalogue of Sculpture in the Archaeological Museum of Thessaloniki 1*. Thessalonike.

———. (2003). *Κατάλογος γλυπτών του Αρχαιολογικού Μουσείου Θεσσα λονικής 2*. Thessalonike.

Dewing, H.B. (trans.). (1914). *Procopius. History of the Wars, Books I and II. The Persian War*. London.

———. (trans.). (1935). *Procopius. The Anecdota or Secret History*. London.

Dewing, H.B. & Downey, G. (trans.). (1941). *Procopius. Buildings*. London.

Dey, H.W. (2015). *The Afterlife of the Roman City: Architecture and Ceremony in Late Antiquity and the Early Middle Ages*. Cambridge.

Di Branco, M. (ed.). (2005). *Expositio totius mundi et gentium*. Rome.

———. (2006). *La città dei filosofi: Storia di Atene da Marco Aurelio a Giustiniano*. Florence.

Di Napoli, V. (2010). Entertainment buildings of the Roman Peloponnese: theatres, *odea*, and amphitheatres and their topographical distribution. In A.D. Rizakis & Cl. E. Lepenioti (eds), *Roman Peloponnese III: Society, Economy and Culture under the Roman Empire: Continuity and Innovation. Meletemata* 63. (pp. 253–66). Athens.

Diakopolos, L. (2006). The Archaeology of Modern Greece. In E.F. Athanassopoulos & L. Wandsnider (eds), *Mediterranean Archaeological Landscapes: Current Issues*. (pp. 183–97). Philadelphia.

Diez, E. & Demus, O. (1931). *Byzantine Mosaics in Greece: Hosios Loucas and Daphni*. Cambridge, Mass.

Dimaio, M. (1988). Smoke in the Wind: Zonaras' Use of Philostorgius, Zosimus, John of Antioch and John of Rhodes. *Byzantion, 58*, 23–55.

Dindorf, L.A. (ed.). (1831). *Ioannis Malalae chronographia*. Bonn.

Dindorf, W. (ed.). (1829). *Aristides*. Leipzig.

Dinsmoor, W.B. (1949). The Largest Temple in the Peloponnese. *Commemorative Studies in Honor of Theodore Leslie Shear*. (pp. 104–15). Princeton.

Dixon, M.D. (2000). Disputed Territories: Interstate Arbitrations in the Northeast Peloponnese, ca. 250–150 B.C. Ph.D. Diss., The Ohio State University.

———. (2014). *Late Classical and Early Hellenistic Corinth, 338–196 B.C.* London.

Dodwell, E. (1819). *A Classical and Topographical Tour through Greece*. London.

Donati, J.C. (2008). Placing the Corinthian Agora: Urban Environment and Civic Space in Archaic and Classical Corinth. *109th Annual Meeting Abstracts*, Vol. 31. Boston.

———. (2010). Marks of State Ownership and the Greek Agora at Corinth. *AJA, 114*, 3–26.

Dörpfeld, W. (1886). Der Tempel von Korinth. *AM, 11*, 297–308.

Doukellis, P. (1994). Le territoire de la colonie romaine de Corinthe. In P.N. Doukellis & L.G. Mendoni (eds), *Structures rurales et societés antiques, Actes du colloque de Corfou, 14–16 mai 1992*. (pp. 359–90). Paris.

Dow, S. (1951). Corinthiaca VI. The Latin Elegiacs of ca. 101 B.C. VII. Greek Elegiacs of the Roman Empire. *HSCP, 60*, 81–100.

Dow, S. (1967). Review of *Corinth* VIII.3. *AHR, 72*, 1359–60.

Downey, G. (1937). The Architectural Significance of the Use of the Words *Stoa* and *Basilike* in Classical Literature. *AJA, 41*, 194–211.

———. (1947). The Composition of Procopius, *De aedificiis*. *TAPA, 78*, 171–83.

———. (1961). *A History of Antioch in Syria from Seleucus to the Arab Conquest*. Princeton.

Downing, F.G. (1998). *Cynics, Paul and the Pauline Churches*. London.

Doxiadis, C.A. (1967). The Ancient Greek City and the City of the Present. *The Living Heritage of Greek Antiquity; L'héritage vivant de l'Antiquité grecque*. (pp. 192–211). The Hague.

Drachmann, A.B. (ed.). (1903). *Scholia vetera in Pindari carmina.* Leipzig.
Drakopoulos, J.C. (1983). *Seismicity and Seismic Risk Studies in the Area of Archaea Nemea.* Athens.
Drijvers, J.W. & Hunt, D. (eds). (1999). *The Late Roman World and its Historian: Interpreting Ammianus Marcellinus.* London.
Dubbini, R. (2011). *Dei nello spazio degli uomini: i culti dell'agora e la costruzione di Corinto arcaica.* Rome.
Dübner, F. & Cougny, E. (eds). (1888). *Epigrammatum anthologia palatina cum Planudeis et appendice nova epigrammatum veterum ex libris et marmoribus ductorum.* Paris.
Duchesne, L. (ed.). (1981). *Le Liber pontificalis* (Reprint of 1955 rev. ed. of 1886–92 ed.). Paris.
Dudley, D.R. (1998). *A History of Cynicism from Diogenes to the 6th century AD* (2nd ed.). London.
Dunand, F. (1973). *Le culte d'Isis dans le bassin oriental de la Méditerranée.* Leiden.
Dunbabin, K.M.D. (1990). *Ipsa deae vestigia* … Footprints divine and human on Graeco-Roman monuments. *JRA, 3,* 85–109.
Dunbabin, T.J. & Payne, H. (1962). *Potteries, Ivories, Scarabs, and Other Objects* (*Perachora* 2). Oxford.
Duncan-Jones, R. (1996). The Impact of the Antonine Plague. *JRA, 9,* 108–36.
Durliat, J. (1989). La peste du VIe siècle: Pour un nouvel examen des sources byzantines. *Hommes et richesses dans l'Empire byzantin.* Vol. 1 (pp. 1.07–1.19). Paris.
Dyson, S.L. (1989). Classical Archaeology. In P. Culham & L. Edmunds (eds), *Classics, A Discipline and Profession in Crisis.* (pp. 211–20). New York.
———. (1993). From New to New Age Archaeology: Archaeological Theory and Classical Archaeology – a 1990's Perspective. *AJA, 97,* 195–206.
———. (2006). *In Pursuit of Ancient Pasts: A History of Classical Archaeology in the Nineteenth and Twentieth Centuries.* New Haven.
Earle Fox, H.B. (1903). Colonia Laus Julia Corinthus. *JIAN, 1,* 5–16.
Edwards, C.M. (1990). Tyche in Corinth. *Hesperia, 59,* 529–42.
———. (1993). A Complex of Copies at Ancient Corinth. *AJA, 97,* 300.
———. (1994). The Arch over the Lechaion Road at Corinth and Its Sculpture. *Hesperia, 63,* 263–308.
Edwards, K.M. (1933). *Coins, 1896–1929* (*Corinth* VI). Cambridge, Mass.
———. (1937). Report on the Coins Found in the Excavations at Corinth during the Years 1930–1935. *Hesperia, 6,* 241–56.
Eisner, R. (1991). *Travelers to an Antique Land: The History and Literature of Travel to Greece.* Ann Arbor.
Elderkin, G.W. (1910). The Fountain of Glauce at Corinth. *AJA, 14,* 19–50.
———. (1945). Golgotha, Kraneion and the Holy Sepulchre. *Archaeological Papers, 7,* 4–8.
Eliot, C.W.J. & Eliot, M. (1968). The Lechaion Cemetery near Corinth. *Hesperia, 37,* 345–67.

Ellegård, A. (1986). The Ancient Goths and the Concepts of Tribe and Migration. *Vetenskap och omvärdering (Festschrift for Curt Weibull).* (pp. 32–62). Göteborg.
Ellis, S.P. (1988). The End of the Roman House. *AJA, 92*, 565–76.
———. (1991). Power, Architecture, and Decor: How the Late Roman Aristocrat Appeared to His Guests. In E.K. Gazda & A.E. Haeckl (eds), *Roman Art in the Private Sphere: New Perspectives on the Architecture and Decor of the Domus, Villa, and Insula.* (pp. 117–34). Ann Arbor.
Ellis, S.P. & Poehler, E.E. (2015). The Roman Buildings East of the Temple of Poseidon on the Isthmus. In E.R. Gebhard & T.E. Gregory (eds), *Bridge of the Untiring Sea: The Corinthian Isthmus from Prehistory to Late Antiquity. Hesperia* Supplement 48. (pp. 271–88). Princeton.
Engels, D.W. (1990). *Roman Corinth: An Alternative Model for the Classical City.* Chicago.
Ensoli, S. & La Rocca, E. (2000). *Aurea Roma: dalla città pagana alla città cristiana.* Rome.
Evans, J.A.S. (1969). The Dates of the *Anecdota* and the *De aedificiis* of Procopius. *CP, 64*, 29–30.
———. (1972). *Procopius.* New York.
———. (1996). The Dates of Procopius' Works: A Recapitulation of the Evidence. *GRBS, 37*, 301–313.
———. (2000). *The Age of Justinian: The Circumstances of Imperial Power* (Reprint. Original ed., 1996). London.
Fagan, G.G. (1999). *Bathing in Public in the Roman World.* Ann Arbor.
Fantham, E. (2012). Purification in Ancient Rome. In M. Bradley (ed.), *Rome, Pollution and Propriety: Dirt, Disease and Hygiene in the Eternal City from Antiquity to Modernity.* (pp. 59–66). Cambridge.
Faraone, C.A. (1997). Salvation and Female Heroics in the Parodos of Aristophanes' *Lysistrata. JHS, 117*, 38–59.
———. (2006). Priestess and Courtesan: The Ambivalence of Female Leadership in Aristophanes' *Lysistrata.* In C.A. Faraone & L.K. McClure (eds), *Prostitutes & Courtesans in the Ancient World.* (pp. 207–23). Madison.
Farnell, L.R. (1977). *The Cults of the Greek States* (Reprint of 1896 ed.). New Rochelle.
———. (1990). *Greece and Babylon: A Comparative Sketch of Mesopotamian, Anatolian and Hellenic Religions* (Reprint of 1911 ed.). Edinburgh.
Farrer, R.R. (1882). *A Tour in Greece, 1880.* Edinburgh.
Farrington, A. (2010). The origins of victors in the Isthmian games. In A.D. Rizakis & Cl.E. Lepenioti (eds), *Roman Peloponnese III: Society, Economy and Culture under the Roman Empire: Continuity and Innovation. Meletemata* 63. (pp. 421–30). Athens.
Feissel, D. (1988). L'architecte Viktôrinos et les fortifications de Justinien dans les provinces balkaniques. *BAntFr*, 136–46.
———. (2006). *Chroniques d'épigraphie byzantine 1989–2004* (*Monographies du Centre de Recherche d'Histoire et Civilisation de Byzance* 20). Paris.
Feissel, D. & Philippidis-Braat, A. (1985). Inventaires en vue d'un recueil des inscriptions historiques de Byzance, III: Inscriptions du Péloponnèse (à l'exception de Mistra). *TravMem, 9*, 267–395.

Festugière, A.J. & Martin, R. (1959). *Antioche païenne et chrétienne: Libanius, Chrysostome et les moines de Syrie (Bibliothèque des Écoles françaises d'Athènes et de Rome* 194). Paris.

Finley, J.H., Jr. (1932). Corinth in the Middle Ages. *Speculum, 7*, 477–99.

Fisher, J.E. (1980). Coins: Corinth Excavations, 1976, Forum Southwest. *Hesperia, 49*, 1–29.

Flemming, N.C. & Webb, C.O. (1986). Tectonic and Eustatic Changes During the Last 10,000 Years Derived from Archaeological Data. *Zeitschrift für Geomorphologie, 62*, 1–29.

Fletcher, R.A. (1998). *The Barbarian Conversion: From Paganism to Christianity*. New York.

Fluck, C., Helmecke, G. & E.R. O'Connell (eds). (2015). *Egypt: Faith after the Pharaohs*. London.

Foerster, G. (1981). Remains of a Synagogue at Corinth. In L.I. Levine (ed.), *Ancient Synagogues Revealed*. (p. 185). Jerusalem.

Foerster, R. (ed.). (1903). *Libanii Opera*. (Reprint ed.). Hildesheim.

Forbes, H.A. (1976). "We have a little of everything": The ecological basis of some agricultural practices in Methana, Trizinia. *Annals of the New York Academy of Sciences, 268*, 236–50.

———. (1982). *Strategies and Soils: Technology, Production and Environment in the Peninsula of Methana, Greece*. Ph.D. Diss., University of Pennsylvania.

———. (1995). The Identification of Pastoral Sites within the Context of Estate-Based Agriculture in Ancient Greece. *BSA, 90*, 325–38.

Fornara, C.W. (1989). Eunapius' *Epidemia* in Athens. *The Cambridge Quarterly, 39*, 517–23.

Forsell, R. (2002). Argolid Countryside in the Roman Period. In E.N. Ostenfeld (ed.), *Greek Romans and Roman Greeks: Studies in Cultural Interaction*. (pp. 64–9). Aarhus.

Foss, C. (1979). *Ephesus after Antiquity: A Late Antique, Byzantine, and Turkish City*. Cambridge.

———. (1996). Stephanus, Proconsul of Asia, and Related Statues. *Cities, Fortresses, and Villages of Byzantine Asia Minor* (Reprint. Original ed., 1979). Aldershot.

Fotiadis, M. (1985). *Economy, Ecology and Settlement among Subsistence Farmers in the Serres Basin, Northeastern Greece*. Ph.D. Diss., Indiana University.

Fowden, G. (1978). Bishops and Temples in the Eastern Roman Empire: A.D. 320–435. *JTS ser. 2, 29*, 53–78.

———. (1995). Late Roman Achaea: Identity and Defence. *JRA, 8*, 549–67.

Fowler, H.N. (1922). The American School of Classical Studies at Athens: The Excavations at Corinth. *Art and Archaeology, 14*, 193–225.

Fowler, H.N. & Stillwell, R. (1932). *Introduction, Topography, Architecture* (*Corinth* I). Cambridge, Mass.

Frakes, R.M. & Digeser, E.D. (eds). (2006). *Religious Identity in Late Antiquity*. Toronto.

Frantz, A. (1965). From Paganism to Christianity in the Temples of Athens. *DOP, 19*, 185–205.

———. (1969). Herculius in Athens: Pagan or Christian? *Akten des VII. Internationalen Kongresses für Christliche Archäologie, Trier, 5–11 September 1965*. (pp. 527–30). Vatican City.

———. (1979). A Public Building of Late Antiquity in Athens (IG II2, 5205). *Hesperia, 48*, 194–203.

———. (1988). *Late Antiquity: A.D. 267–700* (*Agora* XXIV). Princeton.

Frazer, J.G. (1898). *Pausanias's Description of Greece* (1st ed.). London.

———. (1913). *Pausanias's Description of Greece* (2nd ed.). London.

Frey, J.B. (ed.). (1975). *Corpus Inscriptionum Iudaicarum (Corpus of Jewish Inscriptions) 1: Europe* (Reprint. Original ed., Rome 1936). New York.

Frey, J.M. (2006). *Speaking Through Spolia: The Language of Architectural Reuse in the Fortifications of Late Roman Greece*. Ph.D. Diss., U.C. Berkeley.

———. (2008). Pausanias, William Martin Leake and the "Depopulation" of Ancient Greece. In W.R. Caraher, L.J. Hall & R.S. Moore (eds), *Archaeology and History in Roman, Medieval and Post-Medieval Greece: Studies on Method and Meaning in Honor of Timothy E. Gregory*. (pp. 67–84). Aldershot.

———. (2015a). The Archaic Colonnade at Ancient Corinth: A Case of Early Roman Spolia. *AJA, 119*, 147–75.

———. (2015b). Work Teams on the Isthmian Fortress and the Development of a Later Roman Architectural Aesthetic. In E.R. Gebhard & T.E. Gregory (eds), *Bridge of the Untiring Sea: The Corinthian Isthmus from Prehistory to Late Antiquity. Hesperia* Supplement 48. (pp. 311–26). Princeton.

———. (2016). Spolia *in Fortifications and the Common Builder in Late Antiquity*. Leiden.

Frey, J.M. & Gregory, T.E. (2016). Old Excavations, New Interpretations: The 2008–2013 Seasons of The Ohio State University Excavations at Isthmia. *Hesperia, 85*, 437–90.

Friesen, S.J. (2010). The Wrong Erastus: Ideology, Archaeology, and Exegesis. In S.J. Friesen, D.N. Schowalter & J.C. Walters (eds), *Corinth in Context: Comparative Studies on Religion and Society*. (pp. 231–56). Leiden.

Friesen, S.J., Schowalter, D.N., & Walters, J.C. (eds). (2010). *Corinth in Context: Comparative Studies on Religion and Society*. Leiden.

Friesen, S.J., James, S.A., & Schowalter, D.N. (eds). (2014). *Corinth in Contrast: Studies in Inequality*. Leiden.

Fulford, M.G. (1996). Economic Hotspots and Provincial Backwaters: Modelling the Late Roman Economy. *Coin Finds and Coin Use in the Roman World. The Thirteenth Oxford Symposium on Coinage and Monetary History, 25–27.3.1993*. (pp. 153–77). Berlin.

Furnish, V.P. (1988). Corinth in Paul's Time. *Bulletin de l'Association des Amis de Rabelais et de La Devinière, 15.3*, 15–27.

Furtwängler, Adolf. (1895). *Masterpieces of Greek Sculpture: A Series of Essays on the History of Art*. London.

Futrell, A. (2006). *The Roman Games: A Sourcebook*. Malden, Mass.

Gabba, E. (1958). *Iscrizioni greche e latine per lo studio della Bibbia* (*Sintesi dell'Oriente e della Bibbia* 3). Turin.

Gadbery, L.M. (1992). The Statue of Armed Aphrodite on Acrocorinth. *AJA, 96*, 358.

———. (1993). Roman Wall Painting at Corinth: New Evidence from East of the Theater in the Roman Period. In T.E. Gregory (ed.), *The Corinthia in the Roman Period*. (pp. 47–64). Ann Arbor.

Gallant, T.W. (1991). *Risk and Survival in Ancient Greece: Reconstructing the Rural Domestic Economy*. Stanford.
Garnett, K.S. (1975). Late Roman Corinthian Lamps from the Fountain of the Lamps. *Hesperia, 44*, 173–206.
Garnsey, P. (1988). *Famine and Food Supply in the Graeco-Roman World: Responses to Risk and Crisis*. Cambridge.
Geagan, D.J. (1968). Notes on the Agonistic Institutions of Roman Corinth. *GRBS, 9*, 69–80.
———. (1975). A Letter of Trajan to a Synod at Isthmia. *Hesperia, 44*, 396–401.
———. (1989). The Isthmian Dossier of P. Licinius Priscus Juventianus. *Hesperia, 58*, 349–60.
———. (2005). Kyrbeis at Roman Isthmia. *Ancient World, 36*, 146–55.
Gebhard, E.R. (1973). *The Theater at Isthmia*. Chicago.
———. (1979). New Museum on the Corinthian Isthmus. *JFA, 6*, 125.
———. (1990). Excavations at Isthmia and the Work of Oscar Broneer. In E. Guralnick (ed.), *The Ancient Eastern Mediterranean*. (pp. 43–8). Chicago.
———. (1992). Oscar Theodore Broneer, 1894–1992. *AJA, 96*, 543–6.
———. (1993). The Isthmian Games and the Sanctuary of Poseidon in the Early Empire. In T.E. Gregory (ed.), *The Corinthia in the Roman Period*. (pp. 78–94). Ann Arbor.
———. (2005). Rites for Melikertes-Palaimon in the Early Roman Corinthia. In D.N. Schowalter & S.J. Friesen (eds), *Urban Religon in Roman Corinth: Interdisciplinary Approaches*. (pp. 165–204). Cambridge, Mass.
———. (2007, June 15). Isthmia: City of Elusive Ancient Greece. *Athens News*, p. A28.
———. (2013). Pausanias at the Isthmian Sanctuary. The principles governing his narrative. In K. Kissas & W.-D. Niemeier (eds), *The Corinthia and the Northeast Peloponnese: Topography and History from Prehistoric Times until the End of Antiquity*. (pp. 263–74). Munich.
Gebhard, E.R. & Dickie, M.W. (1999). Melikertes-Palaimon, Hero of the Isthmian Games. In R. Hägg (ed.), *Ancient Greek Hero Cult*. (pp. 159–65). Stockholm.
Gebhard, E.R. & Gregory, T.E. (eds). (2015). *Bridge of the Untiring Sea: The Corinthian Isthmus from Prehistory to Late Antiquity. Hesperia* Supplement 48. Princeton.
Gebhard, E.R. & Hemans, F.P. (1992). University of Chicago Excavations at Isthmia, 1989: I. *Hesperia, 61*, 1–77.
Gebhard, E.R., Hemans, F.P., & Hayes, J.W. (1998). University of Chicago Excavations at Isthmia, 1989: III. *Hesperia, 67*, 405–56.
Gebhard, E.R. & Reese, D. (2005). Sacrifices to Poseidon and Melikertes-Palaimon at Isthmia. In R. Hägg & B. Alroth (eds), *Greek Sacrificial Ritual, Olympian and Chthonian*. Proceedings of the Sixth International Seminar on Ancient Greek Cult, Göteborg University, 25–27 April 1997. ActaAth 8. 18. (pp. 125–54). Stockholm.
Georgiades, A.S. (1907). *Les ports de la Grèce dans l'Antiquité qui subsistent encore aujourdhoui: Exposition Maritime*. Athens.
Georgopoulou, M. et al. (eds). (2007). *Following Pausanias: The Quest for Greek Antiquity*. Athens.

Gerster, B. (1884). L'isthme de Corinthe: Tentatives de percement dans l'antiquité. *BCH*, *8*, 225–32.
Gibbon, E. (1994). *The History of the Decline and Fall of the Roman Empire* (Reprint. Original ed., 1788). London.
Gill, D.W.J. (1994). Achaia. In D.W.J. Gill & C.H. Gempf (eds), *The Book of Acts in its Graeco-Roman Setting*. (pp. 433–54). Grand Rapids.
Goffart, W. (1971). Zosimus, The First Historian of Rome's Fall. *AHR*, *76*, 412–41.
———. (1980). *Barbarians and Romans, A.D. 418–584: The Techniques of Accomodation*. Princeton.
———. (1981). Rome, Constantinople, and the Barbarians. *AHR*, *86*, 275–306.
———. (1989). The Theme of "*The* Barbarian Invasions" in Late Antique and Modern Historiography. In *Rome's Fall and After*. (pp. 111–32). London.
———. (1996). What's Wrong with the Map of the Barbarian Invasions? In S.J. Ridyard & R.G. Benson (eds), *Minorities and Barbarians in Medieval Life and Thought*. (pp. 159–74). Sewanee, Tenn.
Golden, M. (1998). *Sport and Society in Ancient Greece*. Cambridge.
Goldhill, S. (ed.). (2001). *Being Greek under Rome: Cultural Identity, the Second Sophistic and the Development of Empire*. Cambridge.
Goldschmidt, A. & Weitzmann, K. (1930). *Die byzantinischen Elfenbeinskulpturen des X–XIII Jahrhunderts*. Berlin.
Goulet, R. (1980). Sur la chronologie de la vie et des oeuvres d'Eunape de Sardes. *JHS*, *100*, 60–72.
———. (2001). *Études sur les vies de philosophes de l'antiquité tardive: Diogène Laërce, Porphyre de Tyr, Eunape de Sardes*. Paris.
Gourdin, H. (1999). *Genséric: soleil barbare*. Paris.
Grabar, A. (1972). *Martyrium: Recherches sur le culte des reliques et l'art chrétien antique* (Originally published 1946. Paris.
Graindor, P. (1930). *Un milliardaire antique: Hérode Atticus et sa famille*. Cairo.
Grant, R.M. (1980). *Eusebius as Church Historian*. New York.
Greatrex, G. (1994). The Date of Procopius' Works. *BMGS*, *18*, 101–14.
———. (1995). Procopius and Agathias on the Defences of the Thracian Chersonese. In C. Mango & G. Dagron (eds), *Constantinople and its Hinterland*. (pp. 127–9). Aldershot.
———. (2003). Recent Work on Procopius and the Composition of *Wars* VIII. *BMGS*, *27*, 45–67.
Greenberg, J. (2003). Plagued by Doubt: Reconsidering the Impact of a Mortality Crisis in the 2nd c. AD. *JRA*, *16*, 413–25.
Greenewalt, C.H., Jr. & Rautman, M.L. (2000). The Sardis Campaigns of 1996, 1997, and 1998. *AJA*, *104*, 643–81.
Grégoire, H. (1950). *Les persécutions dans l'Empire romain*. Brussels.
Grégoire, H., & Kugener, M.-A. (eds). (1930). *Vie de Porphyre, Évêque de Gaza*. Paris.
Gregory, T.E. (1979). The Late Roman Fortification Wall at Corinth. *Hesperia*, *48*, 264–80.
———. (1982). Fortification and Urban Design in Early Byzantine Greece. In R.L. Hohlfelder (ed.), *City, Town, and Countryside in the Early Byzantine Era*. (pp. 43–64). New York.

———. (1983). Urban Violence in Late Antiquity. In R.T. Marchese (ed.), *Aspects of Graeco-Roman Urbanism: Essays on the Classical City*. (pp. 138–61). Oxford.

———. (1984). Cities and Social Evolution in Roman and Byzantine South-East Europe. In J. Bintliff (ed.), *European Social Evolution*. (pp. 267–76). Bradford.

———. (1985). An Early Byzantine Complex at Akra Sophia near Corinth. *Hesperia, 54*, 411–28.

———. (1986). The Survival of Paganism in Christian Greece: A Critical Essay. *AJP, 107*, 229–42.

———. (1992). Kastro and Diateichisma as Responses to Early Byzantine Frontier Collapse. *Byzantion, 52*, 235–53.

———. (1993). An Early Byzantine (Dark Age) Settlement at Isthmia: Preliminary Report. In T.E. Gregory (ed.), *The Corinthia in the Roman Period. JRA Suppl.* 8. (pp. 149–60). Ann Arbor.

———. (1993). *The Hexamilion and the Fortress (Isthmia V)*. Princeton.

———. (1994). Archaeology and Theoretical Considerations on the Transition from Antiquity to the Middle Ages in the Aegean Region. In P.N. Kardulias (ed.), *Beyond the Site: Regional Studies in the Aegean Area*. (pp. 137–59). Lanham.

———. (1995). The Roman Bath at Isthmia: Preliminary Report 1972–1992. *Hesperia, 64*, 279–313.

———. (2000). Procopius on Greece. *Antiquité Tardive, 8*, 105–14.

———. (2007). Contrasting Impressions of Land Use in Early Modern Greece: Kythera and the Eastern Korinthia. In S.A. Davies & J.L. Davis (eds), *Between Venice and Istanbul: Colonial Landscapes in Early Modern Greece. Hesperia Suppl.* 40. Princeton.

———. (2010). Religion and Society in the Roman Eastern Corinthia. In S.J. Friesen, D.N. Schowalter & J.C. Walters (eds), *Corinth in Context: Comparative Studies on Religion and Society*. (pp. 433–76). Leiden.

———. (2013a). Η ανατολική Κορίνθια στην παλαιοχριστιανική εποχή. In K. Kissas & W.-D. Niemeier (eds), *The Corinthia and the Northeast Peloponnese: Topography and History from Prehistoric Times until the End of Antiquity*. (pp. 275–84). Munich.

———. (2013b). People and Settlements of the Northeastern Peloponnese in the Late Middle Ages: An Archaeological Exploration. In S.E.J. Gerstel (ed.), *Viewing the Morea: Land and People in the Late Medieval Peloponnese*. (pp. 276–306). Washington, D.C.

Gregory, T.E. & Kardulias, P.N. (1990). Geophysical and Surface Surveys in the Byzantine Fortress at Isthmia 1985–6. *Hesperia, 59*, 467–511.

Gregory, T.E. & Mills, H. (1984). The Roman Arch at Isthmia. *Hesperia, 53*, 407–45.

Griffiths, J.G. (1975). *Apuleius of Madauros: The Isis-Book*. Leiden.

Grigoriadis, I. (1998). *Linguistic and Literary Studies in the* Epitome Historion *of John Zonaras*. Thessalonike.

Gritsopoulos, T.A. (1972). Ἐκκλησιαστικὴ Ἱστορία Κορινθίας. *Peloponnesiaka, 9*, 77–84.

Groag, E. (1939). *Die römischen Reichsbeamten von Achaia bis auf Diokletian*. Vienna.

———. (1946). *Die Reichsbeamten von Achaia in spätrömischer Zeit.* Budapest.
Guidoboni, E., Comastri, A., & Traina, G. (1994). *Catalogue of Ancient Earthquakes in the Mediterranean Area up to the 10th Century.* Rome.
Gunn, J.D. (ed.). (2000). *The Years without Summer: Tracing AD 536 and Its Aftermath.* Oxford.
Haas, C. (1997). *Alexandria in Late Antiquity: Topography and Social Conflict.* Baltimore.
Habicht, C. (1985). *Pausanias' Guide to Ancient Greece.* Berkeley.
Haensch, R. (1997). *Capita provinciarum: Statthaltersitze und Provinzialverwaltung in der römischen Kaiserzeit* (*Kölner Forschungen* 7). Mainz.
Halkin, F. (ed.). (1957). *Bibliotheca Hagiographica Graeca.* (*BHG*, 3rd ed.). Brussels.
———. (1971). *Recherches et documents d'hagiographie byzantine.* Brussels.
Hall, J.B. (1986). *Prolegomena to Claudian.* London.
Halstead, P. & O'Shea, J. (eds). (1989). *Bad Year Economics: Cultural Responses to Risk and Uncertainty.* Cambridge.
Hamilton, F.J. & Brooks, E.W. (trans.). (1899). *The Syriac Chronicle known as that of Zachariah of Mitylene.* London.
Hammond, N.G.L. (1954). The Main Road from Boeotia to the Peloponnese through the N. Megarid. *BSA, 49,* 104–8.
Hannestad, N. (1999). How Did Rising Christianity Cope With Pagan Sculpture? In E.K. Chrysos & I.N. Wood (eds), *East and West: Modes of Communication. Proceedings of the First Plenary Conference at Mérida.* (pp. 173–204). Leiden.
Hansen, M.H. (2006a). *Polis: An Introduction to the Ancient Greek City-State.* Oxford.
———. (2006b). *The Shotgun Method: The Demography of the Ancient Greek City-State Culture.* Columbia.
Hansen, M.H. & Nielsen, T.H. (2004). *An Inventory of Archaic and Classical Poleis.* Oxford.
Harris, J.M. (1941). Coins found at Corinth, 1936–1939. *Hesperia, 10,* 143–62.
Harrison, E.B. (1953). *Portrait Sculpture (Agora* I*).* Princeton.
Harrison, S.J. (ed.). (1999). *Oxford Readings in the Roman Novel.* Oxford.
———. (2000). *Apuleius: A Latin Sophist.* Oxford.
Haskell, P.B. (1980). Temple E at Corinth: A Re-evaluation. *AJA, 84,* 210–1.
Hattersley-Smith, K.M. (1996). *Byzantine Public Architecture between the Fourth and Early Eleventh Centuries AD with Special Reference to the Towns of Byzantine Macedonia.* Oxford D.Phil. Diss., 1988. Thessalonike.
Haury, J. (1891). *Procopiana.* Augsburg.
Havé-Nikolaus, F. (1998). *Untersuchungen zu den kaiserzeitlichen Togastatuen griechischer Provenienz: Kaiserliche und private Togati der Provinzen Achaia, Creta (et Cyrene) und Teilen der Provinz Macedonia.* Mainz.
Havelock, C.M. (1995). *The Aphrodite of Knidos and Her Successors: A Historical Review of the Female Nude in Greek Art.* Ann Arbor.
Hawthorne, J.G. (1958). The Myth of Palaemon. *TAPA, 89,* 92–8.
———. (1965). Cenchreae, Port of Corinth. *Archaeology, 18,* 191–200.

Hayes, J.W. (1972). *Late Roman Pottery*. London.
———. (1973). Roman Pottery from the South Stoa at Corinth. *Hesperia, 42*, 416–70.
Hayward, C.L. (2003). Geology of Corinth: The Study of a Basic Resource. In C.K. Williams, II & N. Bookidis (eds), *Corinth, the Centenary: 1896–1996* (*Corinth* XX). (pp. 15–42). Princeton.
Heath, S., Rife, J.L., Bravo, J.J., III, and Blasdel, G. (2015). Preliminary Report on Early Byzantine Pottery from a Building Complex at Kenchreai (Greece). *ISAW Papers, 10*, http://dlib.nyu.edu/awdl/isaw/isaw-papers/10/
Heather, P.J. (1991). *Goths and Romans, 332–489*. Oxford.
———. (2005). *The Fall of the Roman Empire*. London.
Heather, P.J. & Matthews, J. (1991). *The Goths in the Fourth Century*. Liverpool.
Heermance, T.W. (1903). Excavations at Corinth: 1903. *AJA, 7*, 350.
———. (1904). Excavations at Corinth in 1904: Preliminary Report. *AJA, 8*, 433–41.
Hellenkemper Salies, G. (1986). Römische Mosaiken in Griechenland. *Bonner Jahrbücher, 186*, 241–84.
Hendy, M.F. (1985). *Studies in the Byzantine Monetary Economy, c. 300–1450*. Cambridge.
———. (1989). *The Economy, Fiscal Administration, and Coinage of Byzantium*. Northampton.
Henrichs, A. (1995). Graecia Capta: Roman Views of Greek Culture. *HSCP, 97*, 243–61.
Henry, R. (ed.). (1959). *Photius. Bibliothèque*. Paris.
Herbert, S. (1986). The Torch-Race at Corinth. In M. Del Chiaro (ed.), *Corinthiaca: Studies in Honor of Darrell A. Amyx*. (pp. 12–24). Columbia.
Hicks, R.D. (trans.). (2000). *Diogenes Laertius. Lives of Eminent Philosophers* (Reprint. Original ed., 1925). Cambridge, Mass.
Higgins, M.D. & Higgins, R.A. (1996). *A Geological Companion to Greece and the Aegean*. London.
Hill, B.H. (1926). Excavations at Corinth, 1925: Preliminary Report. *AJA, 30*, 44–9.
———. (1927). Excavations at Corinth 1926. *AJA, 31*, 70–9.
———. (1964). *The Springs: Peirene, Sacred Spring, Glauke* (*Corinth* I.6). Princeton.
Hiller von Gärtringen, F. (1932). Review of Meritt 1931 (*Corinth* VIII.1). *Philologische Wochenschrift, 13*, 361–4.
Hjohlman, J. (2002). *Farming the Land in Late Antiquity: The Case of Berbati in the Northeastern Peloponnese*. Ph.D. Diss., Stockholm University.
Hjort, Ø. (1993). Augustus Christianus—Livia Christiana: Sphragis and Roman Portrait Sculpture. In L. Rydén & J.O. Rosenqvist (eds), *Aspects of Late Antiquity and Early Byzantium*. (pp. 99–112). Istanbul.
Hodges, R. & Bowden, W. (eds). (1998). *The Sixth Century: Production, Distribution and Demand*. Leiden.
Hofmann, H. (ed.). (1999). *Latin Fiction: The Latin Novel in Context*. London.
Hohlfelder, R.L. (1970a). Pausanias, II,2,3: A Collation of Archaeological and Numismatic Evidence. *Hesperia, 39*, 326–331.

———. (1970b). A Small Deposit of Bronze Coins from Kenchreai. *Hesperia, 39,* 68–72.
———. (1973). A Sixth Century Hoard from Kenchreai. *Hesperia, 42,* 89–101.
———. (1975). Barbarian Incursions in Central Greece in the Late Sixth Century A.D.: New Evidence from Kenchreai. *Eastern European Quarterly, 9,* 251–8.
———. (1976). Kenchreai on the Saronic Gulf: Aspects of its Imperial History. *The Classical Journal, 71,* 217–26.
———. (1978). *The Coins* (*Kenchreai* 3). Leiden.
Hope, V.M. & Marshall, E. (eds). (2000). *Death and Disease in the Ancient City*. London.
Horden, P. & Purcell, N. (2000). *The Corrupting Sea: A Study of Mediterranean History*. Oxford.
Horrell, D.G. (2004). Domestic Space and Christian Meetings at Corinth: Imagining New Contexts and the Buildings East of the Theatre. *NTS, 50,* 349–69.
Horsley, G. (1987). An Archisynagogos of Corinth? *New Documents Illustrating Early Christianity, 4* (1979), 213–4.
Hort, A.F. (trans.). (1916). *Theophrastus: Enquiry into Plants, Volume I: Books 1–5*. Cambridge, MA.
Høgel, C. (ed.). (1996). *Metaphrasis: Redactions and Audiences in Middle Byzantine Hagiography*. Oslo.
———. (2002). *Symeon Metaphrastes: Rewriting and Canonization*. Copenhagen.
Hunger, H. (1978). *Die hochsprachliche profane Literatur der Byzantiner*. Munich.
Hunt, E. (trans.) (1957). *Saint Leo: Letters*. New York.
Hutton, W. (2005). *Describing Greece: Landscape and Literature in the Periegesis of Pausanias*. Cambridge.
Ibrahim, L., Scranton, R.L., & Brill, R. (1976). *The Panels of Opus Sectile in Glass* (*Kenchreai* 2). Leiden.
Iliffe, J.H. & Mitford, T.B. (1952). Excavations at Aphrodite's Sanctuary at Paphos. *Liverpool Bulletin, 2,* 28–66.
Imhoof-Blumer, F.W. & Gardner, P. (1885). Numismatic Commentary on Pausanias. *JHS, 6,* 50–101.
Inan, J. & Rosenbaum, E. (1966). *Roman and Early Byzantine Portrait Sculpture in Asia Minor*. London.
Inan, J. & Alföldi-Rosenbaum, E. (1979) *Römische und frühbyzantinische Porträtplastik aus der Türkei: neue Funde*. Mainz.
Innes, D. (2001). Why Isthmos Ephyrea? In A. Kahane & A. Laird (eds), *A Companion to the Prologue to Apuleius' Metamorphoses*. Oxford.
Ivison, E.A. (1996). Burial and Urbanism at Late Antique and Early Byzantine Corinth (c. AD 400–700). In N. Christie & S.T. Loseby (eds), *Towns in Transition: Urban Evolution in Late Antiquity and the Early Middle Ages*. (pp. 99–125). Aldershot.
Jackson, A.H. (2013). Polybius and Mummius' Isthmian victory, 146 B.C. In K. Kissas & W.-D. Niemeier (eds), *The Corinthia and the Northeast Peloponnese: Topography and History from Prehistoric Times until the End of Antiquity*. (pp. 143–54). Munich.

Jackson, J.A. & White, N. (1989). Normal Faulting in the Upper Continental Crust. *Journal of Structural Geology, 11*, 15–36.
Jacobs, I. (2013). *Aesthetic Maintenance of Urban Space: The Classical City from the 4th to the 7th Century*. Leuven.
Jacoby, F. (ed.). (1923). *Die Fragmente der griechischen Historiker 1–3*. Berlin.
James, S. (2005). Tombs and Tomes at Corinth. *ákoue, 53–54*, 4.
Jeffrey, L.H. (1988). Poseidon on the Acropolis. *Πρακτικά του XII Διεθνούς Συνεδρού Κλασικής Ἀρχαιολογίας (Sept. 4–10, 1983)*. Vol. 3. (pp. 124–6). Athens.
Jeffreys, E.M. et al. (trans.). (1986). *The Chronicle of John Malalas: A Translation* (*Byzantine Australiensia* 4). Melbourne.
Jenkins, R.J.H. & Megaw, H. (1934). Researches at Isthmia. *BSA, 32* (1931–2), 68–89.
Jerningham, H.E.H. (1873). *To and From Constantinople*. London.
Jesse, L. (1992). Ein spätantikes Frauenbildnis aus Korinth In O. Brehm & S. Klie (eds) *Μουσικός ανήρ. Festschrift für Max Wegner zum 90. Geburtstag*. Bonn.
Johnson, F.P. (1924). Byzantine Sculpture at Corinth. *AJA, 28*, 253–65.
———. (1926). The Imperial Portraits at Corinth. *AJA, 30*, 158–76.
———. (1931). *Sculpture, 1896–1923* (*Corinth* IX). Cambridge, Mass.
Jones, A.H.M. (1940) (1998 reprint ed.). *The Greek City: From Alexander to Justinian*. Oxford.
———. (1960). Church Finance in the Fifth and Sixth Centuries. *JTS, 11*, 84–94.
———. (1964). *The Later Roman Empire, 284–602: A Social, Economic and Administrative Survey*. Oxford.
———. (1974). *The Roman Economy: Studies in Ancient Economic and Administrative History*. Oxford.
Jones, A.H.M., Martindale, J.R., & Morris, J. (1971). *The Prosopography of the Later Roman Empire*. Berlin.
Jones, C.P. (1978). *The Roman World of Dio Chrysostom*. Cambridge, Mass.
Jones, W.H.S. (trans.). (1918) (1975 reprint ed.). *Pausanias. Description of Greece: Books I and II*. London.
Jordan, D.P. (1971). *Gibbon and his Roman Empire*. Urbana.
Jordan, D.R. (1994a). Inscribed Lamps from a Cult at Corinth in Late Antiquity. *HTR, 87*, 223–9.
———. (1994b). Inscribed Lead Tablets from the Games in the Sanctuary of Poseidon. *Hesperia, 63*, 111–26.
Jordan, D.R. & Spawforth, A.J.S. (1982). A New Document from the Isthmian Games. *Hesperia, 51*, 65–8.
Kaibel, G. (1878). *Epigrammata graeca ex lapidibus conlecta*. Berlin.
Kaldellis, A. (2004). *Procopius of Caesarea: Tyranny, History, and Philosophy at the End of Antiquity*. Philadelphia.
Kaplan, L.K. (2001). *A Good Considerable Country Town: Visions of a Greek Village in European Travel Narratives*. Ph.D. Diss., University of Pennsylvania.
Kaplan, M. (1976). *Les Propriétés de la couronne et de l'Église dans l'empire byzantin, Ve–VIe siècles: Documents*. Paris.

Kardulias, P.N. (1995). Architecture, Energy, and Social Evolution at Isthmia, Greece: Some Thoughts about Late Antiquity in the Korinthia. *JMA, 8*, 33–59.

———. (2005). *From Classical to Byzantine: Social Evolution in Late Antiquity and the Fortress at Isthmia, Greece.* Oxford.

Kardulias, P.N., Gregory, T.E., & Sawmiller, J. (1995). Bronze Age and Late Antique Exploitation of an Islet in the Saronic Gulf, Greece. *JFA, 22*, 3–21.

Karivieri, A. (1996). *The Athenian Lamp Industry in Late Antiquity*. Helsinki.

Kasas, S.E. (1974). *Corinth and its Environs in Antiquity*. Athens.

Kastriotis, P. (1900). Κεφάλη Αφροδίτης. *ArchEph*, 87–90.

———. (1923). Head of Julian the Apostate. *ArchEph*, 118.

Katakis, S.E. (2002). *Επίδαυρος: Τα γλυπτά των Ρωμαϊκών χρόνων από τό ιερό του Απόλλωνος Μαλεάτα και του Ασκληπιού.* Athens.

Kazhdan, A.P. (1999). *A History of Byzantine Literature, 650–850*. Athens.

Keesling, C. (2006). Heavenly Bodies: Monuments to Prostitutes in Greek Sanctuaries. In C. Faraone & L. McClure (eds), *Prostitutes & Courtesans in the Ancient World*. (pp. 59–76). Madison.

Kelly, J.N.D. (1975). *Jerome*. London.

Kent, J.H. (1950). A Byzantine Statue Base at Corinth. *Speculum: A Journal of Medieval Studies, 25*, 544–6.

———. (1966). *The Inscriptions, 1926–1950* (*Corinth* VIII.3). Princeton.

Keraudren, B. & Sorel, D. (1987). The Terraces of Corinth (Greece): A Detailed Record of Eustatic Sea-Level Variations during the Last 500,000 Years. *Marine Geology, 77*, 99–107.

Kiel, M. (1997). The Rise and Decline of Turkish Boeotia, 15th–19th Century. In J. Bintliff (ed.), *Recent Developments in the History and Archaeology of Central Greece*. (pp. 315–58). Oxford.

Kiilerich, B. (1993). *Late Fourth Century Classicism in the Plastic Arts: Studies in the So-Called Theodosian Renaissance*. Odense.

Kingsley, S.A. (2003). Late Antique Trade: Research Methodologies & Field Practices. In L. Lavan & W. Bowden (eds), *Theory and Practice in Late Antique Archaeology*. (pp. 113–38). Leiden.

Kingsley, S.A. & Decker, M. (eds). (2001). *Economy and Exchange in the East Mediterranean during Late Antiquity*. Oxford.

Kissas, K. (2013). Οργάνωση, λειτουργία και έργο της ΛΖ′ Εφορείας Αρχαιοτήτων Κορίνθου. In K. Kissas & W.-D. Niemeier (eds), *The Corinthia and the Northeast Peloponnese: Topography and History from Prehistoric Times until the End of Antiquity*. (pp. 1–10). Munich.

Kissas, K. & Niemeier, W.-D. (eds). (2013). *The Corinthia and the Northeast Peloponnese: Topography and History from Prehistoric Times until the End of Antiquity*. Athenaia Band 4. Munich.

Kleist, J.A. (trans.). (1961). *The Epistles of St. Clement of Rome and St. Ignatius of Antioch*. Westminster, Md.

Kock, T. (ed.). (1884). *Comicorum Atticorum fragmenta*. Leipzig.

Koder, J. (1996). Climatic Change in the Fifth and Sixth Centuries? In P. Allen & E. Jeffreys (eds), *The Sixth Century: End or Beginning?* (*Byzantina Australiensia* 10). (pp. 270–85). Brisbane.

Koehler, C.G. (1978a). Evidence around the Mediterranean for Corinthian Export of Wine and Oil. In J.B. Arnold III (ed.), *Beneath the*

Waters of Time (Proceedings of the Ninth Conference on Underwater Archaeology, San Antonio 1978). (pp. 231–9). Austin.

———. (1978b). *Corinthian A and B Transport Amphoras.* Ph.D. Diss., Princeton University.

———. (1981). Corinthian Developments in the Study of Trade in the Fifth Century. *Hesperia, 50,* 449–58.

Koepke, E.S. (ed.). (1856). *De Chamaeleontis Heracleotae vita librorumque reliquiis.* Berlin.

Koester, H. (1990). Melikertes at Isthmia: A Roman Mystery Cult. In D.L. Balch & e. al. (eds), *Greeks, Romans, and Christians. Essays in Honor of A.J. Malherbe.* (pp. 355–66). Minneapolis.

Kolarik, R. (1981). The Episcopal Basilica at Stobi. In A. Blaksova & J.R. Wiseman (eds), *Studies in the Antiquities of Stobi 3.* (pp. 61–80). Titov Veles.

———. (1987). Mosaics of the Early Church at Stobi. *DOP, 41,* 295–306.

Kollwitz, J. (1941). *Oströmische Plastik der theodosianischen Zeit.* Berlin.

Kondoleon, C. (2000). *Antioch: The Lost Ancient City.* Princeton.

Kopestonsky, T. (2016). The Greek Cult of the Nymphs at Corinth. *Hesperia, 85,* 711–77.

Kordoses, M.S. (1981). *Συμβολὴ στὴν ἱστορία καὶ τοπογραφία τῆς περιοχῆς Κορίνθου στοὺς μέσους χρόνους.* Athens.

Korka, E. & Rife, J.L. (2013). Systematic excavations undertaken by the Ministry of Culture and the American School of Classical Studies at Athens for promoting the Roman cemetery on the Koutsongila Ridge at Kenchreai. In K. Kissas & W.-D. Niemeier (eds), *The Corinthia and the Northeast Peloponnese: Topography and History from Prehistoric Times until the End of Antiquity.* (pp. 285–96). Munich.

Kosso, C. (2003). *The Archaeology of Public Policy in Late Roman Greece.* BAR 1126. Oxford.

Koukis, G.C. (1990). Peloponnesus: History, Geology, and Engineering Geology Aspects. In P.G. Marinos & G.C. Koukis (eds), *The Engineering Geology of Ancient Works, Monuments and Historical Sites.* Vol. 4. (pp. 2213–34). Rotterdam.

Kourelis, K. (2004). Early Travelers in Greece and the Invention of Medieval Architectural History. In D.M. Lasansky & B. McLaren (eds), *Architecture and Tourism: Perception, Performance, and Place.* (pp. 37–52). Oxford.

———. (2007). Byzantium and the Avant-Garde: Excavations at Corinth, 1920s-1930s. *Hesperia, 76,* 391–442.

Kouroumali, M. (2001). Catastrophe and Conspiracy: The Evidence of the Sixth Century Byzantine Sources for the AD 536 Environmental Event. *Medieval Life, 16,* 2–5.

Koutibas, S. (1966). *Ἱστορία τῆς Κορινθίας.* Athens.

Koutsouba, D. & Nakas, I. (2013). Δίολκος. Ενα σημαντικό τεχνικό έργο της αρχαιότητας. In K. Kissas & W.-D. Niemeier (eds), *The Corinthia and the Northeast Peloponnese: Topography and History from Prehistoric Times until the End of Antiquity.* (pp. 191–206). Munich.

Kraeling, C.H. (1938). *Gerasa, City of the Decapolis.* New Haven.

Krause, J.U., & Witschel, C. (eds). (2006). *Die Stadt in der Spätantike: Niedergang oder Wandel?* Stuttgart.

Krauss, S. (1922). *Synagogale Altertümer*. Berlin and Vienna.

Krautheimer, R. (1986). *Early Christian and Byzantine Architecture* (4th ed.). London.

Kristensen, T.M. (2012). Miraculous Bodies: Christian Viewers and the Transformation of 'Pagan' Sculpture in Late Antiquity. In S. Birk & B. Poulsen (eds), *Patrons and Viewers in Late Antiquity*. (pp. 31–66). Aarhus.

Kristensen, T.M. & Stirling, L. (eds). (2016). *The Afterlife of Greek & Roman Sculpture: Late Antique Responses and Practices*. Ann Arbor.

Kritsas, C. (1979). Ἀργολιδοκορινθία. *ArchDelt, 29* (1973–4), B2.212–49.

Krueger, P., Mommsen, T., Schöll, R., & Kroll, W. (eds). (1954). *Corpus Iuris Civilis*. Berlin.

Kulikowski, M. (2002). Nation vs. Army: A Necessary Contrast? In A. Gillett (ed.), *On Barbarian Identity: Critical Approaches to Ethnicity in the Early Middle Ages*. (pp. 69–84). Turnhout.

———. (2007). Plague in Spanish Late Antiquity. In L.K. Little (ed.), *Plague and the End of Antiquity: The Pandemic of 541–750*. Cambridge.

Kurke, L. (1996). Pindar and the Prostitutes, or Reading Ancient 'Pornography.' *Arion, 4*, 49–75.

———. (1997). Inventing the *Hetaira*: Sex, Politics, and Discursive Conflict in Archaic Greece. *ClAnt, 16*, 106–50.

Kyle, D.G. (2007). *Sport and Spectacle in the Ancient World*. Malden, Mass.

L'Orange, H.P. (1933). *Studien zur Geschichte des spätantiken Porträts*. Oslo.

———. (1961). Der subtile Stil: Eine Kunstströmung aus der Zeit um 400 nach Christus. *AntK, 4*, 68–74.

Lafond, Y. (2010). Concours et identité civique dans le Péloponnèse d'époque romaine (IIe s. av. J.-C. – IIIe s. apr. J.-C.). In A.D. Rizakis & Cl. E. Lepenioti (eds), *Roman Peloponnese III: Society, Economy and Culture under the Roman Empire: Continuity and Innovation. Meletemata* 63. (pp. 407–20). Athens.

Laiou, A. (ed.). (2002). *The Economic History of Byzantium: From the Seventh through the Fifteenth Century (EHB)*. Washington, D.C.

Laiou, A.E. & Morrison, C. (2007). *The Byzantine Economy*. Cambridge.

Lambropoulou, A. (1993). Μορφὴς ἐπικοινωνίας Ἑβραίων καὶ Χριστιανῶν στὴν Πελοπόννησο κατὰ τὴν Πρωτοβυζαντινὴ περίοδο. In N. Moschonas (ed.), *Πρακτικά τοῦ Β΄ Διεθνοῦς Συμποσίου, Ἡ ἐπικοινωνία στὸ Βυζάντιο, 1990*. (pp. 657–682). Athens.

Lampros, S.P. (1877). Über das korinthische Amphitheater. *AthMitt, 2*, 282–8.

Lanci, J.R. (2005). The Stones Don't Speak and the Texts Tell Lies: Sacred Sex at Corinth. In S.J. Friesen & D.N. Schowalter (eds), *Urban Religon in Roman Corinth: Interdisciplinary Approaches*. (pp. 205–20). Cambridge, Mass.

Lançon, B. (2000). *Rome in Late Antiquity: Everyday Life and Urban Change, AD 312–609*. New York.

Landon, M.E. (1994). *Contributions to the Study of the Water Supply of Ancient Corinth*. Ph.D. Diss., U.C. Berkeley.

———. (2003). Beyond Peirene: Toward a Broader View of Corinthian Water Supply. In C.K. Williams, II & N. Bookidis (eds), *Corinth, the Centenary: 1896–1996* (*Corinth* XX). (pp. 43–62). Princeton.

Lane Fox, R. (1987). *Pagans and Christians*. New York.
Lang, M. (1977). *Cure and Cult in Ancient Corinth: A Guide to the Asklepieion* (*Corinth Notes* 1). Princeton.
Langridge-Noti, E. (1996). *A Corinthian Scrapbook: One Hundred Years of American Excavations in Ancient Corinth*. Athens.
Larsen, J.A.O. (1933). Roman Greece. In T. Frank (ed.), *An Economic Survey of Ancient Rome 4*. Baltimore.
Lattimore, S. (1976). *The Marine Thiasos*. Los Angeles.
———. (1996). *Sculpture II: Marble Sculpture, 1967–1980 (Isthmia* VI). Princeton.
Lavan, L. (1999). Residences of Late Antique Governors: A Gazetteer. *AntTard, 7*, 135–64.
———. (2001a). Late Antique Urbanism: A Bibliographic Essay. In L. Lavan (ed.), *Recent Research in Late Antique Urbanism*. (pp. 9–26). Portsmouth, R.I.
———. (2001b). The Praetoria of Civil Governors in Late Antiquity. In L. Lavan (ed.), *Recent Research in Late Antique Urbanism*. (pp. 39–56). Portsmouth, R.I.
———. (ed.). (2001c). *Recent Research in Late-Antique Urbanism*. Portsmouth, R.I.
———. (2003a). Late Antique Archaeology: An Introduction. In L. Lavan & W. Bowden (eds), *Theory and Practice in Late Antique Archaeology*. (pp. vii–xvi). Leiden.
———. (2003b). Late Antique Urban Topography: From Architecture to Human Space. In L. Lavan & W. Bowden (eds), *Theory and Practice in Late Antique Archaeology*. (pp. 171–95). Leiden.
———. (2003c). The Political Topography of the Late Antique City. In L. Lavan & W. Bowden (eds), *Theory and Practice in Late Antique Archaeology*. (pp. 314–40). Leiden.
———. (2006). Fora and Agorai in Mediterranean Cities: Fourth and Fifth Centuries AD. In W. Bowden, C. Machado, & A. Gutteridge (eds), *Social and Political Life in Late Antiquity*. (pp. 195–249). Leiden.
Lavan, L., & Bowden, W. (eds). (2003). *Theory and Practice in Late Antique Archaeology*. Leiden.
Lawrence, A.W. (1983). A Skeletal History of Byzantine Fortification. *BSA, 78*, 171–227.
Lawton, C.L. (2005). *Marbleworkers in the Athenian Agora*. Excavations of the Athenian Agora. Picture book no. 27. Athens.
Le Bas, P. & Waddington, W.H. (1870). *Inscriptions grecques et latines recueillies en Asie Mineure* (Reprint ed., Vols. 1–2). Hildesheim.
Le Roy, J.-D. (2004). *The Ruins of the Most Beautiful Monuments of Greece* (D. Britt, trans.). Los Angeles.
Leake, W.M. (1830). *Travels in the Morea*. London.
———. (1967). *Peloponnesiaca: A Supplement to Travels in the Moréa* (Reprint. Original ed. 1846). Amsterdam.
Lemerle, P. (1979). *Les plus anciens recueils des miracles de Saint Démétrius et la pénétration des Slaves dans les Balkans*. Paris.
Lenski, N. (ed.). (2006). *The Cambridge Companion to the Age of Constantine*. Cambridge.

Leone, A. (2007). *Changing Townscapes in North Africa from Late Antiquity to the Arab Conquest.* Bari.

———. (2013). *The End of the Pagan City. Religion, Economy and Urbanism in Late Antique North Africa.* Oxford.

Leontsini, S. (1989). *Die Prostitution im frühen Byzanz.* Vienna.

Lepinski, S. (2008). Roman Wall Painting from Panayia Field, Corinth, Greece: A Contextual Study. Ph.D. Diss., Bryn Mawr College.

———. (2014). Painting Practices in Roman Corinth: Greek or Roman? In S.J. Friesen, S.A. James & D.N. Schowalter (eds), *Corinth in Contrast: Studies in Inequality.* (pp. 74–100). Leiden.

———. (2015). Methodologies and Materiality: Excavating and Analyzing Fragmentary Mural Painting, a Case Study from Ancient Corinth. In S. Lepinski & S. McFadden (eds), *Beyond Iconography: Material, Methods, and Meaning in Ancient Surface Decoration.* Selected Papers on Ancient Art and Architecture 1. (pp. 19–34). Boston.

Lévêque, P. (1960). Observations sur l'iconographie de Julien. *MonPiot, 51*, 105–28.

Levi, P. (trans.). (1979). *Pausanias. Guide to Greece* (2nd ed.). London.

Levine, L.I. (ed.). (1981). *Ancient Synagogues Revealed.* Jerusalem.

———. (2005). *The Ancient Synagogue: The First Thousand Years* (2nd ed.). New Haven.

Levinskaya, I.A. (1996). *The Book of Acts in its Diaspora Setting* (*The Book of Acts in its First Century Setting* 5). Grand Rapids.

Levy, H.L. (1948). Claudian's *In Rufinum* and an Epistle of St. Jerome. *AJP, 69*, 62–8.

———. (1971). *Claudian's In Rufinum: An Exegetical Commentary.* Cleveland.

Liebeschuetz, J.H.W.G. (1972). *Antioch: City and Imperial Administration in the Later Roman Empire.* Oxford.

———. (2001). *Decline and Fall of the Roman City.* Oxford.

———. (2003). Pagan Historiography and the Decline of the Empire. In G. Marasco (ed.), *Greek and Roman Historiography in Late Antiquity, Fourth to Sixth Century A.D.* (pp. 177–218). Leiden.

Lietzmann, H. (ed.). (1911). *Die drei ältesten Martyrologien* (2nd ed.). Bonn.

Lieu, J.M. (2004). *Christian Identity in the Jewish and Graeco-Roman World.* Oxford.

Lightfoot, C.S. (2012). Business as Usual? Archaeological Evidence for Byzantine Commercial Enterprise at Amorium in the Seventh to Eleventh Centuries. In C. Morrisson (ed.), *Trade and Markets in Byzantium.* (pp. 177–91). Washington, D.C.

Limberis, V. (2005). Ecclesiastical Ambiguities: Corinth in the Fourth and Fifth Centuries. In D.N. Schowalter & S.J. Friesen (eds), *Urban Religon in Roman Corinth: Interdisciplinary Approaches.* (pp. 443–57). Cambridge, Mass.

Lintott, A.W. (1993). *Imperium Romanum: Politics and Administration.* London.

Lippold, A. (1998). *Die Historia Augusta: eine Sammlung römischer Kaiserbiographien aus der Zeit Konstantins.* Stuttgart.

Lisle, R. (1955). *The Cults of Corinth.* Ph.D. Diss., Johns Hopkins University.

Little, L.K. (ed.). (2007). *Plague and the End of Antiquity: The Pandemic of 541–750.* Cambridge.

Lohmann, H. (2013). Der Diolkos von Korinth-eine entike Schiffsschleppe? In K. Kissas & W.-D. Niemeier (eds), *The Corinthia and the Northeast Peloponnese: Topography and History from Prehistoric Times until the End of Antiquity*. (pp. 207–30). Munich.

Löhr, C. (2000). *Griechische Familienweihungen: Untersuchungen einer Repräsentationsform von ihren Anfängen bis zum Ende des 4. Jhs. v. Chr.* Rahden.

Lolos, Y.A. (1997). The Hadrianic Aqueduct of Corinth. *Hesperia, 66*, 271–314.

Long, J. (1996). *Claudian's In Eutropium, or, How, When, and Why to Slander a Eunuch*. Chapel Hill.

Longfellow, B. (2009). The Legacy of Hadrian: Roman Monumental Civic Fountains in Greece. In C. Kosso & A. Scott (eds), *The Nature and Function of Water, Baths, Bathing and Hygiene from Antiquity through the Renaissance*. (pp. 211–32). Leiden.

López Quiroga, J. (2016). Early Byzantine Urban Landscapes in the Southwest and Southeast Mediterranean. In *Proceedings of the 23rd International Congress of Byzantine Studies, Belgrade, 22–27 August 2016, Plenary Papers*. (pp. 69–105). Belgrade.

Lord, L.E. (1947). *A History of the American School of Classical Studies at Athens, 1882–1942: An Intercollegiate Project*. Cambridge, Mass.

Lyttelton, M. (1974). *Baroque Architecture in Classical Antiquity*. Ithaca.

Mabrouk, A. (1998). *Puissant par la gloire: Genséric roi des vandales: récit historique*. Paris.

Mac Isaac, J.D. (1987). Corinth: Coins, 1925–1926: The Theater District and the Roman Villa. *Hesperia, 56*, 97–157.

MacDonald, B.R. (1986). The Diolkos. *JHS, 106*, 191–5.

MacKay, P.A. (1963). Procopius' De Aedificiis and the Topography of Thermopylae. *AJA, 67*, 241–55.

———. (1967). The Fountain at Hadji Mustafa. *Hesperia, 36*, 193–5.

———. (1968). Acrocorinth in 1668: A Turkish Account. *Hesperia, 37*, 386–97.

———. (1980). Evliya in the Corinthia. *SN* 8.257a4–259b7. From *The* Travel Journal *of Evliya Çelebi, Book 8: Travels in Mainland Greece*. Unpublished translation in the Corinth Excavations library, also deposited in the Research Works Archive of the Department of Classics Faculty Papers, University of Washington, http://hdl.handle.net/1773/25311.

MacMullen, R. (1986). What Difference Did Christianity Make? *Historia, 35*, 322–43.

Maehler, H. (ed.). (1987–9). *Pindari carmina cum fragmentis post Brunonem Snell*. Leipzig.

Mahaffy, J.P. (1878). *Rambles and Studies in Greece* (2nd ed.). London.

Maier, F.G. (1979). The Paphian Shrine of Aphrodite. *Acts of the International Archaeological Symposium: The Relations between Cyprus and Crete, ca. 2000–500 B.C.* (pp. 228–34). Cyprus.

Maier, P.L. (trans.). (1999). *Eusebius: The Church History: A New Translation with Commentary*. Grand Rapids.

Malherbe, R.d. (1846). *L'Orient, 1718–1845*. Paris.

Mallan, C., & Davenport, C. (2015). Dexippus and the Gothic Invasions: Interpreting the New Vienna Fragment. *JRS, 105*, 203–26.
Mango, C. (1975). *Byzantine Literature as a Distorting Mirror*. Oxford.
———. (1981a). Discontinuity with the Classical Past in Byzantium. In M. Mullett & R. Scott (eds), *Byzantium and the Classical Tradition*. (pp. 48–57). Birmingham.
———. (1981b). Daily Life in Byzantium. *JÖB, 31/32*, 337–53.
———. (1993a). The Church of Sts Sergius and Bacchus at Constantinople and the Alleged Tradition of Octagonal Palatine Churches. *Studies on Constantinople*. (Reprint. Original ed., JÖB 21 (1972) 189–93). Aldershot.
———. (1993b). The Church of Sts Sergius and Bacchus once again. *Studies on Constantinople*. (Reprint. Original ed., *BZ* 68 (1975) 385–92). Aldershot.
———. (1993c). The Date of the Studius Basilica at Istanbul. *Studies on Constantinople*. (Reprint. Original ed., *BMGS* 4 (1978) 115–22). Aldershot.
———. (2000). The Triumphal Way of Constantinople and the Golden Gate. *DOP, 54*, 173–88.
Mango, C. & Scott, R. (trans.). (1997). *The Chronicle of Theophanes Confessor: Byzantine and Near Eastern History, AD 284–813*. Oxford.
Mango, M.M. (2001). The Porticoed Street at Constantinople. In N. Necipoglu (ed.), *Byzantine Constantinople: Monuments, Topography, and Everyday Life*. (pp. 29–52). Leiden.
Marangou, L. (1976). *Bone Carvings from Egypt 2: The Graeco-Roman Period*. Tübingen.
Marasco, G. (ed.). (2003). *Greek and Roman Historiography in Late Antiquity, Fourth to Sixth Century A.D.* Leiden.
Marchand, J. (2003). *Well-built Kleonai: A History of the Peloponnesian City Based on a Survey of the Visible Remains and a Study of the Literary and Epigraphic Sources*. Ph.D. Diss., U.C. Berkeley.
———. (2009). Kleonai, the Corinth-Argos Road, and the "Axis of History." *Hesperia, 78*, 107–63.
———. (2013). Investigations in the territory of Kleonai in the northeastern Peloponnesos. In K. Kissas & W.-D. Niemeier (eds), *The Corinthia and the Northeast Peloponnese: Topography and History from Prehistoric Times until the End of Antiquity*. (pp. 313–22). Munich.
Marcovich, M. (ed.). (1999). *Diogenis Laertii Vitae philosophorum*. Stuttgart.
Marcus, R.A. (1970). Gregory the Great and a Papal Missionary Strategy. In G.J. Cumming (ed.), *The Mission of the Church and the Propogation of the Faith*. Cambridge.
Mariolopoulos, E.G. (1961). *An Outline of the Climate of Greece*. Athens.
Martin, T.R. (1977). Inscriptions at Corinth. *Hesperia, 46*, 178–98.
Matson, F.R. (1948). Technological Study of the Glass from the Corinth Glass Factory. *AJA, 44*, 325–7.
Matthews, J.F. (1985). *Political Life and Culture in Late Roman Society*. London.
Matthews, J. (1989). *The Roman Empire of Ammianus*. London.
Mattusch, C.C. (1977). Corinthian Metalworking: The Forum Area. *Hesperia, 46*, 380–9.

———. (1991). Corinthian Metalworking: The Gymnasium Bronze Foundry. *Hesperia, 60,* 383–95.

Mau, A. & Kelsey, F.W. (1902). *Pompeii, its Life and Art.* New York.

Max, H.v.S. (1918). *Das Christliche Hellas.* Leipzig.

McClure, L. (2003). *Courtesans at Table: Gender and Greek Literary Culture in Athenaeus.* New York.

McCormick, M. (2015). Tracking mass death during the fall of Rome's empire (I). *JRA, 28,* 325–57.

McDonald, W.A. (1942). Archaeology and St. Paul's Journeys in Greek Lands: Corinth. *Biblical Archaeology, 5,* 36–48.

McGinn, T.A.J. (2004). *The Economy of Prostitution in the Roman World: A Study of Social History and the Brothel.* Ann Arbor.

———. (2006). Zoning Shame in the Roman City. In C.A. Faraone & L.K. McClure (eds), *Prostitutes and Courtesans in the Ancient World.* (pp. 161–76). Madison.

Mee, C. & Forbes, H.A. (eds). (1997). *A Rough and Rocky Place: The Landscape and Settlement History of the Methana Peninsula, Greece: Results of the Methana Survey Project, sponsored by the British School at Athens and the University of Liverpool.* Liverpool.

Meeks, W.A. (1983). *The First Urban Christians: The Social World of the Apostle Paul.* New Haven.

Megaw, A.H.S. (1962). Archaeology in Greece, 1962–3. *Archaeological Reports, 9,* 3–33.

Meier, M. (2002). Das Ende des Konsulats im Jahr 541/42 und seine Gründe: Kritische Anmerkungen zur Vorstellung eines 'Zeitalters Justinians'. *ZPE, 138,* 290–9.

———. (2003). *Das andere Zeitalter Justinians: Kontingenzerfahrung und Kontingenzbewältigung im 6. Jahrhundert n. Chr.* Göttingen.

Meimaris, Y.E. et al. (eds). (1992). *Chronological Systems in Roman-Byzantine Palestine and Arabia: The Evidence of the Dated Greek Inscriptions* (*Meletemata* 17). Athens.

Meleti, P. (2013). Παλαιοχριστιανικό νεκροταφείο στην Αρχαία Κορίνθο. In K. Kissas & W.-D. Niemeier (eds), *The Corinthia and the Northeast Peloponnese: Topography and History from Prehistoric Times until the End of Antiquity.* (pp. 161–8). Munich.

Meritt, B.D. (1931). *Greek Inscriptions, 1896–1927* (*Corinth* VIII.1). Cambridge, Mass.

Meritt, L.S. (1984). *History of the American School of Classical Studies at Athens, 1939–1980.* Princeton.

Merker, G.S. (2000). *The Sanctuary of Demeter and Kore: Terracotta Figurines of the Classical, Hellenistic, and Roman Periods* (*Corinth* XVIII.4). Princeton.

Merrills, A.H. (2005). *History and Geography in Late Antiquity.* Cambridge.

Michaud, J.-P. (1970). Chroniques des fouilles en 1968 et 1969. *BCH, 94,* 934–49.

Mierow, H.E. (1926). *The Roman provincial governor as he appears in the Digest and Code of Justinian.* Colorado Springs.

Miliarakis, A. (1886). *Γεωγραφία πολιτικὴ νέα καὶ ἀρχαία τοῦ νομοῦ Ἀργολίδος καὶ Κορινθίας.* Athens.

Millar, F. (1969). P. Herennius Dexippus: The Greek World and the Third-Century Invasions. *JRS, 59,* 12–29.

———. (1999). The World of the *Golden Ass*. In S.J. Harrison (ed.), *Oxford Readings in the Roman Novel*. (pp. 247–68). Oxford.
———. (2006). *A Greek Roman Empire: Power and Belief under Theodosius II (408–450)*. Berkeley.
Milleker, E. (1985). Three Heads of Sarapis from Corinth. *Hesperia, 54,* 121–35.
Miller, S.G. (1972). A Mosaic Floor from a Roman Villa at Anaploga. *Hesperia, 41,* 332–54.
———. (1986). Poseidon at Nemea. *Φίλια έπη εις Γεώργιον Ε. Μυλωνάν* Vol. 1. (pp. 261–71). Athens.
———. (2004). *Ancient Greek Athletics*. New Haven.
Millis, B.W. (2004). Work on Corinth Guide Progresses. *ákoue, 51,* 4,16.
———. (2010). The Social and Ethnic Origins of the Colonists in Early Roman Corinth. In S.J. Friesen, D.N. Schowalter & J.C. Walters (eds), *Corinth in Context: Comparative Studies on Religion and Society*. (pp. 13–36). Leiden.
———. (2014). The Local Magistrates and Elite of Roman Corinth. In S.J. Friesen, S.A. James & D.N. Schowalter (eds), *Corinth in Contrast: Studies in Inequality*. (pp. 38–53). Leiden.
Moe, D.L. (1977). The Cross and the Menorah. *Archaeology, 30,* 148–59.
Moles, J. (1995). Dio Chrysostom, Greece, and Rome. In D. Innes, H.M. Hine, & C.B.R. Pelling (eds), *Ethics and Rhetoric: Classical Essays for Donald Russell on his Seventy-fifth Birthday*. Oxford.
Monceaux, P. (1884). Fouilles et recherches archéologiques au sanctuaire des Jeux Isthmiques. *GazArch, 8,* 273–85, 354–63.
———. (1885). Fouilles et recherches archéologiques au sanctuaire des Jeux Isthmiques. *GazArch, 9,* 205–14, 402–12.
Moore, R.S. (2000). *Trade in the Eastern Mediterranean, 100–700 AD: The Ceramic Evidence*. Ph.D. Diss., The Ohio State University.
Morgan, C.H., II. (1935). Several Vases from a Byzantine Dump at Corinth. *AJA, 39,* 76–78.
———. (1936). Excavations at Corinth, 1935–1936. *AJA, 40,* 466–84.
———. (1937). Excavations at Corinth, 1936–1937. *AJA, 41,* 539–52.
———. (1938). Excavations at Corinth, Autumn 1937. *AJA, 42,* 362–70.
———. (1939). Excavations at Corinth, 1938. *AJA, 43,* 255–67.
———. (1942). *The Byzantine Pottery* (*Corinth* XI). Cambridge, Mass.
Mourtzas, N.D. & Marinos, P.G. (1994). Upper Holocene Sea-Level Changes: Paleographic Evolution and its Impact on Coastal Archaeological Sites and Monuments. *Environmental Geology, 23,* 1–13.
Müller, K. (ed.). (1882). *Geographi Graeci minores*. Paris.
Murphy-O'Connor, J. (1983). *St. Paul's Corinth: Texts and Archaeology*. Wilmington.
Musti, D. & Torelli, M. (1986). *Pausania, Guida della Grecia II: La Corinzia e l'Argolide*. Rome.
Musurillo, H. (1954). *The Acts of the Pagan Martyrs. Acta Alexandrinorum*. Oxford.
Mylonas, G.E. (1961). *Eleusis and the Eleusinian Mysteries*. Princeton.
Neils, J. (2000). Others within the Other: An Intimate Look at Hetairai and Maenads. In B. Cohen (ed.), *Not the Classical Ideal: Athens and the Construction of the Other in Greek Art*. (pp. 203–226). Leiden.

Nelson, R.S. (1996). Living on the Byzantine Borders of Western Art. *Gesta, 35*, 3–10.
Newton, G.W.A. et al. (1988). Clay Sources and Corinthian Amphorae. In E.A. Slater & J.O. Tate (eds), *Science and Archaeology, Glasgow 1987 (Proceedings of a Conference on the Application of Scientific Techniques to Archaeology, Glasgow, September 1987)*. (pp. 59–81). Oxford.
Nilsson, M.P. (1957). *Griechische Feste von religiöser Bedeutung, mit Ausschluss der Attischen* (Reprint.). Darmstadt.
———. (1972). *Greek Folk Religion* (Reprint. Original ed., 1940). Philadelphia.
Nock, A.D. (1998). *Conversion: The Old and the New in Religion from Alexander the Great to Augustine of Hippo*. Baltimore.
Noller, J.S. (2001). Archaeoseismology: Shaking Out the History of Humans and Earthquakes. In P. Goldberg, V.T. Holliday, & C.R. Ferring (eds), *Earth Sciences and Archaeology*. (pp. 143–70). New York.
Noller, J.S. et al. (1997). Subsidence of the Harbor at Kenchreai, Saronic Gulf, Greece, during the Earthquakes of A.D. 400 and A.D. 1928. *Eos, Transactions, American Geophysical Union, 78*, 636.
Noy, D., Panayotov, A., & Bloedhorn, H. (eds). (2004). *Inscriptiones Judaicae Orientis 1: Eastern Europe*. Tübingen.
Odorico, P. & Agapitos, P.A. (eds). (2002). *Pour une "nouvelle" histoire de la littérature byzantine: problèmes, méthodes, approches, propositions*. Paris.
Oehler, J. (1909). Epigraphische Beiträge zur Geschichte des Judentums. *MGWJ, 53*, 292–302, 443–52, 525–38.
Økland, J. (2010). Ceres, Κόρη, and Cultural Complexity: Divine Personality Definitions and Human Worshippers in Roman Corinth. In S.J. Friesen, D.N. Schowalter & J.C. Walters (eds), *Corinth in Context: Comparative Studies on Religion and Society*. (pp. 199–230). Leiden.
Oliver, A. (2001). A Glass Opus Sectile Panel from Corinth. *Hesperia, 70*, 349–63.
Oliver, J.H. (1953). *The Ruling Power: A Study of the Roman Empire in the Second Century after Christ through the Roman Oration of Aelius Aristides*. Philadelphia.
———. (1968). *The Civilizing Power: A Study of the Panathenaic Discourse of Aelius Aristides against the Background of Literature and Cultural Conflict, with text, translation, and commentary*. Philadelphia.
Olson, S.D. (ed.). (2007). *Athenaeus: The Learned Banqueters, Books 1–3.106e*. Cambridge, Mass.
O'Neill, J.G. (1930). *Ancient Corinth, with a Topographical Sketch of the Corinthia I: From the Earliest Times to 404 B.C.* Baltimore.
Osborne, R. (1985). *Demos: The Discovery of Classical Attika*. Cambridge.
Osland, D. (2016). Abuse or Reuse? Public Space in Late Antique Emerita. *AJA, 120*, 67–97.
Ott, J. (2016). Mortuary Practices in Late Antique Corinth. Ph.D. Diss., New York University.
Özgür, M.E. (2008). *Sculptures of the Museum in Antalya* (3rd ed.). Ankara.
Page, D.L., Dawe, R.D. & Diggle, J. (eds). (1981). *Further Greek Epigrams*. Cambridge.
Palagia, O. (2010). Sculptures from the Peloponnese in the Roman Imperial period. In A.D. Rizakis & Cl. E. Lepenioti (eds), *Roman*

Peloponnese III: Society, Economy and Culture under the Roman Empire: Continuity and Innovation. Meletemata 63. (pp. 431–45). Athens.
Palinkas, J. (2005). A Productive Year of Work on Panaghia Street and Propylaia. *ákoue, 53–54,* 14–15.
Palinkas, J. & Herbst, J.A. (2005). Road Works in Roman Corinth: A Newly Excavated Street in the Panaghia Field. *106th Annual Meeting Abstracts,* Vol. 28. Boston.
——— (2011). A Roman Road Southeast of the Forum at Corinth: Technology and Urban Development. *Hesperia, 80,* 287–336.
Pallas, D.I. (1956). Ἀνασκαφὴ ἐν Παλαιᾷ Κορίνθῳ. *Prakt, 1953,* 175–83.
———. (1957a). Ἀνασκαφὴ ἐν Παλαιᾷ Κορίνθῳ. *Prakt, 1954,* 210–8.
———. (1957b). Πρωτοχριστιανικὴ Κόρινθος. *Πελοποννησιακὴ Πρωτοχρόνια.* (pp. 52–62). Athens.
———. (1959). Scoperte archeologiche in Grecia negli anni 1956–1958. *RACrist, 35,* 187–233.
———. (1960a). Ἀνασκαφὴ τῆς βασιλικῆς τῆς Σκουτέλας ἐν Κορίνθου. *Prakt, 1955,* 193–200.
———. (1960b). Ἀνασκαφὴ ῥωμαϊκῆς ἐπαύλεως παρὰ τὴν Κόρινθον. *Prakt, 1955,* 201–16.
———. (1961). Ἀνασκαφὴ βασιλικῆς ἐν Λεχαίῳ. *Prakt, 1956,* 164–78.
———. (1962). Ἀνασκαφὴ τῆς βασιλικῆς τοῦ Λεχαίου. *Prakt, 1957,* 95–104.
———. (1963a). Ἀνασκαφαὶ Λεχαίου (1956–1960). *ArchDelt, 17* (1961–1962), B.69–78.
———. (1963b). Τὸ Ἑξαμίλιον τεῖχος ἐπὶ τοῦ Ἰσθμοῦ. *ArchDelt, 17* (1961–1962), B.78–83.
———. (1964). Ἀνασκαφὴ ἐν Λεχαίῳ. Τὸ Βαπτιστήριον τῆς παλαιοχριστια αλαιοχριστιανικῆς βασιλικῆς *Prakt, 1961,* 137–54.
———. (1965a). Ἀνασκαφὴ τῆς παλαιοχριστιανικῆς βασιλικῆς τοῦ Λεχαίου. *Prakt, 1958,* 119–34.
———. (1965b). Ἀνασκαφὴ βασιλικῆς Λεχαίου. *Prakt, 1959,* 126–40.
———. (1966). Ἀνασκαφὴ ἐν Λεχαίῳ. *Prakt, 1960,* 144–70.
———. (1967a). Ἀνασκαφικαὶ ἔρευναι ἐν Λεχαίῳ. *Prakt, 1965,* 137–66.
———. (1967b). *Πρωτοχριστιανική Κόρινθος.* Athens.
———. (1970). Über der Datierung eines Kapitells der Basilika von Lechaion (Korinth). *ByzZeit, 63,* 69–75.
———. (1972). Ἀνασκαφικὴ ἔρευνα ἐν τὴν βασιλικὴν τοῦ Κρανείου ἐν Κορίνθῳ. *Prakt, 1970,* 98–117.
———. (1974). Ἀνασκαφὴ τῆς βασιλικῆς τοῦ Κρανείου. *Prakt, 1972,* 205–50.
———. (1977). *Les monuments paléochrétiens de Grèce découverts de 1959 à 1973.* Vatican City.
———. (1978). Ἀνασκαφὴ τῆς βασιλικῆς τοῦ Κρανείου ἐν Κορίνθῳ. *Prakt, 1976,* 163–95.
———. (1980). Ἀνασκαφὴ τῆς βασιλικῆς τοῦ Κρανείου ἐν Κορίνθῳ. *Prakt, 1977,* 162–83.
———. (1981). Corinthe et Nikopolis pendant le bas moyen-âge. *FelRav, 118* (1979), 93–142.
———. (1987). Η βασιλική των Κέγχρεων. *EpetByz, 47,* 295–309.
———. (1990). Korinth. *Reallexikon zur byzantinischen Kunst.* Vol. 4. (pp. 746–811). Stuttgart.

Pallas, D.I. & Dantis, S.P. (1979). Επιγραφές από την Κόρινθο. *ArchEph, 1977*, 61–83.

Palmer, R. (2001). Bridging the Gap: The Continuity of Greek Agriculture from the Mycenaean to the Historical Period. In D.W. Tandy (ed.), *Prehistory and History: Ethnicity, Class and Political Economy*. (pp. 41–84). Montreal.

Palumbo Stracca, B.M. (1985). Lettura critica di epigrammi (I). *Bolletino dei Classici, 3*, 58–65.

Panagiotide, M. (1970). Βυζαντινὰ κιονόκρανα μὲ ἀνάγλυφα ζῷα. *ArchDelt, 24* (1969), 98, 117.

Papachatzis, N. (1985). *Ancient Corinth: The Museums of Corinth, Isthmia and Sicyon* (K. Cicellis, trans. Reprint. Original ed., 1983). Athens.

Papachatzis, N.D. (1963). *Κορινθιακὰ καὶ Λακωνικά. Παυσανίου Ἑλλάδος Περιήγησις* 2. Athens.

Papadopoulos, G.A. & Chalkis, B.J. (1984). Tsunamis observed in Greece and the Surrounding Area from Antiquity up to the Present Times. *Marine Geology, 56*, 509–17.

Papaphotiou, A.E. (2002). *Σεισμοί και κατασκευές στην Κορινθία. Ιστορική αναδρομή*. Corinth.

———. (2007). *Ο Δίολκος στον Ισθμό της Κορίνθου*. Corinth.

Paris, J. (1915). Contributions à l'étude des ports antiques du monde grec. *BCH, 39*, 5–16.

Parkins, H.M. (ed.). (1997). *Roman Urbanism: Beyond the Consumer City*. London.

Paschoud, F. (ed.). (1971–1989). *Zosime. Histoire nouvelle*. Paris.

———. (1975). *Cinq études sur Zosime*. Paris.

———. (2006). *Eunape, Olympiodore, Zosime: scripta minora: recueil d'articles, avec addenda, corrigenda, mise à jour et indices*. Bari.

Patlagean, E. (1977). *Pauvreté économique et pauvreté sociale à Byzance, 4e–7e siècles*. Paris.

Payne, H. et al. (1940). *Perachora: The Sanctuaries of Hera Akraia and Limenia. Architecture, Bronzes, Terracottas* (*Perachora* 1). Oxford.

Pelling, C.B.R. (2007). De Malignitate Plutarchi: Plutarch, Herodotus, and the Persian Wars. In E. Bridges, E. Hall, & P.J. Rhodes (eds), *Cultural Responses to the Persian Wars: Antiquity to the Third Millennium*. Oxford.

Pemberton, E.G. (1989). *The Sanctuary of Demeter and Kore: The Greek Pottery* (*Corinth* XVIII.1). Princeton.

Penella, R.J. (1990). *Greek Philosophers and Sophists in the Fourth Century: Studies in Eunapius of Sardis*. Leeds.

Peppers, J.M. (1979). *Selected Roman Pottery, Isthmia Excavations*. Ph.D. Diss., University of Pennsylvania.

Perry, M. (1975). A Greek Bronze in Renaissance Venice. *Burlington Magazine, 117*, 204–11.

Petrole, K. & Tzonou-Herbst, I. (2016). Outreach in Ancient Corinth: Educational Enrichment in the United States and Greece. *Archaeological Institute of America 117th Annual Meeting Abstracts*, vol. 39, 161.

Pettegrew, D.K. (2006). *Corinth on the Isthmus: Studies of the End of an Ancient Landscape*. Ph.D. Diss., The Ohio State University.

———. (2007). The Busy Countryside of Late Roman Corinth: Interpreting Ceramic Data Produced by Regional Archaeological Surveys. *Hesperia, 76*, 743–84.

———. (2008). The End of Ancient Corinth? Views from the Landscape. In W.R. Caraher, L.J. Hall and R.S. Moore (eds), *Archaeology and History in Roman, Medieval and Post-Medieval Greece: Studies on Method and Meaning in Honor of Timothy E. Gregory*. (pp. 249–66). Aldershot.

———. (2011). The *Diolkos* of Corinth. *AJA, 115*, 549–74.

———. (2014). The Diolkos and the Emporion: How a Land Bridge Framed the Commercial Economy of Roman Corinth. In S.J. Friesen, S.A. James & D.N. Schowalter (eds), *Corinth in Contrast: Studies in Inequality*. (pp. 126–42). Leiden.

———. (2015). Corinthian Suburbia: Patterns of Roman Settlement on the Isthmus. In E.R. Gebhard & T.E. Gregory (eds), *Bridge of the Untiring Sea: The Corinthian Isthmus from Prehistory to Late Antiquity. Hesperia* Supplement 48. (pp. 289–310). Princeton.

———. (2016). *The Isthmus of Corinth: Crossroads of the Mediterranean World*. Ann Arbor.

Pickett, J. (2017). Water and Empire in the *de Aedificiis* of Procopius. *DOP, 70*.

Pfaff, C.A. (1999). The Early Iron Age Pottery from the Sanctuary of Demeter and Kore at Corinth. *Hesperia, 68*, 55–134.

———. (2003). Archaic Corinthian Architecture ca. 600 to 480 B.C. In C.K. Williams, II & N. Bookidis (eds), *Corinth, the Centenary: 1896–1996* (*Corinth* XX). (pp. 95–140). Princeton.

———. (2007). Geometric Graves in the Panayia Field at Corinth. *Hesperia, 76*, 443–537.

Pharr, C. (trans.). (1952). *The Theodosian Code and Novels and the Sirmondian Constitutions*. Princeton.

Philadelpheus, A. (1921a). Ἀρχαία ἐπαυλὶς μετὰ νυμφαίου ἐν Λεχαίῳ τῆς Κορινθίας. *ArchDelt, 4* (1918), 125–35.

———. (1921b). Εὐπρεπισμὸς καὶ νέα προκτήματα τοῦ Μουσείου Κορίνθου. *ArchDelt, 4* (1918), 1–9.

———. (1924). Βυζαντινὰ ἀγγεῖα ἐκ τῶν ἀνασκαφῶν Παλαιᾶς Κορίνθου. *DCAE, 1*, 22–47.

Philippson, A. (1892). *Der Peloponnes: Versuch einer Landeskunde auf geologischer Grundlage*. Berlin.

———. (1948). *Das Klima Griechenlands*. Bonn.

Pickard-Cambridge, A.W. (1968). *The Dramatic Festivals of Athens* (2nd rev. ed.), Gould, J. & Lewis, D.M. (eds). Oxford.

Pietri, C. (1976). *Roma Christiana: Recherches sur l'Eglise de Rome, son organisation, sa politique, son idéologie de Miltiade à Sixte III (311–440)*. Rome.

Pietrogrande, A.L. (ed.). (1977). *Le fulloniche*. Rome.

Pirazzoli, P.A. (1988). Sea-level Changes and Crustal Movements in the Hellenic Arc (Greece): The Contribution of Archaeological and Historical Data. *BAR International Series*, 404, 157–184.

Pirazzoli, P.A. et al. (1994). Episodic Uplift Deduced from Holocene Shorelines in the Perachora Peninsula, Corinth Area, Greece. *Tectonophysics, 229*, 201–9.

Poehlman, W. (1981). The Polycharmos Inscription and Synagogue I at Stobi. In A. Blaksova & J.R. Wiseman (eds), *Studies in the Antiquities of Stobi 3*. (pp. 235–48). Titov Veles.

Pollini, J. (1987). *The Portraiture of Gaius and Lucius Caesar*. New York.

———. (2007). Christian Destruction and Mutilation of the Parthenon. *AthMitt 122*, 207–28.

———. (2008). The Imperial Cult in the East: Images of Power and the Power of Intolerance. In Y.Z. Eliav, E.A. Friedland & S. Herbert (eds), *The Sculptural Environment of the Roman Near East: Reflections on Culture, Ideology, and Power*. (pp. 165–96). Leuven.

Pomeroy, S.B. (2007). *The Murder of Regilla: A Case of Domestic Violence in Antiquity*. Cambridge, Mass.

Potter, D.S. & Mattingly, D.J. (eds). (1999). *Life, Death, and Entertainment in the Roman Empire*. Ann Arbor.

Poulter, A.G. & Blagg, T.F.C. (1995). *Nicopolis ad Istrum: A Roman, Late Roman and Early Byzantine City: Excavations, 1985–1992* (*JRS Monographs* 8). London.

Pouqueville, F.C.H.L. (1805). *Voyage en Morée et à Constantinople*. Paris.

Powell, B. (1903). Greek Inscriptions from Corinth. *AJA*, *7*, 26–71.

———. (1905). The Temple of Apollo at Corinth. *AJA*, *9*, 44–63.

Prentice, W.K. (1908). *Greek and Latin Inscriptions* (*Publications of an American Archaeological Expedition to Syria 1899–1900* 3). New York.

Pretzler, M. (2004a). Pausanias: Another Turn-of-the-Century Boom? *Hermathena*, *176*, 39–57.

———. (2004b). Turning Travel into Text: Pausanias at Work. *Greece & Rome*, *51*, 235–49.

———. (2005a). Pausanias and Oral Tradition. *The Cambridge Quarterly*, *55*, 199–216.

———. (2005b). Strabo and Pausanias: Approaches towards history and geography of Greece. In D. Dueck, H. Lindsay, & S. Pothecary (eds), *Strabo's Cultural Geography: The Making of a Kolossourgia*. (pp. 144–60). Cambridge.

———. (2007a). Pausanias' Intellectual Background: The Travelling Pepaideumenos. In C. Adams & J. Roy (eds), *Travel, Geography and Culture in Ancient Greece and the Near East*. (pp. 123–38). London.

———. (2007b). *Pausanias. Travel Writing in Ancient Greece*. London.

Price, M.J. (1967). Coins from Some Deposits in the South Stoa at Corinth. *Hesperia*, *36*, 348–88.

Pritchett, W.K. (1969). *Studies in Ancient Greek Topography 2: Battlefields*. Berkeley.

———. (1980). *Studies in Ancient Greek Topography 3: Ancient Greek Roads*. Berkeley.

Puech, B. (1983). Grand-prêtres et helladarques d'Achaïe. *REA*, *85*, 15–43.

Pummer, R. (2002). *Early Christian Authors on Samaritans and Samaritanism: Texts, Translations and Commentary*. Tübingen.

Quast, H.W. (1987). *Geiserich: Vandale ohne Vandalismus*. Gernsbach.

Quentin, H. (1969). *Les martyrologes historiques du moyen âge: étude sur la formation du martyrologe romain* (Reprint. Original ed. Paris 1908). Aalen.

Quinet, E. (1830). *La Grèce moderne et de ses rapports avec l'antiquité*. Paris.

Rackham, O. (1983). Observations on the Historical Ecology of Boeotia. *BSA, 78*, 291–351.

Rackham, O. & Moody, J.A. (1996). *The Making of the Cretan Landscape.* Manchester and New York.

Raepsaet, G. (1993). Le Diolkos de l'isthme à Corinthe: Son tracé, son fonctionnement. *BCH, 117*, 233–56.

Rapp, C. (2005). *Holy Bishops in Late Antiquity: The Nature of Christian Leadership in an Age of Transition* (The Transformation of the Classical Heritage 37). Berkeley.

Rapp, G., Jr. (1986). Assessing Archaeological Evidence for Seismic Catastrophes. *Geoarchaeology, 1*, 365–79.

Ratté, C. (2000). New Research on the Urban Development of Aphrodisias in Late Antiquity. In D. Parrish (ed.), *Urbanism of Roman Asia Minor: The Status of Current Research.* Ann Arbor.

Raubitschek, I.K. (1998). *The Metal Objects (1952–1989)* (*Isthmia* VII). Princeton.

Remijsen, S. (2016). *The End of Athletics in Late Antiquity: Greek Culture in the Roman World.* Cambridge.

Renfrew, C. (1972). *The Emergence of Civilisation: The Cyclades and the Aegean in the Third Millennium B.C.* London.

Reynolds, P. (1995). *Trade in the Western Mediterranean, AD 400–700 AD: The Ceramic Evidence.* Oxford.

Rhodes, R.F. (1984). *The Beginnings of Monumental Architecture in the Corinthia.* Ph.D. Diss., University of North Carolina, Chapel Hill.

———. (1987a). Early Corinthian Architecture and the Origins of the Doric Order. *AJA, 91*, 477–80.

———. (1987b). Early Stoneworking in the Corinthia. *Hesperia, 56*, 229–32.

———. (1987c). Rope Channels and Stone Quarrying in the Early Corinthia. *AJA, 91*, 545–51.

Riccardi, L.A. (1998). The Mutilation of the Bronze Portrait of a Severan Empress From Sparta: "*Damnatio Memoriae*" Or Christian Iconoclasm? *RM 113*, 259–69.

———. (2007). The Bust-Crown, the Panhellenion, and Eleusis: A New Portrait from the Athenian Agora. *Hesperia, 76*, 365–90.

———. (2008). Emperors as Conquerors and the Barbarians Beneath Their Feet: A New Example from the Athenian Agora. *109th AIA Annual Meeting Abstracts*, Vol. 31. Boston.

Richardson, R.B. (1896). Notes from Corinth. *AJA, 11*, 371–2.

———. (1897). The Excavations at Corinth in 1896. *AJA, 1*, 455–80.

———. (1898). The Excavations at Corinth in 1898: Preliminary Report. *AJA, 2*, 233–6.

———. (1900a). The Fountain of Glauce at Corinth. *AJA, 4*, 458–75.

———. (1900b). Pirene. *AJA, 4*, 204–39.

———. (1902a). An Ancient Fountain in the Agora of Corinth. *AJA, 6*, 306–20.

———. (1902b). A Series of Colossal Statues at Corinth. *AJA, 6*, 7–22.

———. (1904). A Group of Dionysiac Sculptures Found at Corinth. *AJA, 8*, 288–96.

Richter, G.M.A. (1965). *The Portraits of the Greeks.* London.

Rickman, G. (1971). *Roman Granaries and Store Buildings*. Cambridge.
Ridgway, B.S. (1981). Sculpture at Corinth. *Hesperia, 50,* 422–48.
Ridley, R.T. (1969). Eunapius and Zosimus. *Helikon, 9/10,* 574–92.
———. (1972). Zosimus the Historian. *BZ, 65,* 277–302.
———. (trans.). (1982). *Zosimus: New History*. Canberra.
Rife, J.L. (2008). Leo's Peloponnesian Fire-Tower and the Byzantine Watch-Tower on Acrocorinth. In W.R. Caraher, L.J. Hall & R.S. Moore (eds), *Archaeology and History in Roman, Medieval and Post-Medieval Greece: Studies on Method and Meaning in Honor of Timothy E. Gregory*. (pp. 281–306). Aldershot.
———. (2010). Religion and Society at Roman Kenchreai. In S.J. Friesen, D.N. Schowalter & J.C. Walters (eds), *Corinth in Context: Comparative Studies on Religion and Society*. (pp. 391–432). Leiden.
———. (2012). *The Roman and Byzantine Graves and Human Remains* (*Isthmia* IX). Princeton.
Rife, J., Dunn, R.K., Morison, M.M., Ubelaker, D.H., Barbet, A. & Monier, F. (2007). Life and Death at a Port in Roman Greece: The Kenchreai Cemetery Project, 2002–6. *Hesperia, 76,* 143–81.
Rizakis, A.D. (1995). *Achaie I: Sources textuelles et histoire regionale. Meletemata* 20. Athens.
———. (2010). Peloponnesian Cities under Roman Rule: the new political geography and its economic and social repercussions. In A.D. Rizakis & Cl.E. Lepenioti (eds), *Roman Peloponnese III: Society, Economy and Culture under the Roman Empire: Continuity and Innovation. Meletemata* 63. (pp. 1–18). Athens.
Rizakis, A.D. & Lepenioti, Cl.E. (eds). (2010). *Roman Peloponnese III: Society, Economy and Culture under the Roman Empire: Continuity and Innovation. Meletemata* 63. Athens.
Rizakis, A.D. & Zoumbaki, S. (2001). *Roman Peloponnese I: Roman Personal Names in their Social Context (Achaia, Arcadia, Argolis, Corinthia and Eleia)*. Athens.
Robert, L. (ed.). (1940). *Hellenica. Recueil d'épigraphie de numismatique et d'antiquités grecques*. Limoges.
———. (1966). Inscriptions de l'antiquité et du bas-empire à Corinthe. *RÉG, 79,* 733–70.
———. (1971). *Les gladiateurs dans l'Orient grec* (Reprint. Original ed. Paris 1940). Amsterdam.
Roberts, S.C. & Jackson, J.A. (1991). Active Normal Faulting in Central Greece: An Overview. In A.M. Roberts, G. Yielding, & B. Freeman (eds), *The Geometry of Normal Faults*. (pp. 125–42). London.
Robinson, B.A. (2000). The Fountain of Peirene at Corinth: A Fresh Look at the Triconch Court. *AJA, 104,* 326.
———. (2001). *Fountains and the Culture of Water at Roman Corinth*. Ph.D. Diss., University of Pennsylvania.
———. (2011). *Histories of Peirene: A Corinthian Fountain in Three Millennia*. Princeton.
———. (2012). "Good Luck from Corinth": A Mosaic of Allegory, Athletics, and City Identity. *AJA, 116,* 105–32.
———. (2013). Hydraulic Euergetism: American Archaeology and Waterworks in Early-20th-Century Greece. *Hesperia, 82,* 101–30.

Robinson, H.S. (1943). The Tower of the Winds and the Roman Market-Place. *AJA, 47*, 291–305.
———. (1962). Excavations at Ancient Corinth, 1960. *Hesperia, 31*, 95–133.
——— (1965a). Excavations at Corinth. *ArchDelt, 18* (1963), 76–80.
——— (1965b). *The Urban Development of Ancient Corinth*. Athens.
——— (1966). American Excavations at Corinth. *ArchDelt, 19* (1964), 100–2.
——— (1967). Excavations in Corinth, 1964. *ArchDelt, 20* (1965), 144–5.
——— (1968a). Excavations at Corinth. *ArchDelt, 21* (1966), 133–41.
——— (1968b). Church of Haghia Paraskevi, Ancient Corinth. *ArchDelt, 22* (1967), 218–19.
——— (1969a). Chiron at Corinth. *AJA, 73*, 193–7.
——— (1969b). *Corinth: A Brief History of the City and a Guide to the Excavations* (Rev. Original ed., 1964). Athens.
——— (1969c). A Sanctuary and Cemetery in Western Corinth. *Hesperia, 38*, 1–35.
——— (1972). A Green-Glazed 'Modiolus' from Kenchreai. *Hesperia, 41*, 355–356.
——— (1974a). A Monument of Roma at Corinth. *Hesperia, 43*, 470–84.
——— (1974b). Excavations on Temple Hill. *ArchDelt, 26* (1971), 96–100.
———. (1976a). Excavations at Corinth: Temple Hill, 1968–72. *Hesperia, 45*, 203–39.
———. (1976b). Temple Hill, Corinth. In U. Jantzen (ed.), *Neue Forschungen in griechischen Heiligtümern*. (pp. 239–60). Tübingen.
Robinson, H.S. & Weinberg, S.S. (1960). Excavations at Corinth, 1959. *Hesperia, 29*, 225–53.
Rocha-Pereira, M.H. (ed.). (1989). *Pausaniae Graeciae Descriptio* (2nd ed.). Leipzig.
Rodenwaldt, G. (1919). Griechische Porträts aus dem Ausgang der Antike. *BWPr, 76*.
Roebuck, C.A. (1951). *The Asklepieion and Lerna* (*Corinth* XIV). Princeton.
Rohrbacher, D. (2002). *The Historians of Late Antiquity*. London.
Romano, D.G. (1993a). *Athletics and Mathematics in Archaic Corinth: The Origins of the Greek Stadion*. Philadelphia.
———. (1993b). Post–146 B.C. Land Use in Corinth, and Planning of the Roman Colony of 44 B.C. In T.E. Gregory (ed.), *The Corinthia in the Roman Period*. (pp. 9–30). Ann Arbor.
———. (1994). Greek Land Division and Planning at Corinth. *AJA, 98*, 296.
———. (1996). Remote Sensing and GIS in the Study of Roman Centuriation in the Corinthia, Greece. In H. Kamermans & K. Fennema (eds), *Interfacing the Past: Computer Applications and Quantitative Methods in Archaeology*. (pp. 457–63). Leiden.
———. (1998a). GIS-Based Analysis of Ancient Land Division in the Corinthia, Greece. In J. Peterson (ed.), *Paysages antiques et structures rurales*. (pp. 21–30). Luxembourg.
———. (1998b). Planning the Forum in Roman Corinth. *AJA, 102*, 377.
———. (2000). A Tale of Two Cities: Roman Colonies at Corinth, Colonia Laus Iulia Corinthiensis, Colonia Iulia Flavia Augusta Corinthiensis. In E. Fentress (ed.), *Romanization and the City: Creation, Transformations, and Failures*. (pp. 83–104). Portsmouth, R.I.

———. (2003). City Planning, Centuriation, and Land Division in Roman Corinth: *Colonia Laus Iulia Corinthiensis* and *Colonia Iulia Flavia Augusta Corinthiensis*. In C.K. Williams, II & N. Bookidis (eds), *Corinth, the Centenary: 1896–1996* (*Corinth* XX). (pp. 279–301). Princeton.

———. (2005). A Roman Circus in Corinth. *Hesperia, 74*, 585–611.

———. (2010). Romanization in the Corinthia: urban and rural developments. In A.D. Rizakis & C.E. Lepenioti (eds), *Roman Peloponnese III: Society, Economy and Culture under the Roman Empire: Continuity and Innovation. Meletemata* 63. (pp. 155–72). Athens.

———. (2013). Roman colonies in the Corinthian landscape. In K. Kissas & W.-D. Niemeier (eds), *The Corinthia and the Northeast Peloponnese: Topography and History from Prehistoric Times until the End of Antiquity*. (pp. 155–60). Munich.

Romano, D.G. & Schoenbrun, B.C. (1993). A Computerized Architectural and Topographical Survey of Ancient Corinth. *JFA, 29*, 177–90.

Romano, D.G. & Stapp, N.L. (1998). Piecing Together the City and Territory of Roman Corinth. *Archaeological Computing Newsletter, Institute of Archaeology, Oxford, 52*, 1–7.

Romano, D.G. & Tolba, O. (1995). Remote Sensing, GIS, and Electronic Surveying: Reconstructing the City Plan and Landscape of Roman Corinth. In J. Huggett & N. Ryan (eds), *Computer Applications and Quantitative Methods in Archaeology 1994*. (pp. 163–74). Oxford.

Rose, C.B. (2005). The Parthians in Augustan Rome. *AJA, 109*, 21–75.

Rothaus, R.M. (1992). Pagans and Christians in Early Byzantine Corinth: The Archaeology of Sacred Space. *Byzantine Studies Conference Abstract, 18*, 72–3.

——— (1994). Urban Space, Agricultural Space and Villas in Late Roman Corinth. In P.N. Doukellis & L.G. Mendoni (eds), *Structures rurales et sociétés antiques*. (pp. 391–6). Paris.

——— (1995). Lechaion, Western Port of Corinth: A Brief Archaeology and History. *OJA, 14*, 293–306.

——— (1996). Earthquakes and Temples in Late Antique Corinth. In S.C. Stiros & R.E. Jones (eds), *Archaeoseismology*. (pp. 105–12). Athens.

——— (2000). *Corinth: The First City of Greece, An Urban History of Late Antique Cult and Religion*. Leiden.

Rothaus, R.M., Reinhardt, E.G., & Noller, J.S. (2008). Earthquakes and Subsidence at Kenchreai: Using Recent Earthquakes to Reconsider the Archaeological and Literary Evidence. In W.R. Caraher, L.J. Hall & R.S. Moore (eds), *Archaeology and History in Roman, Medieval and Post-Medieval Greece: Studies on Method and Meaning in Honor of Timothy E. Gregory*. (pp. 53–66). Aldershot.

Roueché, C. (1989). *Aphrodisias in Late Antiquity: The Late Roman and Byzantine Inscriptions*. Journal of Roman Studies Monographs 5. London.

———. (1993). *Performers and Partisans at Aphrodisias*. London.

———. (1998). The Functions of the Governor in Late Antiquity: Some observations. *Les Gouverneurs de province dans l'antiquite tardive*. (pp. 31–6). Turnhout.

Rougé, J. (ed.). (1966). *Expositio totius mundi et gentium*. Paris.

Roullet, A. (1972). *The Egyptian and Egyptianizing Monuments of Imperial Rome*. Leiden.
Rousset, D., Camp, J., & Minon, S. (2015). The Phokian City of Panopeus/Phanoteus. Three New Rupestral Inscriptions, and the Cippus of the Labyadai of Delphi. *AJA, 119*, 441–63.
Roux, G. (1958). *Pausanias en Corinthie*. Paris.
Rubin, B. (1954). *Prokopios von Kaisareia* (Reprinted *RE* 23.1 (1957)). Stuttgart.
———. (1960). *Das Zeitalter Justinians*. Berlin.
Rubini, M. (2008). La Terribile peste di Giustiniano. *Archeologia Viva, 128*.
Ruebel, J.S. (ed.). (2000). *Apuleius. Metamorphoses Book 1*. Wauconda, Ill.
Russell, J.C. (1968). That Earlier Plague. *Demography, 5*, 174–84.
Sacks, K.S. (1986). The Meaning of Eunapius' History. *History and Theory, 25*, 52–67.
Sakellariou, M. & Faraklas, N. (1971). *Corinthia-Cleonaea* (*Ancient Greek Cities* 3). Athens.
Sallares, R. (1991). *The Ecology of the Ancient Greek World*. Ithaca, N.Y.
Salmon, J.B. (1984). *Wealthy Corinth: A History of the City to 338 B.C.* Oxford.
Sande, S. (1975). Zur Porträtplastik des sechsten nachchristlichen Jahrhunderts. In H.P. L'Orange, P.J. Nordhagen, & M. Malmanger (eds), *Institutum Romanum Norvegiae, Acta ad archaeologiam et artium historiam pertinentia 6*. (pp. 65–106). Rome.
Sanders, G.D.R. (1999). A Late Roman Bath at Corinth: Excavations in the Panayia Field, 1995–6. *Hesperia, 68*, 441–80.
———. (2002a). Corinth. In A.E. Laiou (ed.), *The Economic History of Byzantium: From the Seventh through the Fifteenth Century*. (pp. 2.647–2.654). Washington, D.C.
———. (2002b). Corinth Excavations Explore Two Areas of Panayia Field. *ákoue, 48*, 10,17.
———. (2003a). Corinth Excavations Unearth Geometric Grave in Panayia Field. *ákoue, 49*, 5,15.
———. (2003b). Recent Developments in the Chronology of Byzantine Corinth. In C.K. Williams, II & N. Bookidis (eds), *Corinth, the Centenary: 1896–1996* (*Corinth* XX). (pp. 385–400). Princeton.
———. (2004). Problems in Interpreting Rural and Urban Settlement in Southern Greece, AD 365–700. In N. Christie (ed.), *Landscapes Of Change: Rural Evolutions in Late Antiquity and the Early Middle Ages*. (pp. 163–93). Aldershot.
———. (2005). Archaeological Evidence for Early Christianity and the End of Hellenic Religion in Corinth. In D.N. Schowalter & S.J. Friesen (eds), *Urban Religion in Roman Corinth: Interdisciplinary Approaches*. (pp. 419–42). Cambridge, Mass.
———. (2014). Landlords and Tenants: Sharecroppers and Subsistence Farming in Corinthian Historical Context. In S.J. Friesen, S.A. James & D.N. Schowalter (eds), *Corinth in Contrast: Studies in Inequality*. (pp. 103–25). Leiden.
———. (2016). *Recent Finds from Ancient Corinth: How Little Things Make Big Differences*. Tenth BABESCH Byvanck Lecture. Leiden.

Sanders, G.D.R. & Boyd, M.J. (2008). Moving Homes: A Resistivity Survey of the Late Antique City Wall East of the Forum at Corinth. *109th Annual Meeting Abstracts, Vol. 31*. Boston.

Sanders, G.D.R., James, S.A., & Carter Johnson, A. (2017). *Corinth Excavations Archaeological Manual*. Grand Forks.

Sanders, G.D.R., Palinkas, J. & Tzonou-Herbst, I., with Herbst, J. (forthcoming). *Ancient Corinth: Site Guide. Seventh Edition*. Princeton.

Sanders, G.D.R. & I. Whitbread. (1990). Central Places and Major Roads in the Peloponnese. *BSA, 85*, 333–61.

Saradi, H.G. (2006). *The Byzantine City in the Sixth Century*. Athens.

Sarris, P. (2002). The Justinianic Plague: Origins and Effects. *Continuity and Change, 17*, 169–82.

———. (2004). Rehabilitating the Great Estate: Aristocratic Property and Economic Growth in the Late Antique East. In W. Bowden, L. Lavan, & C. Machado (eds), *Recent Research on the Late Antique Countryside*. (pp. 55–71). Leiden.

———. (2006). *Economy and Society in the Age of Justinian*. Cambridge.

Sauer, E.W. (2003). *The Archaeology of Religious Hatred in the Roman and Early Medieval World*. Stroud.

Saunders, F.S. (1999). *The Cultural Cold War: The CIA and the World of Arts and Letters*. New York.

Scahill, D. (2012). The South Stoa at Corinth: Design, Construction and Function of the Greek Phase. Ph.D. Diss., University of Bath.

Schaff, P. (ed.). (1898). *A Select Library of the Nicene and Post-Nicene Fathers of the Christian Church (NPNF)*. New York.

Scheidel, W. (ed.). (1998). *Cities, Peasants, and Food in Classical Antiquity: Essays in Social and Economic History*. Cambridge.

———. (2002). A Model of Demographic and Economic Change in Roman Egypt after the Antonine Plague. *JRA, 15*, 97–113.

Schliemann, H. (1869). *Ithaka, der Peloponnes und Troja: Archäologische Forschungen*. Leipzig.

Schmeling, G.L. (ed.). (1996). *The Novel in the Ancient World*. Leiden.

Schneider, R.M. (1986). *Bunte Barbaren: Orientalenstatuen aus farbigem Marmor in der römischen Repräsentationskunst*. Worms.

———. (1998). Die Faszination des Feindes: Bilder der Parther und des Orients in Rom. In J. Wiesehöfer (ed.), *Das Partherreich und seine Zeugnisse: The Arsacid Empire: Sources and Documentation*. (pp. 95–146). Stuttgart.

Schönberger, R. (1969). The Roman Frontier in Germany: An Archaeological Survey. *JRS, 59*, 144–97.

Schowalter, D.N. (2010). Seeking Shelter in Roman Corinth: Archaeology and the Placement of Paul's Communities. In S.J. Friesen, D.N. Schowalter & J.C. Walters (eds), *Corinth in Context: Comparative Studies on Religion and Society*. (pp. 327–42). Leiden.

———. (2014). Regilla Standing By: Reconstructed Statuary and Re-inscribed Bases in Fourth-Century Corinth. In S.J. Friesen, S.A. James & D.N. Schowalter (eds), *Corinth in Contrast: Studies in Inequality*. (pp. 166–83). Leiden.

Schowalter, D.N. & Friesen, S.J. (eds). (2005). *Urban Religion in Roman Corinth: Interdisciplinary Approaches*. Cambridge, Mass.

Schürer, E. (1973). *The History of the Jewish People in the Age of Jesus Christ (175 B.C.–A.D. 135)*. Edinburgh.
Scorza, G. (1934). Il Peripatetico Cameleonte. *Rivista Indo-Greco-Italica di filologia-lingua-antiquità, 18*, 1–48.
Scott, R. (1987). Justinian's Coinage and Easter Reforms, and the Date of the *Secret History*. *BMGS, 11*, 215–21.
Scotton, P.D. (1997). *The Julian Basilica at Corinth: An Architectural Investigation*. Ph.D. Diss., University of Pennsylvania.
———. (2002). Scotton on Rothaus on Scotton on Rothaus. *Bryn Mawr Classical Review* 2002.10.31.
———. (2005). A New Fragment of an Inscription from the Julian Basilica at Roman Corinth. *Hesperia, 74*, 95–100.
———. (2015). A Sixth-Century Church in Corinth. *Archaeological Institute of America 116th Annual Meeting Abstracts, vol. 38*, 61–2. New Orleans.
———. (2016a). The Antonine Julian Basilica in Corinth. *Archaeological Institute of America 117th Annual Meeting Abstracts, vol. 39*, 162. San Francisco.
———. (2016b). The Julian Basilica at Corinth and Its Possible Commercial Use. In U. Fellmeth, J. Krüger, K. Ohr and J.J. Rasch (eds), *Wirtschaftsbauten in der antiken Stadt*. (pp. 125–134). Karlsruhe.
Scotton, P.D. & Vanderpool, C. de G., with C. Roncaglia. (forthcoming). *The Julian Basilica: An Architectural, Epigraphical, and Sculptural Investigation*. Princeton.
Scranton, R.L. (1944). Two Temples of Commodus at Corinth. *Hesperia, 13*, 315–48.
———. (1951). *Monuments in the Lower Agora and North of the Archaic Temple* (*Corinth* I.3). Princeton.
———. (1957). *Mediaeval Architecture in the Central Area of Corinth* (*Corinth* XVI). Princeton.
———. (1965). Excavation at Kenchreai. *CJ, 61*, 6–8.
———. (1967). Glass Pictures from the Sea. *Archaeology, 20*, 163–73.
Scranton, R.L. & Ramage, E.S. (1964). Investigations at Kenchreai, 1963. *Hesperia, 33*, 134–45.
———. (1967). Investigations at Corinthian Kenchreai. *Hesperia, 36*, 124–86.
Scranton, R.L., Shaw, J.W., & Ibrahim, L. (1978). *Topography and Architecture* (*Kenchreai* 1). Leiden.
Sears, J.M., Jr. (1902). The Lechaeum Road and the Propylaea at Corinth. *AJA, 6*, 439–54.
Segal, A. (1997). *From Function to Monument: Urban Landscapes of Roman Palestine, Syria and Provincia Arabia*. Oxbow Monograph 66. Oxford.
Seibel, V. (1857). *Die grosse Pest zur Zeit Justinians I. und die ihr voraus und zur seite gehenden ungewöhnlichen Natur-Ereignisse: Ein Beitrag zur Geschichte des sechsten Jh. christl. Zeitrechnung*. Dilingen.
Seltman, C.T. (1928). Miscellanea: The Sculptor Hermogenes of Cythera. *NC, 8*, 98–9.
Setton, K.M. (1950). The Bulgars in the Balkans and the Occupation of Corinth in the Seventh Century. *Speculum, 25*, 502–43.
Sevcenko, I. (1981). Levels of Style in Byzantine Prose. *JÖB, 31*, 289–312.

Sevcenko, N.P. (1990). *Illustrated Manuscripts of the Metaphrastian Menologion*. Chicago.
Seymour, T.D. (1902). The First Twenty Years of the ASCSA. *Bulletin of the American School of Classical Studies at Athens, 5*.
Shaw, J.W. (1967a). A Double-Sheaved Pulley Block from Kenchreai. *Hesperia, 36*, 389–401.
———. (1967b). Shallow-Water Excavation at Kenchreai. *AJA, 71*, 223–31.
———. (1969). A Foundation in the Inner Harbor at Lechaeum. *AJA, 73*, 370–2.
———. (1970). Shallow-Water Excavation at Kenchreai: II. *AJA, 74*, 179–80.
———. (1972). Greek and Roman Harbourworks. In G.F. Bass (ed.), *A History of Seafaring Based on Underwater Archaeology*. (pp. 100–105). New York.
Shear, T.L. (1925). Excavations at Corinth in 1925. *AJA, 29*, 391–7.
———. (1926). Excavations in the Theatre District of Corinth in 1926. *AJA, 30*, 444–63.
———. (1928a). Color at Corinth. *AJA, 32*, 330–2.
———. (1928b). Excavations in the Theatre District and Tombs of Corinth in 1928. *AJA, 32*, 474–95.
———. (1929). Excavations in the Theatre District and Tombs of Corinth in 1929. *AJA, 33*, 515–46.
———. (1930). Excavations in the North Cemetery at Corinth in 1930. *AJA, 34*, 403–31.
———. (1930). *The Roman Villa* (*Corinth* V). Cambridge, Mass.
———. (1931a). The Excavation of Roman Chamber Tombs at Corinth in 1931. *AJA, 35*, 424–41.
———. (1931b). A Hoard of Coins Found in the Theatre District of Corinth in 1930. *AJA, 35*, 139–51.
Shear, T.L., Jr. (1973). The Athenian Agora: Excavations of 1971. *Hesperia, 42*, 121–79.
Shelley, J.M. (1943). The Christian Basilica near the Cenchrean Gate at Corinth. *Hesperia, 12*, 166–89.
Shumate, N. (1996). *Crisis and Conversion in Apuleius' Metamorphoses*. Ann Arbor.
Signes Codoñer, J. (2000). *Procopio de Cesarea. Historia Secreta*. Madrid.
———. (2003). Prokops Anekdota und Justinians Nachfolge. *JÖBG, 53*, 47–82.
Simopoulos, K. (1979). *Πως είδαν οι ξένοι την Ελλάδα του '21*. Athens.
———. (1984–5). *Ξένοι ταξιδιώτες στην Ελλάδα*. Athens.
Simpson, R.H. (1965). *A Gazetteer and Atlas of Mycenaean Sites*. London.
Sinn, U. (1991). 'Ο Νέρωνας' και 'οι Έρουλοι': δύο μοιραία γεγονότα στην ιστορία της Ολυμπίας? In A.D. Rizakis (ed.), *Αρχαία Αχαΐα και Ηλεία, Achaia und Elis in der Antike*. (pp. 365–71). Athens.
Sironen, E. (1992). The Edict of Diocletian and a Theodosian Regulation at Corinth. *Hesperia, 61*, 223–6.
———. (1994). Life and Administration of Late Roman Attica in the Light of Public Inscriptions. In P. Castrén (ed.), *Post-Herulian Athens: Aspects of Life and Culture in Athens, A.D. 267–529*. (pp. 15–62). Helsinki.

———. (1995). Statue Base Epigrams in Honor of a Restorer from Early Byzantine Athens. *Arctos, 29*, 163–73.

———. (1997). Formulae in Early Christian Epitaphs of Corinthia. *XI Congresso internazionale di epigrafia greca e latina (Preatti)*. (pp. 741–5). Rome.

———. (2001). Lateinische Ehreninschriften für Constantin den Grossen und seine Nachfolger und andere Inschriften der Spätzeit aus Attika. *ZPE, 136*, 257–66.

———. (2008). *Inscriptiones Graecae* II/III, 2nd edition. *Inscriptiones Atticae Euclidis anno posteriores pars* 5. *Inscriptiones Atticae aetatis quae est inter Heulorum incursionem et Imp. Mauricii tempora*. Berlin. = *IG* II/III^2 5.

———. (2016). *Inscriptiones Graecae* IV, 2nd edition. *Inscriptiones Argolidis fasciculus* 3. *Inscriptiones Corinthiae saeculorum IV. V. VI*. Berlin. = *IG* IV^2 3.

Skias, A.N. (1894). Ἀνασκαφαὶ ἐν Κορίνθῳ. *Prakt, 1892*, 109–36.

———. (1907). Ἀνασκαφαὶ ἐν Κορίνθῳ. *Prakt, 1906*, 145–66.

Sklavou Mavroeide, M. (1999). *Γλυπτά του Βυζαντινού Μουσείου Αθηνών*. Athens.

Slane, K.W. (1987). Roman Pottery from East of the Theater: Quantifying the Assemblages. *AJA, 91*, 483–5.

———. (1990). *The Sanctuary of Demeter and Kore: The Roman Pottery and Lamps* (*Corinth* XVIII.2). Princeton.

———. (1994). Tetrarchic Recovery in Corinth: Pottery, Lamps and Other Finds from the Peribolos of Apollo. *Hesperia, 63*, 127–68.

———. (2000). East-West Trade in Fine Wares and Commodities. The View from Corinth. *Rei Cretariae Romanae Fautorum Acta, 36*, 299–312.

———. (2003). Corinth's Roman Pottery: Quantification and Meaning. In C.K. Williams, II & N. Bookidis (eds), *Corinth, the Centenary: 1896–1996* (*Corinth* XX). (pp. 321–35). Princeton.

———. (2004). Amphoras – used and re-used – at Corinth. In J.J. Eiring & J. Lund (eds), *Transport Amphorae and Trade in the Eastern Mediterranean*. Athens.

———. (2012). Remaining Roman in Death at an Eastern Colony. *JRA*, 25, 442–55.

———. (2015). Tombs, Burials, and Commemoration in Corinth's North Cemetery. *Archaeological Institute of America 116th Annual Meeting Abstracts, vol. 38*, 120. New Orleans.

———. (2017). *Tombs, Burials, and Commemoration in Corinth's North Cemetery* (*Corinth* XXI). Princeton.

Slane, K.W. & Sanders, G.D.R. (2005). Corinth: Late Roman Horizons. *Hesperia, 74*, 243–97.

Slootjes, D. (2006). *The Governor and his Subjects in the Later Roman Empire*. Leiden and Boston.

Slusser, M. (trans.). (1998). *St. Gregory Thaumaturgus: Life and Works*. Washington, D.C.

Smith, D.E. (1977). The Egyptian Cults at Corinth. *HTR, 70*, 200–31.

Smith, R.R.R. (1990). Late Roman Philosopher Portraits from Aphrodisias. *JRS, 80*, 127–55.

———. (1999). Late Antique Portraits in a Public Context: Honorific Statuary at Aphrodisias in Caria, AD 300–600. *JRS, 89*, 155–89.

———. (2001). A Portrait Monument for Julian and Theodosius at Aphrodisias. In C. Reusser (ed.), *Griechenland in der Kaiserzeit: Neue Funde und Forschungen zu Skulptur, Architektur und Topographie*. Zurich.

———. (2002). The Statue Monument of Oecumenius: A New Portrait of a Late Antique Governor From Aphrodisias. *JRS, 92*, 134–156.

———. (2007). Statue Life in the Hadrianic Baths at Aphrodisias, AD 100–600: Local Context and Historical Meaning. In F.A. Bauer & C. Witschel (eds), *Statuen in der Spätantike*. (pp. 203–35). Wiesbaden.

———. (2012). Defacing the Gods at Aphrodisias. In B. Dignas & R.R.R. Smith (eds), *Historical and Religious Memory in the Ancient World*. (pp. 283–326). Oxford.

Smith, R.R.R., Dillon, S., Hallett, C.H., Lenaghan, J. & van Voorhis, J. (2006). *Roman Portrait Statuary from Aphrodisias*. Mainz.

Smith, R.R.R. & Ward-Perkins, B. (eds). (2016). *The Last Statues of Antiquity*. Oxford.

Snively, C.S. (1984). Cemetery Churches in the Early Byzantine Period in Eastern Illyricum. *Greek Orthodox Theological Review, 29*, 117–24.

Snodgrass, A.M. (1987). *An Archaeology of Greece: The Present State and Future Scope of a Discipline*. Berkeley.

Snyder, L.M. & Williams, C.K., II. (1997). Frankish Corinth: 1996. *Hesperia, 66*, 7–47.

Sodini, J.-P. (1984). La sculpture architecturale à l'époque paléochrétien en Illyricum. In D.I. Pallas (ed.), *Actes du Xe Congrès international d'archéologie chrétienne: Thessalonique, 28 septembre–4 octobre, 1980*. (Vol. 1, pp. 207–98). Vatican City.

Soles, M.E.C. (1976). *Aphrodite at Corinth: A Study of the Sculptural Types*. Ph.D. Diss., Yale University.

Sourlas, D. (2013). The Monument within the Monument: Preliminary Results of the Excavation at the "Aiolos" Hotel in Plaka, Athens. In L.M. Caliò, E. Lippolis & V. Parisi (eds), *Gli Ateniesi e il loro modello di città. Seminari di Storia e Archeologia greca I, Roma 25–26 giugno 2012. Thiasos* 5. (pp. 293–300). Rome.

Spaeth, B. (2011). Imperial Cult in Roman Corinth: A Response to "The Cult of the Roman Emperor: Uniter or Divider by Karl Galinsky." In J. Reed & J. Brodd (eds), *Rome and Religion: A Cross-Disciplinary Dialogue on the Imperial Cult*. (pp. 61–82). Atlanta.

Spawforth, A.J.S. (1994). Corinth, Argos and the Imperial Cult: Pseudo-Julian, Letters 198. *Hesperia, 63*, 211–32.

———. (1995). C. Iulius Spartiaticus, "First of the Achaeans": A Correction. *Hesperia, 64*, 225.

Spieser, J.-M. (1982). La ville en Grèce du IIIe au VIIe siècle. *Villes et peuplement dans l'Illyricum protobyzantin*. (pp. 315–40). Rome.

———. (1984). *Thessalonique et ses monuments du IVe au VIe siècle: Contribution a l'étude d'une ville paléochrétienne*. Athens.

———. (2001). Ambrose's Foundations at Milan and the Question of Martyria. *Urban and Religious Spaces in Late Antiquity and Early Byzantium*. (Translation of *DCAE* 20 (1998) 29–34). (pp. 1–12). Aldershot.

Spiro, M. (1978). *Critical Corpus of the Mosaic Pavements on the Greek Mainland, Fourth-Sixth Centuries*. New York.
Starr, J. (1936). Epitaph of a Dyer in Corinth. *BNJ, 12*, 42–9.
Stathakopoulos, D. (2000). The Justinianic Plague Revisited. *BMGS, 24*, 256–76.
———. (2003). Reconstructing the Climate of the Byzantine World: State of the Question and Case Studies. In J. Laszlovszky & P. Szabó (eds), *People and Nature in Historical Perspective*. Budapest.
———. (2004). *Famine and Pestilence in the Late Roman and Early Byzantine Empire: A Systematic Survey of Subsistence Crises and Epidemics*. Aldershot.
Stefanidou-Tiveriou, T. (1987–90). Ο Καλός Ποιμένας της Προκοννήσου. *Αφιερωμένο στην 8ή επέτειο των γενεθλίων του καθηγητού Γεωργίου Μπακαλάκη*. (pp. 247–83). Athens.
———. (1993a). Späte attische Sarkophage und das Ende der attischen Werkstätten. In G. Koch (ed.), *Grabeskunst der römischen Kaiserzeit*. (pp. 133–40). Mainz.
———. (1993b). *Τραπεζοφόρα με πλαστική διακόσμηση. Η Αττική ομάδα*. Athens.
———. (2008). Ein Beamter und ein Philosoph ais dem spätantiken Thessaloniki. *Archaeologia Adriatica, 11*, 659–69.
Stein, E. (1949). *Histoire du Bas-Empire*. Paris.
Stein, F.J. (1957). *Dexippus et Herodianus rerum scriptores quatenus Thucydidem secuti sint*. Bonn.
Steinhauer, G. (2010). C. Iulius Eurycles and the Spartan Dyasty of the Euryclids. In A.D. Rizakis & Cl. E. Lepenioti (eds), *Roman Peloponnese III: Society, Economy and Culture under the Roman Empire: Continuity and Innovation. Meletemata* 63. (pp. 75–88). Athens.
Stern, W.O. & Thimme, D.H. (2007). *Ivory, Bone, and Related Wood Finds* (*Kenchreai* 6). Leiden.
Stevens, G.P. (1934). The Fountain of Peirene in the Time of Herodes Atticus. *AJA, 38*, 55–8.
Stewart, A. (2013). Sculptors' Sketches, Trial Pieces, Figure Studies, and Models in Poros Limestone from the Athenian Agora. *Hesperia, 82*, 615–50.
Stewart, P. (1999). The destruction of statues in Late Antiquity. In R. Miles (ed.), *Constructing Identities in Late Antiquity*. (pp. 159–89). London.
———. (2003). *Statues in Roman Society*. Oxford.
———. (2007). Continuity and Tradition in Late Antique Perceptions of Portrait Statuary. In F.A. Bauer & C. Witschel (eds), *Statuen in der Spätantike*. (pp. 27–42). Wiesbaden.
Stikas, E.G. (1964). Κοιμητηριακή βασιλική Παλαιᾶς Κορίνθου. *Prakt, 1961*, 129–36.
———. (1965). La basilique céméteriale récemment découverte à Corinthe. *Atti del VI congresso internazionale di archeologia cristiana (Ravenna 1962)*. (pp. 471–9). Vatican City.
———. (1966). Ἀνασκαφὴ κοιμητηριακὴ βασιλικὴ Παλαιᾶς Κορίνθου. *Prakt, 1962*, 51–6.
Stillwell, R. (1952). *The Theatre* (*Corinth* II). Princeton.

Stillwell, R., Scranton, R.L., & Freeman, S.E. (1941). *Architecture* (*Corinth* I.2). Cambridge, Mass.
Stirling, L.M. (2005). *The Learned Collector: Mythological Statuettes and Classical Taste in Late Antique Gaul.* Ann Arbor.
———. (2008). Pagan Statuettes in Late Antique Corinth: Sculpture from the Panayia Domus. *Hesperia, 77*, 89–161.
Stiros, S.C. (1988). Earthquake Effects on Ancient Constructions. In R.E. Jones & H.W. Catling (eds), *New Aspects of Archaeological Science in Greece*. (pp. 1–6). Athens.
Stiros, S.C. et al. (1996). On the Date of Construction of Lechaion, Western Harbor of Ancient Corinth, Greece. *Geoarchaeology, 11*, 251–63.
Stiros, S.C. & Pirazzoli, P.A. (1995). Palaeoseismic Studies in Greece: A Review. *Quaternary International, 25*, 57–63.
Stoneman, R. (1987). *Land of Lost Gods: The Search for Classical Greece.* London.
Storey, G.R. (1999). Archaeology and Roman Society: Integrating Textual and Archaeological Data. *Journal of Archaeological Research, 7*, 203–48.
Stothers, R. & Rampino, M. (1983). Volcanic Eruptions in the Mediterranean before AD 630 from Written and Archaeological Sources. *Journal of Geophysical Research, 88*, 6357–71.
Strong, R.A. (1997). *The Most Shameful Practice: Temple Prostitution in the Ancient Greek World.* Ph.D. Diss., University of California, Los Angeles.
Stroud, R.S. (1965). The Sanctuary of Demeter and Kore on Acrocorinth Preliminary Report I: 1961–2. *Hesperia, 34*, 1–24.
———. (1968). The Sanctuary of Demeter and Kore on Acrocorinth, Preliminary Report II: 1964–5. *Hesperia, 37*, 299–330.
———. (1971). An Ancient Fort on Mount Oneion. *Hesperia, 40*, 127–45.
———. (1972). Greek Inscriptions at Corinth. *Hesperia, 41*, 198–217.
———. (1985). Review: Salmon, *Wealthy Corinth. AJA, 89*, 697–9.
———. (1993). The Sanctuary of Demeter on Acrocorinth in the Roman Period. In T.E. Gregory (ed.), *The Corinthia in the Roman Period.* (pp. 65–74). Ann Arbor.
———. (2013). *The Sanctuary of Demeter and Kore: The Inscriptions*. (*Corinth* XVIII.6). Princeton.
———. (2014). Religion and Magic in Roman Corinth. In S.J. Friesen, S.A. James & D.N. Schowalter (eds), *Corinth in Contrast: Studies in Inequality*. (pp. 187–202). Leiden.
Sturgeon, M.C. (1975). A New Group of Sculptures from Ancient Corinth. *Hesperia, 44*, 280–301.
———. (1977). *Sculpture: The Reliefs from the Theater* (*Corinth* IX.2). Princeton.
———. (1987). *Sculpture I: 1952–1967* (*Isthmia* IV). Princeton.
———. (1997). The Corinth Theater Sculptures: Self–Presentation of the Roman City. *AJA, 101*, 380.
———. (1998a). Hellenistic Sculpture at Corinth: The State of the Question. In O. Palagia & W.D.E. Coulson (eds), *Regional Schools in Hellenistic Sculpture*. (pp. 1–13). Oxford.
———. (1998b). Hellenistic Sculptures in Ancient Corinth. *AJA, 102*, 408.

———. (1998c). A Peloponnesian Aphrodite: The Corinth Theater Type. In K. Hartswick & M.C. Sturgeon (eds), *Στέφανος: Studies in Honor of Brunilde Sismondo Ridgway*. (pp. 223–33). Philadelphia.

———. (2003). Sculpture at Corinth, 1896–1996. In C.K. Williams, II & N. Bookidis (eds), *Corinth, the Centenary: 1896–1996* (*Corinth* XX). (pp. 351–68). Princeton.

———. (2004). *The Assemblage from the Theater* (*Corinth* IX.3). Princeton.

———. (2015). New Sculptures from the Isthmian Palaimonion. In E.R. Gebhard & T.E. Gregory (eds), *Bridge of the Untiring Sea: The Corinthian Isthmus from Prehistory to Late Antiquity*. *Hesperia* Supplement 48. (pp. 159–92). Princeton.

Sullivan, C.T. (1975). *The Architecture of the Egyptian Cult in Roman Italy*. Ph.D. Diss., U.C. Berkeley.

Swain, S. (1996). *Hellenism and Empire: Language, Classicism and Power in the Greek World, A.D. 50–250*. Oxford.

Swain, S. (ed.). (2000). *Dio Chrysostom: Politics, Letters, and Philosophy*. Oxford.

Sweetman, R.J. (2015). Memory, Tradition, and Christianization of the Peloponnese. *AJA*, *119*, 501–31.

Sweetman, R. & Sanders, G.D.R. (2005). A New Group of Mosaics from Corinth in their Domestic Context and in the Context of the Colony. In H. Morlier (ed.), *Colloque international pour l'étude de la mosaïque antique (09.2001 Rome)*. (pp. 359–69). Rome.

Swift, E.H. (1916). Marble Head from Corinth. *AJA*, *20*, 350–5.

———. (1921a). A Group of Roman Imperial Portraits at Corinth, I: Augustus. *AJA*, *25*, 142–59.

———. (1921b). A Group of Roman Imperial Portraits at Corinth, II: Tiberius. *AJA*, *25*, 248–65.

———. (1921c). A Group of Roman Imperial Portraits at Corinth, III: Gaius and Lucius Caesar. *AJA*, *25*, 337–63.

———. (1922). A Group of Roman Imperial Portraits at Corinth, IV: The Four Torsos. *AJA*, *26*, 131–47.

———. (1923). *Imagines* in Imperial Portraiture. *AJA*, *27*, 286–301.

———. (1934). Byzantine Gold Mosaics. *AJA*, *38*, 81–2.

———. (1935). Latins at Hagia Sophia. *AJA*, *39*, 458–74.

———. (1940). *Hagia Sophia*. New York.

———. (1951). *Roman Sources of Christian Art*. New York.

———. (1958). Review of *Corinth* XVI. *AJA*, *62*, 352–3.

Swinglehurst, E. (1982). *Cook's Tours: The Story of Popular Travel*. Poole.

Sydow, W. von. (1969). *Zur Kunstgeschichte des spätantiken Porträts im 4. Jhr. n. Chr.* Leiden.

Syme, R. (1971). *Emperors and Biography: Studies in the "Historia Augusta"*. Oxford.

Talbert, R.J.A. (2010). *Rome's World: The Peutinger Map Reconsidered*. Cambridge.

Tartaron, T.F. et al. (2006). The Eastern Korinthia Archaeological Survey: Integrated Methods for a Dynamic Landscape. *Hesperia*, *75*, 453–523.

Tartaron, T.F. et al. (2011). The Saronic Harbors Archaeological Research Project (SHARP): Investigations at Mycenaean Kalamianos, 2007–9. *Hesperia*, *80*, 559–634.

Tartaron, T.F. & Pullen, D.J. (2008). The Saronic Harbors Archaeological Research Project (SHARP): Report on the First Season, 2007. *109th AIA Annual Meeting Abstracts, Vol. 31*. Boston.

Tartaron, T.F., Pullen, D.J., & Noller, J.S. (2006). Rillenkarren at Vayia: Geomorphology and a New Class of Early Bronze Age Fortified Settlement in Southern Greece. *Antiquity, 80*, 145–60.

Tataki, A.B. (1994). *Rhodes, Lindos, Kamiros, Filerimos: The Palace of the Grand Masters and the Museum*. Athens.

Taymaz, T., Jackson, J.A., & McKenzie, D.P. (1991). Active Tectonics of the North and Central Aegean Sea. *Geophysical Journal International, 106*, 433–90.

Teall, J.L. (1977). Byzantine Urbanism in the Military Handbooks. In H.A. Miskimin, D. Herlihy, & A.L. Udovitch (eds), *The Medieval City: Essays written in Honor of Robert S. Lopez*. (pp. 201–5). New Haven.

Telilis, I. (2004). *Μετεωρολογικά φαινόμενα και κλίμα στο Βυζάντιο*. Athens.

Temple, G., Sir. (1836). *Travels in Greece and Turkey, and the Mediterranean*. London.

Themelis, P.G. (2003). *Ancient Messene*. Athens.

———. (2010). The Economy and Society of Messene under Roman Rule. In A.D. Rizakis & C.E. Lepenioti (eds), *Roman Peloponnese III: Society, Economy and Culture under the Roman Empire: Continuity and Innovation. Meletemata* 63. (pp. 89–110). Athens.

Thiselton, A.C. (2000). *The First Epistle to the Corinthians: A Commentary on the Greek Text*. Grand Rapids.

Thomas, C.M. (2010). Greek Heritage in Roman Corinth and Ephesos: Hybrid Identities and Strategies of Display in the Material Record of Traditional Mediterranean Religions. In S.J. Friesen, D.N. Schowalter & J.C. Walters (eds), *Corinth in Context: Comparative Studies on Religion and Society*. (pp. 117–50). Leiden.

Thompson, C. (1752). *The Travels of the Late Charles Thompson, Esq*. Reading.

Thompson, D.B. & Griswold, R.E. (1982). *Garden Lore of Ancient Athens*. Princeton.

Thompson, E.A. (1948). *A History of Attila and the Huns*. Oxford.

———. (1966). *The Visigoths in the Time of Ulfila*. Oxford.

Thompson, H.A. (1950). Excavations in the Athenian Agora: 1949. *Hesperia, 19*, 313–37.

———. (1959). Athenian Twilight: A.D. 267–600. *JRS, 49*, 61–72.

———. (1984). Necrology: Charles Hill Morgan (1902–1984). *AJA, 88*, 439–440.

Thompson, H.A. & Wycherley, R.E. (1972). *The Agora of Athens* (*Agora* XIV). Princeton.

Tobin, J. (1993). Some New Thoughts on Herodes Atticus's Tomb, His Stadium of 143/4, and Philostratus *VS* 2.550. *AJA, 97*, 81–9.

———. (1997). *Herodes Atticus and the City of Athens*. Amsterdam.

Tod, M.N. (1962). *A Selection of Greek Historical Inscriptions* (Reprint. Original ed., 1933–1948). Oxford.

Tod, M.N. & A.J.B. Wace. (1906). *A Catalogue of the Sparta Museum*. Oxford.

Tomlinson, R.A. (1992). *From Mycenae to Constantinople: The Evolution of the Ancient City*. London.
Torelli, M. (2001). Pausania a Corinto. Un intellettuale greco del secondo secolo e la propaganda imperiale romana. In D. Knoepfler & M. Piérart (eds), *Éditer, traduire, commenter Pausanias en l'an 2000*. (pp. 135–84). Geneva.
Toynbee, A.J. (1971). *An Ekistical Study of the Hellenic City-State*. Athens.
Tran, V.T.T. (1964). *Essai sur le culte d'Isis à Pompéi*. Paris.
Trapp, E. (1993). Learned and Vernacular Literature in Byzantium: Dichotomy or Symbiosis? *DOP*, *47*, 115–29.
Travlos, J. (1971). *Pictorial Dictionary of Ancient Athens*. London.
Trigger, B.G. (1989). *A History of Archaeological Thought*. Cambridge.
Tritle, L. (1997). Ammianus Marcellinus and the Historical Geography of the Balkans. *Balkan Studies*, *38*, 5–19.
Trombley, F.R. (1993). *Hellenic Religion and Christianization, ca. 370–529*. Leiden.
Trümper, M. (2004). The Oldest Original Synagogue Building in the Diaspora: The Delos Synagogue Reconsidered. *Hesperia*, *73*, 513–98.
Tsigakou, F.-M. (1981). *The Rediscovery of Greece: Travellers and Painters in the Romantic Era*. London.
Tucker, J., Jr. (1902). Various Statues from Corinth. *AJA*, *6*, 422–38.
Turner, J. (1999). *The Liberal Education of Charles Eliot Norton*. Baltimore.
Ubelaker, D.H. & Rife, J.L. (2007). The Practice of Cremation in the Roman-era Cemetery at Kenchreai, Greece. The Perspective from Archaeology and Forensic Science. *Bioarchaeology of the Near East*, *1*, 35–57.
Urse, M.P. (1988). *Rural Settlement in the Korinthia in Roman Times*. Ph.D. Diss., The Ohio State University.
van de Paverd, F. (1991). *St John Chrysostom, the Homilies on the Statues: An Introduction*. Orientalia Christiana Analecta 239. Rome.
van der Vin, J.P.A. (1980). *Travellers to Greece and Constantinople: Ancient Monuments and Old Traditions in Medieval Travellers' Tales*. Istanbul.
van Groningen, B.A. (1956). Théopompe ou Chamaeléon? à propos de Simonide 137B, 104D. *Mnemosyne: Bibliotheca Classica Batava*, *9*, 11–22.
van Uytfanghe, M. (1993). L'hagiographie: un "genre" chretien ou antique tardif? *AnBoll*, *111*, 135–88.
Vandiver, P.B. & Koehler, C.G. (1986). Structure, Processing, Properties, and Style of Corinthian Transport Amphoras. In W.D. Kingery (ed.), *Ceramics and Civilization 2: Technology and Style*. (pp. 173–215). Columbus.
Vasiliev, A. (ed.). (1910). *Agapius (Mahboud) of Menbidj. Kitab al-'Unvan. Histoire universelle*. Paris.
Vasiliev, A.A. (1936). *The Goths in the Crimea*. Cambridge, Mass.
Veh, O. (1950). *Zur Geschichtsschreibung und Weltauffassung des Prokop von Caesarea*. Bayreuth.
Veikou, M. (2012). *Byzantine Epirus: A Topography of Transformation*. Leiden.

Verdelis, N.M. (1956). Der Diolkos am Isthmus von Korinth. *AM, 71*, 51–9.
———. (1958). Die Ausgrabung des Diolkos während der Jahre 1957–9. *AM, 73*, 140–5.
———. (1959). Συνέχισις τῆς ἀνασκαφῆς τοῦ Διόλκου. *ArchEph, 1956*, 1–3.
———. (1960 (1962)). *Ἀρχαιότητες Ἀργολιδοκορινθίας, 16*, 79–82.
———. (1966). Ἀνασκαφὴ τοῦ Διόλκου. *Prakt, 1960*, 136–43.
———. (1966). Ἀνασκαφὴ τοῦ Διόλκου. *Prakt, 1962*, 48–50.
Vermeule, C.C., III. (1968). *Roman Imperial Art in Greece and Asia Minor.* Cambridge, Mass.
———. (1986). Figural Pillars: From Asia Minor to Corinth to Rome. In M. Del Chiaro (ed.), *Corinthiaca: Studies in Honor of Darrell A. Amyx.* (pp. 71–80). Columbia.
Vidman, L. (ed.). (1969). *Sylloge inscriptionum religionis Isiacae et Sarapiacae.* Berlin.
Vikela, E. & Vollkommer, R. (1992). Melikertes. *LIMC* (6.1–2:436–44).
Vischer, W. (1875). *Erinnerungen und Eindrücke aus Griechenland* (2nd ed.). Basel.
Vita-Finzi, C. & King, G.C.P. (1985). The Seismicity, Geomorphology, and Structural Evolution of the Corinth Area of Greece. *Philosophical Transactions of the Royal Society of London, A314*, 379–407.
Vogeikoff-Brogan, N. (2007). *Triumph over Time (1947): The American School of Classical Studies at Athens in Post-War Greece.* Princeton.
Vogt, J. (1993). Historical Seismology: Some Notes on the Sources for Seismologists. In M. Stucchi (ed.), *Historical Investigation of European Earthquakes.* (pp. 15–24). Milan.
von Freyberg, B. (1973). *Die Geologie des Isthmus von Korinth* (*Erlangen Geologische Abhandlungen* 95). Erlangen.
von Hesberg, H. (1983). Zur Datierung der Gefangenenfassade in Korinth: Eine wiederverwendete Architektur augusteischer Zeit. *AM, 98*, 215–38.
Vryonis, S., Jr. (1981). The Panegyris of the Byzantine Saint: A Study in the Nature of a Medieval Institution, its Origins and Fate. In S. Hackel (ed.), *The Byzantine Saint.* (pp. 196–228). Birmingham.
Waagé, F.O. (1934). Preliminary Report on the Medieval Pottery from Corinth, I: The Prototype of the Archaic Italian Majolica. *Hesperia, 3*, 129–39.
———. (1935) Bronze Objects from Old Corinth, Greece. *AJA* 39:79–91.
Wachsmuth, C. (ed.). (1897). *Ioannis Laurentii Lydi Liber de ostentis et calendaria Graeca omnia.* Leipzig.
Walbank, Mary E. Hoskins (1986a). *The Nature and Development of Roman Corinth to the End of the Antonine Period.* Ph.D. Diss., Open University.
——— (1986b). The Nature of Early Roman Corinth. *AJA, 90*, 220–1.
——— (1989). Pausanias, Octavia, and Temple E at Corinth. *BSA, 84*, 361–94.
——— (1996). Evidence for the Imperial Cult in Julio-Claudian Corinth. In A. Small (ed.), *Subject and Ruler: The Cult of the Ruling Power in Classical Antiquity, Papers Honoring D. Fishwick.* (pp. 201–13). Ann Arbor.

——— (1997). The Foundation and Planning of Early Roman Corinth. *JRA*, *10*, 95–130.
——— (2003). Aspects of Corinthian Coinage in the Late 1st and Early 2nd Centuries A.C. In N. Bookidis & C.K. Williams, II (eds), *Corinth, the Centenary: 1896–1996* (*Corinth* XX). (pp. 337–50). Princeton.
——— (2010a). Image and Cult: The Coinage of Roman Corinth. In S.J. Friesen, D.N. Schowalter & J.C. Walters (eds), *Corinth in Context: Comparative Studies on Religion and Society*. (pp. 151–98). Leiden.
——— (2010b). The Cults of Roman Corinth: Public Ritual and Personal Belief. In A.D. Rizakis & C.E. Lepenioti (eds), *Roman Peloponnese III: Society, Economy and Culture under the Roman Empire: Continuity and Innovation. Meletemata* 63. (pp. 357–74). Athens.
——— (2014). Remaining Roman in Death at Corinth: A Debate with Kathleen Slane. *JRA*, *27*, 403–417.
——— (2015). Prospectus for Palaimon. In U. Wartenberg & M. Amandry (eds), *ΚΑΙΡΟΣ: Contributions to Numismatics in Honor of Basil Demetriadi*. (pp. 327–46). New York.
Walbank, Mary E. Hoskins & Walbank, Michael B. (2006). The Grave of Maria, Wife of Euplous: A Christian Epitaph Reconsidered. *Hesperia*, *75*, 267–88.
Walbank, Michael B. (2010). Where Have All The Names Gone? The Christian Community in Corinth in the Late Roman and Early Byzantine Eras. In S.J. Friesen, D.N. Schowalter & J.C. Walters (eds), *Corinth in Context: Comparative Studies on Religion and Society*. (pp. 257–326). Leiden.
Wallace, P.W. (1969). Strabo on Acrocorinth. *Hesperia*, *38*, 495–9.
Walton, F.R. (1965). A Neglected Historical Text. *Historia*, *14*, 236–51.
Ward-Perkins, B. (2001). Specialisation, Trade and Prosperity: An Overview of the Economy of the Late Antique Eastern Mediterranean. In S.A. Kingsley & M. Decker (eds), *Economy and Exchange in the East Mediterranean during Late Antiquity*. (pp. 167–78). Oxford.
———. (2005). *The Fall of Rome and the End of Civilization*. Oxford.
Ward-Perkins, J.B. (1951). The Art of the Severan Age in Light of Tripolitanian Discoveries. *Proceedings of the British Academy*, 297–8.
Watkins, C. (2014). *Trees, Woods and Forests: A Social and Cultural History*. London.
Watts, E. (2010). Riot in Alexandria: Tradition and Group Dynamics in Late Antique Pagan and Christian Communities. Berkeley.
Waywell, S.E. (1979). Roman Mosaics in Greece. *AJA*, *83*, 293–321.
Webb, R. (1999). The Aesthetics of Sacred Space: Narrative, Metaphor, and Motion in 'Ekphraseis' of Church Buildings. *DOP*, *53*, 59–74.
Weber, S.H. (1952). *Voyages and Travels in the Near East Made during the XIX Century*. Princeton.
———. (1953). *Voyages and Travels in Greece, the Near East, and Adjacent Regions Made Previous to the Year 1801*. Princeton.
Wehrli, F. (ed.). (1944). *Die Schule des Aristoteles: Texte und Kommentare*. Basel.
Weinberg, S.S. (1939). On the Date of the Temple of Apollo at Corinth. *Hesperia*, *8*, 191–9.

———. (1948). A Cross-Section of Corinthian Antiquities (Excavations of 1940). *Hesperia, 17*, 197–241.
———. (1949). Investigations at Corinth, 1947–8. *Hesperia, 18*, 148–57.
———. (1960). *The Southeast Building, the Twin Basilicas, the Mosaic House* (*Corinth* I.5). Princeton.
Weinberg, S.S. & Weinberg, G.R. Davidson (1946). Corinth: The Ancient City Revealed. *CJ, 42*, 66–76.
Weitzmann, K. (ed.). (1979). *Age of Spirituality: Late Antique and Early Christian Art, Third to Seventh Century*. New York.
———. (1986). The Contribution of the Princeton University Department of Art and Archaeology to the Study of Byzantine Art. In S. Curcic & A. St Clair (eds), *Byzantium at Princeton: Byzantine Art and Archaeology at Princeton University*. (pp. 11–30). Princeton.
Welch, K. (1999). Negotiating Roman Spectacle Architecture in the Greek World: Athens and Corinth. In B. Bergmann & C. Kondoleon (eds), *The Art of Ancient Spectacle*. (pp. 124–45). New Haven.
Wesolowsky, A.B. (1973). The Skeletons of Lerna Hollow. *Hesperia, 42*, 340–51.
West, A.B. (1931). *Latin Inscriptions, 1896–1926* (*Corinth* VIII.2). Cambridge, Mass.
West, M.L. (1997). *The East Face of Helicon: West Asiatic Elements in Greek Poetry and Myth*. Oxford.
———. (2002). 'Eumelos': A Corinthian Epic Cycle? *JHS, 122*, 109–33.
Westholm, A. (1933). The Paphian Temple of Aphrodite. *ActaArch, 4*, 201–36.
Wheeler, J.R. (1909). American School of Classical Studies at Athens: Excavations at Corinth. *Yearbook of the Carnegie Institution, 8*, 203–4.
———. (1910). American School of Classical Studies at Athens: Excavations at Corinth. *Yearbook of the Carnegie Institution, 9*, 205.
Wheeler, J.R. & Hill, B.H. (1907). Twenty-Sixth Annual Report of the Managing Committee of the American School of Classical Studies at Athens. *AJA Supplement: Annual Reports 1906–1907, 11*, 9–21.
———. (1908). Twenty-Seventh Annual Report of the Managing Committee of the American School of Classical Studies at Athens. *AJA Supplement: Annual Reports 1907–1908, 12*, 9–18.
Whitbread, I.K. (2003). Clays of Corinth: The Study of a Basic Resource for Ceramic Production. In C.K. Williams, II & N. Bookidis (eds), *Corinth, the Centenary: 1896–1996* (*Corinth* XX). (pp. 1–14). Princeton.
Whitby, M. (1985). Justinian's Bridge over the Sangarius and the Date of Procopius' *De Aedificiis*. *JHS, 105*, 129–48.
———. (1995). Recruitment in Roman Armies from Justinian to Heraclius (ca. 565–615). In A. Cameron & L.I. Conrad (eds), *The Byzantine and Early Islamic Near East 3: States, Resources and Armies*. (pp. 92–103). Princeton.
White, L.M. (2005). Favorinus's "Corinthian Oration": A Piqued Panorama of the Hadrianic Forum. In D.N. Schowalter & S.J. Friesen (eds), *Urban Religon in Roman Corinth: Interdisciplinary Approaches*. (pp. 61–110). Cambridge, Mass.

Whitehouse, D. (1991). Glassmaking at Corinth: A Reassessment. In D. Foy & G. Sennequier (eds), *Ateliers de verriers: De l'antiquité à la période pre-industrielle*. (pp. 73–8). Rouen.

———. (1993). The Date of the Agora South Central Workshop at Corinth. *Archeologia Medievale, 20*, 659–62.

Whitmarsh, T. (1998). Reading Power in Roman Greece: The Paideia of Dio Chrysostom. In Y.L. Too & N. Livingstone (eds), *Pedagogy and Power: Rhetorics of Classical Learning*. Cambridge.

———. (2001). *Greek Literature and the Roman Empire: The Politics of Imitation*. Oxford.

Whittaker, C.R. (1983). Late Roman Trade and Traders. In P. Garnsey, K. Hopkins, & C.R. Whittaker (eds), *Trade in the Ancient Economy*. (pp. 163–80). London.

———. (2004). *Rome and its Frontiers: The Dynamics of Empire*. London.

Wickham, C. (1988). Marx, Sherlock Holmes and Late Roman Commerce. *JRS, 78*, 183–93.

———. (2001). Society. In R. McKitterick (ed.), *The Early Middle Ages*. (pp. 59–94). Oxford.

Wickkiser, B.L. (2010). Asklepios in Greek and Roman Corinth. In S.J. Friesen, D.N. Schowalter & J.C. Walters (eds), *Corinth in Context: Comparative Studies on Religion and Society*. (pp. 37–66). Leiden.

Wilamowitz-Moellendorff, U.v. (1889). Commentariolum grammaticum IV. *NAkG*, 3–7.

Wilhelm, A. (1905). Zu griechischen Epigrammen IX. *BCH, 29*, 415–6.

Wilisch, E. (1908). Zehn Jahre amerikanischer Ausgrabung in Korinth. *NJbb, 31*, 414–39.

Wilkes, J.J. (1989). Civil Defence in Third-Century Achaea. In S. Walker & Av. Cameron (eds), *The Greek Renaissance in the Roman Empire*. (pp. 187–92). London.

Will, E. (1955). *Korinthiaka: Recherches sur l'histoire et la civilisation de Corinthe, des origins aux guerres mediques*. Paris.

Williams, C.K., II (1969). Excavations at Corinth, 1968. *Hesperia, 38*, 36–63.

———. (1970a). Corinth, 1969: Forum Area. *Hesperia, 39*, 1–39.

———. (1970b). Excavations at Corinth. *ArchDelt, 24* (1969), 112–6.

———. (1974). Excavations at Corinth. *ArchDelt, 26* (1971), 94–6.

———. (1976). Corinth Excavations. *ArchDelt, 27* (1972), 220–4.

———. (1977). Excavations at Corinth. *ArchDelt, 28* (1973), 136–43.

———. (1978a). Corinth 1977, Forum Southwest. *Hesperia, 47*, 1–39.

——— (1978b). *Pre-Roman Cults in the Area of the Forum of Ancient Corinth*. Ph.D. Diss., University of Pennsylvania.

———. (1979). Corinth, 1978: Forum Southwest. *Hesperia, 48*, 105–44.

———. (1980). Corinth Excavations, 1979. *Hesperia, 49*, 107–34.

———. (1981). The City of Corinth and Its Domestic Religion. *Hesperia, 50*, 408–41.

———. (1982). Zeus and Other Deities: Notes on Two Archaistic Piers. *Studies in Athenian Architecture, Sculpture, and Topography Presented to Homer A. Thompson*. (pp. 175–81). Princeton.

———. (1986). Corinth and the Cult of Aphrodite. *Corinthiaca: Studies in Honor of Darrell A. Amyx*. Columbia.

———. (1987a). Laus Julia Corinthiensis et Diana Nemorensis? *ΦΙΛΙΑ ΕΠΗ ΕΙΣ ΓΕΩΡΓΙΟΝ Ε. ΜΥΛΩΝΑΝ (Mylonas Festschrift) 2*. (pp. 384–9). Athens.
———. (1987b). The Refounding of Corinth: Some Roman Religious Attitudes. In S. Macready & F.H. Thompson (eds), *Roman Architecture in the Greek World*. (pp. 26–37). London.
———. (1989). A Re-evaluation of Temple E and the West End of the Forum of Corinth. In S. Walker & Av. Cameron (eds), *The Greek Renaissance in the Roman Empire*. (pp. 156–62). London.
———. (1993). Roman Corinth as a Commercial Center. In T.E. Gregory (ed.), *The Corinthia in the Roman Period*. (pp. 31–46). Ann Arbor.
———. (1995). Archaic and Classical Corinth. In *Corinto e l'Occidente (Atti del trentaquattresimo convegno di studi sulla Magna Grecia, Taranto, 7–11 ottobre 1994)*. (pp. 31–45). Taranto.
———. (2005). Roman Corinth: The Final Years of Pagan Cult Facilities along East Theater Street. In D.N. Schowalter & S.J. Friesen (eds), *Urban Religon in Roman Corinth: Interdisciplinary Approaches*. (pp. 221–48). Cambridge, Mass.
———. (2013a). Corinth 2011: Investigations of the West Hall of the Theater. *Hesperia, 82*, 487–549.
——— (2013b). In Corinth with Pausanias as Guide. In K. Kissas & W.-D. Niemeier (eds), *The Corinthia and the Northeast Peloponnese: Topography and History from Prehistoric Times until the End of Antiquity*. (pp. 11–26). Munich.
Williams, C.K., II, Angel, J.L., Burns, P. & Fisher, J.E. (1973). Corinth, 1972: The Forum Area. *Hesperia, 42*, 1–44.
Williams, C.K., II & Bookidis, N. (eds). (2003). *Corinth, the Centenary: 1896–1996* (*Corinth* XX). Princeton.
Williams, C.K., II & Fisher, J.E. (1971). Corinth, 1970: Forum Area. *Hesperia, 40*, 1–51.
———. (1972). Corinth, 1971: Forum Area. *Hesperia, 41*, 143–84.
———. (1975). Corinth, 1974: Forum Southwest. *Hesperia, 44*, 1–50.
———. (1976). Corinth, 1975: Forum Southwest. *Hesperia, 45*, 99–162.
Williams, C.K., II, MacIntosh, J., & Fisher, J.E. (1974). Excavation at Corinth, 1973. *Hesperia, 43*, 1–73.
Williams, C.K., II & Russell, P. (1981). Corinth: Excavations of 1980. *Hesperia, 50*, 1–44.
Williams, C.K., II, Snyder, L.M., Barnes, E., & Zervos, O.H. (1998). Frankish Corinth: 1997. *Hesperia, 67*, 223–281.
Williams, C.K., II & Zervos, O.H. (1982). Corinth, 1981: East of the Theater. *Hesperia, 51*, 115–63.
———. (1983). Corinth, 1982: East of the Theater. *Hesperia, 52*, 1–47.
———. (1984). Corinth, 1983: The Route to Sikyon. *Hesperia, 53*, 83–122.
———. (1985). Corinth, 1984: East of the Theater. *Hesperia, 54*, 55–96.
———. (1986). Corinth, 1985: East of the Theater. *Hesperia, 55*, 129–75.
———. (1987). Corinth, 1986: Temple E and East of the Theater. *Hesperia, 56*, 1–46.
———. (1988). Corinth, 1987: South of Temple E and East of the Theater. *Hesperia, 57*, 95–146.
———. (1989). Corinth, 1988: East of the Theater. *Hesperia, 58*, 1–50.

———. (1990). Excavations at Corinth, 1989: The Temenos of Temple E. *Hesperia, 59*, 325–69.
———. (1991). Corinth, 1990: Southeast Corner of Temenos E. *Hesperia, 60*, 1–58.
———. (1992). Frankish Corinth: 1991. *Hesperia, 61*, 133–91.
———. (1993). Frankish Corinth: 1992. *Hesperia, 62*, 1–52.
———. (1994). Frankish Corinth: 1993. *Hesperia, 63*, 1–56.
———. (1995). Frankish Corinth: 1994. *Hesperia, 64*, 1–60.
———. (1996). Frankish Corinth: 1995. *Hesperia, 65*, 1–55.
Williams, H. (1981). *The Lamps* (*Kenchreai* 5). Leiden: Brill.
Williams, H.W. (1829). *Select Views in Greece with Classical Illustrations*. 2 vols. London.
Williamson, G.A. (trans.). (1966). *Procopius: The Secret History*. Baltimore.
Winkes, R. (1969). *Clipeata Imago: Studien zu einer römischen Bildnisform*. Bonn.
Wiseman, J.R. (1963). A Trans-Isthmian Fortification Wall. *Hesperia, 32*, 248–75.
———. (1967a). Excavations at Corinth, the Gymnasium Area, 1965. *Hesperia, 36*, 13–41.
———. (1967b). Excavations at Corinth, the Gymnasium Area, 1966. *Hesperia, 36*, 402–28.
———. (1969a). Ancient Corinth: The Gymnasium Area. *Archaeology, 22*, 216–25.
———. (1969b). Excavations in Corinth, The Gymnasium Area, 1967–8. *Hesperia, 38*, 64–106.
———. (1970). The Fountain of the Lamps. *Archaeology, 23*, 130–7.
———. (1972). The Gymnasium Area at Corinth, 1969–1970. *Hesperia, 41*, 1–42.
———. (1974). The Road to Oenoe. *Hesperia, 43*, 535–43.
———. (1978). *The Land of the Ancient Corinthians*. Göteborg.
———. (1979). Corinth and Rome I: 228 B.C. – A.D. 267. *ANRW, II.7.1*, 438–548.
———. (2015). Agonistic Festivals, Victors, and Officials in the Time of Nero: An Inscribed Herm from the Gymnasium Area of Corinth. In E. R. Gebhard & T.E. Gregory (eds), *Bridge of the Untiring Sea: The Corinthian Isthmus from Prehistory to Late Antiquity. Hesperia* Supplement 48. (pp. 193–246). Princeton.
Witakowski, W. (1987). *The Syriac Chronicle of Pseudo-Dionysius of Tel-Mahre: A Study in the History of Historiography*. Uppsala.
Wohl, B.L. (2015). In E.R. Gebhard & T.E. Gregory (eds), *Bridge of the Untiring Sea: The Corinthian Isthmus from Prehistory to Late Antiquity. Hesperia* Supplement 48. (pp. 341–51). Princeton.
Wolfram, H. (1988). *History of the Goths* (T. J. Dunlop, trans.). Berkeley.
———. (1997). *The Roman Empire and Its Germanic Peoples* (T. J. Dunlop, trans.). Berkeley.
Wörrle, M. (1992). Neue Inschriftenfunde aus Aizanoi I. *Chiron* 22, 337–76.
Wozniak, F.E. (1982). The Justinianic Fortification of Interior Illyricum. In R.L. Hohlfelder (ed.), *City, Town, and Countryside in the Early Byzantine Era*. New York.

Wright, W.C. (trans.). (1921). *Philostratus and Eunapius: The Lives of the Sophists*. London.

Wycherley, R.E. (1962). *How the Greeks Built Cities*. New York.

Wyse, T., Sir. (1865). *An Excursion in the Peloponnesus in the Year 1858*. London.

Yannopoulos, P. (1993). Métropoles du Péloponnèse mésobyzantin: un souvenir des invasions avaro-slaves. *Byzantion, 63*, 388–400.

Yegül, F.K. (2015). Roman Baths at Isthmia and Sanctuary Baths in Greece. In E.R. Gebhard & T.E. Gregory (eds), *Bridge of the Untiring Sea: The Corinthian Isthmus from Prehistory to Late Antiquity. Hesperia* Supplement 48. (pp. 247–70). Princeton.

Young, P.H. (2005). The Cypriot Aphrodite Cult: Paphos, Rantidi, and Saint Barnabas. *JNES, 64*, 23–44.

Zangger, E. (1993). *The Geoarchaeology of the Argolid*. Berlin.

Zarinebaf, F., Bennet, J., & Davis, J.L. (2005). *A Historical and Economic Geography of Ottoman Greece: The Southwestern Morea in the 18th Century* (*Hesperia Suppl.* 34). Princeton.

Zavagno, L. (2009). *Cities in Transition: Urbanism in Byzantium between Late Antiquity and the Early Middle Ages (500–900 A.D.)*. Oxford.

Zervos, O.H. (1986). Coins Excavated at Corinth, 1978–1980. *Hesperia, 55*, 183–205.

———. (1988). Corrigenda: Corinth 1986: Temple E and East of Theater. *Hesperia, 57*, 146.

———. (1997). Frankish Corinth, 1996: The Coins. *Hesperia, 66*, 173–92.

Ziskowski, A. (2016). Athena at Corinth: Revisiting the Attribution of the Temple of Apollo. *Archaeological Institute of America 117th Annual Meeting Abstracts, vol. 39*, 160. San Francisco.

INDEX

CPSIA information can be obtained
at www.ICGtesting.com
Printed in the USA
LVHW042126221019
634998LV00014B/178/P

9 781350 124981